The
Book
of
Rules

*A visual guide to the laws
of every commonly played
sport and game*

The
Book
of
Rules

*A visual guide to the laws
of every commonly played
sport and game*

EP
EBURY
PRESS

First published in 1997 by Ebury Press

1 3 5 7 9 10 8 6 4 2

Ebury Press
Random House
20 Vauxhall Bridge Road, London SW1V 2SA

Random House Australia (Pty) Limited
20 Alfred Street, Milsons Point, Sydney
New South Wales 2061, Australia

Random House New Zealand Limited
18 Poland Road, Glenfield
Auckland 10, New Zealand

Random House South Africa (Pty) Limited
Endulini, 5A Jubilee Road, Parktown 2193, South Africa

Random House UK Limited Reg. 954009

Conceived, edited and designed by
Duncan Petersen Publishing Ltd,
31, Ceylon Road, London W14 OPY

Printed by Graficromo, S.A. , Cordoba, Spain

Typeset by Duncan Petersen Publishing Ltd

A CIP catalogue record for this book is available from the British Library

ISBN 0-09-185403-2

Introduction

The ambitious goal of this book was to create a supremely easy-to-use, functionally (rather than superficially) illustrated guide to the rules of sport - something much more friendly and stimulating than the dense text of the official rule books; quicker to use; easily understood by readers of all ages - perhaps from ten upwards.

By assembling within two covers a full set of rules for all the commonly played sports - a major feat of compilation - we hoped also to create a uniquely valuable reference work that might serve individuals, families, schools, clubs and indeed sports writers.

We devised the colour pages of the book (those headed 'Essentials') with accessibility and simplicity uppermost. The illustrations linked to the captions are the ideal way to get to grips with the essentials, and to solve everyday queries on how the games should be played. They are designed to give the reader an easy 'handle' on the game.

These 'Essential' pages would, of course, be superficial if they stood on their own. We therefore back them up with the text of the rule books, point by point, on double-page spreads that follow the 'Essentials' spreads alternately, with clear cross-referencing. These two strands of contrasting information - summary and detailed back-up - thread their way through the whole book making, we believe, a stimulating contrast. Many people will, we hope, enjoy using the 'Essentials' pages and find them helpful; but the rules point by point remain the hard core of the book - a unique and invaluable resource. For further details about our criteria in compiling the rules point by point, see page 9.

Acknowledgements

It would have been impossible to put together a book such as this without the talents of our main researcher-compiler, Angela Koo; and without the help of experts. The texts of all but a handful of sports have been vetted by the governing body concerned. Those few that could not vet their text were prevented from doing so by constraints of time; and even these texts have been taken from the most up-to-date sources available. The rules are therefore up to date at time of first printing, August 1997.

We thank the governing bodies of the sports in this book for their invaluable help. A list of all their names and addresses is given on page 223. We are, however, especially indebted to the following individuals for their particularly useful contributions:

- **American football** David Rossell
- **Athletics** David Littlewood and Pat Liddiard •
Australian rules football Andrew Watt • **Baseball**
Steve Meyerhoff and Wendy Macadam • **Basketball**
Alan Richardson and Albert Schencking
- **Bowls** David Johnson • **Boxing** Karl-Heinz Wehr
- **Cricket** John Jamieson
- **Croquet** Paul Campion • **Football** David Barber • **Hockey**
Jane Nuckolds, George Croft and Mary Coyle • **Men's
lacrosse** Rodney Burns and Mark Coups • **Netball** Maria
Harding • **Rounders** Brian Mackinney • **Rugby
League** Neil Tunnicliffe • **Softball** Merle Butler •
Squash Ted Wallbutton • **Table tennis** Colin Clemett • **Tennis**
Nicola Bickord
- **Volleyball** Bernard Kilkenny

Main contents list

The sports and games as they appear in the book

Alphabetical contents list

How to use this book

What's in, what's out

You will find in *The Book of Rules* all the mainstream sports and games most people expect to play or to watch. The emphasis is on sports with a substantial physical element, and on those that don't need specialized equipment. Thus rowing, sailing, cycling and shooting are outside the scope of this book - at any rate the first edition; similarly billiards, snooker and darts.

Although some important 'local' sports are included, such as Australian rules football, it's essentially an international selection.

Topics covered

For ease of access, each sport is covered under a consistent sequence of headings:

Playing surface, equipment, players and officials

The information given in the captions, the illustrations and the annotation on the diagrams and artwork is taken from the official rule book.

How to play/win

This information provides a brief summary of how play progresses, again based on the official rule book.

Measurements
Both Imperial and metric measurements are given. When the official rule book of a sport uses Imperial, that is given first, followed by an approximate metric conversion. When a rule book uses metric, that is put first, followed by an approximate Imperial conversion.

5.18 m (17 ft)

76 cm (2 ft 6 in)

1.98 m (6 ft 6 in)

1.55 m (5 ft 1 in)

3.96 m (13 ft)

76 cm (2 ft 6 in)

13.40 m (44 ft)

6.10 m (20 ft)

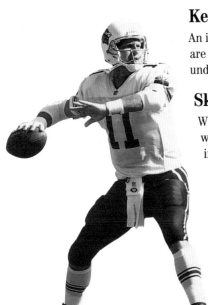

Key rules

An important feature, simplifying points that are essential, controversial or difficult to understand.

Skills and tactics

Whole books have been written on these; here we give a necessarily brief summary of the important points.

Grey areas

Most have been suggested by experts in the governing bodies of the sports concerned.

The rules point by point

Generally we give the most 'senior' official version available - typically the international rules. Otherwise we give the most widely used version. Note that for boxing we give the amateur, rather than the professional, rules.

For each sport, some of the most important rules, such as those governing playing surface and equipment, are covered simply by a cross-reference to an 'Essentials' page, where they are explained in simple terms, and illustrated.

The rules are given as completely as possible for every sport, but constraints of space have meant that in some instances the rules have been abridged. Where abridgements or summaries occur, they are made clear by italics or notes in the text.

Thus the rules as given are a true working version, which will provide rulings on most issues experienced by most people.

Please note that some sports update their rule books regularly.

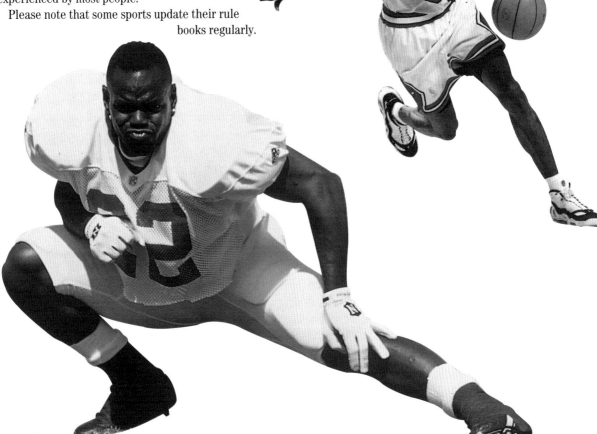

Football
Essentials

This was once a riotous game played between whole villages in the Middle Ages, but it became formalized in 1863 with the foundation of the Football Association which drew up a set of rules to co-ordinate the way it was played. The game founded on these rules – now known as Association Football, soccer or just plain football – is today the most popular game in the world as well as the most popular spectator sport.

Manchester United 1996

The field

Must be rectangular, traditionally with a grass surface, and be divided into two equal halves. Its length must be between 110 and 120 yds (100–110 m) and its breadth between 70 and 80 yds (64–73 m).

Corner flag
Touch line
20 yds
Corner flag
44 yds
18 yds
Optional halfway flagstaff
Halfway
Centre circle
20 yds
Line
70 - 80 yds
Touch line
110 - 120 yds
1 yd
Penalty area
6 yds
10 yds
Corner flag
Goal line
12 yds
Penalty mark
Goal area
Goal line
Corner flag

The teams

Two teams of eleven players each, including one goalkeeper. A maximum of three substitutes is permitted. Any of the other players may change places with the goalkeeper.

The goals

These are placed on the centre of the goal-lines at each end of the field and must consist of two upright posts, 8 yards (7.3 m) apart and joined by a horizontal crossbar. Both posts and crossbars should be of equal width, not exceeding 5 in (12.7 cm). A net attached to posts, bars and the ground behind them is optional, and the whole structure must stand 8 feet (2.4 m) above the ground (inside measurement).

Football fans
Perhaps the biggest ever football crowd was the 199,854 who crammed into the Maracaña Municipal Stadium in Rio de Janeiro in Brazil to watch the World Cup final on the 16th of July 1950. Pictured right is Wembley Stadium.

The ball

Spherical with an outer casing of leather or approved substitute material. Its circumference must be 27-28 in (68-70 cm) and it must weigh between 14 and 16 oz (410 and 450 g). Its pressure should be equal to 0.6 - 1.1 atmospheres.

HOW TO PLAY

Each team endeavours to score goals by kicking or heading the ball into the goal net defended by the opposing side. The ball must not be deliberately played with the hands by any player other than the goalkeeper.

Starting

The team who wins the toss opts either to choose an end or to take the kick-off. At least two players from the team taking the kick-off then position themselves behind the halfway line and inside the centre circle. At this point each player must be within his own half of the field. The defending team's players must in addition remain outside the centre circle. The ball is placed on the centre spot and the game starts on the Referee's whistle. The first kick must enter the opponent's half.

How to win

The team scoring the highest number of goals by kicking or heading the ball into the opposition's goal wins the game. The goal zone is defined in *Law 10, Method of Scoring (page 12).*

Officials

A referee and two assistant referees (linesmen).

Dressing for goal
The goalkeeper must wear colours that distinguish him from the other players – so that he is instantly identifiable. Some goalkeepers may wear gloves to help them grip the ball and occasionally a peaked cap to shade their eyes.

Dress

A jersey or shirt with shorts and socks. These must be the same colour for a whole team, although the goalkeeper must wear colours that distinguish him from the other players. Suitable footwear and protective shin guards (covered entirely by the socks) are also worn. A player must not wear anything which is dangerous to another player.

Getting stripped
Football clubs are identified by their own distinctively coloured strip but most teams have at least one alternative strip – so they can be clearly distinguished when playing away to opponents with a similar colour strip. Here one of the stars of the early 90s, Frenchman Eric Cantona, is wearing the away strip of his former team Manchester United. Normally he would have been playing in red.

KEY RULES

A game lasts 90 minutes and is divided into two halves of 45 minutes each, with teams changing ends at half-time. (For cup matches this may be extended by another 30 minutes of 'extra time' in the case of a draw).

• A player will be penalized for being offside, i.e., being in front of the ball, in the opposite side's half and without at least two opponents between him and the goal. *See Law 11, Offside (page 12).*

• If a player commits a major physical offence such as kicking, striking or pushing an opponent, a direct free-kick is awarded to the opposing team. This also applies if the ball is deliberately handled by any player other than the goalkeeper. Other offences such as time-wasting or indulging in dangerous play are penalized with an indirect free-kick for the other team.

For any free-kick, the kicker's opponents must keep a distance of 10 yards, between themselves and the ball.

• A player who argues with the referee or persistently breaks the rules will be shown the yellow card (an official caution), while more serious conduct such as violent behaviour or foul language will result in the player being sent immediately off the field (shown the red card). See page 16 for *Law 12, Fouls and Misconduct.*

• Some offences, if they take place within the penalty area, will incur a penalty kick against the offending team. *See Law 14, Penalty Kick (page 13).*

FOOTBALL
THE RULES

Law 1

The Field of Play
See The field (page 10).

Law 2

The Ball
See The ball (page 10).

Law 3

Number of Players
See The teams (page 10).

Law 4

Players' Equipment
See The Ball (page10).

Laws 5 & 6

Refer to referees

Law 7

Duration of the Game
The duration of the game shall be two equal periods of 45 minutes, unless otherwise mutually agreed upon, subject to the following:-
a) Allowance shall be made in either period for all time lost through substitution, the transport from the field of injured players, time-wasting or other cause, the amount of which shall be a matter for the discretion of the Referee.
b) Time shall be extended to permit of a penalty kick being taken at or after the expiration of the normal period in either half.
   The half-time interval shall not exceed 15 minutes.
   Competition rules shall clearly stipulate the duration of the half-time interval.
   The duration of the half-time interval may be altered only with the consent of the Referee.

Law 8

The Start of Play
a) At the beginning of the game, choice of ends and the kick-off shall be decided by the toss of a coin. The team winning the toss shall have the option of choice of ends or the kick-off. The Referee having given a signal, the game shall be started by a player taking a place-kick (i.e., a kick at the ball while it is stationary on the ground in the centre of the field of play) into his opponents' half of the field of play. Every player shall be in his own half of the field and every player of the team opposing that of the kicker shall remain not less than 10 yards from the ball until it is kicked-off; it shall not be deemed in play until it has

travelled the distance of its own circumference. The kicker shall not play the ball a second time until it has been touched or played by another player.
b) After a goal has been scored, the game shall be restarted in like manner by a player of the team losing the goal.
c) After half-time: when restarting after half-time, ends shall be changed and the kick-off shall be taken by a player of the opposite team to that of the player who started the game.

Punishment
For any infringement of this Law, the kick-off shall be retaken, except in the case of the kicker playing the ball again before it has been touched or played by another player; for this offence, an indirect free-kick shall be taken by a player of the opposing team from the place where the infringement occurred, subject to the over-riding conditions imposed in Law 13. A goal shall not be scored direct from a kick-off.
d) After any other temporary suspension: when restarting the game after a temporary suspension of play from any cause not mentioned elsewhere in these Laws, provided that immediately prior to the suspension the ball has not passed over the touch line or goal lines, the Referee shall drop the ball at the place where it was when play was suspended, unless it was within the goal area at that time, in which case it shall be dropped on that part of the goal area line which runs parallel to the goal line, at the point nearest to where the ball was when play was stopped. It shall be deemed in play when it has touched the ground; if, however, it goes over the touch line or goal lines after it has been dropped by the Referee, but before it is touched by a player, the Referee shall again drop it. A player shall not play the ball until it has touched the ground. If this section of the Law is not complied with the Referee shall again drop the ball.

Law 9

Ball In and Out of Play
The ball is out of play:
a) When it has wholly crossed the goal line or touchline, whether on the ground or in the air.
b) When the game has been stopped by the Referee.
The ball is in play at all other

Keeping it clean
Football is not a physical contact sport and any kind of interference with an opponent is regarded as a foul and is penalised by a direct free kick.

times from the start of the match to the finish including:
a) If it rebounds from a goalpost, crossbar or corner flag post into the field of play.
b) If it rebounds off either the Referee or Assistant Referees when they are in the field of play.
c) In the event of a supposed infringement of the Laws, until a decision is given.

Law 10

Method of Scoring
Except as otherwise provided by these Laws, a goal is scored when the whole of the ball has passed over the goal line, between the goalposts and under the cross bar, provided it has not been thrown, carried or intentionally propelled by hand or arm, by a player of the attacking side, except in the case of a goalkeeper, who is within his own penalty area. The team scoring the greater number of goals during a game shall be the winner; if no goals, or an equal number of goals are scored, the game shall be termed a 'draw'.

Law 11

Offside
1. A player is in an offside position if he is nearer to his opponents' goal line than the ball, unless:
a) he is in his own half of the field of play, or
b) he is not nearer to his

opponents' goal line than at least two of his opponents.

2. It is not an offence in itself to be in an offside position. A player shall only be penalized for being in an offside position if, at the moment the ball touches, or is played by one of his team, he is, in the opinion of the Referee, involved in active play by:
a) interfering with play, or
b) interfering with an opponent, or
c) gaining an advantage by being in that position.

3. A player shall not be declared offside by the Referee
a) merely because of his being in an offside position, or
b) if he receives the ball, direct from a goal kick, a corner kick, or a throw-in.

4. If a player is declared offside, the Referee shall award an indirect free-kick, which shall be taken by a player of the opposing team from the place where the infringement occurred, unless the offence is committed by a player in his opponents' goal area, in which case the free-kick shall be taken from any point within the goal area.

Law 12

Fouls and Misconduct
A player who commits any of the following six offences in a

manner considered by the Referee to be careless, reckless or involving disproportionate force:
a) kicks or attempts to kick an opponent; or
b) trips an opponent; or
c) jumps at an opponent; or
d) charges an opponent; or
e) strikes or attempts to strike an opponent; or
f) pushes an opponent;

or who commits any of the following four offences:
g) when tackling an opponent makes contact with the opponent before contact is made with the ball; or
h) holds an opponent; or spits at an opponent; or
i) handles the ball deliberately, i.e., carries, strikes or propels the ball with his hand or arm (this does not apply to the goalkeeper within his own penalty area);

shall be penalized by the award of a **direct free-kick** to be taken by the opposing team from the place where the offence occurred, unless the offence is committed by a player in his opponents' goal area, in which case the free-kick shall be taken from any point within the goal area. Should a player of the defending team commit one of the above ten offences within the penalty area, he shall be penalized by a **penalty-kick.** A penalty-kick can be awarded irrespective of the position of the ball, if in play, at the time an offence within the penalty-area is committed.

A player committing any of the following five offences:
1. playing in a manner considered by the referee to be dangerous;
2. charging fairly, i.e. with the shoulder, when the ball is not within playing distance of the players concerned and they are definitely not trying to play it;
3. when not playing the ball, impeding the progress of an opponent, i.e. running between the opponent and the ball, or interposing the body so as to form an obstacle to an opponent;
4. charging the goalkeeper except when he:
a) is holding the ball
b) is obstructing an opponent;
c) has passed outside his goal area;
5. when playing as a goalkeeper and within his own penalty-area:
a) from the moment he takes

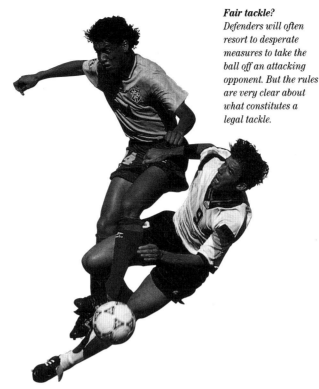

Fair tackle?
Defenders will often resort to desperate measures to take the ball off an attacking opponent. But the rules are very clear about what constitutes a legal tackle.

control of the ball with his hands, he takes more than four steps in any direction whilst holding, bouncing or throwing the ball in the air and catching it again, without releasing it into play, or
b) having released the ball into play before, during or after the four steps, he touches it again with his hands, before it has

been touched or played by a player of the opposing team either inside or outside of the penalty area, or by a player of the same team outside the penalty area, subject to the overriding conditions of 5c), or
c) touches the ball with his hands after it has been deliberately kicked to him by a team-mate, or

Playing dirty
If the referee spots an encounter like this, the guilty party is likely to be shown the yellow card but often players will hide their offence on the referee's blind side.

d) indulges in tactics which, in the opinion of the Referee, are designed merely to hold up the game and thus waste time and so give an unfair advantage to his own team, shall be penalized by the award of an **indirect free-kick** to be taken by the opposing side from the place where the infringement occurred, subject to the overriding conditions imposed in Law 13.

A player shall be **cautioned** and shown the **yellow card** if:-
j) he enters or re-enters the field of play to join or rejoin his team after the game has commenced, or leaves the field of play during the progress of the game (except through accident) without, in either case, first having received a signal from the Referee showing him that he may do so. If the Referee stops the game to administer the caution, the game shall be restarted by an indirect free-kick taken by a player of the opposing team from the place where the ball was when the Referee stopped the game, subject to the overriding conditions imposed in Law 13.

If, however, the offending player has committed a more serious offence, he shall be penalized according to that section of the law he infringed;
k) he persistently infringes the Laws of the Game;
l) he shows, by word or action, dissent from any decision given by the Referee;
m) he is guilty of ungentlemanly conduct.

For any of these last three offences, in addition to the caution an **indirect free-kick** shall be awarded to the opposing side from the place where the offence occurred, subject to the overriding conditions imposed in Law 13, unless a more serious infringement of the Laws of the Game was committed.

A player shall be sent off the field of play and shown the **red card** if, in the opinion of the Referee, he:
n) is guilty of violent conduct;
o) is guilty of serious foul play;
p) uses foul or abusive language;
q) is guilty of a second cautionable offence after having received a caution.

If play is stopped by reason of a player being ordered from the

➡ *page 16*

SKILLS
• • • • •

Although all players require
stamina, speed and the ability
to control a ball, particular
qualities are desirable for each
for the four play positions
within a team. *Defenders* must
be skilled at tackling and
heading. *Midfield Players* need
the stamina to keep up with
play at all times and the
flexibility to play defence or
attack as required. *Strikers*
need to be especially skilful
with the ball and good at
heading. They also need to be
able to respond quickly and
accurately to goal opportunities.
Goalkeepers must have the
agility and reflexes to be able to
block balls coming in from all
kinds of angles. They also need
a high level of concentration
and good judgement.

Passing

There are a number of different
passes which can be used by a
player, depending on the
direction and distance that the
ball needs to travel. The
direction the ball takes will
depend on which part of it is
kicked and what part of the foot
is used e.g. the heel, toe, instep
etc., while the distance will
depend on the length of the
backswing (the backwards lift
of the foot prior to kicking). For
example, a *lofted pass* combines
a long backswing with an instep
kick to the lower part of the ball
to produce a high, long passage
through the air, whereas a
swerving pass, made by kicking
the ball to left or right of centre
with the inside or outside of the
foot, may be used to curve the
ball round an opponent.

Ball control

Controlling the ball with the
feet is the foremost of all
football skills. The most skilled
players can dribble the ball
rapidly down the field changing
direction at will to deceive an
opponent.

Playing on
The ball is much easier
to control when it is
travelling away from
you. Players try to pass
the ball in front of a
team mate so he can run
on to it.

Foul play
This is an illegal tackle. The
defender has gone over the top of
the ball with the danger of kicking
the attacker's legs and missed the
ball completely..

Tackling

The *block tackle* is used by a
player to take posession of the
ball from an opponent by
approaching him head-on or
from the side, snatching the
ball from his control and
continuing on with it in another
direction. The *sliding tackle*
simply clears the ball from the
opponent's control without
actually taking posession of it.
Successful tackling requires
balance, tenacity and a good
sense of timing.

Attacker

Defender

Fair play
This is a legal tackle. The defender has gone for
the ball and is striking it cleanly.

Defender

Attacker

Kicking

The direction and distance
a ball travels when kicked
depends not only on the
length and power of the leg
swing but what part of the foot
makes contact with the ball – and
where on the ball it contacts.

Too late
A late tackle – that is,
an attempt to tackle an
attacker after the ball
has gone past – will
almost certainly lead to
a penalty if it occurs
within the goal area

Ball control and dribbling

The ball can be received and brought under control with any part of the body other than the arms and hands. A player can then travel down the field with it by dribbling, i.e., keeping it rolling slightly in front of him with quick, deft taps. A skilled player will be able to incorporate sudden changes in direction and pace to outwit opponents.

Body control
A player may bring down and control a high ball with his chest but he must take care not to let the ball touch his arms or hands.

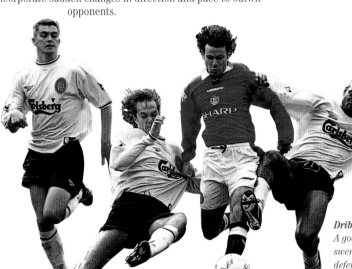

Dribbling
A good forward can feint and swerve through a whole bank of defenders and leave them lunging in his wake.

Striking the ball

Ideally shots should be kept low, since the course of a high shot is clearly visible, more predictable and therefore easier to block or intercept. But when a direct ground shot is not possible different techniques must be employed. A *volley shot* directs the ball into the goal while it is still in the air. A *chip shot* is a steep, short shot which takes advantage of a goalkeeper who has moved off the goal line. The ball enters the net over his head. Heading is another way of deflecting the ball neatly into the net.

Heading
Heading can be used for scoring, passing and defence. By meeting the ball with the forehead and using the body to provide force, the ball can be directed forwards, backwards or to one side.

No 'climbing'
Players are allowed to strike the ball with their forehead as well as their feet but they are not allowed to "climb" up an opponent to reach the ball for a header.

Goalkeeping

The goalkeeper is the only player permitted to use his hands and taking advantage of this to catch the ball is generally the safest way of saving a goal. He will have to be consistently on the alert, ready to leap into the air, plunge to the ground or stand securely front-on to receive balls. When it is not possible to catch the ball, a goalkeeper can 'palm' or punch it, diverting its course away from the goal.

Striking
The best strikers like England's Gary Lineker here swoop in on balls in the goal area to get a shot in before defenders can intercept

continued from page 13

field for an offence without a separate breach of the Law having been committed, the game shall be resumed by an **indirect free-kick** awarded to the opposing side from the place where the infringement occurred, subject to the over-riding conditions imposed in Law 13.

Law 13
Free-Kick

Free-kicks shall be classified under two headings: 'Direct' (from which a goal can be scored direct against the **offending side**), and 'Indirect' (from which a goal cannot be scored unless the ball has been played or touched by a player other than the kicker before passing through the goal).

When a player is taking a direct or an indirect free-kick inside his own penalty area, all of the opposing players shall be at least 10 yards (9.4 m) from the ball and shall remain outside the penalty area until the ball has been kicked out of the area. The ball shall be in play immediately it has travelled the distance of its own circumference and is beyond the penalty area. The goalkeeper shall not receive the ball into his hands, in order that he may thereafter kick it into play. If the ball is not kicked direct into play, beyond the penalty area, the kick shall be retaken.

When a player is taking a direct or an indirect free-kick outside his own penalty area, all of the opposing players shall be at least 10 yds (9.4 m) from the ball, until it is in play, unless they are standing on their own goal-line, between the goal-posts. The ball shall be in play when it has travelled the distance of its own circumference.

If a player of the opposing side encroaches into the penalty-area, or within 10 yards (9.4 m) of the ball, as the case may be, before a free-kick is taken, the Referee shall delay the taking of the kick, until the Law is complied with.

The ball must be stationary when a free-kick is taken, and the kicker shall not play the ball a second time, until it has been touched or played by another player.

Notwithstanding any other reference in these Laws to the point from which a free-kick is to

The yellow card
Any player who persistently breaks the rules or argues with the referee is given an official warning with a yellow card held high in the air.
A player guilty of violent behaviour or foul language is shown a red card and sent off the field immediately.

be taken:
1. any free-kick awarded to the defending team, within its own goal area, may be taken from any point within the goal-area,
2. any indirect free-kick awarded to the attacking team within its opponent's goal area shall be taken from the part of the goal-area line which runs parallel to the goal line, at the point nearest to where the offence was committed.

Punishment

If the kicker, after taking the free-kick, plays the ball a second time before it has been touched or played by another player an indirect free-kick shall be taken by a player of the opposing team from the spot where the infringement occurred, unless the offence is committed by a player in his opponents' goal area, in which case the free-kick shall be taken from any point within the goal area.

Law 14
Penalty Kick

A penalty-kick shall be taken from the penalty mark and, when it is being taken, all players with the exception of the player taking the kick, properly identified, and the opposing goalkeeper, shall be within the field of play but outside the

penalty area, at least 10 yds (9.4m) from the penalty mark and must stand behind the penalty mark.

The opposing goalkeeper must stand (without moving his feet) on his own goal line, between the goalposts, until the ball is kicked. The player taking the kick must kick the ball forward; he shall not play the ball a second time until it has been touched or played by another player. The ball shall be deemed in play directly it is kicked, i.e., when it has travelled the distance of its circumference. A goal may be scored directly from a penalty kick. When a penalty kick is being taken during the normal course of play, or when time has been extended at half-time or full-time to allow a penalty kick to be taken or retaken, a goal shall not be nullified if, before passing between the posts and under the crossbar, the ball touches either or both of the goalposts, or the crossbar, or the goalkeeper, or any combination of these agencies, providing that no other infringement has occurred.

Punishment

For any infringement of this Law:
a) by the defending team, the

kick shall be retaken if a goal has not resulted;
b) by the attacking team, other than by the player taking the kick, if a goal is scored it shall be disallowed and the kick retaken;
c) by the player taking the committed after the ball is in play, a player of the opposing team shall take an indirect free-kick from the spot where the infringement occurred, subject to the overriding conditions imposed in **Law 13.**

Law 15
Throw-In

When the whole of the ball passes over the touchline, either on the ground or in the air, it shall be thrown in from the point where it crossed the line, in any direction, by a player of the team opposite to that of the player who last touched it. The thrower at the moment of delivering the ball must face the field of play and part of each foot shall be either on the touchline or on the ground outside the touchline. The thrower shall use both hands and shall deliver the ball from behind and over his head. The ball shall be in play immediately it enters the field of play, but the thrower shall not again play the ball until it has been touched or played by another player. A goal shall not be scored direct from a throw-in.

Punishment

a) If the ball is improperly thrown in, the throw-in shall be taken by a player of the opposing team.
b) If the thrower plays the ball a second time before it has been touched or played by another player, an indirect free-kick shall be taken by a player of the opposing team from the place where the infringement occurred, subject to the over-riding conditions imposed in Law 13.

Law 16
Goal Kick

When the whole of the ball passes over the goal line excluding that portion between the goalposts, either in the air or on the ground, having last been played by one of the attacking team, it shall be kicked direct into play beyond the penalty area from any point within the goal area, by a player of the defending team. A goalkeeper shall not receive the ball into his hands from a goal kick in order that he may thereafter kick it into play. If the ball is not kicked beyond the penalty-area, i.e., direct into play, the kick shall be retaken. The kicker shall not play the ball a second time until it has been touched or been played by another player. A goal shall not be scored direct from such a kick. Players of the team opposing that of the player taking the goal kick shall remain outside the penalty area until the ball has been kicked out of the penalty area.

Punishment

If a player taking a goal kick plays the ball a second time after it has passed beyond the penalty-area, but before it has touched or been played by another player, an indirect free-kick shall be awarded to the opposing team, to be taken from the place where the infringement occurred, subject to the overriding conditions imposed in Law 13.

Law 17

Corner Kick

When the whole of the ball passes over the goal line, excluding that portion between the goalposts, either in the air or on the ground, having last been played by one of the defending team, a member of the attacking team shall take a corner kick, i.e., the whole of the ball shall be placed within the quarter circle at the nearest corner flag-post, which must not be moved, and it shall be kicked from that position.

A goal may be scored direct from such a kick. Players of the team opposing that of the player taking the corner kick shall not approach within 10 yds (9.4 m) of the ball until it is in play, i.e., it has travelled the distance of its own circumference, nor shall the kicker play the ball a second time until it has been touched or played by another player.

Punishment

a) If the player who takes the kick plays the ball a second time before it has been touched or played by another player, the referee shall award an indirect free-kick to the opposing team, to be taken from the place where the infringement occurred, subject to the conditions imposed in Law 13.
b) For any other infringement the kick shall be retaken.

Women, children and veterans

Laws may be modified in their application to matches for players of under 16 years of age, for women's football and for Veterans' football (over 35 years).

International Board decisions

Above are listed all the basic rules of Association Football. However, these rules are continually qualified year-by-year by additional rulings called International Board Decisions. For the latest Decisions, contact your national Association Football governing body.

Reprinted by permission of The Football Association. A complete set of rules including laws relating to children, women and veterans, plus the latest International Board decisions, is available from the national association.

TACTICS

Most teams choose one of three main formations to make effective use of their players. Defence - midfield - strikers are detailed as 4-2-4 (four defenders, two midfield and four strikers), 4-3-3 or 4-4-2. This last formation is the most defensive. The arrangement chosen will depend on a number of factors such as the strengths of the individual players and those of the opposing team, the conditions and the venue.

The decision may be made to change the formation during play if, for example, a team urgently needs to score. In this instance more strikers will be allocated to strengthen the attack.

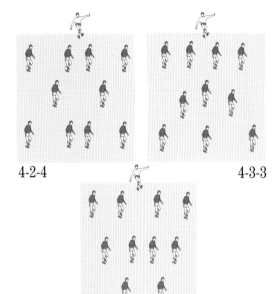

4-2-4   4-3-3

4-4-2

GREY AREA

Q. Player A passes the ball up the field to Player B who is currently standing in an offside position. In running back to receive the pass, Player B passes two opponents, thus placing them between him and the goal. Would he be penalized for being offside?

A. Yes. Player B cannot return himself to an onside position by running back down the field once the ball has been played to him. *See Law 11, Offside (page 12).*

Drop-kick
A goalkeeper can send the ball upfield either by kicking it or throwing it with a single arm. A goalkeeper who holds the ball too long may be penalised for time wasting.

Australian rules football
Essentials

A winter sport previously restricted to just a few states in Australia at the professional level, most notably Victoria, the popularity of this game has increased so much in recent years that it is now a national sport, controlled by the Australian Football League. It is played widely in schools and in various leagues throughout the country, as well as at AFL level.

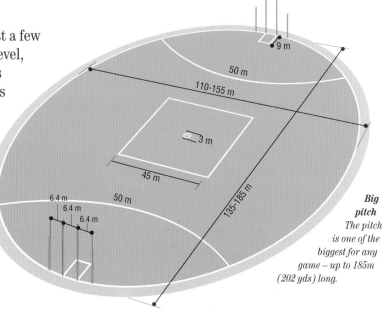

Big pitch
The pitch is one of the biggest for any game – up to 185m (202 yds) long.

The ground

Oval, grass, 135–185 m (148–202 yds) in length and 110–155 m (120–170 yds) in width. Two goalposts, 6.4 m (21 ft) apart and at least 6 m (20 ft) in height) are placed at each end of the ground. Two behind posts, 3 m (10 ft) minimum height are placed in line with the goalposts, at a distance of 6.4 m (21 ft) from each. The line between the goalposts is the goal line and the lines between the goalposts and the behind posts are the behind lines. A goal square is marked out using the goal line as one of its sides, as well as two 9 m (30 ft) lines drawn out at right angles from the goalposts (kick-off lines) and a line connecting the outer end of these kick-off lines. The centre circle is 3 m (10 ft) in diameter, divided into two semicircles and enclosed in a square of 45 m (49 yds).

The players

Two teams of 14 – 18 players on the field at a time, plus up to four interchange players.

Officials

A field umpire, two boundary umpires and two goal umpires.

The ball

Oval, 720–730 mm (29 in) by 545–555 mm (approx 21 in) and weighing 450-500 g (approx 17 oz).

Dress

Sleeveless shirts (referred to as 'guernseys' in Australia), shorts, socks and boots. Players must not wear anything which may cause injury during a match, such as jewellery, guards or dangerous bootstuds.

Grand final day
The biggest date of the Australian rules calendar is Grand Final day at the Melbourne Cricket Ground, below.

Basic dress
Surprisingly for such a tough physical game, Australian rules players wear no protective clothing.

Player positions

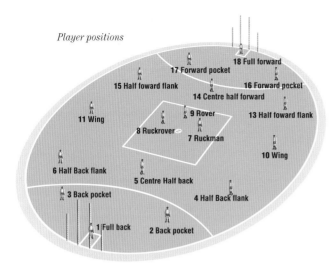

18 Full forward
17 Forward pocket
15 Half foward flank
16 Forward pocket
14 Centre half forward
9 Rover
13 Half foward flank
11 Wing
8 Ruckrover
7 Ruckman
10 Wing
6 Half Back flank
5 Centre Half back
3 Back pocket
4 Half Back flank
1 Full back
2 Back pocket

Playing positions

In Australian rules the forwards main function is to score goals, the midfield players pass the ball up the field and the backs prevent the opponents scoring.

Little rover

Australian rules is not only for big men. Rovers are often small, for they need to be nimble and quick to grab the ball from a spill and dart away up the field with it taking it to the forwards.

HOW TO PLAY

Players attempt to score goals by kicking the ball in between their opponents' goalposts. They may run with the ball, kick it or hit it but they are not allowed to throw it.

Starting

A toss decides the choice of ends. The umpire then starts the quarter with a centre bounce. This takes place inside the centre circle, with a maximum of four players from each team allowed inside the centre square at the time. The umpire holds up the ball, blows the whistle and then bounces the ball in the circle. Only one player from each team may then try to contact the ball. They must be outside the circle. In muddy conditions the umpire may need to throw the ball up into the air rather than bounce it – a 'ball-up'.

Ball up

Australian rules games begin with the umpire bouncing the ball in a circle between up to four players from each team.

How to win

A ball kicked between the goalposts scores a goal (six points). If it passes between a goalpost and a behind post, a behind is scored (one point). Following either, the field umpire must signal the 'All clear' (if there are no penalties to be incurred) to the goal umpire who then signals the score. If a defender causes the ball to cross the goal or behind line, a behind is scored. The team with the most points wins the match.

KEY RULES

A match consists of four quarters of 20 to 25 minutes each. Teams change ends after every quarter.

• Play is fast-moving and restricted by just a few basic rules. The ball may be kicked or handballed (held in one hand and then punched with the fist of the other hand) in any direction. Throwing is not allowed as a means of passing the ball.

See Law 9, Ball Disposal (page 21).

• Players may also run with the ball, unless tackled, provided they bounce it on the ground at every 15 m (approx 16 yds).

See Law 10, Ball Possession (page 21).

• If a player marks the ball from a kick he is in possession and has the choice of either playing on or stopping to take an unobstructed kick. If he marks the ball from a hand pass he must play on.

• Breaches of the laws are penalized by a free-kick to the opposition. These include throwing the ball while it is still in play, illegal tackling (see Law 11, How a Player May be Checked or Tackled, page 22), deliberate obstruction, charging an opponent and kicking the ball out of bounds.

See Law 12, Free-kicks (page 22).

AUSTRALIAN RULES FOOTBALL
· · · · · · · ·

THE LAWS

1 Playing Ground, Oval, Goal and Behind Posts
See The ground (page 18).
2 The Ball
See The ball (page 18).
3 Teams
See The players (page 18).
4 Players' Boots, Jewellery and Protective Equipment
See Dress (page 18).
5 Starting the Match
See How to play (page 19).

6 Goals and Behinds
6.1 A goal shall register six points and a behind one point. The team scoring the greater number of points shall win the match. If the points are equal, the match shall be drawn.
6.2 When a ball crosses a goal or behind line or hits a goalpost, the field umpire shall give the goal umpire an "All clear" signal if there have not been any incidents in play which the field umpire intends to penalize.
6.3 A score cannot be registered unless the field umpire calls or indicates "All clear", or "Touched, all clear" to the goal umpire.
6.4 Subject to the "All clear" signal, a goal shall be scored

when the ball is kicked over the goal line by a player of the attacking team without touching a player or a goalpost. A behind shall be scored in any other case when the ball passes over the goal line, or touches or passes over a goalpost or passes over a behind line without touching or passing over a behind post.

6.4.1 If a defending player kicks or takes the ball over the goal or behind line, a behind shall be scored.

6.4.2 If the ball touches or passes over a behind post, it shall be out of bounds.

6.4.3 The fact that the ball has struck or touched an umpire (or any other authorized official or replaced player) shall not prevent the scoring of a goal or a behind.

6.4.4. While the ball is on the ground and a player has his hands on it, and if another player kicks the ball, it shall be deemed to have been touched in transit. If the ball goes over the goal or behind lines, the field umpire shall call "Touched, all clear" and a behind shall be registered.

6.4.5 In the event that the ball crosses a goal or behind line, or hits a goalpost, and the goal umpire does not receive an all clear from the field umpire and play continues, the goal umpire shall run after the field umpire

and notify him at once.
On receipt of such advice, the field umpire shall stop play and give the all clear.
The goal umpire shall signal and record the score and play shall recommence in accordance with these laws.
In the event that a free-kick has been awarded after the ball crosses the line and before the all-clear has been given, the field umpire shall give the all-clear and the goal umpires shall signal and record the score. The free-kick shall then be taken where the infringement occurred or where the ball is at the time, whichever is the greater penalty against the offending team.

6.4.6 In the event that, after the all-clear has been given for a goal, an infringement occurs to a player of the defending team prior to the ball being bounced in the centre circle, the resultant free-kick shall be taken at the spot where the infringement occurred, or at the centre circle, whichever is the greater penalty against the offending team.

6.4.7 In the event that, after the all clear has been given for a behind, an infringement occurs to a player of the defending team prior to the ball being kicked off after the behind, the resultant free-kick shall be taken at the spot where the infringement

occurred, or at the back line of the centre square, whichever is the greater penalty against the offending team.

6.5 The goal umpires shall be the sole judges of goals and behinds and their decisions are final, except when the ball has become dead by a decision of the field umpire.

6.5.1 Upon receiving "All clear", the goal umpire shall initially indicate a goal by raising both index fingers, and a behind by raising one index finger.

6.5.2 The goal umpire shall then signal a goal by waving two flags, and a behind by waving one flag. A score cannot be annulled unless the goal umpire immediately rectifies a mistake by notifying the field umpire before the ball is bounced in the centre if he has wrongly signalled a goal or before the ball is kicked off in the case of a behind except when the ball has been signalled out of bounds and the signal has not been seen by the field umpire.

6.5.3 When a score has been annulled, the goal umpire shall immediately stand on the centre of the goal line and hold both flags above his head in crossed position.

6.6 At the first sound of the siren, the ball shall be dead, but a player who has, prior to the first sound of the siren, taken a mark or been awarded a free-kick shall be allowed to kick or handball the ball. A goal or behind obtained therefrom or from a ball which is in transit prior to the first sound of the siren shall be counted.

In the event that the siren sounds whilst the ball is in transit, or whilst the player taking a kick after the siren is preparing to kick the ball, or after he has kicked the ball, an infringement occurs to a player of the attacking team before the all-clear has been given, the field umpire shall blow his whistle and consult with the goal umpire as to whether a goal or behind has been kicked.

If a goal has been kicked the field umpire shall give the all-clear and the goal shall be registered. In the event that a behind has been kicked, the

Swooping pack
Packs swoop quickly on a loose ball and players have to be deft at making a clean pick-up on the run while surrounded by opponents – they can be tackled the moment they touch the ball.

player offended against shall be given the option of taking the free-kick at the spot the infringement occurred, or allowing the behind to be registered.

Should the siren sound whilst the ball is in transit, or whilst the player taking a kick after the siren is preparing to kick the ball, or after he has kicked the ball, an infringement occurs to a player of the defending team before the all-clear has been given, the field umpire shall award a free-kick to the player offended against at the spot where the infringement occurred.

6.6.1 In the event that two or more field umpires are officiating, the ball shall be deemed dead when one of the field umpires hears the first sound of the siren. That field umpire shall be the sole judge of whether the ball has been kicked or handled or whether a free-kick has been awarded prior to the first sound of the siren.

6.6.2 If the ball is touched in transit the field umpire must be satisfied that the score was not assisted by another player, but if the ball touches any player below the knee it shall become dead and no score recorded.

6.7 Controlling bodies shall authorize such officials as they deem appropriate to record scores, separate from the goal umpires. In the event of the goal umpires disagreeing on the final scores, the controlling body may take the separately recorded scores into consideration in determining the result of the match.

7 Kicking Off from Behind

7.1 When a behind has been scored, unless a subsequent free-kick has been given, any player of the defending team shall kick the ball into the field of play from within the kick-off lines, the ball contact being made before the ball completely crosses the line. When the ball is being kicked off, no player shall be allowed within 5 m (approx 16 ft) of the kick-off lines.

7.2 The player kicking off may regain possession provided the ball has been kicked into the field of play beyond the kick-off lines.

7.3 If the ball is not brought into play correctly, the field umpire shall bounce the ball on the centre of the kick-off line.

7.4 The ball shall not be kicked off until the goal umpire has

finished waving the flag.

7.5 If an opposing player attempts to delay play by moving to, or standing within, 5 m (approx 16 ft) of the kick-off line or prevents the player from kicking off, the field umpire shall penalize the offending team by advancing the mark from the kick-off line to the back line of the centre square – the kick to be taken at the centre of the line by the nearest player of the team offended against.

In the event of a further offence against this law, the mark to be advanced to the forward line of the centre square – the kick to be taken at the centre of the line by the nearest player of the team offended against.

7.6 If after the goal umpire has finished waving the flag a player will not kick off (time being added) when directed to do so by the field umpire, or kicks the ball over the goal or behind line, the field umpire shall bounce the ball on the centre of the kick-off line.

8 Marking the Ball

8.1 A mark is catching the ball directly from the kick of another player, not less than 10 m (33 ft) distant, the ball being held a reasonable time and not having been touched in transit from kick to catch.

8.1.1 A mark shall be awarded to a player who crosses the boundary line from the playing ground but controls the ball before it has passed completely over the boundary line. If the field umpire is in doubt he should consult the boundary umpire.

8.1.2 A mark shall be allowed when the ball is caught and controlled on the goal, behind or boundary lines.

8.1.3 A mark will be awarded where a ball in flight strikes an umpire, or any other authorized official or replaced player.

8.2 When a player takes a mark or is given a free-kick, an opponent is permitted to stand on the mark or spot where this occurrence took place.

8.2.1 Only one opponent may stand on a player's mark.

8.2.2 No other player is allowed within a corridor which extends from 5 m (approx 16 ft) either side of the mark to 5 m either side of, and a 5 m radius behind, the player with the ball. This corridor is to be known as the 10 m protected area.

8.2.3 In the event of an opponent encroaching over the

mark when a player is kicking for goal and a goal is kicked, the field umpire shall give the "All clear" and the goal shall be registered. If a goal has not been kicked, the player shall be given the option of another kick, and the mark shall be advanced 50 m (approx 55 yds).

9 Ball Disposal

The ball may be kicked or handballed.

9.1 A player shall handball the ball by holding the ball in one hand and hitting it with the clenched fist of the other hand. If the ball is not handballed correctly, a free-kick shall be given to the nearest opponent.

See 9.1.

9.2 A player may kick the ball by making contact with the ball below the knee.

9.2.1 A player who takes a mark or is awarded a free-kick shall play the ball from directly behind the spot where the mark or free-kick was awarded. The 10 m protected area shall apply. If the player attempts to play the ball other than in a direct line over the mark, the field umpire shall call "Play on" and the ball shall immediately be in play.

9.2.2 When it is necessary for a defending player, from a free-kick or mark, to play the ball from beyond the goal or behind line, the player on the mark shall not be permitted to come within 5 m (16 ft) of the goal or behind lines. In such cases, the ball must be played directly over the mark. If there is no player on the mark, the ball may be played in any direction provided it is brought into play over the goal,

behind or boundary line originally crossed.

9.2.3 When a player is kicking for goal from a mark or a free-kick, the kick shall be taken along a direct line through the mark to the centre of the goal line.

9.2.4 The ball shall be deemed to be brought into play when any portion of it is on or above the boundary line.

9.2.5 If a player taking his kick from outside the boundary line after having been awarded a mark or a free-kick, fails to take the ball into play, or attempts to play on outside the boundary line, the ball shall be deemed to be out of bounds. The ball will then be thrown into play by the boundary umpire from the spot where the original mark or free-kick took place.

9.2.6 If a player on the defending team, from a free-kick or mark, kicks from behind the goal or behind lines and the ball hits either a goalpost or behind post, the field umpire shall direct the timekeepers to add time on and give the player another kick to put the ball into play.

10 Ball Possession

10.1 A player may hold the ball for any length of time provided he is not held by an opponent.

10.2 If he runs with the ball he must bounce it or touch it on the ground at least once within every 15 m (approx 16 yds) from the commencement of his run, whether running in a straight line or turning and dodging.

10.3 If a player with the ball bounces it, he is deemed to be in

➠ *page 22*

Below, see 10.20.

Good shepherd
Players help a team-mate pick up a loose ball by shepherding. This means using the body to protect the team-mate and stop an opponent tackling or spoiling – that is, knocking the ball away.

SKILLS AND TACTICS

The overall aim of both teams is to keep possession of the ball, moving it swiftly into the forward area to score maximum points.

Marking is an acquired skill. The high mark is one of the game's main characteristics – leaping into the air to catch the ball directly from a kick. The ball is difficult to catch due to slippery winter conditions and also because of its shape. Players need the strength to mark the ball against the pressure of leaping opponents trying to do the same. Being able to *kick* with the left or right foot, for distance and accuracy, is essential for all players, particularly when kicking for goal. *Handballing* too is left- or right-handed. The emphasis is on accuracy and speed. *Running with the ball* requires agility and strength as players must bounce the ball as they run, dodging opponents as they go. *Tapping* the ball in *ruck duels* to fellow players is frequently used to clear blocked play. As with the centre bounce, the umpire blows his whistle to restart play and bounces the ball between two rucks.

Shepherding is using the body to stop an opponent tackling or spoiling (knocking the ball away from) a team-mate. Players must be able to *tackle* effectively, bringing an opponent to a halt and preventing him from disposing of the ball in order to gain possession.

continued from page 21

possession of the ball.

10.4 If he runs with the ball and handballs it over an opponent's head and catches it, he must, within 15 m (approx 16 yds) of commencing his run or striking the ball on the ground, bounce it or touch the ground with it or dispose of the ball.

10.5 A player who lies on or over the ball is deemed to be in possession of the ball.

11 How a Player May Be Checked or Tackled

11.1 A player may be fairly met or checked by an opponent by the use of the hip, shoulder, chest, arms or open hand provided the ball is not more than 5 m (16 ft) away.

11.2 A player may be pushed in the chest or side or shepherded by an opponent provided the ball

is not more than 5 m (16 ft) away.

11.3 A player in possession of the ball may fend off a prospective tackler by pushing him with an open hand in the chest, shoulder or side.

11.4 A player in possession of the ball may be tackled and grasped in the area below the top of the shoulders and on or above the knees. The tackle may be from front, side or behind provided that the tackle from behind does not thrust forward the player with the ball.

11.5 Procedures for administering this law are as follows:

11.5.1 A player in possession of the ball, when held by an opponent firmly enough to retard his progress, should be given a reasonable chance of disposing of it by kicking or handball, otherwise a free-kick shall be

awarded to his opponent for holding the ball.

11.5.2 The field umpire shall bounce the ball when the player with the ball has the ball held to his body by an opponent, unless the player has had a reasonable time to dispose of the ball prior to being tackled, in which case a free-kick shall be awarded for holding the ball.

11.5.3 A player not in possession of the ball when held by an opponent, shall be awarded a free-kick.

11.5.4 When a player claims a mark, the ball having been touched in transit, and retains possession when held by an opponent, the field umpire shall not award a free-kick but bounce the ball if he is satisfied that the player did not hear his call of "Play on". But if the ball has been taken away from the player by another player, the field

umpire's call "Play on" shall hold good.

11.5.5 The field umpire shall allow play to continue if a player in the act of kicking or handball, is swung off balance and his foot or hand does not connect with the ball.

11.5.6 The field umpire shall allow play to continue if a player is bumped and the ball falls from his hands.

11.5.7 The field umpire shall allow play to continue when a player's arm is knocked, causing him to drop the ball.

11.5.8 The field umpire shall allow play to continue if a player has his arms pinned to his sides causing him to drop the ball.

11.5.9 The field umpire shall allow play to continue if a player is pulled by one arm or swung causing the ball to fall from his hand.

12 Free-kicks

Making your mark

One of the most distinctive moments in Australian rules is the dramatic high jump or mark as a player leaps to catch a ball kicked by a team-mate. A good, clean catch gives the player a free kick. Here the leaping player in black has gone up to make a mark but his opponent has spoiled his catch by punching the ball away.

Losing control

When tackled, a player must be allowed to kick or handball the ball away – if he is still holding the ball. So opponents usually try to force him to drop the ball – for example, by swinging him off balance, as here – so that he loses possession.

12.1 The spirit of the laws relating to awarding free-kicks is:

12.1.1 The player who makes the ball his sole objective shall be given every opportunity to gain possession of the ball.

12.1.2 The player who has possession of the ball and is held by an opponent shall be given a reasonable time to kick or handball the ball.

12.1.3 The ball shall be kept in motion. The field umpire shall call "Play on" even though a free kick should have been awarded but by doing so would penalize the team offended against.

12.2 All breaches of the laws shall be penalized whether the ball is dead or in play. The field umpire shall sound his whistle for the awarding of a free-kick. Unless otherwise specified, the player nearest to the opponent who commits a breach of the Laws shall receive the free-kick.

12.2.1 If the field umpire has sounded his whistle for a free-kick, he may cancel such a free kick by calling "Play on" if the side offended against will be penalized by enforcing the free-kick.

Should the field umpire cancel a free-kick he may reverse the decision if it is obvious that it is not to the advantage of the team concerned.

12.2.2 A player awarded a free-kick must go back to the spot where the breach occurred before being allowed to kick or play the ball. If such a player kicks or plays the ball without complying to this law, the field umpire shall stop play and enforce compliance.

12.2.3 A free-kick shall be awarded against a player who throws or hands the ball to another player, or to the advantage of play, while the ball is in play.

12.2.4 When a player who has taken a mark or been awarded a free-kick is, in the opinion of the field umpire, unable to dispose of the ball through accident or

➡ *page 24*

continued from page 23

the deliberate action of an opponent, the field umpire shall award a free-kick to the nearest player of the same team at the time the incident occurred. The kick shall be taken at the spot nearest to where the incident occurred.

12.2.5 If a player has been awarded a free-kick or a mark, and before the kick is taken a further breach of the laws is made by a player on the same side as the first offender, the field umpire shall sound his whistle and direct the free-kick to be taken by a team mate at the spot where the subsequent breach took place, if doing so will penalize the offending team. Where a subsequent breach is committed by a team-mate of the player taking the kick, a free-kick shall be given to the nearest opponent at the spot of the original free-kick, if doing so will penalize the offending team.

12.2.6 If a breach of the laws is committed, regardless of the position on the field, the free-kick is to be taken at the spot where the infringement occurred, or where the ball is at the time, whichever would be the greater penalty for the offending team.

12.2.7 A free-kick shall be given if a player infringes any of the laws between the time the field umpire sounds his whistle and bounces the ball.

12.3 Free-kicks for infringements concerning the field umpire bouncing the ball will be awarded against the player who:

12.3.1 Enters the centre circle when the field umpire is in the act of bouncing the ball at the start of the match, the start of the quarter, and after a goal has been scored.

12.3.2 Interferes with an opponent from the time the ball has been bounced in the centre circle until the ball subsequently makes contact with a player or the ground.

12.3.3 Unduly interferes with the bouncing of the ball by the field umpire or deliberately interferes with an umpire during the progress of the match.

12.4 A free-kick will be awarded against a player who interferes with an opponent in the following manner:

12.4.1 Interferes with an opponent from the time the ball goes out of bounds, until the ball, after being thrown in by the boundary umpire, makes contact with a player or the ground.

12.4.2 When a goal is kicked by a player, and while the ball is being kicked or is in transit a breach of the laws is made by an opponent, the field umpire shall give the "All clear" signal and the goal shall be registered; but in the event of a behind being scored the ball not having touched the ground or player, the player shall be given the option of another kick.

12.4.3 After the ball has been kicked and an infringement occurs, and the ball crosses the behind line on the full or hits the goalpost on the full, the option of another kick shall be given to the player who originally kicked the ball at the spot from where the kick originated. If the breach of the laws occurred before or during the act of kicking or handball, a free-kick shall be taken by the player offended against, at the spot where the breach occurred, provided that the team offended against will not be penalized by the taking of such a free-kick.

12.4.4 If a breach of the laws is made by a player of the attacking side, the field umpire shall not signal "All clear" but must award a free-kick, to the nearest player of the defending team.

12.4.5 If a player is fouled immediately after scoring a goal or behind and after the field umpire has given the "All clear", the field umpire shall award such player a free-kick at the spot where the offence took place. Another score may then be registered without the ball having been bounced in the centre circle or kicked off.

12.4.6 If a breach of the laws is committed against a player who has disposed of the ball, or who is shepherding for a team-mate with the ball, and this occurs after the ball has been kicked or handballed, a penalty free-kick shall be awarded to a player of the team offended against at the spot where the ball first touched the ground, a player, was marked or went out of bounds. If the awarding of

See
12.4.7

such a free-kick will penalize the team offended against, the free-kick shall be given to the player who originally kicked the ball.

12.4.7 Trips or kicks, attempts to trip or kick or slings an opponent, or when not in possession of the ball, kicks in a manner likely to cause injury to an opponent, or strikes or attempts to strike an opponent with either hand or arm or deliberately with the knee.

12.5 A free-kick shall be awarded against a player who kicks the ball out of bounds in the following manner:

12.5.1 Kicks the ball out of bounds on the full. The free-kick shall be taken at the spot where the ball went out of bounds.

12.5.2 When kicking off after a behind has been registered, the ball is kicked out of bounds without it having been touched by any player, a free-kick shall be given at the spot where the ball went out of bounds.

12.5.3 Wilfully kicks or forces the ball out of bounds without it being touched by another player.

12.6 A free-kick shall be awarded against the player who checks or tackles an opponent in the following manner:

12.6.1 Catches hold of an opponent below the knee or by the neck or head, which includes the top of the shoulder.

12.6.2 Charges an opponent.

12.6.3 Pushes an opponent from behind in any way, except when legitimately going for a mark, a player may interfere with an opponent from behind.

12.6.4 Pushes, bumps or shepherds an opponent in the face, head, neck or in the shoulder.

12.6.5 Pushes, bumps or

See
12.6.1

See
12.6.3

shepherds an opponent who is in the air for a mark.

12.6.6 Shepherds an opponent when the ball is more than 5 m (16 ft) away or is out of play.

12.6.7 Deliberately holds back or throws an opponent after that opponent has kicked or handballed the ball. No free-kick shall be given if the player, unable to release his hold at once, throws the opponent down.

12.7 A free-kick shall be awarded against a player who interferes with play as follows:

12.7.1 If the ball is in transit towards goal from a free-kick, mark or field kick and an opponent shakes the goalpost, the field umpire shall give the player the option of another kick if in the umpire's opinion, the opponent's action could have affected the result.

12.7.2 If a team-mate shakes the goalpost, the field umpire shall award a free-kick to the nearest opponent at the spot from where the ball was kicked.

12.8 A free-kick shall be awarded against a player who wilfully wastes time by not allowing the ball to be brought into play prior to, or when directed to do so, by the field umpire.

12.9 A free-kick shall be awarded against the team as follows:

12.9.1 Any official runner, trainer, medical officer, other approved team official or replaced player who interferes with the ball, the play or a player of the opposing team during the course of the game shall cause the field umpire to award a free-kick to the nearest player of the team offended against at the spot of the infringement, or where the ball is at the time, whichever would be a greater penalty to the offending team. When a player is awarded a set kick at goal and an opposition player climbs on the shoulders of a team-mate before the kick is taken, the mark shall be advanced to the centre of the goal line and the player with the kick shall be permitted to kick from directly in front of goal.

12.9.2 A free-kick shall be awarded against a player who carries the ball across the boundary line, and after a boundary umpire signals out of bounds, does not give the ball immediately to the boundary umpire or drop it directly to the ground.

12.9.3 A free-kick shall be awarded against a player who touches the ball after it has passed outside the boundary line and been signalled out of bounds by the boundary umpire, except for a player of the team to receive the free-kick when the ball has been kicked out on the full, kicked out directly from a kick-off from a behind, or wilfully kicked or forced out without being touched by another player.

13. 50 Metre Penalty

13.1 A 50 m penalty (55 yds) will be applied in instances where the actions of a player encroach over the mark, waste time and/or delay the play.

13.2 When the umpire applies a 50 m penalty, he shall signal "time on". The player receiving the penalty shall not be permitted to play on. The mark shall then be advanced 50 m in a direct line with the centre of the goal. The player receiving the penalty shall be given free access to take up a position behind the advanced mark. When the umpire is satisfied the player has taken up a correct position, he will instruct the timekeepers to stop adding time, irrespective of whether an opponent is standing on the mark.

13.3 A 50 m penalty shall have the same implication as a free-kick.

13.4 If a free-kick or mark has been awarded and a player of the opposing team runs through the 10 m protected area , unless accompanying or following an opponent within 5m, a 50 m penalty shall be awarded.

13.5 Where a 50 m penalty advances the mark to the centre of the goal line, the kick shall be taken from directly in front of the advanced mark.

13.6 Where a player has been awarded a mark or free-kick and another player of the same team is unlawfully prevented from running past the spot of the mark or free-kick, a 50 m penalty shall be awarded to the player originally awarded the mark or free-kick.

13.7 Where a free-kick is awarded for intentionally tripping, a 50 m penalty shall automatically apply.

13.8 To suit local requirements controlling bodies may reduce the distance of the penalty to 25 m (27 yds).

14 Play On

The field umpire shall call and indicate "Play on" and the ball shall immediately remain in play in any of the following circumstances:

14.1 When an umpire, or any other authorized official or player is struck by the ball while it is in play.

14.2 When the ball, having been kicked, is touched while still in transit.

14.3 When the ball is caught directly from a kick of another player less than 10 m (33 ft) distant.

14.4 When the field umpire cancels a free-kick.

14.5 When a player who has taken a mark or been awarded a free-kick, attempts to run, handball or kick otherwise than over his mark.

15 Bouncing the Ball

15.1 The field umpire shall bounce the ball in the following circumstances:

15.1.1 At the start of the match, at the start of each quarter and after each goal has been kicked, except when a breach of the laws has been penalized by the awarding of a free-kick.

15.1.2 When in doubt as to which player has taken a mark.

15.1.3 When a player, in kicking off after a behind has

been registered, fails to correctly bring the ball into play, the ball to be bounced on the centre of the kick-off line.

15.1.4 In a scrimmage where players are struggling in undue confusion for possession of the ball.

15.1.5 When the field umpire has bounced the ball and it goes over the goal, behind or boundary line without having been touched by any player.

15.1.6 When a player claims a mark, the ball having been touched, and retains possession of the ball when held by an opponent, the field umpire will bounce the ball if he is satisfied that the player did not hear his call of "Play on".

15.1.7 When a goal umpire is unable to see whether the ball goes over the goal or behind lines, and cannot give a decision, the ball shall be bounced on the centre of the kick-off line in front of the goal.

15.1.8

When there is simultaneous encroachment of players from opposing teams, into the centre square prior to the ball being bounced.

16 Umpires: Duties and Instructions

17 Match-Time, Duties And Responsibilities of Umpires and Timekeepers

18 Controlling Body

19 Doping Policy

20 Infectious Diseases

These laws are reprinted by permission of the Australian Football League who hold the copyright. The complete Laws of Australian rules football can be obtained from the AFL.

Possession
Gaining possession of the ball is crucial in Australian rules and whenever a ball goes loose you will see players hurtling in to grab it before their opponents. But picking up a slippery, oval shaped ball on the run can be extraordinarily difficult and players often resort to kicking it on.

American football

Essentials

This massively popular and lucrative sport – known also as 'gridiron' football – is often described as a warlike game of chess. A team's coaches formulate a complex set of moves, tactics and formations and then guide their players strategically as a game progresses. The National Football League season culminates each year in the Super Bowl.

The field (or gridiron)

Rectangular, 360 by 160 ft (110 by 49 m). Grass (natural or artificial). Bounded by the sidelines and end lines, with goal lines marked parallel to the end lines, 10 yds (9 m) in. Yard lines are marked at intervals of 5 yds (4.5 m) along the field, parallel to the goal lines, to mark the ground gained by a team.

The goals

Two bright gold goalposts are offset from each end line, at the center, and are connected by a horizontal crossbar, 18 ft 6 in long, 10 ft (3 m) above the ground. The posts extend 30 ft (9 m) above this bar and the goal is the vertical plane extending indefinitely above the crossbar and between the two posts.

The ball

Oval, tan. An inflated rubber bladder enclosed in a pebble-grained leather case. Standard measurements are: long axis, 11 to 11¼ in (approx 28 cm); long circumference (around the middle), 28-28½ in (approx 71 cm); weight, 14 to 15 oz (approx 397 g). There must be 24 balls available for stadium matches.

The gridiron game
Unlike other football games where pitch measurements are only approximate, all pitches in American football are very precisely measured out with lines every five yards. Each of the five-yard lines has two lines at 90° to it called hash marks which mark the limits of each play.

Armour plating
American footballers are amongst the most heavily protected of all sportsmen and look almost like Medieval knights of armour when they enter the field. Underneath his shirt the footballer wears a full body jacket with massive shoulder pads, a complete pelvic guard and hip pads.

Pylons
Inbound yard markers
20-yd line
Goal
10 yds
Goal line
120 yds
Side view

Super Bowl
The top teams in the National Football League compete to play in the Super Bowl, the match which decides the year's champions. Since it was first held in 1967, the Super Bowl has been won most by the San Fransisco 49ers and the Dallas Cowboys.

The players

Overall squads consist of 45 men each and from these a coach will pick a team of 11 players to be on the field at any one time. Within the squad there is an 'offense' team, 'defense' team and a special team which is brought in for kick-offs, punts, (kicks to the opposition), extra points (or conversion kicks) and field goals.

Dress

Helmet, shoulder pads, thigh pads, knee pads, trousers, jerseys, wristbands, gloves, stockings and shoes. Jerseys feature the player's numbers on the front, back and sleeves and the player's surname on the back. Numbers are:
1 – 19 quarterbacks, punters, place-kickers
20 – 49 running backs and defensive backs
50 – 59 centers
60 – 79 offensive guards and tackles
80 – 89 wide receivers and tight ends
90 – 99 defensive linesmen (if 60 – 79 unavailable)
90 – 99 linebackers (if 50 – 59 unavailable).

Officials

A referee, umpire, head lines-man, line judge, back judge, side judge and field judge.

Target
The player running with the ball is the only player who may be tackled in each play.

Kicking for goal
If the team gets close enough to their opponents' line on the fourth down, the team's kicker may come on and try to score a field goal by kicking the ball over the bar.

Quarterback pass
Unlike in rugby, a forward pass is allowed in American football and it is usually the quarterback who makes it.

Short run
Players rarely get to run far with the ball before they are brought down.

GREY AREAS

One of the most commonly called penalties in American football is for **holding**. The offensive team are allowed to use their arms or hands to block their opponents, but they are not allowed to actually hold on to them. There is often a fine line between a legal and an illegal block and linemen are frequently pulled up for holding on to the arm or jersey of an opponent in their attempts to break through the defense.

Although it is not as common an offence, **pass interference** causes much debate, partly because it incurs quite a harsh penalty. While a player is allowed to intercept a pass, he must not unfairly impede the attempts of an opponent to catch the ball. It is up to the official to decide in certain cases whether a player was making a genuine attempt to get the ball himself, or whether he was trying intentionally to restrict his opponent's chances of doing so.

HOW TO PLAY

The team in possession of the ball (the offense) advances down the field to score points by crossing their opponents' goal line with the ball for a touchdown or by kicking the ball over the crossbar for a goal. The offense is allowed four downs (attempts) to advance 10 yds while in possession and, if they do so, another four downs to advance a further 10 yds and so on.

Yardage is recorded progressively. The number of the down is given, followed by the yds still to be gained to make the required 10 yd total. For example, with the first down, when there are 10 full yds yet to be gained, the offensive are declared to be 'first and 10'. If on their second play they manage to travel six yds further, they are then said to be '2nd and 4'.

Yardage lost is subtracted from the second digit.

Players run with the ball or pass it, while the defense try to stop them gaining ground and make them lose possession.

Starting

The winner of the toss can choose which goal to defend or whether to receive first. The defense starts the game with a kick-off from their 35-yd line. The ball is placed on a kicking tee and kicked down the field towards the opposing team who then attempt to advance with it in the other direction.

How to win

A touchdown is worth six points, a field goal scores three points. A successful try (or conversion – a kick taken from the 2-yd line following a touchdown) is worth one or two points and a safety (if the offense are caught in possession in their own end zone) is worth two points. The team with the most points wins.

If a game's score is tied, the sudden-death system is used to determine a winner. Periods of 15 minutes are played until either team manages to score.

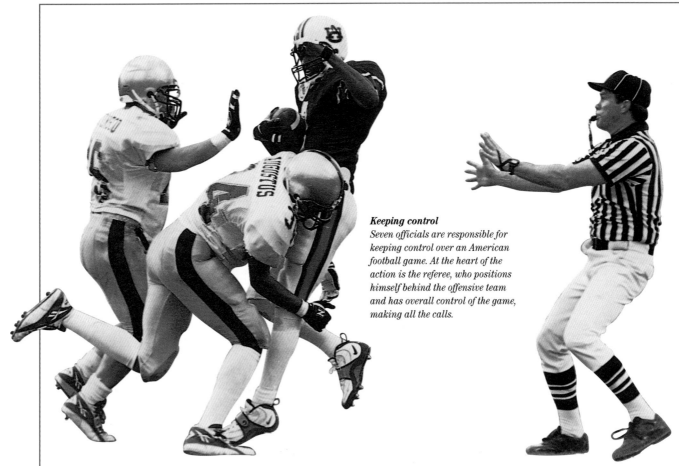

Keeping control
Seven officials are responsible for keeping control over an American football game. At the heart of the action is the referee, who positions himself behind the offensive team and has overall control of the game, making all the calls.

AMERICAN FOOTBALL – NATIONAL FOOTBALL LEAGUE RULES
• • • • • • • • • •

These rules are abridged and summarized.

Rule 1 The Field
See The field (page 26).

Rule 2 The Ball
See The ball (page 26).

Rule 3 Definitions

Rule 4 Game Timing

Rule 5 Players, Substitutes, Equipment
See The players and Dress (page 26).

Rule 6 Free-Kick
Section 1 Putting Ball in Play
Article 1 A free-kick called a kick-off puts the ball in play:
(a) at the start of each half;
(b) after a try; and
(c) after a successful field goal.
Article 2 A free-kick also puts the ball in play:
(a) after a safety;
(b) following a fair catch when this method is chosen;
(c) when there is a replay for a short free-kick; and
(d) when enforcement for a foul during a free-kick is from the previous spot.

Article 3 A free-kick may be made from any point on or behind the offensive team's free-kick line and between inbounds lines. A drop-kick, place-kick, or punt may be used.
Penalty: For illegal kick at free-kick: loss of 5 yds from previous spot.
Article 4 The initial free-kick lines during a given free-kick shall be as follows (plus or minus any distance they might be moved because of a distance penalty enforced prior to the kick):
   For the kicking team:
(a) Kick off – offensive 30
(b) Safety kick – offensive 20
(c) Fair-catch kick – the yard line through the mark of the catch.
   For the receiving team:
A yard line 10 yards in advance of the offensive team's free-kick line.
Article 5 After the referee's whistle prior to a free-kick:
(a) All receiving players (Team B) must be inbounds and behind their line until the kick.
(b) All kicking players (Team A) must be inbounds and behind the ball when kicked except the holder of the placekick may be beyond the line and the kicker may be beyond the line but his kicking foot may not be.
Penalty: For violation of free-

kick formation: the free-kick is made again. New free-kick lines are set 5 yds nearer the offender's end line unless a half-distance penalty is being enforced.
Section 2 Ball in Play After Free-kick
Article 1 A free-kick is short when it does not go to or across the receiving team's free-kick line unless, before doing so, it is first touched by a player of the receiving team, or goes out of bounds.
Penalties:
(a) For the first short free-kick: loss of 5 yds from the previous spot, and rekick must be made.
(b) For the second (or more) consecutive short free-kick illegally touched:
the receiving team takes possession of the ball at the spot of illegal touch or recovery. If a re-kick is to be made, new free-kick lines are set.
Article 2 Free-Kick Recovery
(a) If a free-kick is recovered by the receiving team it may advance.
(b) If a free-kick(legal or illegal) is recovered by the kicking team, the ball is dead. If the recovery is legal, the kicking team next puts the ball in play at the spot of recovery. Undue advance by the kicking team recovering (legal or illegal) is delay of

game.
(c) If a free-kick is simultaneously recovered by two opposing players, the ball is awarded to the receiving team.
Article 3 All general rules apply - when play continues after a free-kick (loose ball) ends.
Article 4 No player of the kicking team may touch or recover a kick-off or safety kick before:
(a) it is touched by the receiving team (B) if that kicking team player has been out of bounds during the kick; or
(b) it has crossed the receiving team's restraining line, unless before doing so, it has first been touched by the receiving team.
Penalty: For illegal touching of a free-kick by the kicking team: loss of 5 yds from the previous spot. New free-kick lines are set if enforced.
Article 5 If there is a foul other than a personal foul (blocking) after a fair-catch signal, fair-catch interference or an invalid fair-catch signal during a free-kick, any enforcement, if made, is from the previous spot and the free-kick must be made again.

Section 3 Free-Kick Out of Bounds or in Touch
Article 1 The kicking team may not kick a free-kick out of bounds between the goal lines.
Penalties:

(a) Receivers' ball 30 yds from the spot of the kick or the team may elect the option of taking possession of the ball at the out-of-bounds spot.
(b) For the second (or more) consecutive onside kick out of bounds: receiving team takes possession of the ball at the out-of-bounds spot.
Article 2 Rule 11 governs if a free-kick:
(a) goes out of bounds behind the receiving team's goal line;
(b) kick-off or safety kick becomes dead because the ball strikes the receiving team's goalpost; or
(c) is downed in the end zone.

Rule 7 Scrimmage
Section 1 Necessary Gain on Downs
Article 1 A new series (first-and-10) is awarded to the offensive team when the following conditions exist; subject, however, to the specific rules of enforcement (Rule 12).
(a) When, during a given series, the ball is declared dead in possession of offensive team while it is on, above, or across the necessary line, or unless a

penalty places it there, or unless a touchback for them results.
(b) When the ball is dead in the field of play in the offense's possession, after having been in the defensive team's possession during the same down.
(c) When a foul is made by the defense, except as otherwise specified, or when an impetus by them results in a touchback for the offensive team.
(d) When the kicking team recovers a scrimmage kick anywhere in the field of play after it first has been touched beyond the line by the receivers.
Article 2 The forward part of the ball in its position when declared dead in the field of play shall be taken as the determining point in measuring any distance gained. The ball shall not be rotated when measuring.
Article 3 If offensive team fails to advance ball to necessary line during a given series, it is awarded to defensive team for a new series at the spot:
(a) where dead at end of fourth down; or
(b) where it is placed because of a combination penalty or a

touchback for defensive team.
Section 2 Position of Players at Snap
Article 1 The offensive team must have:
(a) seven or more players on its line at the snap.
(b) all players who are not on line, other than the snap receiver under center, must be at least 1 yd behind it at snap.
Penalty: For violation of snap formation: loss of 5 yds from previous spot.
Article 2 After the neutral zone starts, no player of either team at snap may:
(a) encroach upon it; or
(b) be offside.
Penalty: For encroachment, offside, or a neutral zone infraction: loss of 5 yds from previous spot. Number of down and necessary line remain the same.
Article 3 An offensive player who comes into game wearing an illegal number for the position he takes must report to the referee who in turn will report same to the defensive captain. The clock shall not be stopped and the ball may not be put in play until the referee take his

normal position.
Penalties:
(a) 5 yds for illegal substitution if player in above category enters the game and/or his team's huddle without reporting and later reports his player position status to the referee prior to snap.
(b) For failure to notify referee of change in eligibility or ineligibility status (when required) prior to snap: loss of 5 yds for illegal susbstitution.
Article 4 At the snap, a center, guard, or tackle of the offensive team may be anywhere on his line, but he may not be behind it unless he is at least 1-yd behind it and has informed the referee of his change of position to that of an eligible receiver.
Penalty: For center, guard, or tackle not on the line at the snap: loss of five yards from the previous spot.
Article 5 At the snap, all offensive players must be stationary in their positions:
(a) without any movement of feet, head, or arms;
(b) without swaying of body; and
(c) without moving directly forward except that one player only and he, provided he is moving, parallel to, obliquely backward from, or directly backward from the line of scrimmage at snap.
Penalty: For player illegally in motion at snap: loss of 5 yds from previous spot. In case of doubt, this penalty shall be enforced.
Article 6 After a shift or huddle all offensive players after assuming a set position must come to an absolute stop. They also must remain stationary in their position without any

➡ *page 31*

Head to head
Players line up at a scrimmage – ready for action.

Scrimmage
After every dead ball play restarts with a scrimmage.

Scrimmage positions
Offense:
B	*back*
QB	*quarterback*
E	*end*
T	*tackle*
G	*guard*

Defense:
LB	*line backer*
DE	*defense end*
DT	*defense tackle*
DB	*defense back*

Offside
Any other player but the snapper who moves across the scrimmage line is offside.

The snap
One of the key actions in American football is the 'snap'. This is when the centre snaps the ball back through his legs from a scrimmage to his quarterback in one quick and continuous action. The centre and every other player must remain completely still while the snap is made.

The snap

Centre   Quarterback   Back

Special plays
Tactically American football is an incredibly elaborate game and teams play each down with a series of 'plays', carefully worked out by the coach and executed with military precision. These include running plays,

such as: the 'sweep', in which the ball carrier is protected by two blockers as he runs wide around his linesmen; the 'trap', in which the offensive players leave

a gap to fool their opponents; and the 'quarterback sneak', which creates a gap in the defense for the quarterback to run through. There are also passing plays, and a variety of defensive plays.

KEY RULES

A game consists of four periods of 15 minutes each, with intervals of two minutes between the first and second periods and then the third and fourth periods, and a 12 minute intermission at half-time. The clock only runs, though, when the ball is in play, so a game will often last for about three hours. Teams change goals at the end of the first and third periods and are also allowed three time-outs of two minutes each during each half.

• Players are allowed to run with the ball, pass it or kick it. Forward passes are permitted, but only one is allowed to an offensive player per scrimmage, made from behind the line of scrimmage. A backwards pass can occur at any time during the game.
See Rule 8, Forward Pass, Backward Pass, Fumble (page 32).

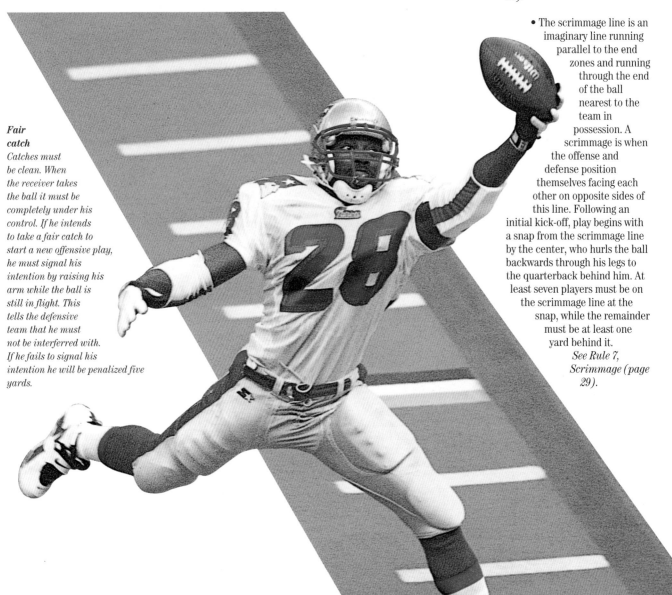

Fair catch
Catches must be clean. When the receiver takes the ball it must be completely under his control. If he intends to take a fair catch to start a new offensive play, he must signal his intention by raising his arm while the ball is still in flight. This tells the defensive team that he must not be interferred with. If he fails to signal his intention he will be penalized five yards.

• The scrimmage line is an imaginary line running parallel to the end zones and running through the end of the ball nearest to the team in possession. A scrimmage is when the offense and defense position themselves facing each other on opposite sides of this line. Following an initial kick-off, play begins with a snap from the scrimmage line by the center, who hurls the ball backwards through his legs to the quarterback behind him. At least seven players must be on the scrimmage line at the snap, while the remainder must be at least one yard behind it.
See Rule 7, Scrimmage (page 29).

• A fair catch is made by a player after a punt or kick-off from the opposing team. The catcher must signal his intention to receive the ball by waving one arm above his head and a player who then interferes with this catcher before the ball is caught incurs a penalty. Following a fair catch, the team of the player responsible then has the option of restarting play with a free kick or a snap.

See Rule 10, Fair Catch (page 35).

• A defensive player may tackle an opponent who is carrying the ball using his hands or arms to bring him down or hold him. The offensive player can also be blocked by the opposing team to stop his progress down the field. However, the rules place several restrictions on physical contact. A player must not hit an opponent with a clenched hand. In a blocking situation he may not hit an opponent with his elbows or forearms by turning unneccesarily. At no time must the face mask of a player be pulled. It is also forbidden to trip, kick or knee another player. Any foul or unsportsmanlike behaviour results in a penalty – either the loss of a down, a loss of yards (or a combination of both) or even automatic disqualification.

See Rule 12, Player Conduct (page 37).

SKILLS

Within a squad there are players to fill each specific position on the field. Overall the game calls for a combination of brute strength, intelligence and skill.

The offense

The quarterback is a powerful thrower and an alert player who leads the offense, liaising between the coach and the other players. He must have a quick eye to sum up the best play for his team. Offensive play begins when the center passes the ball to the quarterback (the snap) who then runs with it himself, and passes it to an open receiver or to a *running back*. The running backs are either *half-backs* (quick, agile and evasive enough to dodge tackles) or *full-backs* (strong enough to plough through tacklers when only a few yards are needed to make a first down). *Wide receivers* are fast players who also must be expert at catching the ball from short-, medium-

or long-range passes from the quarterback. The tight end is a well-built player, capable of blocking opponents as well as being able to run with the ball if need be. The biggest players are the *tackles* who must hold back the opposition in order to create openings for their teammates to carry the ball down the field. Guards reinforce the tackles, often running ahead of the ball-carrier to clear a path for him through the defense.

The defense

The *defensive ends* are tall and quick and head off runners from the sides of the field. *Defensive tackles* are tenacious, powerful players who face the offense head-on from the centre of the defense formation. *Linebackers* must be flexible defense players – blocking a particular part of the field, or running to intercept and tackle the quarterback. *Cornerbacks* require the same versatility – the strength to tackle effectively and the agility to run and intercept. The two *safeties* stand at the back of the defense and are mostly used to block passes from the offense to receivers down the field.

Tackled
A defensive player may only grab, that is, tackle his offensive opponent carrying the ball.

---

continued from page 29

movement of their feet, head or arms, or swaying of their body for a period of at least one second before snap.
Penalty: For illegal pause or motion after a shift: loss of 5 yds from previous spot. In case of doubt the penalty is to be enforced.
Article 7 No player may be out of bounds at the snap.
Penalty: For player out of bounds at snap: loss of 5 yds from the previous spot.
Section 3 Putting the Ball in Play
Article 1 The offensive team must put the ball in play by a snap at the spot where previous down ended, unless otherwise specifically provided for, unless a free-kick is prescribed or is chosen after a fair catch.
Penalty: For not using a snap when prescribed: loss of 5 yds.
Article 2 When a foul occurs, the ball shall not be put in play again until the penalty has been:

(a) enforced;
(b) declined;
(c) offset;
(d) annulled by a choice; or
(e) disregarded.
Article 3 The snap may be made by any offensive player who is on the line but must conform to the following provisions:
(a) The snap must start with ball on ground with is long axis horizontal and at right angles to line; and
(b) The impulse must be given by one quick and continuous motion of hand or hands of snapper. The ball must actually leave or be taken from his hands during this motion.
(c) The snapper may not:
(1) move his feet abruptly from the start of snap until the ball has left his hands;
(2) have quick plays after the neutral zone starts if the referee has not had a reasonable time to assume his normal stance. The ball remains dead. No penalty unless for a repeated act after warning (delay of game).

Penalty: For illegally snapping ball: loss of 5 yds from spot of snap for false start.
Article 4 From the start of the neutral zone until the snap, no offensive player, if he assumed a set position, shall charge or move in such a way as to simulate the start of a play (false start).
Penalty: For false start: loss of 5 yds from spot of snap.
Article 5 Prior to the snap no defensive player shall enter the neutral zone and touch the ball.
Penalty: For actions interfering with the ball prior to or during the snap: loss of 5 yds for delay from the spot of snap.
Article 6 The snap must be to a player who was not on his line at the snap, unless it has first struck the ground. The play continues as after any other backward pass if the snap either:
(a) first touches the ground; or
(b) first touched or is caught by an eligible backfield receiver.
Penalty: For snapping to ineligible snap receiver: loss of

5 yds from the spot of snap.
Article 7 Ball is next put in play (snap) at inbounds spot by the team entitled to possession when:
(a) a loose ball is out of bounds between goal lines;
(b) a runner is out of bounds between goal lines;
(c) the ball is dead in a side zone;
(d) the ball is placed there as a result of an enforcement; or
(e) the mark of a fair catch is in a side zone.
Section 4 Dead Ball
Article 1 An official shall declare dead ball and the down ended:
(a) when a runner is out of bounds, cries "down", or falls to the ground and makes no effort to advance.
(b) any time a quarterback immediately drops to his knee (or simulates dropping to his knee) to the ground behind the line of scrimmage during the last two minutes of a half. The game

➡ *page 32*

continued from page 29

clock will not stop during this action.

(c) whenever a runner declares himself down by sliding feet first on the ground. The ball is dead at the spot of the ball at the instant the runner so touches the ground.

(d) when a runner is so held or otherwise restrained that his forward progress ends.

(e) when a runner is contacted by a defensive player and he touches the ground with any part of his body except his hands or feet, ball shall be declared dead immediately. The contact by the defensive player must the the cause of runner going down.

(f) when an opponent takes a ball (hand in hand) in possession of a runner who is down on the ground.

(g) when any forward pass (legal or illegal) is incomplete.

(h) when any legal kick touches receivers' goalposts or crossbar unless it later scores a goal from field.

(i) when any scrimmage kick crosses receivers' goal line from the impetus of kick and no attempt is made to run it out, or if it is lying loose in the end zone from the impetus of the kick.

(j) when any legal kick or a short free-kick is recovered by the kickers, except one kicked from behind line which is recovered behind line (not a try-kick).

(k) when defense gains possession during a try, or a try-kick ceases to be in play.

(l) when a touchdown, touchback, safety, field goal, or try has been made.

(m) when any receiver catches after a fair-catch signal (valid or invalid) before kick is touched in flight by an opponent.

(n) when any official sounds his whistle, even though inadvertently.

(o) when any fourth down fumble by offensive team is recovered or caught by any offensive player other than the fumbling player.

Article 2 If a loose ball comes to rest anywhere in field and no player attempts to recover, official covering the play should pause momentarily before signaling dead ball (official's time-out). Any legal kick is awarded to receivers and any other ball to team last in possession. When awarded to a team behind the goal line, the ball is placed on its 1-yd line.

Article 3 If an official inadvertently sounds his whistle during a play, the ball becomes dead immediately:

(a) If during a run, it is the offensive team's ball at the spot of the ball at the time of the whistle.

(b) If during a backward pass or fumble, it is the offensive team's ball at the spot of the ball at the time of the whistle.

(c) If during a kick, it is the receiver's ball at the spot of the ball at the time of the whistle.

(d) If during a forward pass from behind the line, the ball reverts to the passers at the previous spot. It is an incomplete pass.

(e) If during a forward pass from beyond the line, the ball reverts to the passers at the spot of the pass. It is an illegal pass. The penalty is assessed from the spot of the pass.

(f) If during a forward pass not from the scrimmage, the ball reverts to the passers at the spot of the pass. The penalty is assessed from the spot of the pass.

Article 4 When the ball is dead, it is next put in play at spot designated by official so declaring it. This is usually the spot of the ball when his whistle sounded, but may be some other spot, when referee is informed by an official that the ball should have been dead at another spot or when the rules prescribe otherwise.

Article 5 The ball is not dead because of touching an official who is inbounds or because of a signal by an official other than a whistle.

Section 5 Possession of Ball After Out of Bounds

Article 1 If any legal kick, except for a free-kick, is out of bounds between the goal lines, ball is next put in play at inbounds spot by the receivers, unless there is a spot of illegal touching nearer kickers' goal line.

Article 2 If it is a play from scrimmage, any possession by offensive team after an out of bounds during fourth down is governed by the location of the necessary line.

Article 3 If a runner is out of bounds between goal lines, the ball is next put in play by his team at inbounds spot.

Article 4 If a forward pass is out of bounds between the goal lines, the ball is next put in play by passing team as provided for an incompletion or for an illegal pass.

Article 5 If a backward pass is out of bounds between the goal lines, the ball is next in play at the inbounds spot by the team last in possession.

Article 6 A fumble by the offensive team cannot result in an advance by that team if the ball is not recovered in the field of play or end zone.

(a) A fumble that goes forward and out of bounds is to return to that team at the spot of the fumble.

(b) A fumble in the field of play that goes backward and out of bounds belongs to the offense at the out-of-bounds spot.

(c) A fumble in the field of play that goes forward into the opponent's end zone and over the end line or sideline results in the ball being given over to the defensive team and a touchback awarded.

(d) A fumble which occurs in a team's own end zone and goes forward into the field of play and out of bounds will result in a safety if that team provided the impetus that put the ball into the end zone. If the impetus was provided by the opponent, the play will result in a touchback.

(e) A fumble which occurs in a team's own end zone or in the field of play and the ball goes out of bounds in the end zone will result in a safety if that team provided the impetus that put the ball into the end zone. If the

Warming up
Unlimited substitution is allowed from among the squad of 45 players and throughout the game players are limbering up on the touchline ready to be called on.

impetus was provided by the opponent, the play will result in a touchback.

Rule 8 Forward Pass, Backward Pass, Fumble
Section 1 Forward Pass
Article 1 The offensive team may make one forward pass from behind the line during each play from scrimmage provided the ball does not cross the line and return behind line prior to the pass.
(a) Any other forward pass by either team is illegal and is a foul by the passing team.
(b) When any illegal pass is intercepted, the ball may be advanced and the penalty declined.
(c) When illegal pass is caught by an offensive player, the ball is dead immediately.
Penalties:
a) For a forward pass not from scrimmage: loss of 5 yds from the spot of the pass. It is a safety when the spot of the pass is behind the passer's goal line.
b) For a second forward pass from behind line, or for a pass that was thrown after the ball returned behind the line: loss of down from the previous spot. (This is an offset foul).
c) For a forward pass from beyond the line: loss of down and 5 yds from the spot of the pass.
Article 2 A forward pass from behind the line may be touched or caught by any eligible player. (Pass in flight may be tipped, batted, or deflected in any direction by any eligible player at any time.)
(a) Defensive players are eligible at all times.
(b) Offensive players who are on either end of the line (other than a center, guard, or tackle) are eligible.
(c) Offensive players who are at least (legally) 1 yd behind the line at the snap are eligible, except T-formation quarterback.
Article 3 an eligible receiver becomes ineligible if he goes out of bounds (prior to or during a pass) and remains ineligible until an eligible receiver or any defensive player touches the pass.
Article 4 An ineligible offensive player is one who:
(a) was originally ineligible;
(b) loses his eligibility by going out of bounds;
(c) fails to notify the referee of being eligible when indicated; or
(d) is a T-formation quarterback, who takes his stance behind center,
(1) receives a hand-to-hand pass

or snap from him while moving backward;
(2) does not receive a hand-to-hand pass or snap from him and is not legally 1 yd behind the line of scrimmage; or
(3) ever receives a forward pass (handed or thrown) from a team-mate during a play from scrimmage.
Article 5 Any forward pass (legal or illegal) becomes incomplete and the ball is dead immediately if the pass strikes the ground, goes out of bounds, touches the goalpost of either team, or is caught by any offensive player after it has touched an ineligible offensive player before any touching by any eligible receiver. It is a foul if a forward pass (legal or illegal):
(a) first touches or is caught by an ineligible offensive player on or behind the line of scrimmage. Penalty: oss of down at previous spot. (This foul offsets a foul by the defense).
(b) is first touched or caught by an ineligible offensive player beyond the line (including a T-formation quarterback). Penalty: loss of 10 yds or loss of down from the previous spot. (This foul offsets a foul by the defense).
Article 6 A legal forward pass thrown from behind the line is complete and may be advanced if it is:
(a) caught by an eligible offensive player before any illegal touching by a teammate;
(b) caught by any offensive player after it is first touched by any eligible player; or
(c) intercepted by the defense (defense may also intercept and advance an illegal forward pass).
Section 2 Pass Interference/Ineligible Player Downfield
Article 1 There shall be no pass interference beyond line of scrimmage when there is a forward pass thrown from behind the line. This applies regardless of whether the pass crosses the line.
(a) The restriction for the offensive team begins with the snap.
(b) The restriction for the defensive team begins when the ball leaves the passer's hands.
Article 2 It is a foul when an ineligible offensive player (including a T-formation quarterback), prior to a legal forward pass:
(a) advances beyond his line, after losing contact with an opponent at the line of

scrimmage;
(b) loses contact with an opponent downfield after the initial charge and then continues to advance or move laterally; or
(c) moves downfield without contacting an opponent at the line of scrimmage.
The above restrictions end when the ball leaves the passer's hand.
Penalty: Ineligible offensive player downfield: loss of 5 yds from previous spot.
Article 3 It is not a foul for an ineligible receiver downfield when ineligible receivers:
(a) block an opponent at the line of scrimmage and drive him downfield, then lose the block and remain stationary;
(b) are forced behind their line;
(c) move laterally behind their line (before or after contact of their initial charge) provided they do not advance beyond their line until the ball leaves the passer's hands; or
(d) have legally crossed their line in blocking an opponent (eligible offensive player A1 may complete a pass between them and the offensive line).
Article 4 After the ball leaves the passer's hand, ineligible forward pass receivers can advance:
(a) from behind their line;
(b) from their own line; or
(c) from their initial charge position, provided they do not block or contact a defensive player until the ball is touched by a player of either team. Such prior blocking and/or contact is forward-pass interference.
When an ineligible lineman, who has legally crossed his line in blocking an opponent or a T-formation quarterback is touched by a forward-pass while beyond his line, enforcement is for Penalty (b) under 8-1-5 (loss of down or 10 yds).
Article 5 It is pass interference by either team when any player movement beyond the offensive line significantly hinders the progress of an eligible player or such player's opportunity to catch the ball during a forward pass. When players are competing for position to make a play on the ball, any contact by hands, arms, or body shall be considered incidental unless prohibited. Prohibited conduct

Centre of attention
The quarterback is the linchpin of the side and is often a team's star player.

shall be when a player physically restricts or impedes the opponent in a manner that is visually evident and materially affects the opponent's opportunity to gain position or retain his position to catch the ball. If a player has gained position, he shall not be considered to have impeded or restricted his opponent in a prohibited manner if all of his actions are a bona fide effort to go to and catch the ball.
Provided an eligible player is not interfered with in such a manner, the following exceptions to pass interference will prevail:
(a) If both players are looking for the ball or if neither player is looking for the ball and there is incidental contact in the act of moving to the ball that does not materially affect the route of an eligible player, there is not interference. If there is any question whether the incidental contact materially affects the route, the ruling shall be no interference.
(b) Any eligible player looking for and intent on playing the ball who initiates contact however severe, while attempting to move to the spot of completion or

➥ *page 34*

TACTICS

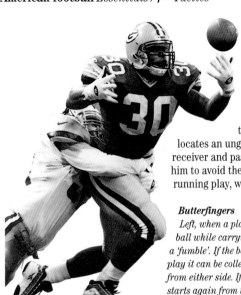

Generally speaking, the offense may opt for a passing play, in which the quarterback locates an unguarded receiver and passes the ball to him to avoid the defense, or a running play, with the player carrying the ball running as far towards the end zone as possible before being tackled. Moves and plays are well-rehearsed. Before each new play the quarterback forms a huddle with his team-mates and passes on the coach's instructions for a particular plan of action. This will often involve the use of a 'fake' play – fooling the defense into expecting one approach and thereby gaining time to carry out a completely different set of manoeuvers before they spot the deception. It is up to the quarterback ,too, to make last minute changes whenever he senses that the defense have anticipated their intentions and have set up a formation to counteract them. He does this by calling out coded instructions on the field.

The defense's aim then is to break up offensive plays by tackling the ball carrier or intercepting passes, whilst also blocking the rest of the offense, preventing them from providing support for their ball carrier and progressing up the field.

Butterfingers

Left, when a player drops the ball while carrying it, it is called a 'fumble'. If the ball then stays in play it can be collected by a player from either side. If it goes out play starts again from the place where it was fumbled.

Stopper

The linebackers are the ultimate part of the defensive team. They stand directly behind the linesmen to act as a final defense against all offensive players. If the ball carrier gets past a linebacker he usually has a clear run for the line.

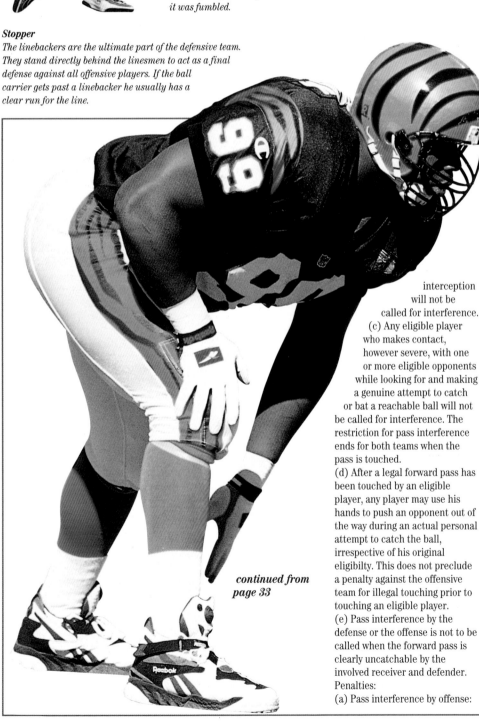

continued from page 33

interception will not be called for interference.

(c) Any eligible player who makes contact, however severe, with one or more eligible opponents while looking for and making a genuine attempt to catch or bat a reachable ball will not be called for interference. The restriction for pass interference ends for both teams when the pass is touched.

(d) After a legal forward pass has been touched by an eligible player, any player may use his hands to push an opponent out of the way during an actual personal attempt to catch the ball, irrespective of his original eligibilty. This does not preclude a penalty against the offensive team for illegal touching prior to touching an eligible player.

(e) Pass interference by the defense or the offense is not to be called when the forward pass is clearly uncatchable by the involved receiver and defender.

Penalties:

(a) Pass interference by offense: loss of 10 yds from previous spot.

(b) Pass interference by defense: first down for offensive team at the spot of any such foul. If the interference is also a personal foul, the usual distance penalty for such a foul is also enforced (from spot of foul). If the interference is behind the defensive goal line, it is first down for the offensive team on the defense's 1-yd line, or, if the previous spot was inside the 2-yd line, then halfway between the previous spot and the goal line.

Section 3 Fouls on Passes and Enforcement

Article 1 Intentional grounding will be called when a passer, facing an imminent loss of yardage because of pressure from the defense, throws a forward pass without a realistic chance of completion.

Penalty: For intentional grounding: loss of down and 10 yds from the previous spot, or if foul occurs more than 10 yds from line of scrimmage or where it is more advantageous to the defense, loss of down at spot of foul, or safety if passer is in his end zone when ball is thrown.

Article 2 If there is a foul by either team from the time of the snap until a forward pass from behind the line ends, the penalty is enforced from the previous spot.

Article 3 When the defense commits a personal foul prior to a completion of a legal forward pass

Flattened
When a runner is brought down by a lineman he certainly knows it. Linemen are the biggest men in football and are quite often 6 ft 8 in (2 m) tall and weigh 275 lbs 124 kg)or more. Crunches like this are the reason why body armour is essential.

Hands off
Above, the offensive player running with the ball can ward off his opponents with his hands or arms. His team-mates may also help by blocking opponents, but they may not use their hands or arms. Once the runner has got three yards beyond the line of the scrimmage downfield a defender is only allowed to make one attempt to tackle.

from behind the line, the offense shall have the choice of either:
(a) the usual penalty – 15 yds from the previous spot; or
(b) a 15-yd penalty enforced from the spot where the ball is dead.
Article 4 When the offense commits a personal foul prior to an interception of a legal forward pass from behind the line, the defense will have a 15-y penalty enforced from the spot where the ball is dead.
Article 5 If there is a foul by the defense from the start of the snap until a legal forward pass ends, it is not offset by an incompletion by the offensive team.

Section 4 Backward Pass and Fumble
Article 1 A runner may pass backward at any time.
(a) An offensive player may catch a backward pass or recover it after the pass touches the ground and advance.
(b) A defensive player may catch a backward pass or recover it after the pass touches the ground and advance.
Article 2 Any player of either team may recover or catch and advance a fumble:
(a) before the fumble strikes the ground; or
(b) after the fumble strikes the ground.
Article 3 If a backward pass goes out of bounds between the goal lines, the ball is next put in play at the inbounds spot by the team

in last possession. The ball is dead.
Article 4 When a foul occurs during a backward pass or fumble, the basic spot of enforcement is the spot of the fumble or the spot of the backward pass. If the offensive team fouls behind the spot of the fumble or backward pass, the spot of enforcement is the spot of the foul.

Rule 9 Scrimmage Kick
Section 1 Kick from Scrimmage
Article 1 The kicking team, behind the scrimmage line, may:
(a) punt;
(b) drop-kick; or
(c) place-kick.
Penalty: For a punt, drop-kick, or place-kick not kicked from behind the line of scrimmage: 10 yds from the spot of the kick.
Article 2 If the receivers recover any kick, they may advance.
Article 3 During a kick from scrimmage, only the end men as eligible receivers on the line of scrimmage at the time of the snap, are permitted to go beyond the line before the ball is kicked.
Penalty: Loss of 5 yds from the previous spot for leaving before the ball is kicked.
Article 4 No player of the kickers may illegally touch a scrimmage kick before it has been touched by a receiver (first touching).
Penalty: For illegal touching of a scrimmage kick: receivers' ball at any spot of illegal touching or possession. Officials' time out

when the ball is declared dead. This illegal touch does not offset a foul by the receivers during the down.
Article 5 No player of the kicker's team, who has been out of bounds, may touch or recover a scrimmage kick beyond the line until after it has been touched by B.
Penalty: loss of 5 yds from the previous spot.
Article 6 A ball is dead if the kickers recover a kick made from behind the line (other than one recovered on or behind the line unless a try-kick).
Article 7 If a kick from behind the line is touched in the immediate vicinity of the neutral zone or behind A's line by B, such touching does not make A eligible to recover the kick beyond the line.
Article 8 Any touching behind the line by a kicking team player is legal, even if the kick crosses the line and returns behind the line before touching a receiver beyond the line.
Article 9 When a legal kick is simultaneously recovered anywhere by two eligible opposing players, or if it is lying on the field of play with no player attempting to recover, it is awarded to the receivers.
Article 10 Ordinarily there is no distinction between a player touching a ball or being touched by it.
Article 11 During a kick a kicking team player, after he has

crossed his scrimmage line, may use his hands to ward off, push, or pull aside a receiver who is legally or illegally attempting to obstruct him.
Article 12 When a scrimmage kick from behind the line is recovered by the kicking team behind the line, the kicking team may advance.
Article 13 When a kick from scrimmage, or unsuccessful field goal crosses the receivers' goal line from the impetus of the kick it is a touchback unless:
(a) there is a spot of illegal touching by the kickers outside the receivers' 20-yd line; or
(b) the receivers after gaining possession, advance with the ball into the field of play; or
(c) kickers recover in end zone after receivers first touch ball in field of pay.
Ruling: Touchdown for kickers; or
(d) kickers recover in end zone after receivers first touch ball in end zone.
Ruling: Touchdown for kickers; or
(e) the ball goes out of bounds in the field of play after being touched by a receiver.
Ruling: Receiving team's ball at inbounds spot.
Article 14 If a scrimmage kick touches the receivers' goalposts or crossbar either before or after touching a player of either team, it is a touchback unless it later

➡ *page 36*

continued from page 35

scores a field goal.
Article 15 If a scrimmage kick touches the kickers' goalpost or crossbar (irrespective of where it was made from, or how it occurred), it is a safety. Goalpost is out of bounds.
Article 16 For a scrimmage kick out of bounds between goal lines, see Rule7, Article 5, Section 1.
Article 17 If there is a foul from the time of the snap until a legal scrimmage kick ends, enforcement is from the previous spot. This includes a foul during a run prior to the legal kick and running into or roughing the kicker. If the offensive team commits a foul in its own end zone, it is a safety.

Rule 10 Fair Catch
Section 1 Fair Catch
Article 1 A fair catch signal is valid beyond the line while kick is in flight when one arm is fully extended above the head and waved from side to side.
Penalty: For invalid fair catch signal: snap by receivers 5 yds behind the spot of the signal.
Article 2 If a receiver signals (valid or invalid) for a fair- catch during any kick except one which does not cross the line, the ball is dead when caught by any receiver. If the catcher did not signal, the ball is put in play by the receivers at the spot of the catch.
Article 3 If a player signals (valid or invalid) for a fair-catch, he may not until the ball touches a player:
(a) block; or
(b) initiate contact with one of the kickers.
Penalty: For illegal block after a fair catch signal: snap by receivers 15 yds from the spot of the foul. (Personal Foul).
Article 4 During any kick (except one which fails to cross the scrimmage line), if any receiver could reach the kick in flight, no player of the kickers shall interfere with either:
(a) the receiver;
(b) the ball; or
(c) the receiver's path to the ball.
Penalty (a): For fair-catch interference following a signal: loss of 15 yds from the spot of the

A score

Here the referee is signalling a score.

foul. Fair catch also awarded irrespective of a catch.
Penalty (b): For interference with the opportunity to make a catch (no prior signal made): loss of 15 yds from the spot of the foul and offended team is entitled to put the ball in play by a snap from scrimmage.
Article 5 After a receiver has made a fair catch following a valid signal, an opponent:
(a) may not tackle him;
(b) may not block him; and
(c) must avoid contact with him.
Penalty: For illegal contact with the maker of a fair catch: loss of 15 yds from the mark of the catch (snap or free-kick).
Article 6 When a fair catch is declared for a team, the captain must choose (and his first choice is not revocable) either:
(a) A fair-catch kick (punt, drop-kick, or place-kick without "tee"), or
(b) A snap to next put the ball in play.

Rule 11 Scoring
Section 1 Value of Scores
Article 1 The team that scores the greater number of points during the entire game is the winner. Points are scored as follows:
(a) Touchdown   6 points
(b) Field goal   3 points
(c) Safety 2 points
(d)Successful try after touchdown   1 or 2 points
Article 2 To insure a winner in all National Football League games the sudden-death method of deciding a tie game is Rule 16.
Section 2 Touchdown
Article 1 It is a touchdown:
(a) when a runner advances from the field of play and the ball touches the opponents' goal line (plane); or
(b) while inbounds any player catches or recovers a loose ball on or behind the opponents' goal line.

Section 3 Try   *Just scored.*
Article 1 After a touchdown, the scoring team is allowed a try. This try is an attempt to score one or two additional points, during one scrimmage down with the spot of snap:
(a) anywhere between the inbounds lines and
(b) which is also 2 or more yds from the defensive team's goal line.
During this try:
(a) if a try-kick is good, one point is scored. If a kick cannot score, the ball becomes dead as soon as failure is evident.
(b) if a try results in what would ordinarily be a touchdown by the offense, two points are awarded. If a touchdown is not scored, the try is over at the end of play or if there is a change of possession.
(c) if there is no kick and the try results in what would ordinarily be a safety by the defense, one point is awarded to the offensive team.
Article 2 The try begins when the referee sounds his whistle for play to start.
Article 3 During a try:
(a) if any play or a foul by the offense would ordinarily result in a touchback or loss of down, the try is unsuccessful and there shall be no replay.
(b) if any play or a foul by the defense would ordinarily result in a safety, one point is awarded to the offensive team.
(c) if a foul by the defense does not permit the try to be attempted, the down is replayed and the offended team has the option to have the distance penalty assessed on the next try or on the ensuing kick-off.
(d) if the defensive team commits a foul and the try is attempted and is unsuccessful, the offensive team may either accept the penalty yardage to be assessed or decline the distance penalty before the down is replayed.
(e) all fouls committed by the defense on a successful try will result in the distance penalty being assessed on the ensuing kick-off or retry B1.
(f) if there is a false start, encroachment, or a neutral-zone infraction which normally causes play to be whistled dead during ordinary scrimmage plays, they

are to be handled the same way during try situations.
Article 4 If fouls are signalled against both teams during a try, it must be replayed.
Article 5 During a try the defensive team can never score. When it gains possession, the ball is dead immediately.
Article 6 After a try the team on defense during the try shall receive.

Section 4 Safety
Article 1 When an impetus by a team sends the ball in touch behind its own goal, it is a safety if the ball is either:
(a) dead in the end zone in its possession; or
(b) out of bounds behind the goal line.
Article 2 It is a safety when the offense commits a foul (anywhere) and the spot of enforcement is behind its own goal line.
Article 3 After a safety, the team scored upon must next put the ball in play by a free-kick (punt, drop-kick, or place-kick). No tee can be used.

Section 5 Field Goal
Article 1 A field goal is scored when all of the following conditions are met:
(a) The kick must be a place-kick or drop-kick made by the offense from behind the line of scrimmage or from the spot of a fair catch (fair-catch kick).
(b) The ball must not touch the ground or any player of the offensive team before it passes through the goal.
(c) The entire ball must pass through the goal. In case wind or other forces cause it to return through the goal, it must have struck the ground or some object or person before returning.
Article 2 All field goals attempted and missed when the spot of the kick is beyond the 20-yd line will result in the defensive team taking possession of the ball at the spot of the kick. On any field goal attempted and missed when the spot of the kick is on or inside the 20-yd line, the ball will revert to the defensive team at the 20-yd line.
Article 3 On a free-kick following a fair-catch all general rules apply as for a field-goal attempt from scrimmage. The clock starts when the ball is kicked.
Article 4 No artificial media shall

be permitted to assist in the execution of a field goal and/or try after touchdown attempt.
Article 5 After a field goal, the team scored upon will receive.
Section 6 Touchback
Article 1 When an impetus by a team sends a ball in touch behind its opponents' goal line, it is a touchback:
(a) if the ball is dead in the opponents' possession on their end zone;
(b) if the ball is out of bounds behind the goal line if the impetus was a scrimmage kick unless there is a spot of first touching by the kickers outside the receivers' 20-yd line or if the receivers after gaining possession advance with the ball into the field of play; or
(d) if any legal kick touches the receivers' goalposts or crossbar other than one which scores a field goal.
Article 2 It is a touchback:
(a) when the kickers interfere with a fair catch behind the receivers' goal line; or
(b) when the kickers first touch a scrimmage kick behind the receivers' goal line.
(c) when a kicking team player illegally recovers or catches a punt inside the receiver's 5-yd line and carries the ball across the defender's goal line or his body touches the end zone.
Article 3 When the spot of enforcement for a foul by the defense is behind the offensive goal line, the distance penalty is enforced from the goal line.
Article 4 After a touchback, the touchback team next snaps from its 20 (any point between the inbounds lines and the forward point of the ball on that line).

Rule 12 Player Conduct
Section 1 Use of hands, Arms, and Body
Article 1 No offensive player may:
(a) assist the runner except by individually blocking opponents for him.
(b) use interlocking interference. Interlocked interference means the grasping of one another by encircling the body to any

degree with the hands or arms; or
(c) push the runner or lift him to his feet.
Penalty: For assisting runner or interlocked interference: loss of 10 yds.
Article 2 A runner may ward off opponents with his hands and arms, but no other offensive player may use them to obstruct an opponent, by grasping with hands or encircling with arm in any degree any part of body, during a block.
Article 3 No player on offense may push or throw his body against a team-mate either:
(a) in such a way as to cause him to assist runner;
(b) to aid him in an attempt to obstruct an opponent or to recover a loose ball;
(c) to trip an opponent; or
(d) in charging, falling, or using

hands on the body into the back from behind above the waist of an opponent.
Penalty: For holding, illegal use of hands, arms or body of offense: loss of 10 yds.
Article 4 A defensive player may not tackle or hold any opponent other than a runner. Otherwise, he may use his hands, arms, or body only to defend or protect himself against an obstructing opponent in an attempt to reach a runner. On a punt, field-goal attempt, or try-kick attempt, a defensive player (B1) may not grab and pull an offensive player out of the way which allows another defensive player(s) (B2) to shoot the gap (pull and shoot) in an attempt to block the kick, unless the defensive player (B1) is advancing toward the kicker.
Penalty: For illegal contact, illegal cut, or holding by the defense: loss of 5 yds and automatic first down.
Section 2 Personal Fouls
Article 1 All players are prohibited from:
(a) striking with the fists;
(b) kicking or kneeing; or
(c) striking, swinging, or clubbing to the head, neck, or face with the heel, back, or side of the hand, wrist, forearm, elbow, or clasped hands.
Penalty: For fouls in (a), (b), and (c): loss of 15 yds. If any of the above acts is judged by the official(s) to be flagrant, the offender may be disqualified as long as the

entire action is observed by the official(s).
Articles 2 – 14 define personal fouls in detail.
Section 3 Unsportsmanlike Conduct
Article 1 There shall be no unsportsmanlike conduct. This applies to any act which is contrary to the generally understood principles of sportsmanship. Such acts specifically include, among others:
(a) The use of abusive, threatening or insulting language or gestures to opponents, teammates, officials, or representatives of the League.
(b) The use of baiting or taunting acts or words that engender ill will between teams.
(c) Unnecessary physical contact with a game official.
Penalty: (a), (b), and (c): loss of 15 yds from succeeding spot or whatever spot the referee, after consulting with the crew, deems equitable.
Article 2 The defense, when near its goal line, shall not commit successive or continued fouls (half-distance penalties) to prevent a score.
Penalty: For continuous fouls to prevent a score: if the violation is repeated after a warning, the score involved is awarded to the offensive team.
Article 3 A player or substitute shall not interfere with play by any act which is palpably unfair.
Penalty: For a palpably unfair act: offender may be disqualified. The referee, after consulting his crew, enforces any such distance penalty as they consider equitable and irrespective of any other specified code penalty. The referee could award a score.

These rules are reprinted by permission of the National Football League. For a complete copy of the rules, including Rules 13–18, as well as various Exceptions to the Rules, contact the NFL.

When two teams match each other closely with their precision play, it is often individual flashes of brilliance which make the difference between a match won and a match lost. A player who can regularly make a few yards with a surprise run or a quarterback who can spiral the ball forward with unfailing accuracy is a match winner.

Rugby League
Essentials

Played mostly in Australasia and in the north of England, this game was established in 1895 when a number of rugby clubs broke away from the Rugby Football Union, protesting against the amateur status of the game. It involves teams of 13 players (as opposed to Rugby Union's 15) and places the emphasis on running and passing, which makes for a hard, fast-moving game.

Headgear
An increasing number of players have taken to wearing a helmet to protect head and ears. The rules state that protective clothing may be worn provided it contains nothing of a rigid nature.

The teams
Two teams of 13 players, with a maximum of four replacements. Positions and numbers *(see diagram below)* are as follows:

Backs
1 Full-back
2 Right wing
3 Right centre
4 Left centre
5 Left wing
6 Stand-off half or five eighth
7 Scrum-half

Forwards
8 Prop
9 Hooker
10 Front row
11 Second row
12 Second row
13 Loose forward

Super League teams now wear squad numbers which belong to individual players rather than to their positions on the field.

Officials
A referee and two touch judges plus in-goal judges at the professional level.

The field
A grass pitch with a maximum length of 100 m (109 yds) and width of 68 m (74 yds).

The goals
Two posts 4 m (4.5 yds) minimum height), 5.5 m (6yds) apart and joined by a crossbar 3 m (10 ft) from the ground.

Touch in-goal line
In-goal
Dead ball line
Goal line
Touch in-goal
Touch
Touchline
10 m
10 m
Halfway line
5.5 m
40 m line
30 m line
20 m line
10 m line
100 m maximum
4 m minimum
3 m
11 m maximum
5 m minimum

Below, Central park, Wigan.

Flying tackle
Rugby League is one of the most physical of all games – tackle involves a player launching himself full length at an opponent who is running with the ball.

The ball
Oval, inflated, with an outer casing of leather or approved material. It must be between 27 and 29 cm (approx 11 in) long, have a longest circumference of 73–5 cm (approx 29 in), a width of 58–61 cm (approx 24 in) and a weight of 380-440 g (approx 14 oz).

HOW TO PLAY

Both teams attempt to gain possession of the ball so as to be able to ground it in the opponents' in-goal to score a try and, if this is successful, kick it over the opponents' crossbar to score a conversion goal. Players can run with the ball, kick it in any direction or pass it (although only to the side or behind, not forward), in order to avoid being tackled by the opposition.

Starting

The team that wins the toss chooses an end and the team that loses the toss starts the game, with one of their players taking the kick-off – a place-kick (for which the ball is placed on the ground) from the centre of the halfway line. The kick must travel at least 10 m (33 ft) forward and all other players must remain at this same distance away from the kicker until the kick has been made. The opposition kicks off to start the second half.

How to win

A try is worth four points, a conversion or penalty goal is worth two points and a drop goal is worth one point. (A penalty goal is scored from a penalty kick – *see Section 6, The Penalty (page 41);* and a drop goal is scored from a kick over the opposition's crossbar from anywhere in the field). The team scoring the highest number of points wins the game.

Dress

A jersey featuring player's number, shorts, socks and studded boots. Players must not wear anything that might be dangerous to other players.

Running with the ball
Running with the ball demands tremendous speed, strength and stamina. The ball should be carried in complete control, either in both hands or against the chest, not tucked under the arm as some inexperienced players do. Holding in both hands means the player can quickly and accurately pass the ball on if a tackle threatens. Holding the ball with one arm against the chest means the runner has one hand free to generate pace and fend off tackles. This kind of grip is used when the player is running clear ahead of the field.

KEY RULES

A game is normally 80 minutes long, with a half-time break of five minutes, although time is extended to allow for injuries, conversion or penalty kicks. Teams change ends at half-time.

Restarts

After points have been scored, the scoring team restarts play with a place kick from the half-way line. However, the restart is a placekick from the centre of the 20 m line if a player: sends the ball over the opposition's dead-ball or touch in-goal line; infringes the rules in the opposition's in-goal area; or takes a kick in general play from the opposition on the full while in his own in-goal. It is a drop kick from the 20 m line if the ball crosses the dead-ball or touch in-goal line from a penalty kick. (A drop kick is when the ball is dropped on the ground and kicked immediately as it rebounds). It is a drop kick from the goal-line if a player: sends the ball over his own dead-ball or touch in-goal line; does this from a kick-off at the half-way line; commits a breach or is tackled in his own in-goal area or kicks the ball into touch on the full from his own in-goal area.

A player may be tackled by one or more opponents only when he is in possession of the ball. He is said to be 'tackled' when he is held by his opponent(s) and the ball, his hand or his arm holding the ball touches the ground.

One of the main differences between Rugby Union and Rugby League is the procedure following a tackle. In Rugby League, a team is allowed to be tackled five times in succession, but on the sixth tackle they lose possession to the opposition. *See Section 2, The Tackle (page 40).*

Until this loss of possession, a tackled player is released to immediately 'play the ball'. For this one opponent may mark him and another player from each team (acting half-backs) may position himself immediately behind his own tackled player/marker. The tackled player then places the ball on the ground and plays it backwards with his foot. *See Section 3, The Play-the-Ball (page 40).*

Minor offences are penalized by the formation of a scrum to re-establish possession of the ball. For example, if a player fumbles with the ball and knocks it forward (a 'knock-on'), passes it forward or accidentally becomes offside. *See Section 5, The Scrum (page 41).*

Any player who deliberately breaks the rules incurs a penalty kick to the opposition. This is taken by punting (dropping the ball and kicking it before it touches the ground), drop-kicking, placekicking or tapping the ball from the point where the offence took place. *See Section 6, The Penalty (page 41).*

Technical offences, committed persistently, result in a player being suspended for ten minutes (placed in the 'Sin Bin'). Serious offences, such as violent behaviour, result in a player being dismissed.

RUGBY LEAGUE
THE RULES

Section 1 Start of Play
See page 39.

Section 2 The Tackle

2.1 The Tackle

2.1.1 A player in possession may be tackled by any number of opposing players.

2.1.2 It is illegal to tackle or obstruct a player who is not in possession.

2.1.3 A player in possession is tackled:

a) When he is held by one or more opposing players and the ball or the hand or arm holding the ball comes into contact with the ground.

b) When he is held by one or more opposing players in such a manner that he can make no further progress and cannot part with the ball.

c) When being held by an opponent and the tackled player makes it evident he has succumbed to the tackle and wishes to be released in order to play the ball.

d) When he is lying on the ground and an opponent places a hand on him.

2.1.4

a) A tackle is not effected if the player in possession is brought to the ground and the hold on the player in possession is broken before he is grounded.

b) The referee should be sure in his own mind that the tackle was indeed broken and the tackler had not released the player having thought the tackle was completed.

2.1.5 A tackler must not use any special holds or throws which are likely to cause injury.

2.1.6 Bringing a player to the ground by pulling him over the outstretched leg is permissible provided both arms make contact with the opponent before the leg.

2.1.7 A tackler must not use his knees in making a tackle.

2.1.8 Where opponents, whilst making a tackle, attempt to push, pull or carry the player in possession, the tackled player's colleagues may lend their weight in order to avoid losing ground. Immediately this happens the referee should call 'Held'.

2.1.9 Once a player in possession has been tackled it is illegal for any player to move or try to move him from the point where the tackle is effected.

2.1.10 When a tackled player is tackled within easy reach of the

Dangerous tackle
Tacklers are not allowed to use any holds or throws that might cause injury, so this kind of tackle in which the tackler has grabbed his opponent by the neck is definitely out of order.

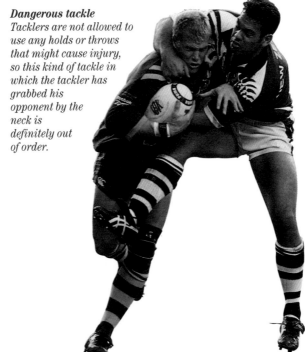

goal line he should be penalised if he makes a second movement to place the ball over the line for a try.

2.1.11 If an attacking player in possession is brought down near the goal line and the ball is not grounded it is permissible to place the ball over the line for a try. In this case the tackle has not been completed.

2.1.12 A player in possession shall not deliberately or unnecessarily allow himself to voluntarily fall to the ground when not held by an opponent.

2.1.13 If a player drops on a loose ball he shall not remain on the ground waiting to be tackled if he has time to regain his feet and continue play.

2.1.14 If a tackled player slides along the ground because of his momentum the tackle is effected where his slide ends.

2.1.15 If any doubt arises as to a tackle, the referee should give a verbal instruction to "play on" or shout "held" as the case may be.

2.1.16 If there is no acting half-back, it is permissible for a player to dive behind the tackled player to drop on the ball after he has played it. He should then immediately try to regain his feet and play on.

2.2 Sixth Tackle

2.2.1 A team in possession of the ball shall be allowed five successive play-the-balls.

2.2.2 If tackled for a sixth time the referee will rule a handover.

2.2.3 If an infringement occurs by the team in possession after the fifth play-the-ball, the referee will rule a handover.

2.2.4 A handover play-the-ball will not be counted in the tackle count.

2.2.5 If the ball is kicked out on the full after the fifth tackle the handover takes place at the point from where the ball was kicked.

2.2.6 If the ball is kicked out after landing in the field of play after the fifth tackle a scrum will be formed. The scrum shall be formed 20 m (22 yds) in from where the ball crosses the touch line and no closer than ten metres to the goal line.

2.2.7 The referee will indicate the fifth tackle by raising one arm vertically with fingers and thumb outstretched.

2.2.8 He will indicate the sixth tackle by blowing his whistle and signalling the player to release the ball for his opponents to play the ball.

2.3 Zero Tackle

2.3.1 When a player gathers the ball from an opposition kick in general play and does not subsequently pass or kick the ball himself, the initial kick will be a zero tackle.

2.3.2 If a player knocks-on and an opponent gathers the ball and is tackled before gaining any territorial advantage the play-the-ball will not be counted as a tackle in the tackle count.

2.3.3 A tackled player shall not intentionally lose the ball.

2.3.4 If after being tackled a player accidentally loses possession, a scrum shall be formed, except after the fifth play-the-ball.

2.3.5 A player in possession brought to his knees or brought

to the ground on his back may still pass the ball provided he has not made it evident he has succumbed to the tackle.

2.4 Stealing the Ball

2.4.1 Once a tackle has been completed, no player shall take or attempt to take the ball from the tackled player.

2.4.2 If more than one player makes no effort to complete a tackle of the player in possession but simply hold him so that a colleague can take the ball from him, they should be penalized.

2.4.3 In tackles involving only one tackler, it is permissible to steal the ball prior to the tackle being effected. In tackles involving two or more tacklers, the ball cannot be intentionally stolen.

Section 3 The Play the Ball

3.1 Playing the Ball

3.1.1 The tackled player shall be immediately released and shall not be touched until the ball has been played.

3.1.2 If any doubt arises as to which player should play the ball (disputed possession) the referee should nominate the team in possession.

3.1.3 In the case of a player lying on the ground and not holding the ball with both hands or arms, circumstances may arise where there is some doubt as to whether he is 'in possession'.

3.1.4 If he is holding the ball with a hand or arm to some part of his person then he is 'in possession'.

3.1.5 The tackled player shall without delay regain his feet where he was tackled.

3.1.6 No part of the tackled player's person other than his feet should be in contact with the ground when he releases the ball.

3.1.7 One opponent may take up a position immediately opposite the tackled player, known as the 'marker'.

3.1.8 The tackled player shall lift the ball clear of the ground, face his opponents' goal line and drop or place the ball in front of his foremost foot.

3.1.9 The ball must be played

Below: see 3.1.9

backwards with the foot and it is clear of the ruck when it passes behind the heel of the tackled player.

3.1.10 The marker is not allowed to strike for the ball.

3.1.11 A player from each team, to be known as the acting half-back, may stand immediately and directly behind his own player taking part in the play-the-ball.

3.1.12 He must remain in this position until the ball has come clear of the two players in the play-the-ball movement.

3.1.13 Players of the side not in possession other than the marker and the acting half-back are out of play if they fail to retire 10 m (33 ft) from the point at which the ball is played or to their own goal line. They should only be penalized if they intentionally interfere with the play.

3.1.14 Players of the side in possession other than the player playing the ball and the acting half-back are out of play if they fail to retire 5 m (16 ft) from the point at which the ball is played or to their own goal line.

3.1.15 If the interference with play is accidental, a scrum should be formed.

3.1.16 Having retired the distance required a player may not advance until the ball has cleared the ruck.

3.1.17 A player who is out of play may take part in the game when the advantage gained by not retiring has been lost.

3.1.18 The play-the-ball must be performed as quickly as possible.

3.1.19 Any player who intentionally delays the bringing of the ball into play shall be penalized.

3.1.20 If part of the tackled player is on or over the goal line but the ball is in the field of play, the tackled player shall play-the-ball where the ball lies.

3.1.21 If a player is tackled in an upright position bestriding the goal line he is deemed to be tackled in the in-goal area.

Section 4 The Knock-On and Forward Pass

4.1 Knock-On

4.1.1 Play shall stop after a knock-on and a scrum formed, except after the fifth tackle.

4.1.2 The referee should allow play to proceed long enough after the knock-on to allow the opposing team the advantage of gaining possession.

4.1.3 An opponent may charge

Knock-on.

down a kick and this is not a knock-on.

4.1.4 A player shall be penalized if he deliberately knocks on.

4.1.5 If after an accidental knock-on the player knocking on regathers or kicks the ball before it hits the ground, goal post or an opponent, play shall be allowed to proceed.

4.1.6 If a player knocks on in the field of play, and the ball goes into the in-goal area before being touched down by that player or a colleague, play is restarted with a scrum.

4.2 Forward Pass

4.2.1 A player shall be penalized if he deliberately passes the ball forward.

4.2.2 If the ball is passed correctly and then bounces forward or is blown forward by the wind there is no infringement and play should continue.

4.2.3 The direction of a pass is relative to the player making it and not to the actual path relative to the ground.

4.2.4 A player running towards his opponents' goal line may pass the ball to a colleague who is behind him but because of his momentum the ball travels forward relative to the ground. This is not a forward pass as the player has not passed the ball forward in relation to himself. A good example is a high lobbed pass made by a running player.

4.2.5 If the referee forms the opinion that a forward pass was not deliberate he will restart play with a scrum.

4.2.6 It is illegal to head the ball in a forward direction.

Section 5 The Scrum

5.1 Formation of Scrum

5.1.1 A scrum is formed to restart play when play is not being restarted with a kick-off, drop out, penalty kick or play-the-ball.

5.1.2 A maximum of six forwards will be used to form a scrum in a 3-2-1 formation.

5.1.3 A minimum of three forwards can form a scrum if a

team is depleted.

5.1.4 It is an infringement resulting in a penalty if there are more than seven backs when a scrum is formed.

5.1.5 The front row is made up of three forwards who interlock arms and bend forward from the hip. The forward in the centre (hooker) must bind with his arms over the shoulders of the prop and front row forward.

5.1.6 Two second row forwards bend from the hip, interlock arms and place their heads in the gaps between the front row forwards.

5.1.7 The loose forward bends from the hip and places his head in the gap between the second row forwards.

5.1.8 All forwards with their bodies bent brace themselves and interlock against the opposing team's forward pack. This forms a tunnel between the front row forwards.

5.1.9 Scrums shall be formed where an infringement occurs, but no closer than 20 m (22 yds) to the touch line or 10 m (33 ft) to the goal line.

5.1.10 Scrums shall be formed at right angles to the touchline.

5.1.11 The forwards take the weight and hold the scrum on the mark until the ball has been put in.

5.1.12 The non-offending team will have the loose head and put-in except when a mutual infringement occurs; in this case the attacking team have the loose head and put-in. If the infringement occurs on the halfway line the last team in possession shall have the loose head and put-in.

5.1.13 The ball must be held horizontally and put into the scrum on the referee's side by rolling it along the ground between the outside feet of the two prop forwards. The outside feet must also be the forward-most foot of the two props.

5.1.14 The ball should be put into the scrum without delay when the scrum has been formed correctly and the half-back shall retire behind his last row of forwards.

5.1.15 The opposing half-back shall retire behind his last row of forwards. The rest of his team shall retire at least 5 m (16 ft) behind this last row of forwards.

5.1.16 When the ball is in the scrum, it can only be played at with the foot.

5.1.17 The hooker can strike for the ball with either foot once the ball is in the tunnel.

5.1.18 The prop must keep both feet on the ground and may only strike for the ball after the hooker.

5.1.19 No player shall wilfully collapse a scrum.

5.1 20 The ball is out of the scrum when it emerges from between and behind the inner feet of the second rowers.

5.1.21 Any forward can detach himself from the scrum to gather or kick the ball when the ball has emerged from the scrum correctly, even if the scrum has wheeled.

5.1.22 Forwards must not butt violently when coming together to form a scrum.

5.2 Held Up In-Goal

5.2.1 If an attacking player is held up in his opponents' in-goal and is unable to ground the ball, play is restarted with a scrum 10 m (33 ft) from the goal line opposite where the player was held. The loose head and put-in shall be awarded to the team in possession and unable to ground the ball.

5.2.2 If the player is held up in-goal after the fifth tackle play will restart with a hand over 10 m (33ft) out from the goal line in line with the tackle.

Section 6 The Penalty

6.1 When Penalties are Awarded

6.1.1 A penalty shall be awarded against a player who deliberately breaks the rules provided that the awarding of the penalty will not disadvantage the opposing team.

6.1.2 The advantage to the opposing team must be apparent if the referee is to allow play to proceed.

6.1.3 Any player can ask the referee the reason why a penalty has been awarded provided he does so respectfully.

6.2 Where Penalties are Awarded

6.2.1 Unless stated the mark is where the offence occurred. The mark is moved in the following circumstances:

6.2.2 If misconduct occurs in-touch, the penalty is awarded 10 m (33 ft) in field opposite where the offence occurred.

6.2.3 Where a kicker is interfered with after a kick, the mark is where the ball lands or is caught in the field of play. If the ball crosses the touchline on the full, or crosses the goal line on the full, the penalty is awarded 10 m (33 ft) in field from where

➡ *page 44*

SKILLS AND TACTICS

The essentials for all players
are speed, power and
endurance. As with any game,
the best strategy is one which
takes account of the
opposition's strengths, and
combats these by placing its
own players in the most suitable
positions.

Tackling – Players must use an
equal mix of force and
determination to overcome
opponents who are often
travelling at top speed with a
tight grip on the ball.

Kicking – Accuracy is always
vital, whether kicking for field
position or shooting for goals. A
good place-kicker, i.e. a player
who can kick at goal or convert
tries with a high degree of
success, is an invaluable
member of a team.

Handling – Catching and
passing the ball are very
important in that the team
which has the ball in its
possession controls the game
and has the capacity to score
tries and points. Drop the ball,
and you give it to the
opposition. When passing, the
ball usually has to be projected
with the points horizontal, so
that it flies through the air like
a torpedo rather than spinning
wildly.

On the wing
*Wingers need
speed, stamina
and agility for
quick breaks rather than
the brute strength of the
forwards.*

Quick break
*Many a scoring situation
is set up when the
scrum-half picks up
the ball from a
scrum and makes a
blind-side break
past the opposing
winger.*

Vital support
*It is essential for anyone running with the
ball to pass it on before he is tackled, so players always follow a player breaking with the
ball to be ready for a timely pass.*

Straight punt
*The straight punt is the most common of all kicks in rugby
league. The aim is to send the ball far upfield to gain ground
for your team – or else to find touch from a
penalty. Typically a stand-off half may
punt the ball far up the field
to clear the ball after a
scrum close to his
own line.*

Place-kick
*Place-kicks are used to
start the game, to kick
for goal or into touch
from a penalty, or for
an attempt to convert
a try.*

Spiral punt
*Above left and left, the
spiral punt is one of the
hardest of all kicks to
master but it proves a very
effective weapon. The aim is
to bring the ball, held at
both ends, down across the
body at an angle of 45°. The
foot then slices across the
ball as it kicks, sending it
spinning far down the field
and making it very difficult
to catch.*

Power play
Since a player doesn't have to release the ball until he is actually brought down, the strength to power on through a tackle and gain vital yards is invaluable in a forward.

Bring 'im down
It often needs at least two players to bring down a strong player once he's got into his stride.

High tackle
A tackle high on the body stands less chance of success because the player with the ball can fend it off with his hand. In this picture, the tackler on the right stands a much better chance.

Passing time
This player has timed his pass perfectly, getting the ball cleanly away to a team-mate just as he is about to be brought down. The important thing to remember when passing under pressure like this is that the ball must not go forward.

Going for it
In a classic flying tackle the tackler launches himself into the air to clasp the runner around the thighs and stop his legs moving – so that his momentum brings him down.

GREY AREA

To avoid a game being slowed down, the play-the-ball rule discourages players from holding on to tackles too long. But just what is 'too long'? The answer is that it is up to the referee to decide – which is why there is often dispute.

Making a pass
The perfect pass travels straight through the air with the ball end-on. The player grips the ball firmly around the middle with fingers outstretched to form a cradle underneath. The passer's fingers guide the ball towards his team-mate as he lets go of it. As the ball leaves the hands the arms follow through in the same direction.

continued from page 41

the ball crossed the line.

6.2.4 Any offence in the in-goal which results in a penalty being awarded, the penalty is awarded 10 m (33 ft) in the field opposite where the offence occurred.

6.3 Further Misconduct

In cases of further offences, the mark shall be advanced once by 10 m (33 ft), towards the offending team's goal line.

6.4 Breaches by the Kicker's Team

In cases of a breach by the kicker's team, a scrum is formed where the penalty kick was awarded.

6.5 Breaches by Opposing Teams

In cases of a breach by the opposing team another penalty shall be awarded opposite where the breach occurred, 10 m (33 ft) from where the original penalty was awarded.

6.6 How Penalty Kicks are Taken

6.6.1 A player may take a penalty kick by punting, drop-kicking or place-kicking the ball from the mark or behind the mark provided it is parallel with the touchline.

6.6.2 The ball may be kicked in any direction, after which it is in play, except when kicking for goal. If the kicker advises the referee that he is kicking for goal from a penalty it is an offence to

Place kick

Drop kick

Punt

do otherwise.

6.6.3 A penalty from a scrum is a differential penalty, which a goal cannot be scored from. If the penalty is for foul play or offensive language a normal penalty is awarded.

6.6.4 The differential penalty applies to all players in the team including those outside the scrum.

6.7 Position of Players

6.7.1 All players from the kicker's team must remain behind the ball when it is kicked from a penalty kick.

6.7.2 The opposing players shall position themselves at least 10 m (33 ft) from the point where the penalty was awarded.

6.7.3 Opposing players who have not retired 10 m (33 ft) at a penalty kick should only be penalized if they interfere with play.

6.7.4 Opposing players shall not interfere with or distract the attention of the kicker at a penalty kick.

6.7.5 Opposing players may only advance after the ball has been kicked.

6.8 Finding Touch

6.8.1 From a penalty kick, if the ball is kicked into touch without touching any other player, the kicking team shall restart play with a free-kick 10 m (33 ft) in the field of play opposite where the ball crossed the line.

6.8.2 If the ball touches an opposing player and goes into touch, a scrum shall be packed 20 m (22 yds) in field from where the ball crossed the line. The kicker's team has the loose head and the put-in.

6.8.3 Play is restarted with a 20 m (22 yds) drop-kick if the ball is kicked dead in the opponents' in-goal from a penalty kick.

6.9 Free-kick

6.9.1 The ball may be kicked in any direction in any manner when bringing it into play after finding touch.

6.9.2 Opposing players shall retire 10 m (33 ft) from the free-kick.

6.9.3 In the event of a breach by the opposing team a penalty kick shall be awarded opposite where the breach occurred and 10 m (33 ft) from the free-kick.

6.9.4 In the event of a breach by the kicker's team, a scrum shall be packed 20 m (22 yds) from the touch line opposite where the free-kick was to be taken.

6.10 No Delay

6.10.1 No player shall deliberately delay the taking of a penalty kick.

6.11 Infringement by Kicker's Team

6.11.1 If the penalty kick is not taken as stated or if a player from the kicker's team infringes, a scrum shall be formed at the mark, not closer than 20 metres (22 yd) from the touch line.

6.12 Offence Against Try Scorer

6.12.1 If a player fouls an opponent who is touching down for a try, an eight-point try is awarded, i.e., a penalty kick at goal shall be taken from in front of the posts after the attempt to convert the try.

6.12.2 After an eight-point try, play is restarted with a kick-off from the centre of the halfway line.

6.13 Drop Goal Foul Play on Kicker

6.13.1 If a player attempting a drop goal is fouled, a penalty kick shall be awarded in front of the goalposts.

6.13.2 If he is successful with the drop goal, a kick at goal must be taken from the penalty kick. Play is then restarted from the centre of the halfway line.

6.13.3 If the drop goal is unsuccessful, the penalty kick can be taken in any manner.

6.14 The Mark

6.14.1 As the mark cannot be marked on the ground, a player who punts or drop-kicks may deviate slightly from it, provided no advantage is gained from it.

6.14.2 Where a player is taking a kick at goal and moves the ball back from the point where the penalty was awarded, the point where the kick is taken becomes the new mark. Opposition players must be at least 10 m (33 ft) from where the kick is being taken from.

Section 7 Scoring Points

7.1 Points Value of a Try, Goal and Field Goal

7.1.1 A try is worth four points.

7.1.2 A conversion or penalty goal is two points.

7.1.3 A field goal is one point.

7.2 Winning the Game

7.2.1 The game shall be decided by the team scoring the higher number of points. If both teams have the same number of points, the game is drawn.

7.3 How a Try is Scored

7.3.1 A try is scored when a player grounds the ball in his opponents' in-goal. The ball must be grounded before the player or

the ball crosses the touch in-goal or dead-ball line.

7.3.2 A player may pick up the ball in his opponents' in-goal, in order to ground it in a more advantageous position.

7.3.3 A try is scored when opposing players ground the ball simultaneously in the in-goal area.

7.3.4 A try is scored when a tackled player's momentum carries him into the opponents' in-goal where he grounds the ball.

7.3.5 A try is scored by grounding the ball on the goal line. A try is not scored by grounding the ball at the foot of the goalposts in the field of play.

7.3.6 When the ball is not grounded correctly play is allowed to continue unless the ball has been knocked on or has gone dead.

7.3.7 A referee should not disallow a try because a player who correctly grounds the ball fails to retain it.

7.3.8 The referee should not disallow a try because he was not in a position to see the grounding of the ball.

7.3.9 When the ball is in the scrum, a try cannot be scored by grounding it.

7.3.10 When the ball is at the base of the scrum, it is permissible for a player to pick it up and bore through his own forwards to ground the ball for a try.

7.4 Penalty Try

7.4.1 The referee can award a penalty try if, in his opinion, a try would have been scored, except for the unfair play of a defender.

7.4.2 A penalty try is awarded between the goalposts.

7.5 Touching Referee (Etc.)

7.5.1 If play is affected following an attacking player coming into contact with the referee, touch judge or spectator in the opposition's in-goal area a try is awarded.

7.6 Where Try is Awarded

7.6.1 Where the ball is grounded as in 7.3.1 and 7.3.2 and 7.3.3.

7.6.2 Where the ball first crosses the goal line if scored as per 7.3.4.

7.6.3 In-between the goalposts if a penalty try is to be awarded.

7.6.4 Where contact took place if scored as per 7.5.1.

7.7 Referee is the Sole Judge

7.7.1 A try can only be awarded by the referee. The referee can take advice from the touch judge before making a decision.

7.7.2 To award a try, the referee points to the spot where the ball was grounded and blows his whistle.

7.7.3 Before awarding the try the referee should look at the two touch judges to ensure that they are not reporting a prior incident.

7.7.4 When approved by the controlling authority of any competition, in-goal judges and the use of audio/visual electronic aids may be used to assist the referee in the decision making process.

7.8 How a Goal is Scored

7.8.1 A goal is scored if the ball passes over the opponents' crossbar and between the uprights after being kicked on the full by a player (and not being touched in flight by any other player) in any of the following circumstances:

7.8.2 By a place-kick after a try has been scored and counts as two points.

7.8.3 By a place-kick or a drop kick when a penalty has been awarded and counts as two points.

7.8.4 If, after completely passing over the crossbar the ball is blown back, a goal is still allowed.

7.8.5 When a kick at goal is being taken a team-mate of the kicker is allowed to hold the ball in position by placing a hand on it.

7.9 No Goal From Kick-Off

7.9.1 A goal cannot be scored from a kick-off or drop-out, or from a drop-kick when bringing the ball into play by a free-kick, or from a differential penalty.

7.10 How a Drop Goal is Scored

7.10.1 By a drop-kick during general play from any position in the field of play, over the crossbar and between the uprights. A drop goal counts as one point.

7.11 Where Kicks at Goal are Taken

7.11.1 A kick at goal after a try may be taken from any point opposite where the try is scored and parallel to the touchline.

7.11.2 A kick at goal from a penalty may be taken from the mark or from any point opposite the mark and parallel to the touchline.

7.11.3 A referee should ensure that a kick at goal is taken from the correct position. If the kick is taken from the incorrect position no goal shall be allowed and the kick shall not be retaken.

7.12 Players' Positions

7.12.1 When a kick at goal is being taken following a try, the opposing players shall stand within their own in-goal area.

7.12.2 Players from the kicker's team must be behind the ball.

7.12.3 When a penalty kick at goal is being taken, the opposing players shall retire to their goal line or not less than 10 m (33 ft) from the mark.

7.13 Illegal to Distract the Kicker

7.13.1 It is illegal to attempt to distract the attention of the kicker.

7.14 Goalposts

7.14.1 For the purpose of judging a kick at goal, the goalposts are assumed to extend indefinitely upwards.

7.15 Judging Kicks at Goal

7.15.1 If a touch judge believes a goal has been kicked he shall raise his flag above his head.

7.15.2 If a touch judge believes the kick at goal is unsuccessful he shall wave his flag in front of him.

7.15.3 If both touch judges are in agreement, their decision shall be final.

7.15.4 In the event of a disagreement, the referee shall decide.

7.16 Wasting Time

7.16.1 If a player wastes time when kicking at goal, the referee may caution him or, in extreme cases, dismiss him. The kick should not be cancelled, but extra time should be allowed.

7.17 Colleague Holds Ball

7.17.1 When a place-kick is being taken it is permissible for a colleague of the kicker to hold the ball in position by placing a hand on it.

7.18 Pretending to Kick at Goal

7.18.1 It shall count as misconduct for a player to pretend to kick at goal from a penalty kick and then deliberately kick it elsewhere. Such misconduct shall result in a penalty being awarded against the kicker.

Section 8 Offside

8.1 When Players are Offside

8.1.1 A player is offside if the ball touches, is touched, held or kicked by one of his own team behind him.

8.1.2 A player cannot be offside in his own in-goal.

8.1.3 When the referee is satisfied that accidental offside has taken place, a scrum should be packed where the accidental offside took place.

8.2 Out of Play

8.2.1 An offside player shall not take any part in the game or attempt in any way to influence the course of the game.

8.3 Players to Retire 10 Metres

8.3.1 An offside player shall not encroach within 10 m (33 ft) of an opponent waiting for the ball.

8.3.2 An offside player shall retire 10 m (33 ft) from an opponent who first secures possession of the ball.

8.4 Player Placed Onside

8.4.1 An offside player is placed onside in the following circumstances:

a) An opposing player runs 10 m (33 ft) or more with the ball.

b) An opposing player touches the ball but does not retain it.

c) A team-mate in possession of the ball runs in front of him.

d) A team-mate kicks or knocks the ball forward and takes up a position in front of him in the field of play.

e) If he retires behind the point where the ball was last touched by one of his team-mates.

8.4.2 Players who are out of play are not put onside in the manner described above.

8.5 Catcher Claims Opponent Offside

8.5.1 A player who catches the ball near an offside opponent must not go out of his way to make interference by the offside player inevitable.

8.5.2 If the catcher deliberately and unnecessarily runs into the offside player then play should proceed.

8.6 Accidental Offside

8.6.1 If the touch judge considers that any interference caused by an offside player is accidental, play should be re-started with a scrum.

Section 9 Touch and Touch-in Goal

Section 10 Obstruction

Section 11 Player's Misconduct

These rules are reprinted by permission of the Rugby Football League. A complete copy of the International Rules of Rugby League can be obtained from the League.

Aggressive double tackle

Rugby Union
Essentials

The original and most widely played version of rugby. The roots of this game are generally traced back to a pupil at Rugby School who, in 1823, breached the rules in a football game by picking up the ball and running with it.

The ground

Grass covered, clay or sand. There are only maximum – not minimum – distance requirements.

Officials
A referee and two touch judges.

At least 3.4 m (11 ft)

3.m (10 ft)

5.6 m (18 ft)

The goals

Two goalposts at each end, at least 3.4 m (11 ft) high. The posts are placed 5.6 m (18 ft) apart and are joined by a crossbar, 3 m (10 ft) above the ground.

Team numbers and positions on the field
1 – 8 Forwards
9 and 10 half-backs
12 and 13 centres
11 and 14 wing three-quarters
15 fullback

Francois Pienaar, captain of South Africa's 1996 World Cup winning team.

The World Cup

Dress

Jerseys, shorts and undergarments, socks and boots. Players may also wear mouth-guards and shin-guards. They must not wear anything which might cause injury to other players. Boot studs must have a maximum length of 18 mm (³/₄ in), minimum diameter of 13 mm (¹/₂ in) at the base and 10 mm (approx ¹/₂ in) at the top.

Major event
Below, teams from Ireland, France, Wales, England and Scotland play for the Five Nations Championship.

Scrum time
Above, the scrum is one of the key parts of a rugby game, occupying much of the playing time.

The players

Two teams of fifteen players (or ten or seven in some cases).

The ball

Oval, with four panels. Its length must be 280–300 mm (approx 11 in), its circumference must be 760–790 mm (approx 30 in) (end on) and its weight, 400-440 g (approx 15 oz). At the start of play the pressure should be 0.67–0.70 kg/squ. cm.

HOW TO PLAY

Each team contests possession of the ball in order to touch it down in their opponents' in-goal to score tries and to kick it over the crossbar (and between the extended line of the posts) for converting a try or kicking a penalty goal. Players may carry, kick or pass the ball. They may also take part in a scrummage, ruck, maul and line-out, which are particular features of the Union game.

Starting

Captains toss for the right to kick-off or the choice of ends. A player from the team taking the kick-off takes a place-kick from the centre of the halfway line. This must reach the opponents' 10–metre line, unless first played by an opponent. The kicker's team must be behind the ball and the opposing team must be on or behind the 10–metre line at the start of play.
See Law 10, Kick-Off (page48).

How to win

A try scores five points, a goal scored after a try scores two points and a goal from a penalty kick scores three, as does a goal scored during play by a place-kick (the ball is kicked from a spot on the ground) or drop kick (the player drops the ball onto his foot), although this goal must not be scored off a free-kick or after a scrum taken in lieu of a free-kick. The team with the most points wins.

KEY RULES

• A game consists of two halves of 40 minutes each (international matches) with an interval of not more than ten minutes. Teams change ends at half-time.

• The ball may be *carried* or *kicked* in a forward direction, but it may only be *passed* to the side or backwards.

• When a player is tackled in rugby union he must release the ball immediately. Both teams will then try to gain possession of it. A *ruck* is formed when one or more players from each team, all on their feet and binding with one another, close around the ball. A *maul* occurs when players bind in a similar manner around a player who is in possession of the ball.
See Law 21 Ruck, and Law 22, Maul (page 53).

• If neither team manages to gain possession with either of these methods, a *scrummage* is ordered. *See Law 20, Scrummage (page 51).* This is formed by players from each team binding in anticipation of the ball being put in between them. The middle player in the front row is the hooker and on either side of him are the props. These players bind together, keeping a clear tunnel between their feet. The players behind them must link up with each other using at least one arm and hand. Both teams' players then come together to complete the scrum formation.

The ball is put in by the scrum-half, who then plays the ball as it emerges from the scrummage. He puts the ball in so that it travels along the imaginary middle line between the two front rows. The hookers must be the first ones to touch the ball with their feet, otherwise the ball must be put in again.

• A *fair catch* is made by a player who is within his own 22-metre area and manages to catch the ball cleanly from a kick by an opponent, exclaiming "Mark!" as he does so. This player is then awarded a free-kick.
See Law 16, Fair Catch (Mark) (page 49).

If the ball is in touch (i.e., if it, or the player carrying it, touches the touchline or the ground beyond it), play must be restarted with a line-out. At least two players from each team form a single line which is parallel to the other team's line, one metre apart from it and at right angles to the touchline. The line-out stretches from five metres to 15 metres from the touchline. The player throwing in the ball does so from outside the field of play. The players in the line-out must try to catch the ball cleanly or guide it towards a team-mate to gain possession for their team.
(See Law 23, Touch and Line-Out Touch and Line-Out (page 53.)

Just for kicks
A rugby ball is such an awkward shape that kicking it is a fine art, so each team has its specialist kicker for penalties and goal kicks. This is Scotland's kicker, full-back Gavin Hastings.

Nice try
The ultimate aim of most moves on the field is to get the ball over the opposing team's goal-line and touch it down for a try which scores a team five points.

RUGBY UNION THE LAWS

International referee, Derek Bevan

These laws are abridged and summarized. P.K. and F.K. stand for the Penalty Kick and Free-Kick provisions for infringements of the laws.

Laws 1–6
These laws are covered on page 47.

Law 7 Mode of Play
A match is started by a kick-off, after which any player who is onside, and provided he does so in accordance with these laws may at any time:
• catch or pick up the ball and run with it,
• pass, throw or knock the ball to another player.
• kick or otherwise propel the ball,
• tackle, push or shoulder an opponent holding the ball,
• fall on the ball,
• take part in a scrummage, ruck, maul or line-out,
• ground the ball in in-goal.

Law 8 Advantage
The referee shall not whistle for an infringement during play which is followed by an advantage gained by the non-offending team. An advantage must be either territorial or such possession of the ball as constitutes an obvious tactical advantage. A mere opportunity to gain advantage is not sufficient.
Notes:
(i) The referee is given a wide discretion as to what constitutes an advantage and is not limited to a territorial advantage. The referee is the sole judge of whether an advantage has been gained.
ii) Neither team may gain an advantage from the following circumstances:
(a) when the ball or a player carrying it touches the referee (Law 9(1));
(b) when the ball emerges from either end of the tunnel at a scrummage not having been played (Law 20, note (xiv)).
iii) When any irregularity of play not provided for in the laws occurs, a scummage shall be formed where the irregularity

occurred. In deciding which team should put in the ball, the referee should apply Law 20(7).

Law 9. Ball or Player Touching Referee
(1) If the ball or a player carrying it touches the referee in the field of play, play shall continue unless the referee considers either team has gained an advantage in which case he shall order a scrummage. The team which last played the ball shall put it in.
(2) (a) If the ball in a player's possession or a player carrying it touches the referee in his opponents' in-goal, play shall continue unless the referee considers an advantage has been gained by that player's team in which case a touchdown shall be awarded at the place where the referee was touched.
(b) If the ball in a player's possession or a player carrying it touches the referee in this opponents' in-goal, play shall continue unless the referee considers an advantage has been gained by that player's team in which case a try shall be awarded at the place where the referee was touched.
Notes:
(i) If the ball, while in play in in-goal at either end but not held by a player, touches the referee, a touch judge, or a spectator, a touchdown shall be awarded provided that a touchdown would otherwise have been obtained or the ball would have gone into touch-in-goal or on or over the dead-ball line.
(ii) If the ball while in play in in-goal at either end, but not held by a player, touches the referee, a touch judge, or a spectator, a try shall be awarded at that place provided an attacking player would otherwise have scored it.

Law 10 Kick-Off
Kick-off is (a) a place-kick taken from the centre of the halfway line by the team which has the right to start the match or by the opposing team on the resumption of play after the half-time interval or (b)a drop kick taken at or from behind the centre of the halfway line by the defending team after the opposing side has scored.
(1) The ball must be kicked from

the correct place and by the correct form of kick; otherwise it shall be kicked off again.
(2) The ball must reach the opponents' 10-metre line, unless first played by an opponent; otherwise it shall be kicked off again, or a scrummage formed at the centre, at the opponents' option. If it reaches the 10-metre line and is then blown back, play shall continue.
(3) If the ball is kicked directly into touch, the opposing team may accept the kick, have the ball kicked off again, or have a scrummage formed at the centre.
(4) If the ball crosses the opposing team's goal line from a kick-off, without touching or being touched by a player, the opposing team has the option of grounding the ball, making it dead, or playing on. If the opposing team grounds the ball or makes it dead or the ball becomes dead by touch-in-goal or by touching or crossing the dead-ball line, they will have the option of either having a scrummage formed at the centre of the halfway line, with the put-in, or having the other team kick off again.
(5) The *kicker's team* must be behind the ball when kicked; otherwise a scrummage shall be formed at the centre.
(6) The *opposing team* must stand on or behind the 10-metre line. If they are in front of that line or if they charge before the ball has been kicked, it shall be kicked off again.

Law 11 Method of Scoring
Try. A try is scored by first grounding the ball in the opponents' in-goal
   A penalty try shall be awarded if one would probably have been scored but for foul play by the opposing team.
   Goal. A goal is scored by kicking the ball over the opponents' crossbar and between the goalposts from the field of play by any place-kick or drop-kick, except a kick-off, drop-out or free-kick, without touching the ground or any player of the kicker's team.
   A goal is scored if the ball has crossed the bar notwithstanding a prior offence of the opposing team.
   A goal is scored if the ball has crossed the bar, even though it may have been blown backwards afterwards, and whether it has touched the crossbar or either goalpost or not.
   A goal may be awarded if the

ball is illegally touched by any player of the opposing team and if the referee considers that a goal would otherwise probably have been scored.
For scoring values, see How to win (page 47).

Law 12 Try and Touchdown
Grounding the ball is the act of a player who
   (a) while holding the ball in his hand (or hands) or arm (or arms) brings the ball in contact with the ground, or
   (b) while the ball is on the ground either
• places his hand (or hands) or arm (or arms) on it with downward pressure, or
• falls upon it and the ball is anywhere under the front of his body from waist to neck inclusive.
A. Try
(1) A player who is onside scores a try when
• he carries the ball into his opponents' in-goal, or
• the ball is in his opponents' in-goal,
and he first grounds it there.
(2) The scoring of a try includes the following cases:
(a) if a player carries, passes, knocks or kicks the ball into his in-goal and an opponent first grounds it;
(b) if, at a scrummage or ruck, a team is pushed over its goal line and before the ball has emerged it is first grounded in in-goal by an attacking player;
(c) if the momentum of a player, when tackled, carries him into his opponents' in-goal and he first there grounds the ball;
(d) if a player first grounds the ball on his opponents' goal line or if the ball is in contact with the ground and a goalpost; and
(e) if a tackle occurs in such a position that the tackled player whilst complying with the law is able to place the ball on or over the goal-line.
(3) If a player grounds the ball in his opponents' in-goal and picks it up again, a try is scored where it was first grounded.
(4) A try may be scored by a player who is in touch or in touch-in-goal provided he is not carrying the ball.
B. Penalty Try
A penalty try shall be awarded between the posts if but for foul play by the defending team
• a try would probably have been scored, or
• it would probably have been scored in a more favourable position than that where the ball was grounded.

C. Touchdown
(1) A touchdown occurs when a player first grounds the ball in his in-goal.
(2) After a touchdown, play shall be restarted either by a drop-out or a scrummage.

D. Scrummage after Grounding in Case of Doubt
Where there is doubt as to which team first grounded the ball in in-goal, a scrummage shall be formed 5 m (16 ft) from the goal line opposite the place where the ball was grounded. The attacking team shall put in the ball.

Law 13 Kick at Goal after a Try
(1) After a try has been scored, the scoring team has the right to take a place-kick or drop kick at goal on a line through the place where the try was scored.
(2) If a kick is taken:
(a) it must be taken without undue delay;
(b) any player including the kicker may place the ball;
(c) the kicker's team, except a placer, must be behind the ball when kicked;
(d) if the kicker kicks the ball from a placer's hands without the ball being on the ground, the kick is void;
(e) the opposing team must be behind the goal line until the kicker begins his run or offers to kick when they may charge or jump with a view to preventing a goal.
(3) Neither the kicker nor a placer shall wilfully do anything which may lead the opposing team to charge prematurely. If either does so, the charge shall not be disallowed.

Penalty:
• For an infringement by the kicker's team – the kick shall be disallowed
• For an infringement by the opposing team – the charge shall be disallowed. If, however, the kick has been taken successfully, the goal shall stand. If it was unsuccessful, the kicker may take another kick under the original conditions without the charge and may change the type of kick.

Law 14 In-Goal
In-goal is the area bounded by a goal line, touch-in-goal lines and dead-ball line. It includes the goal line and goalposts but excludes touch-in-goal lines and dead-ball line.
Touch-in-goal occurs when the ball or a player carrying it touches a corner post or a touch-in-goal line or the ground or a person or object on or beyond it. The flag is not part of the corner post.

Five-Metre Scrummage
(1) A five-metre scrummage is a scrummage formed 5 m (16 ft) from the goal line opposite the place where the ball became dead in in-goal, but no closer than 5 m from the touch-line. The attacking team shall put in the ball.
(2) If a player carrying the ball in in-goal is so held that he cannot ground the ball, the ball becomes dead.
(3) A five-metre scrummage shall be formed:
(a) if a defending player heels, kicks, carries, passes or knocks the ball into his in-goal, and it there becomes dead without an infringement having occurred; except where
• a try is scored, or
• he wilfully knocks or throws the ball from the field of play into touch-in-goal or over his dead-ball line or,
(b) if a defending player carrying the ball in the field of play is forced into his in-goal and he then touches down; or
(c) if, at a scrummage or ruck a defending team, with the ball in its possession, is pushed over its goal line and before the ball has emerged first grounds it in in-goal.

Drop-Out
(4) Except where the ball is knocked on or thrown forward in the field of play or in-goal, if an attacking player kicks, carries, passes or charges down the ball from an opponent's kick and it travels into his opponent's in-goal, either directly or having touched a defender who does not wilfully attempt to stop, catch or kick it, and it is there:
• grounded by a defending player, or
• goes into touch-in-goal or over the dead-ball line
a drop-out shall be awarded.

Penalties:-
(a) A penalty try shall be awarded when by foul play in in-goal the defending team has prevented a try which otherwise would probably have been scored.
(b) A try shall be disallowed and a penalty kick awarded, if a try would probably not have been gained but for foul play by the attacking team.
(c) For foul play in in-goal while the ball is out of play the penalty kick shall be awarded at the place where play would otherwise have restarted and, in addition, the player shall either be ordered off or cautioned that he will be sent off it he repeats the offence.
(d) For wilfully charging or obstructing in in-goal a player who has just kicked the ball the penalty shall be
• a penalty kick in the field of play 5 m (16 ft) from the goal-line opposite the place of infringement, or, at the option of the non-offending team,
• a penalty kick where the ball alights as provided under law 26(3) Penalty (ii) (b).
(e) For other infringements in in-goal, the penalty shall be the same as for a similar infringement in the field of play except that the mark for a penalty kick or free-kick shall be in the field of play 5 m(16 ft) from the goal-line opposite the place of infringement and the place of any scrummage shall be 5 m from the goal line opposite the place of infringement but not within 5 m of the touchline.

Law 15. Drop-Out
A drop-out is a drop kick awarded to the defending team.
(1) The drop kick must be taken from anywhere on or behind the 22-metre line; otherwise the ball shall be dropped out again.
(2) The drop kick must be taken without delay.

Penalty:-
Penalty kick on the 22-metre line.
(3) The ball must cross the 22-metre line; otherwise the opposing team may have it dropped out again, or have a scrummage formed at the centre of the 22- metre line. If it crosses the 22- metre line and is then blown back, play shall continue.
(4) If the ball is kicked directly into touch, the opposing team may accept the kick, have the ball dropped out again, or have a scrummage formed at the centre of the 22-metre line.
(5) The kicker's team must be behind the ball when kicked. However, retiring players of the kicker's team who are in front of the ball will not be penalized if their failure to retire is due to the rapidity with which the kick has been taken but they must not stop retiring and must not enter the game until they have been made onside by an action of their own team as required by Law 25 (1).

Penalty:
Scrummage at the centre of the 22-metre line and the opposing team shall put in the ball.
(6) The opposing team must not charge over the 22 metre line; otherwise the ball shall be dropped out again.
(7) When the ball has been made dead by the attacking team by a kick, other than an unsuccessful kick at goal, which goes into touch-in-goal or on or over the dead-ball line, the defending team will have the option of a drop-out or of a scrummage. If a scrummage is chosen, the scrummage will be ordered at the place from where the ball was kicked but not less than 5 m (16 ft) from the touchline.

Law 16 Fair Catch (mark)
(a) A player makes a fair-catch when, in his 22-metres area or in his in-goal, he cleanly catches the ball direct from a kick, other than from a kick-off, by one of his opponents and at the same time he exclaims "Mark!". A fair catch may be obtained even though the ball on its way touches a goalpost or crossbar.
(b) A free-kick is awarded for a fair catch.
(1) The free kick must be taken by the player making the fair catch, unless he is injured in so doing. If he is unable to take the kick within one minute a scrummage shall be formed at the mark. His team shall put in the ball.
(2) If the mark is in in-goal, any resultant scrummage shall be 5 m (16 ft) from the goal line on a line through the mark.

Law 17 Knock-On or Throw-Forward
A knock-on occurs when the ball travels forward towards the direction of the opponents' dead-ball line after:
• a player loses possession of it, or
• a player propels or strikes it with his hand or arm, or
• it strikes a player's hand or arm and touches the ground or another player before it is recovered by the player.
A throw-forward occurs when a player carrying the ball throws or passes it in the direction of his opponents' dead-ball line. A throw-in from touch is not a throw-forward. If the ball is not thrown or passed forward but it bounces forward after hitting a player or the ground, it is not a throw-forward.
(1) The knock-on or throw-forward must not be intentional.

Penalty:
Penalty kick at the place of infringement or in accordance with Law 14 Penalty (e). A

➥ *page 51*

SKILLS

The *front row* consists of the *props* and the *hooker*. The hooker is responsible for 'hooking' the ball with his feet in a scrum. The props are strong, sturdy players who assist the hooker by channelling the force of their own pack as well as withstanding the pressure of the opposition. The *locks* are the powerhouse of the scrum. Generally tall players, they are also often relied upon to secure possession at the line-out. The *back row* is made up of two *flankers* and the *number eight*. Flankers need to be good tacklers as well as key players in a maul or line-out. The number eight must have the stamina, strength and awareness to be able to control a scrum from its base and the ball as well, when it is channelled back through the scrum. The *scrum-half* works together with the *fly-half* to provide a link between the forwards and the backs. These two have tactical control over the game, deciding whether to kick, pass or run with the ball once the forwards have gained possession. Both must be nimble, quick and cunning. They must also be able to kick and pass well. The *centre three-quarters* play either in attack, setting up try-scoring opportunities for the wingers, or in defence, tackling and blocking the attacks of the opposition's three-quarters. The *wing three-quarters* receive the ball from the centre and must be swift runners, evading opponents with the sidestep, swerve and change of pace. The *full-back* is the last line of defence and must be able to kick to touch accurately.

TACTICS

The forwards contest for control of the ball through a series of 'set pieces', i.e. scrums and line-outs, and then release it in order to set the backs up for an attack. Alternatively, if they are a particularly strong unit, they may choose to head the attack themselves, keeping possession of the ball rather than passing it to the backs, and shifting play towards their opponents' in-goal directly via scrums, mauls and line-outs.

Training session
A second row forward (or lock) practises jumping in the line-out, supported by the props.

Coming together
Forwards bind together in a carefully arranged fashion before a scrum, both to ensure maximum push and a safe encounter.

Number eight
The number eight is the back row of the scrum. His task is to control the ball as it comes out of the scrum, directing the ball to the scrum-half waiting behind.

Small controller
Not all rugby players are big. The fly-half needs to be agile and very good at ball handling, kicking and passing. The fly-half is the team's mid-field general, whose task is to set the three-quarters in motion. He controls not only the direction of their movements but their pace and it is important for him to be able to switch direction in an instant to catch the opposition on the hop.

Hard ruck
When a player goes down with the ball, players pile on in a loose scrum or ruck in order to drive over the top and gain possession of the ball.

Link man
The scrum-half is the essential link between the fowards and the backs. It is the scrum half who must nip in and take the ball as it is cleared by the forwards from a scrum, line-out or ruck and then clear it to the three-quarters.

Kick back
The full-back is often the team's specialist kicker because it is immensely useful to have a man at the back who can sweep up the ball and kick it way upfield.

Flying pass
Scrum-halfs are typically small and nimble. You will often see them diving full length to get the ball quickly away from a scrum and out to the three-quarters.

Winging it
There is nothing more exciting than a swift three-quarter line movement – as the ball is fed out rapidly along the line from player to fast moving player.

On the run
The wingers are the team's speed kings, able to outpace the opposition and swerve and sidestep on a penetrating run upfield.

continued from page 49

penalty try may be awarded.
(2) If the knock-on or throw-forward is unintentional, a scrummage shall be formed either at the place of infringement or, if it occurs at a line-out, 15 m (16 yds) from the touchline along the line of touch unless:
• the ball is knocked on by a player who is in the act of charging down the kick of an opponent but is not attempting to catch the ball, or
• the ball is knocked on one or more times by a player who is in the act of catching or picking it up or losing possession of it and is recovered by that player before it has touched the ground or another player.

Law 18. Tackle, Lying with, on or Near the Ball
A tackle occurs when a player carrying the ball in the field-of-play is held by one or more opponents so that while he is so held he is brought to the ground or the ball comes into contact with the ground. If the ball carrier is on one knee, or both knees, or is sitting on the ground, or is on top of another player who is on the ground, the ball carrier is deemed to have been brought

to the ground.
(1) (a) A tackled player must immediately pass the ball or release the ball and get up or move away from the ball.
(b) Any player who tackles an opponent and, in doing so, goes to ground in the same way as the tackled player, must immediately release the tackled player and get up or move away from the tackled player and the ball. He must not play the ball until he is on his feet.
(c) After a tackle any other player must be on his feet when he plays the ball.
(d) A player who goes to the ground and gathers the ball or with the ball in his possession but who is not tackled must immediately get up on his feet with the ball or pass the ball or release the ball, and get up or move away from the ball.
(2) It is illegal for any player:
(a) to prevent a tackled player from passing or releasing the ball, or getting up or moving away after he has passed or released it;
(b) to pull the ball from a tackled player's possession or attempt to pick up the ball before the tackled player has released it;
(c) while lying on the ground after a tackle to play or interfere with the ball in any way or to

tackle or attempt to tackle an opponent carrying the ball;
(d) to wilfully fall on or over a player lying on the ground with the ball in his possession;
(e) to wilfully fall on or over players lying on the ground with the ball between them or in close proximity; or
(f) while lying on the ground in close proximity to the ball to prevent an opponent from gaining possession of it.
Note:
(viii) Close proximity means within 1 m (3 ft).
(3) A player must not fall on or over the ball emerging from a scrummage or ruck.
Penalty:
Penalty kick at the place of infringement.
(4) A try may be scored if the momentum of a player carries him into his opponents' in-goal even though he is tackled.

Law 19 Lying with, on or near the Ball
The requirements of this law are now incorporated into law 18.

Law 20 Scrummage
A scrummage, which can take place only in the field of play, is formed by players from each team closing up in readiness to

allow the ball to be put on the ground between them but is not to be formed within 5 m (16 ft) of the touchline.
The middle player in each front row is the hooker, and the players on either side of him are the props.
The middle line means an imaginary line on the ground directly beneath the line formed by the junction of the shoulders of the two front rows.
If the ball in a scrummage is on or over the goal line the scrummage is ended.
Forming a Scrummage
(1) A team must not wilfully delay the forming of a scrummage (F.K.).
(2) Every scrummage shall be formed at the place of infringement or as near thereto as is practicable within the field of play. It must be stationary with the middle line parallel to the goal lines until the ball has been put in.
Before commencing engagement, each front row must be in a crouched position with heads and shoulders no lower than their hips and so that they are not more than one arm's length from the opponents'

➡ *page 52*

continued from page 51
shoulders.

In the interest of safety, each front row should engage in the sequence of crouch, then pause and only engage on the call "Engage" given by the referee (F.K.).

Notes:

(i) To the extent that it is necessary, the scrummage is to be moved from the place of infringement so that the scrummage is formed in the field of play and the feet of all the defending players in the scrummage are in the field of play.

(ii) When the place of infringement is within 5 m (16 ft) of a touchline the scrummage is to be formed 5 m from that touchline.

(iii) The referee shall mark the place of engagement with his foot before the scrummage is formed.

(iv) A crouched position is the extension of the normal stance by bending the knees sufficiently to step into the engagement without a charge.

(3) It is dangerous play for a front row to form down some distance from its opponents and rush against them. (P.K.).

Note:

(v) The referee should not call the front rows to engage until the ball is in the hands of the player putting in the ball and is available to be put in immediately. This call is not a command, but an indication that the front rows may engage when ready.

(4) **Experimental Variation:**

A maximum of eight players from each team shall be required to form a scrummage and the number of these players shall not be increased while the scrummage is taking place. These players shall remain bound in the scrummage until it ends. Each front row of a scrummage shall have three players in it at all times. The head of a player in the front row shall not be next to the head of a player of the same team (P.K.).

Exception:

(a) when for any reason the number of players in a team is reduced to less than 15 players, the number of players of each team in the scrummage may be similarly reduced. Any reduction must not be such that the number of players for any team

in the scrummage is less than five;

(5) (a) While a scrummage is forming:

• the shoulders of each player in the front row must not be lower than his hips,

• all players in each front row must adopt a normal stance,

• both feet must be on the ground and not crossed,

• the hookers must be in a hooking position,

• a hooker's foot must not be in front of the forward feet of his props (F.K.).

(b) While the scrummage is taking place, players in each front row must have their weight firmly on at least one foot and be in a position for an effective forward shove and the shoulders of each player must not be lower than his hips (F.K.).

Notes:

(vi) The restriction on the crossing of the feet of the players in the front rows refers only to the feet of individual players. The feet of all players in the front rows must be in a position for an effective forward shove.

(vii) A hooking position is where a hooker in the scrummage has both feet on the ground, the weight retained firmly on one foot and in a position to hook or strike the ball.

(viii) A flank forward in the second or third row of a scrummage may pack at an angle provided he is properly bound. If the ball is emerging from the back of the scrummage and he moves outwards, thereby preventing an opponent from advancing around the scrummage, a penalty kick should be awarded.

(ix) In the event of the scrummage collapsing the referee should whistle immediately so that players do not continue to push. The referee should also whistle immediately if any player in the scrummage is lifted off his feet or is forced upwards out of the scrummage.

(x) The scrummage is ended:

• if the ball in the scrummage is on or over the goal line

• when the ball emerges from the scrummage

• if, in the scrummage, a player whose feet are the 'hindmost' feet in that scrummage, has the ball at his feet, unbinds and picks up the ball.

Binding of Players

(6)(a) The players of each front row shall bind firmly and continuously while the scrummage is forming, while the

ball is being put in and while it is in the scrummage (P.K.).

(b) The hooker may bind either over or under the arms of his props but, in either case, he must bind firmly around their bodies at or below the level of the armpits. The props must bind the hooker similarly. The hooker must not be supported so that he is not carrying any weight on either foot (P.K.).

(c) The outside (loose-head) prop must either (i) bind his opposing (tight-head) prop with his left arm inside the right arm of his opponent, or (ii) place his left hand or forearm on his left thigh.

The tight-head prop must bind with his right arm outside the left upper arm of his opposing loose-head prop. He may *grip* the jersey of his opposing loose head prop with his right hand but only to keep himself and the scrummage steady and he must not exert a downward pull (P.K.).

(d) All players in a scrummage, other than those in a front row, must bind with at least one arm and hand around the body of another player of the same team. The player whose feet are the 'hindmost' feet in the scrummage must bind with at least one arm on to one of his locks (P.K.).

(e) No outside player other than a prop may hold an opponent with this outer arm (F.K.).

Putting the Ball into the Scrummage

(7) When an infringement occurs the team not responsible shall put in the ball. In other circumstances, unless otherwise provided, the ball shall be put in by the team which was moving forward prior to the stoppage or, if neither team was moving forward, by the attacking team.

(8) The ball shall be put in without delay as soon as the two front rows have closed together. A team must put in the ball when ordered to do so and on the side first chosen (F.K.).

(9) The player putting in the ball shall:

(a) stand 1m (3 ft) from the scrummage on the middle line between the two front rows (F.K.);

(b) hold the ball with both hands over the middle line between the two front rows at a level midway between his knees and ankles (F.K);

(c) from that position put in the ball

• without any delay or without feint or backward movement, i.e. with a single forward movement,

and

• at a quick speed straight along the middle line so that it first touches the ground immediately beyond the width of the nearer prop's shoulders (F.K.).

(10) Play in the scrummage begins when the ball leaves the hands of the player putting it in.

(11) If the ball is put in and it comes out at either end of the tunnel, it shall be put in again, unless a free-kick or penalty kick has been awarded. If the ball comes out otherwise than at either end of the tunnel and if a penalty kick has not been awarded play shall proceed.

Notes:

(xiv) Advantage applies as soon as the ball has been put into the scrummage and played.

Restrictions on Front Row Players

(12) All front row players must place their feet so as to allow a clear tunnel. A player must not prevent the ball from being put into the scrummage, or from toughing the ground at the required place (F.K.).

(13) No front row player may raise or advance a foot until the ball has left the hands of the player putting it into the scrummage (F.K.).

(14) When the ball has touched the ground, any foot of any player in either front row may be used in an attempt to gain possession of the ball subject to the following:

players in the front row must not at any time during the scrummage wilfully:

(a) raise both feet off the ground at the same time (P.K.); or

(b) adopt a position or take any action, by twisting or lowering the body or by pulling on an opponent's dress, which is likely to cause the scrummage to collapse (P.K.); or

(c) lift an opponent off his feet or force him upwards out of the scrummage (P.K.); or

(d) kick the ball out of the tunnel in the direction from which it is put in. (F.K.)

Restrictions on Players

(15) Any player who is not in either front row must not play the ball while it is in the tunnel. (F.K.).

(16) A player must not:

(a) return the ball into the scrummage (F.K.); or

(b) handle the ball in the scrummage except in the act of obtaining a 'push-over' try or touchdown (P.K.); or

(c) pick up the ball in the

scrummage by hand or legs (P.K.);

(d) wilfully collapse the scrummage (P.K.); or

(e) wilfully fall or kneel in the scrummage (P.K.); or

(f) attempt to gain possession of the ball in the scrummage with any part of the body except the foot or lower leg (F.K.).

(17) (a) The player putting in the ball and his immediate opponent must not kick the ball while it is in the scrummage (F.K.).

(b) Neither of the players referred to in (a) should take any action while the ball is in the scrummage to convey to the opponents that the ball is out of the scrummage (F.K.).

(18) A scrummage must not be wheeled beyond a position where the middle line becomes parallel to the touchline. The scrummage will be reformed at the site of the stoppage, the ball to be put in by the side that has gained possession or otherwise by the same team.

Penalty:

(a) For an infringement of paragraphs (1), (2), (5) and (6)(e), (9), (9), (12), (13), (14)(d), (15), (16)(a) and (f) and (17)(a) and (b), a free-kick at the place of infringement.

(b)For an infringement of paragraphs (3), (4), (6)(a)(b)(c) and (d), (14)(a)(b) and (c), or (16) (b)(c)(d) and (e), a penalty kick at the place of infringement

For Offside at Scrummage see Law 24 B.

Law 21 Ruck

A ruck, which can take place only in the field of play, is formed when the ball is on the ground and one or more players from each team are on their feet and in physical contact, closing around the ball between them.

Rucking is the act of a player who, in a ruck, is using his feet to retrieve or retain the ball without contravening Law 26.

If the ball in a ruck is on or over the goal line the ruck is ended.

(1) A player joining a ruck must have his head and shoulders no lower than his hips. He must bind with at least one arm around the body of a player of his team in the ruck.

Penalty:-

Free-kick at the place of infringement (F.K.).

Notes:

(i) The placing of a hand on another player is not binding. Binding involves the whole arm, from hand to shoulder.

(2) A player must not:

(a) return the ball into the ruck;

(b) take any action while the ball is in the ruck to convey to the opponents that the ball is out of the ruck;

Penalty:

Free-kick at the place of infringement (F.K.).

(c) or handle the ball in the ruck except in the act of securing a try or touchdown; or

(d) pick up the ball in the ruck by hand or legs; or(e) wilfully collapse the ruck; or

(f) jump on top of other players in the ruck; or

(g) wilfully fall or kneel in the ruck; or

(h) while lying on the ground interfere in any way with the ball in or emerging from the ruck. He must do his best to roll away from it.

Penalty:

For (c) to (h), a penalty kick at the place of infringement (P.K.).

For Offside at Ruck see Law 24 C.

Note:

(ii) Players' safety is of primary importance and players should ruck for the ball and not the players on the ground. Players rucking for the ball should attempt to step over other players lying on the ground and should not intentionally step on them. Players must ruck in close proximity to the ball.

(3) When the ball in the ruck becomes unplayable a scrummage shall be ordered and the ball put in by the team moving forward immediately prior to the stoppage. When neither team was moving forward or when the referee is unable to determine which team was moving forward, the ball shall be put in by the team moving forward immediately before the formation of the ruck and if no team was moving forward by the attacking team.

Law 22 Maul

A Maul, which can take place only in the field of play, is formed by one or more players from each team on their feet and in physical contact closing round a player who is in possession of the ball.

A maul ends when the ball is on the ground or the ball or a player carrying it emerges from the maul or when a scrummage is ordered.

If the ball in a maul is on or over the goal line the maul is ended.

(1) A player joining a maul must have his head and shoulders no lower than his hips.

Penalty:

Free kick at the place of infringement (F.K.).

(2) A player must not:

(a) jump on top of players in a maul;

(b) wilfully collapse a maul;

(c) attempt to drag an opponent out of a maul;

Penalty:

Penalty kick at the place of infringement (P.K.).

(d) take any action while the ball is in the maul to convey to the opponents that the ball is out of the maul.

Penalty:

Free-kick at the place of infringement.

(3) A player is not in physical contact unless he is caught in or bound to the maul and not merely alongside it.

(4) (a) When a maul remains stationary or stops moving forward or the ball in a maul becomes unplayable, a scrummage shall be ordered and the ball shall be put in by the team not in possession at the commencement of the maul, except where the referee is unable to determine which team was in possession then the ball shall be put in by the team which was moving forward prior to the stoppage, or if neither team was moving forward by the attacking team.

(b) If a player catches the ball direct from a kick by an opponent other than from a kick-off or from a drop-out, and is immediately held by an opponent so that a maul ensues and the maul remains stationary or stops moving forward or the ball becomes unplayable, his team shall put in the ball at the ensuing scrummage.

For Offside at Maul see Law 24 C.

LAW 23 TOUCH AND LINE-OUT

A. Touch

(1) The ball is in touch

• when it is not being carried by a player and it touches a touchline or the ground or a person or object on or beyond it, or

• when it is being carried by a player and it or the player carrying it touches a touchline or the ground beyond it.

(2) If the ball is not in touch and has not crossed the plane of the touchline, a player who is in touch may kick the ball or propel it with his hand but not hold it.

(3) The ball is deemed to have been kicked directly into touch if,

from a kick, it is in touch without having pitched on the playing area or without having touched or been touched in flight by a player or the referee.

Notes:

(i) (a) If the ball is kicked directly into touch from a kick-off and the opposing team elects to accept the kick, the line-out shall be formed.

• at the halfway line, or

• where the ball went into touch if that place be nearer to kicker's goal line.

(b) If the ball is kicked directly into touch from a drop-out and the opposing team elects to accept the kick, the line-out shall be formed where the ball went into touch.

(ii) On or beyond the touchline or touch-in goal line refers to all areas except the playing area.

(iii) It is not touch or touch-in goal when a player with both feet in the playing area catches the ball, even though the ball before being caught has crossed the touchline or touch-in-goal line. Such a player may deflect or tap the ball in the playing area provided it is not propelled forward. If a player jumps and catches the ball his feet must land in the playing area.

B. Line-Out

The line of touch is an imaginary line in the field of play at right angles to the touchline through the place where the ball is to be thrown in.

Formation of line-out

(1) A line-out is formed by at least two players from each team lining up in single lines parallel to the line of touch in readiness for the ball to be thrown in between them. The team throwing in the ball shall determine the maximum number of players from either team who so line up. Such players are those 'in the line-out' unless excluded below (F.K.).

(2) Each team must line up half a metre (1 ½ ft) on its side of the line-of-touch so as to leave a clear space of 1 m (3 ft) between the two lines of players (measured between the shoulders of the players, standing upright) (F.K.).

(3) The line-out stretches from 5 m (16 ft) from the touchline from which the ball is being thrown in to a position 15 m (16 yds) from that touchline (F.K.).

(4) Any player of either team who is further than 15 m (16 yds)

➡ *page 55*

Line-out
If the ball goes into touch, play is re-started with a line-out. The opposing forwards stand in two lines and jump to try and catch the ball as it is thrown. The maximum number of players in the line-out is determined by the team taking the throw.

Jump for it
Line-outs are one of the main ways of gaining possession. As players jump for the ball, they try and either catch it, deflect it to the scrum-half or knock it back to another player in the line-out.

Hold up
In any line-out there is usually one target jumper. As soon as he catches the ball, the players in front of him close round to protect him.

Line down
In contrast to a scrum, where the team putting in the ball has the best chance of gaining possession, in a line-out each team has a good chance. The result is often a chaotic scramble for the ball.

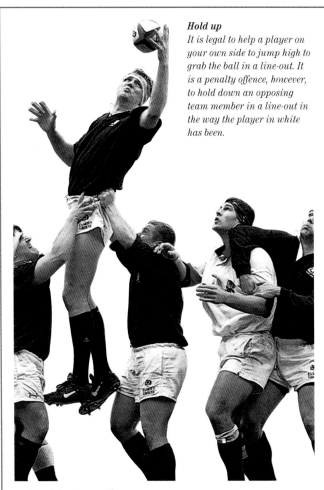

Hold up
It is legal to help a player on your own side to jump high to grab the ball in a line-out. It is a penalty offence, however, to hold down an opposing team member in a line-out in the way the player in white has been.

continued from page 53

from the touchline when the line-out begins is not in the line-out (F.K.).

Note:

(vi) If, at a formed line-out, the team throwing in the ball line up less than the normal number, their opponents must be given a reasonable opportunity to conform. Opposing players who are retiring for that purpose must do so directly and without delay to a line 10 m (33 ft) behind the line of touch. Loiterers must be penalized. Subject to this, when the line-out is ended players so retiring may rejoin play, even if they have not reached the 10 m line.

Throwing in the Ball

(5) When the ball is in touch the place at which it must be thrown in is as follows:

(a) When the ball goes into touch from a penalty kick; or from a kick including a free-kick awarded within 22 m (24 yds) of the kicker's goal line, at the place where it touched or crossed the touchline, except as otherwise provided;

(b) when the kicker has received the ball outside his 22-metre line and retreated behind that line before kicking, and on other occasions when the ball is kicked

directly into touch, after having been kicked otherwise than as stated in (a), opposite the place from which the ball was kicked or at the place where it touched or crossed the touchline if that place be nearer to the kicker's goal line;

(c) when a quick throw-in is taken, from any point along the touchline between where the ball went into touch and the goal line of the team throwing in the ball;

(d) Otherwise when the ball is in touch, at the place where the ball touched or crossed the touch-line.

(6) (a) When kicked into touch from a penalty kick, the ball will be thrown in at the line-out by the team which kicked the ball into touch.

(b) Otherwise the ball is to be thrown in by an opponent of the player whom it last touched, or by whom it was carried before being in touch.

(c) In the event of doubt as to which team should throw in the ball, the attacking team shall do so.

(7) The ball may be brought into play at a formed line-out or by a quick throw-in which can only be taken before the line-out has formed.

If a quick throw-in occurs after

the line-out has formed, it is void and the ball is brought into play at the formed line-out by the same team.

(8) At a formed line-out the player throwing in the ball must:

• not put any part of either foot in the field of play.

• throw the ball in at the place indicated in (5) so that it first touches the ground or touches or is touched by a player at least 5 m (16 ft) from the touchline along the line of touch; otherwise the opposing team shall have the right, as its option, to throw in the ball or to take a scrummage 15 m (16 yds) from the touchline.

(9) (a) At a quick throw-in, the ball that went into touch must be used and, after going into touch and being made dead, unless it has been touched only by the player throwing it in, the ball shall be thrown in at the place indicated in (5) by the same team.

(b) At a quick throw-in, the ball must be thrown straight long the line of touch so that it first touches the ground or touches or is touched by a player at least 5 m (16 ft) from the touchline along the line of touch, otherwise the opposing team shall have the right, at its option, to throw in the ball or to take a scrummage 15 m (16 yds) from the touchline at the place where the quick throw-in occurred;

(c) At a quick throw-in a player must not prevent the ball from being thrown 5 m (16 ft) (F.K.).

(10) If, on the second occasion, the ball is not thrown in correctly, a scrummage shall be formed and the ball shall be put in by the team which threw it in on the first occasion.

Beginning and End of Line-Out

(11) The line-out begins when the ball leaves the hands of the player throwing it in.

(12) The line-out ends when

• a ruck or maul is taking place and all feet of players in the ruck or maul have moved beyond the line of touch, or

• a player carrying the ball leaves the line-out, or

• the ball has been passed, knocked back or kicked from the line-out, or

• the ball is thrown beyond a position 15 m (16 yds) from the touchline, or

• the ball becomes unplayable.

Peeling-Off

'Peeling-off' occurs when a player (or players) moved from his position in the line-out for the purpose of catching the ball when it has been passed or knocked

back by another of his team in the line-out.

(13) When the ball is in touch players who approach the line of touch must always be presumed to do so for the purpose of forming a line-out. Before the ball leaves the hands of the player throwing it in, the players in the line-out must not leave it but may change their position along the line of touch. After the ball has been thrown in such players must not leave the line-out except in a peel off movement (F.K.).

(14) In a peeling off movement a player must move parallel and close to the line-out (F.K.).

Restrictions on Players in Line-Out

(15) **Experimental Variation**

When a line-out is taking place, any player in the line-out must not

(a) stand within 5 m (16 ft) of the touchline or prevent the ball from being thrown 5 m (F.K.); or

(b) be offside (P.K.); or

(c) use an opponent as a support to enable him to jump for the ball (P.K.); or

(d) hold, push, charge, obstruct or grasp an opponent not holding the ball, except when a ruck or a maul is taking place (P.K.); or

(e) charge an opponent except in an attempt to tackle him or to play the ball (P.K); or

(f) use any player of his team as a support to enable him to jump for the ball (F.K.); or

(g) lift a player of his team (F.K.); or

(h) support any player of his team before this player has jumped for the ball (F.K.); or

(i) hold a supported player below the waist (P.K.).

(16) **Experimental Variation**

A player jumping for the ball must do so with either both hands or his inside arm to catch or deflect the ball. When a player plays the ball with both hands above his head, he is allowed to use either hand (F.K.).

(17) Except when jumping for the ball or peeling off, a clear space of 1 m (3 ft) must be left between the two lines of players until the ball has touched or has been touched by a player or has touched the ground (F.K.).

Note:

(xv) The act of jumping for the ball may include a step or steps in any direction provided it takes the jumper up to but not across the line of touch.

(18) A player in the line-out may move into the space between the

➥ *page 56*

continued from page 55

touchline and the 5 m-mark only when the ball has been thrown beyond him, and if he does so, he must not move towards his goal line before the line-out ends, except in a peeling off movement (F.K.).

(19) Until the line-out ends, no player may move beyond a position 15 m (16 yds) from the touchline except as allowed when the ball is thrown beyond that position, in accordance with the Exception following Law 24 D(1)(c) (P.K.).

Note:

(xvi) If the ball in a line-out becomes unplayable, otherwise than as a result of an infringement for which a penalty is prescribed, a scrummage should be ordered.

(20) A player participating in the line-out as defined in Law 24 D may run into a gap in the line-out and take the ball provided he does not charge or obstruct an opponent in the line-out (P.K.).

Restrictions on Players not in Line-out

(21) Players of either team who are not in the line-out may not advance from behind the line-out and take the ball from the throw-in, except only a player advancing at a long throw-in. (P.K.) on offside line.

Penalty:

(a) For an infringement of paragraphs (1), (2), (3), (4), (9)(c), (13), (14), (15)(a), (b), (g), or (h), (16), (17) or (18) a free-kick 15 m (16 yds) from the touchline along the line of touch.

(b) For an infringement of paragraphs (15)(b), (c), (d), (e) or (i), (19) or (20), a penalty kick 15 m (16 yds) from the touchline along the line of touch.

(c) For an infringement of paragraph (21), a penalty kick on the offending team's offside line (as defined in Law 24 D) opposite the place of infringement, but not less than 15 m (16 yds) from the touchline.

Place of Scrummage

Any scrummage taken or ordered under this Law or as the result of any infringement in a line-out shall be formed 15 m (16 yds) from the touchline along the line of touch.

Note:

(xvii) If a player repeatedly infringes, he must be dealt with under Law 26(2).

For Offside at Line-Out, see Law 24 D.

Law 24 Offside

Offside means that a player is in a position in which he is out of the game and is liable to penalty.

In general play the player is in an offside position because he is in front of the ball when it has been last played by another player of his team.

In play at a scrummage, ruck, maul or line-out the player is offside because he remains or advances in front of the line or place stated in, or otherwise infringes, the relevant sections of this Law.

A. Offside in General Play

(1) A player is in an offside position if the ball has been
• kicked, or
• touched, or
• is being carried
by one of his team behind him.

(2) There is no penalty for being in an offside position unless:
(a) the player plays the ball or obstructs an opponent; or
(b) he being within 10 m (33 ft) of an opponent waiting to play the ball or of the place where the ball pitches, does not retire without delay and without interfering with the opponent, or
(c) he, on all other occasions, moves towards the opponents waiting to play the ball or to the place where the ball pitches, before he is put onside.

Exceptions:-

(i) When an offside player cannot avoid being touched by the ball or by a player carrying it, he is 'accidentally offside'. Play should be allowed to continue unless the infringing team obtains an advantage, in which case a scrummage shall be formed at that place.
(ii) A player who receives an unintentional throw-forward is not offside.

Penalty:

Penalty kick at the place of infringement, or, at the option of the non-offending team, a scrummage at the place where the ball was last played by the offending team. If the latter place is in in-goal, the penalty kick shall be taken or the scrummage shall be formed 5 m from the goal line, on a line through the place.

For an infringement of (2)(c) by more than one player, the place of infringement will be that of the offside player closest to the player waiting for the ball or where the ball pitches.

Notes:

(i) A penalty for offside should not be given at once if the non-offending team gains an

advantage or if it appears likely to gain an advantage; but if the expected advantage is not gained, the penalty should in all cases be awarded even if it is necessary to bring play back for that purpose to the place of infringement.

(ii) When a player knocks on and offside player or the same team next plays the ball, a penalty for offside should not be awarded unless the offside deprives the non-offending team of an advantage.

(iii) A player can be offside in his in-goal.

(iv) If a player hands the ball to another player of his team in front of him, the second player is offside. A scrummage for 'accidental offside' should be awarded unless it is considered the player was wilfully offside in which case a penalty kick should be awarded.

(v) The referee should whistle at once if an offside player who cannot be placed onside charges within 10 m (33 ft) of an opponent waiting to receive the ball. Delay may prove dangerous to the latter player. Where there is no opponent waiting to play the ball but one arrives as the ball pitches, an offside player who is near such an opponent must not obstruct or interfere with him in any way whatsoever before he is put onside.

(vi) If an attacking player kicks the ball which is misfielded by an opponent and the ball is then played by another attacking player in an offside position within 10 m (33 ft) of the opponent, a penalty kick should be awarded.

(vii) If an attacking player kicks the ball which is charged down by an opponent and another attacking player within 10 m (33 ft) of the opponent then plays the ball, play should be allowed to continue. The opponent was not 'waiting to play the ball' and the second attacking player is therefore onside under Law 25 (2).

(viii) Law 24 A(2)(b) and (c) also apply where the ball has struck a goalpost or crossbar. Offside players must not approach or remain within 10 m (33 ft) of an opponent waiting to play the ball or the place where the ball pitches.

B. OffSide at Scrummage

The term 'offside line' means a line parallel to the goal lines through the hindmost foot of the player's team in the scrummage.

While a scrummage is forming or is taking place:

(1) A player is offside if
(a) he joins it from his opponent's side, or
(b) he, not being in the scrummage nor the player of either team who puts the ball in the scrummage,
• fails to retire behind the offside line or to his goal line whichever is the nearer, or
• places either foot in front of the offside line while the ball is in the scrummage.

(2) A player is offside if:
(a) he being the player in a scrum-half position whose team has won the ball, places both feet in front of the ball while it is still in the scrummage; or
(b) he being the immediate opponent of the player in a scrum-half position whose team has won the ball, places either foot in front of the ball while it is still in the scrummage.

(3) A player is offside if he, being the immediate opponent of the player putting in the ball, moves to the opposite side of the scrummage or moves away from the scrummage and is in front of the scrummage offside line. (P.K.).

Penalty:

Penalty kick on the offside line.

Notes:

(ix) Players must retire without delay to the scrummage offside line when a scrummage is forming. Loiterers must be penalized.

(x) Any player of either team may at a particular scrummage be the player who puts in the ball or who takes up position as scrum-half when his opponent is putting in the ball; but such player is at that scrummage the only player of his team who has the benefit of Law 24 B(2).

C. Off-side at Ruck or Maul

The term 'offside line' means a line parallel to the goal lines through the hindmost foot of the player's team in the ruck or maul.

(1) Ruck or Maul otherwise than at Line-Out

While a ruck or maul is taking place (including a ruck or maul which continues after a line-out has ended) a player is offside if he:
(a) joins it from his opponents' side; or
(b) joins it in front of the hindmost player of his team in the ruck or maul; or
(c) does not join the ruck or maul but fails to retire behind the offside line without delay; or
(d) unbinds from the ruck or leaves the maul and does not

immediately retire behind the offside line, or once he is on side, if he rejoins the ruck or maul in front of the hindmost player of his team in the ruck or maul; or
(e) advances beyond the offside line with either foot and does not join the ruck or maul.

Penalty: Penalty kick on the offside line.

(2) Ruck or Maul at Line-Out
The term 'participating in the line-out' has the same meaning as in Section D of this Law. A player participating in the line-out is not obliged to join or remain in the ruck or maul and if he is not in the ruck or maul he continues to participate in the line-out until it has ended.

While a line-out is in progress and a ruck or maul takes place, a player is offside if he:
(a) joins the ruck or maul from his opponents' side; or
(b) joins it in front of the hindmost player of his team in the ruck or maul; or
(c) being a player who is participating in the line-out and is not in the ruck or maul, does not retire to and remain at the offside line defined in this Section;
Penalty:
Penalty kick 15 m (16 yds) from the touchline along the line of touch.
(d) or being a player who is not participating in the line-out, remains or advances with either foot in front of the offside line defined in Section D of this Law.
Penalty:
Penalty kick on the offending team's offside line opposite the place of infringement, but not less than 15 m (16 yds) from the touchline.
Note:
(xi) When the line-out has ended but the ruck or maul is still taking place, a player is offside if he infringes Section (1) of these Laws.

D. Offside at Line-out
The term 'participating in the line-out' refers exclusively to the following players:
• those players who are in the line-out, and
• the player who throws in the ball, and
• his immediate opponent who may have the option of throwing in the ball, and
• one other player of either team who takes up position to receive the ball if it is passed or knocked back from the line-out.

All other players are not participating in the line-out.

The term 'offside line' means a line 10 m (33 ft) behind the line of touch and parallel to the goal lines or, if the goal line be nearer than 10 m (33 ft) to the line of touch, the 'offside line' is the goal line.

Offside while participating in line-out
(1) A participating player is offside if:
(a) before the ball has touched a player or the ground he wilfully remains or advances with either foot in front of the line of touch, unless he advances while jumping for the ball, provided that the jump is made from his side of the line of touch; or
(b) after the ball has touched a player or the ground, if he is not carrying the ball, he advances with either foot in front of the ball, unless he is lawfully tackling or attempting to tackle an opponent who is partcipating in the line-out. Such tackle or attempt to tackle must, however, start from his side of the ball; or
(c) before the line-out ends he moves beyond a position 15 m (16 yds) from the touchline.
Exception:
Players of the team throwing in the ball may move beyond a position 15 m from the touchline for a long throw-in to them. They may do so only when the ball leaves the hands of the player throwing it in and if they do so their opponents participating in the line-out may follow them. If players so move and the ball is not thrown to or beyond them they must be penalized for offside.
Penalty:
Penalty kick 15 m from the touchline along the line of touch (P.K.).
Notes:
(xii) Players who advance beyond the offside line or who move beyond a position 15 m from the touchline in the expectation of a long throw-in must be penalized, if for any reason the ball is not thrown beyond that position.
(xiii) A player who has jumped unsuccessfully for the ball and crossed the line of touch should not be penalized if he retires immediately to an onside position.
(2) The player throwing in the ball and his immediate opponent must:
(a) remain within 5 m of the touchline; or
(b) retire to the offside line; or
(c) join the line-out after the ball has been thrown in 5 m; or
(d) move into position to receive

the ball if it is passed or knocked back from the line-out provided no other player is occupying that position at that line-out. If they do not they are offside.
Penalty:
Penalty kick 15 m from the touchline along the line of touch.
Notes:- (xv) If a player other than the wing three-quarter throws in the ball from touch, the wing three-quarter must retire to the offside line, or join the line-out.

Off-side while not participating in line-out
(3) A player who is not participating is offside if before the line-out has ended he advances or remains with either foot in front of the offside line.
Exception:
Players of the team throwing in the ball who are not participating in the line-out may advance for a long throw-in to them beyond the line-out. They may do so only when the ball leaves the hands of the player throwing in the ball and, if they do, their opponents may advance to meet them. If players so advance for a long throw-in to them and the ball is not thrown to them they must be penalized for offside.

Players returning to 'onside' position
(4) A player is not obliged, before throwing in the ball, to wait until players of his team have returned to or behind the line-out but such players are offside unless they return to an on-side position without delay.
Penalty:
Penalty kick on the offending team's offside line (as defined in Section D of this Law) opposite the place of infringement but not less than 15 m from the touchline.
Note:
(xvii) Scrummage, Ruck, Maul and Line-Out – where these Laws state a line which determines the offside position such line stretches continuously from touchline to touchline.

Law 25 Onside
Onside means that a player is in the game and not liable to penalty for offside.

Player made onside by action of his team
(1) Any player who is offside in general play and who is not infringing Law 24(A)(2) becomes onside as a result of any of the following actions of his team:
• when the offside player has retired behind the player of his team who last kicked, touched or

carried the ball, or
• when one of his team carrying the ball has run in front of him, or
• when one of his team has run in front of him after coming from the place or from behind the place where the ball was kicked.

In order to put the offside player onside, this other player must be in the playing area, but he is not debarred from following up in touch or touch-in goal.
Note:
(i) An offside player who is within 10 m (33 ft) of an opponent waiting to play the ball or the place where the ball pitches must retire and continue to do so up to 10 m until he is put onside. If he does not do so, he must be penalized.

Player made onside by action of opposing team
(2) Any player who is offside in general play, except an offside player within 10 m of an opponent waiting to play the ball or the place where the ball pitches, becomes onside as a result of any of the following actions:-
• when an opponent carrying the ball has run 5 m (16 ft), or
• when an opponent kicks or passes the ball, or
• when an opponent intentionally touches the ball and does not catch or gather it.

An offside player within 10 m (33 ft) of an opponent waiting to play the ball or the place where the ball pitches cannot be put onside by any action of his opponents.

Any other offside player in general play is always put onside when an opponent plays the ball.

Player retiring at scrummage, ruck, maul or line-out
(3) A player who is in an offside position when a scrummage, ruck maul or line-out is forming or taking place and is retiring as required by Law 24 (Offside) becomes onside:
• when an opponent carrying the ball has run 5 m (16 ft), or
• when an opponent has kicked the ball.

An offside player in this situation is NOT put onside when an opponent passes the ball.

Law 26 Foul Play
Foul Play is any action by a player which is contrary to the letter and spirit of the game and includes obstruction, unfair play, misconduct, dangerous play, unsporting behaviour, retaliation and repeated infringements.

➡ *page 58*

Forward play

Number eight break

1 *Occasionally the number eight, instead of heeling the ball out to the scrum half, may unbind from the pack and pick up the ball himself.*

Stopper
One of the roles of flankers is to break away rapidly when the opposition gain the ball and make a tackle before they get the ball away.

2 *He runs directly at the opposing forwards on the blind side of the scrum. He inevitably runs into opposition but his aim is to drive on as far as he can to gain valuable ground before he is brought down.*

Mutual support
When a player is running with the ball his team-mates must be there ready to receive the ball as soon as he is tackled.

Getting it away
When a player is tackled, he must get the ball away to a team-mate before he finally hits the deck – taking care not to throw it forward.

Loose head
The prop forwards are usually the biggest players in the team : they have to support the hooker and drive the scrum forward. But they must also be able to run with the ball.

---

continued from page 57

Obstruction

(1) It is illegal for any player:
(a) who is running for the ball to charge or push an opponent also running for the ball, except shoulder to shoulder;
(b) who is in an offside position wilfully to run or stand in front of another player of his team who is carrying the ball, thereby preventing an opponent from reaching the latter player;
(c) who is carrying the ball after if has come out of a scrummage, ruck, maul or line-out, to attempt to force his way through the players of his team in front of him;
(d) who is an outside player in a scrummage to prevent an opponent from advancing around the scrummage.
Penalty:
Penalty kick at the place of infringement. A penalty try may be awarded.

Notes:
(i) There are no circumstances in which a player carrying the ball can be penalized for obstruction.

Unfair Play, Repeated Infringements
(2) It is illegal for any player:
   (a) deliberately to play unfairly or wilfully infringe any law of the game;
(b) wilfully to waste time;
(c) wilfully to knock or throw the ball from the playing area into touch, touch-in-goal or over the dead-ball line;
(d) to infringe repeatedly any law of the game.
Penalty:
Penalty kick at the place of infringement. A penalty try may be awarded if the offence prevents a try which otherwise would have been probably scored.
   For offences under 2(d) a player may be cautioned and, if he repeats the offence, must be

ordered off.
Misconduct, Dangerous Play
(3) It is illegal for any player:
(a) to strike an opponent;
(b) wilfully or recklessly to hack or kick an opponent or to trip him with the foot or to trample on an opponent lying on the ground;
(c) to tackle early, or late or dangerously, including the action known as 'a stiff arm tackle'
(d) who is not running for the ball wilfully or recklessly to charge or obstruct an opponent who has just kicked the ball;
(e) to hold, push, charge, obstruct or grasp an opponent not holding the ball except in a scrummage, ruck or maul;
(Except in a scrummage or ruck the dragging away of a player lying close to the ball is permitted. Otherwise pulling any part of the clothing of an opponent is holding.)
(f) in the front row of a scrummage to form down some

distance from the opponents and rush against them;
(g) in the front row of a scrummage wilfully to lift an opponent off his feet or force him upwards out of the scrummage;
(h) wilfully or recklessly to cause a scrummage, ruck or maul to collapse;
(i) while the ball is out of play to molest, obstruct or in any way interfere with an opponent or be guilty of any form of misconduct;
(j) to commit any misconduct on the playing enclosure which is prejudicial to the spirit of good sportsmanship.
Penalty:
A player guilty of misconduct or dangerous play shall either be ordered off or else cautioned that he will be ordered off if he repeats the offence. For a similar offence after caution, the player must be ordered off.
   In addition to a caution or

Back play

Central run
When the centre runs with the ball, his aim is usually to run straight forward rather than at a diagonal. This not only makes it easier to sidestep opponents but helps maintain the three-quarter line.

Away in time
It is crucial that a three-quarter gets the ball away to a team-mate before he is tackled. Ideally, he will get it away before he has even slowed down so that the line's momentum is maintained.

The three-quarters
The back division of a rugby team is seven players: the scrum half who links the forwards and backs; the fly half who initiates movements in the three-quarter line; the two centre three-quarters; the wing three-quarters, who are the team's main try scorers; and the full-back, who is often the last line of defence.

Offensive defence
Centre three-quarters must be strong tacklers. Timing and strength is essential, but here Scott Gibbs not only stops his opponent but drives him backwards and gains the initiative.

ordering off a penalty try or a penalty kick shall be awarded as follows:
(i) If the offence prevents a try which would otherwise probably have been scored, a penalty try shall be awarded.
(ii) The place for a penalty kick shall be:
  (a) For offences other than under paragraphs (d) and (i), at the place of infringement;
  (b) For an infringement under (d) the non-offending team shall have the option of taking the kick at the place of infringement or where the ball alights, and if the ball alights.
• in touch, the mark is 15 m (16 yds) from the touchline on a line parallel to the goal lines through the place where it went into touch, or
• within 15 m from the touch-line, it is 15 m from the touchline on a line parallel to the goal lines

through the place where it alighted, or
• in in-goal, touch-in-goal, or over or on the dead-ball line, it is 5 m from the goal line on a line parallel to the touchline through the place where it crossed the goalline or 15 m from the touchline whichever is the greater. When the offence takes place in touch the 'place of infringement' in the optional penalty award is 15 m from the touchline opposite to where the offence took place:
  If the offence takes place in touch-in-goal, the 'place of infringement' in the optional penalty award is in the field of play 5 m (16 ft) from the goalline and 15 m (16 yds) from the touchline;
(c) For an offence under (i), at any place where the ball would next have been brought into play if the offence had not occurred,

or, if that place is on the touchline, 15 m from that place, on a line parallel to the goal lines.
(iii) For an infringement in In-goal, a penalty kick is to be awarded as provided for under Law 14 Penalties.
(iv) For an offence under Law 26(3)(i), the penalty kick is to be taken at whichever is the place where play would restart, that is
• at the 22-metre line (at any point the non-offending team may select), or
• at the centre of the halfway line, or
• if a scrummage 5 m (16 ft) from the goal line would otherwise have been awarded, at that place or 15 m from the touchline on a line 5 m from and parallel to the goalline, whichever is the greater.
(v) For an offence which occurs within the playing enclosure and

which is not otherwise covered in the foregoing, the penalty kick shall be awarded in the playing area 15 m (16 yds) from the touchline and opposite to where the offence took place.
(4) It is illegal for a team to adopt ploys knows as:-
(a) The Flying Wedge; and
(b) The Cavalry Charge as described in Notes (xii) and (xiii).
Penalty:
Penalty kick at the place of the original infringement.
Notes:
(iii) 'Playing the man without the ball' and all forms of dangerous tackling including early, late and stiff arm 'tackling' or tackling or attempting to tackle a player around the neck or head or above the line of the shoulders must be punished severely. Players who wilfully resort to this type of foul

➡ *page 60*

continued from page 59

play must be ordered off the field. Advantage should be played, but a penalty try must be awarded if the dangerous tackle prevents a probable try (P.K.).

(iv) It is for the referee to decide what constitutes a dangerous tackle, having regard to the circumstances, e.g. the apparent intentions of the tackler, or the nature of the tackle, or the defenceless position of the player being tackled or knocked over, which may be the cause of serious injury.

(v) The following actions constitute dangerous play:

(a) If a player charges or knocks down an oponent carrying the ball without any attempt to tackle him;

(b) If a player taps or pulls the foot or feet of another player who is jumping in a line-out;

(c) If a player attempts to tackle a player who, when fielding a kick in open play is off the ground jumping for the ball.

(vi) A player shall not 'take the law into his own hands' nor wilfully do anything that is dangerous to an opponent even if the latter is infringing the laws.

(vii) If a player is obstructed after kicking the ball and the ball strikes a goalpost, the optional penalty should be awarded where the ball alights after bouncing off the post.

(viii) If a penalty kick has been awarded and, before the kick has been taken, the offending team infringes Law 26(2)(i), the referee should:

(a) caution or order off the player guilty of misconduct; and

(b) in addition advance the mark for the penalty kick 10 m (33 ft), this to cover both the originaly infringement and the misconduct.

(ix) If a penalty kick is awarded to a team and before the kick is taken, a player of that team infringes Law 26(3)(i) the referee should:

(a) caution or order off the player guilty of misconduct; and

(b) declare the penalty kick void; and

(c) award a penalty kick against the team last guilty of misconduct.

(x) The referee should note that:

(a) Repeated infringement is a question of fact and not a question of whether the offender intended to infringe;

(b) If the same player has to be penalized repeatedly he

should be dealt with under Law 26(2)(d);

(c) Foul play must not be condoned;

(d) Repeated infringements arise mainly in connection with scrummages, offside and line-outs, tackles, rucks and mauls. If a player has been penalized for infringing one of these laws several times in the same match, he should be cautioned and, if he repeats the offence, ordered off;

(e) It is a question for the referee whether or not a series of the same offences by different players of a team amounts to repeated infringement. If he considers that it does, he should give a general warning to that team and, if the offence is repeated, he must order the next offending player off the field;

(f) In deciding the number of offences which should constitute 'repeated infringement', as indicated in (d) and (e) above, the referee should always apply a strict standard in representative and senior matches. On the third occasion a caution must be given.

In the case of junior or minor matches where ignorance of the laws and lack of skill may account for many infringements, a less strict standard may be applied.

(xi) The International Board and the Unions in membership with it will fully support referees in the strict and uniform enforcement of the law as to repeated infringements.

(xii) Flying Wedge.
This move usually occurs close to the opponent's goal line when a penalty kick or a free-kick is awarded to the attacking team, and is initiated by a player either tapping the ball to himself or receiving a short pass, and then driving towards the goal line with his colleagues binding on to either side of him in a V or wedge formation. Frequently the player is isolated illegally by those of his own team in front of him. The dangers inherent in this formation are not for those initiating the move but for those trying to stop it.

(xiii) The Cavalry Charge.
A cavalry charge usually occurs when a penalty kick or free-kick is awarded to the attacking team close to the opponents' goal line. Players of the attacking team line up behind the kicker, spacing themselves across the field in gaps of a metre or two. On a signal from the kicker they begin to charge forward. Only when

they are close to the kicker does he tap kick the ball and pass it to one of them. The defending team has to remain behind a line 10 m (33 ft) from the mark of their own goalline (if nearer) until the ball has been kicked. The move is potentially dangerous.

Players Ordered Off
A player who is ordered off shall take no further part in the match.

Law 27 Penalty Kick
A penalty kick is a kick awarded to the non-offending team as stated in the laws.

It may be taken by any player of the non-offending team and by any form of kick provided that the kicker, if holding the ball, must propel it out of his hands or, if the ball is on the ground, he must propel it a visible distance from the mark.

(1) The non-offending team has the option of taking a scrummage at the mark and shall put in the ball.

(2) When a penalty kick is taken the following shall apply:

(a) the kick must be taken without undue delay;

(b) the kick must be taken at or behind the mark on a line through the mark and the kicker may place the ball for a place-kick. If the place prescribed by the laws for the award of a penalty kick is within 5 m (16 ft) of the opponents' goal line, the mark for the penalty kick or a scrummage taken instead of it shall be 5 m from the goal line on a line through that place;

(c) the kicker may kick the ball in any direction and he may play the ball again, without any restriction, except that if he has indicated to the referee that he intends to attempt a kick at goal or has taken any action indicating such intention he must not kick the ball in any other way. A player kicking for touch may only punt or drop-kick the ball. Any indication of intention is irrevocable;

(d) the kicker's team, except the placer for a place-kick, must be behind the ball until it has been kicked. However, retiring players of the kicker's team who are in front of the ball will not be penalized if their failure to retire is due to the rapidity with which the kick has been taken but they must not stop retiring and must not enter the game until they have been made onside by an action of their own team as required by Law 25 (1);

(e) the opposing team must run

without delay (and continue to do so while the kick is being taken and while the ball is being played by the kicker's team) to or behind a line parallel to the goal lines and 10 m (33 ft) from the mark, or to their own goalline if nearer to the mark. If a kick at goal is taken they must there remain motionless with their hands by their sides until the kick has been taken.

Retiring players will not be penalized if their failure to retire 10 m (33 ft) is due to the rapidity with which the kick has been taken, but they must not stop retiring and must not enter the game until they have retired 10 m (33 ft) back from where the penalty kick was awarded, or until one of their own team who was at least 10 m (33 ft) from the mark has run in front of them.

(f) the opposing team must not wilfully resort to any action which may delay the taking of a penalty kick. This includes actions such as wilfully carrying, throwing or kicking the ball away out of the reach of the kicker or interfering with him;

Penalty:
• For an infringement by the kicker's team – a scrummage at the mark.
• For an infringement by the opposing team – a penalty kick 10 m (33 ft) in front of the mark or 5 m (16 ft) from the goalline whichever is the nearer, on a line through the mark. Any player of the non-offending team may take the kick.

Notes:
(i) The kick must be taken with the ball which was in play unless the referee decides that the ball is defective.
(ii) the use of sand, sawdust or an approved kicking tee is permitted for placing the ball.
(iii) A player taking a penalty kick may not bounce the ball on his knee. The kick must be made with the foot or lower leg. If a player fails to kick the ball, a scrummage should be ordered.
(iv) In addition to the general provision regarding waste of time, the kicker is bound to kick without delay, under penalty.

The instructions in the second paragraphs of note (i) on Law 13 apply also in the case of a penalty kick.

Even without a caution, if the delay is clearly a breach of law the kick should be disallowed and a scrummage ordered.
(vi) If the kickers appears to be about to take a kick at goal, the

referee may ask him to state his intention.

(vii) If the kicker is taking a kick at goal, all players of the opposing team must remain passive from the time the kicker commences his run until the kick has been taken.

(viii) When a penalty kick is taken in in-goal, a penalty try shall be awarded if a defending player by foul play prevents an opponent from first grounding the ball.

(ix) If, from a penalty kick taken in in-goal, the ball travels into touch-in-goal, or over the dead-ball line, a 5-m scrummage should be ordered, the attacking team to put in the ball.

(x) If the kicker takes a drop kick and a goal results, the goal stands even though the kicker has not indicated to the referee an intention to kick at goal.

(xi) If, notwithstanding a prior infringement by the opposing team, a goal is kicked, the goal should be awarded instead of a further penalty kick.

(xii) The referee should not award a further penalty if he is satisfied that the reason for such further penalty has been deliberately contrived by the kicker's team, but should allow play to continue. If the referee awards a further penalty, the penalty kick should not be taken before the referee has made the mark indicating the place of the penalty.

Law 28 Free-Kick

A free-kick is a kick awarded for a fair catch or to the non-offending team as stated in the laws. A goal may not be scored from a free-kick.

The team awarded a free-kick may not score a dropped goal until after the ball next becomes dead or an opposing player has played the ball or has tackled an opponent or a maul has been formed.

A free-kick awarded for an infringement may be taken by any player of the non-offending team.

A free-kick may be taken by any form of kick, unless kicking for touch, provided that the kicker, if holding the ball must propel it out of his hands, or, if the ball is on the ground he must propel it a visible distance from the mark.

(1) The team awarded a free-kick has the option of taking a scrummage at the mark and shall put in the ball.

(2) When a kick is taken, it must be taken without undue delay.

(3) and (4)
As with Law 27 (2b).

(5) The kicker may kick the ball in any direction and he may play the ball again without restriction. A player kicking for touch may only punt or drop kick the ball.

6) *As with Law 27 (2d).*

(7) The opposing team must not wilfully resort to any action which may delay the taking of a free-kick. This includes actions such as wilfully carrying, throwing, or kicking the ball away out of reach of the kicker.

(8) The opposing team must retire without delay to or behind a line parallel to the goal lines and 10 m (33 ft) from the mark or to their own goal line if nearer to the mark, or 5 m (16 ft) from their opponents' goal line if the mark is in in-goal. Having so retired, players of the opposing team may charge with a view to preventing the kick, as soon as the kicker begins his run or offers to kick.

Retiring players will not be penalized if their failure to retire 10 m is due to the rapidity with which the kick has been taken, but they must not stop retiring and must not enter the game until they have retired 10 m back from where the free-kick was awarded, or until one of their own team who was at least 10 m from the mark has run in front of them.

(9) If, having charged fairly, players of the opposing team prevent the kick being taken, it is void.

(10) Neither the kicker nor the placer shall wilfully do anything which may lead the opposing team to charge prematurely. If either does so, the charge shall not be disallowed.

Penalty:

• For an infringement by the kicker's team or for a void kick – a scrummage at the mark and the opposing team shall put in the ball.
If the mark is in-goal, the scrummage shall be awarded 5 m (16 ft) from the goal line on a line through the mark.
• For an infringement by the opposing team – a free-kick 10 m (33 ft) in front of the mark or 5 m (16 ft) from the goalline whichever is nearer on a line through the mark. Any player of the non-offending team may take the kick.

Notes:

(i) *As with Law 27 (2), note (i).*
(ii) *As with Law 27 (2), note (iii).*
(iii) The kicker may not feint to kick and then draw back. Once

SEVEN-A-SIDE AND MINI RUGBY

'Sevens'

The variation of rugby known as 'sevens' is a fast moving game which first originated in Scotland in the 1880's. There are two major competitions for the sport – the Middlesex tournament, which involves hundreds of clubs and is held every year at Twickenham, and the international tournament, the Hong Kong Sevens (held every four years) in which countries such as England, Australia, New Zealand and Fiji compete for the Melrose Cup (named after the place in Scotland where the first sevens tournament was held in 1882). Sevens follows the same basic laws as the 15-a-side game and is played on the same sized pitch.

However, there are only seven players – three forwards and four backs – so the number of players in a scrum or a line-out is reduced to three. Games last only 15 minutes.

Mini rugby

Mini rugby is a fairly recent innovation, designed to introduce young players to the game's laws and skills safely and gradually. A side is made up of nine players – four forwards and five backs – with four players in a scrum. The pitch is much smaller and is generally marked out across a standard sized rugby pitch and measuring approx. 59 x 28 m (under tens) or approx. 69 x 38 m (10 – 13 year olds). Games consist of two halves – 15, 20 or 25 minutes long each. The idea is to allow maximum participation. The reduced pitch ensures that players in all positions have the chance to become involved in the action and make repeated contact with the ball. The laws are the same as for 15-a-side, with a few exceptions, such as: if a kick goes directly into touch from outside the kicker's 15 m area, the opposition is awarded a tap penalty (the ball is tapped with the foot by the player taking the penalty, who then picks up the ball and passes it); a distance of at least 7 m (7¹/2 yds) must be observed by opposition players for all penalties; players may not kick for goal from a penalty kick; under eights do not kick conversions, but under nines and tens may do, although this is from right in front of the goal posts.

he makes any movement to kick, the opponents may charge.
(iv) *As with Law 27 (2), note (iv).*
(v) The referee shall see that the opposing players do not gradually creep up and that they have both feet behind the 10-metre line, otherwise he shall award a penalty in accordance with the penalty provisions of Law 28.
(vi) If the kick is taken from behind the goal line, the ball is in play if an opponent legitimately plays it before it crosses the goal line, and a try may be scored.
(vii) *As with Law 27 (2), note (viii).*
(viii) *As with Law 27 (2), note (ix).*
(ix) If opponents lawfully charge down a free-kick in the playing area, play should be allowed to continue.
(x) If a free-kick has been awarded in the field of play and the player retires to his in-goal to take the kick and his opponents having lawfully charged prevent the kick from being taken, a scrummage shall be awarded 5 m (16 ft) from the goal line on a line through the mark.
(xi) If a free-kick has been awarded in in-goal and the opponents having lawfully charged prevent the kick from being taken, a scrummage shall be awarded 5 m (16 ft) from the goalline on a line through the mark.
(xii) If the referee is satisfied that the reason for a free-kick under the penalty provisions has been contrived, he should allow play to continue. If the referee awards a further penalty, the free-kick should not be taken before the referee has made the mark indicating the place of the free-kick.

These laws are reprinted by permission of the International Rugby Football Board. For a complete copy of the Laws of the Game of Rugby Football, including Laws 1 – 6, various accompanying notes and Under – 19 Variations, contact the IRFB.

Hockey
Essentials

A universally popular stick and ball sport. Fast, vigorous and, sometimes, dangerous, hockey is at its most exhilarating when skill, energy and intelligent teamwork come together.

Crossbar not to exceed sideways beyond goalposts
2 in wide, 3in deep
7 ft
4 yds
2 in wide, 3in deep
Front face must touch outer edge of back-line

The goals

The goalposts and crossbar are white and rectangular, with a loosely fitted net. The whole structure is positioned at the centre of each back-line.

The ball

Spherical, hard, of any material. Must weigh between 5$\frac{1}{2}$ and 5$\frac{3}{4}$ oz (156–163 g) and have a circumference of 8$\frac{13}{16}$ –9$\frac{1}{4}$ in (224–235 mm). Usually white.

The stick

Must weigh between 12 and 28 ounces (340 - 794 g) and be able to pass through a 5.1 cm (interior diameter) ring. With a curved wooden head of no more than 4 inches in length (measured from the lowest part of the flat face) and a flat face on the left hand side only.

Saving the goalkeeper
Hockey balls are very hard and so

The field

A grass or synthetic pitch, rectangular, with a length of 100 yds (91.4 m) and a width of 60 yds (55 m), Flagposts of between 4 and 5 ft high (1.2–1.5 m) are placed at each 25 yds line (22.9 m), 1 yd outside the sidelines and at each corner of the field.

Hockey sticks
Most adults use a stick around 90 cm long. Ideally, the handle of the stick should reach your hips when the head is on the ground beside your feet.

Dress

Shirt and shorts or a skirt. Players of the same team must wear uniform clothing, approved by their association or club, apart from the goalkeeper, who must wear over any upper body protectors a shirt or garment of a different colour to the team and the opposition, plus protective clothing - full helmet, pads, hand protectors and kickers.

Shin protection
For most of the players no special clothing is needed for hockey. However, players usually wear plastic or foam shin guards beneath their socks.

Teams

Two teams of maximum16 players (including substitutes), although only 11 players are allowed on the field at a time.

Officials

Two umpires.

Team extras
Eleven players are allowed on the field for each team at any one time but up to five substitutes may swap with players on the field throughout a match.

HOW TO PLAY

Both teams aim to get possession of the ball using sticks and to hit it down the field into the opposition's goal while blocking the opposition's attempts to do the same.

Starting

The winner of the toss chooses between 1. possession of the ball at the start of the game and 2. which end to attack first. The first pass is made from the centre of the field by a player of the team which has possession of the ball. All the opposing team's players must be at least 5 yds (4.55 m) away from the ball, and all players must be in their own half of the field. The pass is made back into the player's own half to be hit by a team member in an attacking direction.

How to win

The team scoring the highest number of goals by shooting the ball into the opposition's goal, from somewhere inside the shooting circle, wins the game.

KEY RULES

• A game consists of two halves of 35 minutes, with a half-time interval of five to ten minutes.

• A number of rules are concerned with maintaining the highest level of safety possible during a game. Players must not play the ball with their sticks any higher than shoulder height, or raise their sticks in a dangerous manner when approaching the ball. It is also against the rules to kick, charge or hold an opponent, or to use the stick to prevent an opponent from playing the ball.
  See Rule 13, Conduct of Play (page 65).

• The penalty incurred by an infringement of the rules depends on where it occurred and how serious it was.
  Generally, the penalty is a free hit to the opposition, but if, for example, a defender inside his own circle intentionally prevents a goal from being

scored, the opposition will be awarded a penalty stroke. Another penalty is the penalty corner - for unintentional offences inside the defender's own circle, or for intentional offences within their own 25-yards area, but outside the circle. Goals cannot be scored directly from a penalty corner. The ball must be completely stopped outside the circle before the strike; a direct strike must hit the goal back board while an indirect strike does not need to.
  See Rule 14, Penalties (page 65).

• In extreme cases of misconduct, the umpire may decide to caution a player with a green card, or even send him off the field. A yellow card means the player is suspended for at

least five minutes, whereas a red card means suspension for the remainder of the game.

• The *bully* is used when both teams breach the rules simultaneously, or when play has to be stopped due to injury or other unforeseen circumstances. Two players (one from each team) face one another with their own back-line to their right and the ball on the ground between them. The players tap their sticks on the ground and then against each other's sticks alternately three times, after which both are free to try and play the ball.
  See Rule 10.4, Bully (page 64).

Grass pitch kings
In the past, international hockey used to be dominated by teams such as India and Pakistan who were masters on grass pitches. Now that the game at high level is more often played on artificial surfaces, such countries have lost their dominance. Artificial surfaces mean a far faster, more accurate game with fewer errors in ball control and passing.

HOCKEY THE RULES
· · · · · · · · · · · · · · · ·

I: Field and Equipment Section

Rule 1 Field of play
Rule 2 Goals
Rule 3 The ball
Rule 4 The stick
Rule 5 Player' dress and equipment
See page 62.

II: Teams, Captains and Umpires

6. Teams

6.1 A game shall be played between 2 teams of not more than 16 players each, but not more than 11 players of each team shall be on the field at the same time. Each team is permitted to substitute from the maximum of 16 players.

6.2 Substitution:
a. no limit to the number of players who may be substituted at the same time nor to the number of times any player may substitute or be substituted.
b. substitution of a player may be made only after a player from the same team has left the field.
c. time shall not be stopped for substitutions except for goalkeepers.
d. substitutes shall not be permitted for suspended players during their suspension.
e. after completing a suspension, a player may be substituted without first returning to the field.
f. players leaving or entering the field shall do so at the centre-line or such other place on the side of the field decided by the umpires before the game.

6.3 Each team must have one goalkeeper on the field:
a. an incapacitated or suspended goalkeeper shall be replaced immediately by another goalkeeper.
b. where no substitute goalkeeper is available, the field player replacing the goalkeeper must wear protective headgear and a shirt of a colour different from those of either team and shall be permitted to put on, without time-wasting, other protective equipment.
c. during the suspension of a goalkeeper, the team must have one less player on the field.

6.4 During play only players

and umpires may be on the field unless authorised by the umpire.

7. Captains

7.1 Each team must have a captain on the field who must wear a distinctive arm-band.
7.2 Captains shall:
a. toss a coin; the winner shall have choice of ends or possession of the ball to start the game.
b. indicate to the umpires any replacement captain.
c. be responsible for the substitution of players.
d. be responsible for the behaviour of all their team players.

8. Umpires

Two umpires shall control the game and apply the rules; they are the sole judges of fair play. Players and substitutes, whether on or off the field, including any period of temporary or permanent suspension, are under the jurisdiction of the umpires.
8.1 Umpires shall be:
a. primarily responsible for the decisions in their half of the field, for the whole of the game without changing ends.
b. responsible for ensuring that the full or agreed time is played and for indicating the end of the first half and of the game if time is prolonged for completion of the penalty corner.
c. solely responsible for decisions on the ball going out of play for the full length of their nearer side-line and back-line.
d. solely responsible for decisions on corners, penalty corners, penalty strokes and goals in their own half and free hits in their own circle.
e. responsible for keeping a written record of goals scored and warnings/suspensions.
f. debarred from coaching during a game and during half-time.
8.2 Umpires shall blow the whistle to:
a. start and end each half of the game.
b. enforce a penalty.
c. start and end a penalty stroke.
d. indicate, when necessary, that the ball has passed wholly outside the field.
e. signal a goal.
f. re-start the game after a goal has been scored or awarded.

g. re-start the game after a penalty stroke in which a goal was not scored or awarded.
h. stop the game for any other reason and re-start after such a stoppage.

III: Application of the Rules of the Game

9. Duration of Play

Two periods of 35 minutes each unless otherwise agreed:
a. half-time: 5 to 10 minutes as agreed: teams change ends.
b. each half starts when the umpire blows the whistle for the centre pass.

10. To Start and Restart the Game

10.1 Centre pass:
a. played from the centre of the field.
b. a push or hit may be played in any direction; all players other than the player making the pass shall be in their half of the field.
c. made at the start of the game, by a player of the team which did not choose ends.
d. after half-time, by a player of the team which did not start the game.
e. after a goal, by a player of the team against which the goal was scored or awarded.
10.2 Centre pass and putting the ball back into play:
a. all opponents at least 5 yds (4.6 m) from the ball.
Mandatory Experiment
a. no player of either team, other than the taker, shall be within 5 yds of the ball when the ball is put back into play from within the 25-yards (23 m) area; no player of the opposing team shall be within 5 yds of the ball when the ball is put back into play from betwen the 25-yards lines.
b. the ball to be pushed or hit.
c. the ball must move at least 1 yd (0.9 m).
d. after playing the ball, the player may not do so again nor remain or approach within playing distance of it until it has been played by another player.
e. the ball shall not be raised intentionally or such as to be dangerous or lead to dangerous play.
10.3 Ball outside the field:
When the ball passes completely over the side-line or back-line it shall be out of play and it or another ball shall be used to re-start play.

10.3.1 Over the side-line:
a. on the side-line close to where the ball went out of play
b. the player playing the ball is not required to be wholly inside or outside the side-line
c. taken by a player of the opposing team.
10.3.2 Over the back-line: by the attack when no goal is scored:
a. up to 16 yds (14.5 m) from and opposite where, or close to where, it crossed the back-line, in line parallel to the side-line.
b. taken by a defender.
10.3.3 Over the back-line unintentionally by the defence when no goal is scored:
a. on the back-line up to 5 yds from the corner flag nearest to where the ball crossed the back-line
Mandatory Experiment
a. on the side-line 5 yds from the corner flag nearest to where the ball crossed the back-line.
b. taken by an attacker.
10.3.4 Over the back-line: intentionally by the defence when no goal is scored:
a. on the back-line from a spot 10 yds from the nearer goal-post on whichever side the attacking team prefers.
b. taken by an attacker. That is, a penalty corner.
10.4 Bully:
10.4.1 The game shall be re-started with a bully when:
a. the ball in play has to be replaced.
b. there is a simultaneous breach of the Rules by both teams.
c. the ball is lodged in a goalkeeper's pad or player's or umpire's clothing.
d. when time has been stopped for an injury or any other reason and there has been no offence.
10.4.2 The bully:
a. on a spot chosen by the umpire but not within 16 yds (14.5 m) of the back-line.
b. a player of each team shall face one another with

The bully

1
2
3
4
5
6

Charging
Players must not raise their stick above shoulder height or trip, shove, charge, strike or handle an opponent.

their own back-line to their right.

c. ball shall be on the ground between the two players.

d. the two players tap the ground with their stick to the right of the ball then the flat face of the opponent's stick over the ball, three times alternately, after which either player may play the ball to put it into play.

e. all other players at least 5 yds away until the ball is in play.

11. Scoring a Goal

a. a goal is scored when the ball is played in the circle by an attacker and does not go outside the circle before passing completely over the goal-line and under the crossbar.

b. the ball may be played by or touch the stick or body of a defender before or after being played in the circle by an attacker.

c. after a stoppage of play inside the circle, the ball must again be played from inside the circle by an attacker before a goal can be scored.

d. a goal shall be awarded if a goalkeeper breaches the Penalty Stroke Rules preventing a goal being scored.

e. the team scoring the greater number of goals shall be the winner.

12. Offside

12.1 Players are in an offside position if, at the moment the ball is passed or played to them by a member of their team, they are:

a. in their opponents' 25 yard area and

b. in front of the ball and

c. nearer the back-line than two opponents.

12.2 Players so positioned are

not committing an offence unless the ball is passed to them or they gain an advantage for their team. Players level with the second defender (i.e. the one furthest from the goal) are NOT offside. Players off the field next to the 25-yards area or behind their opponents' back-line can be in offside positions.
Mandatory Experiment
There is no offside.

13. Conduct of Play

Unless played with consideration for others, hockey can be a dangerous game. This Rules prohibits or explains actions which affect the safety of all players. Players shall not:

13.1.1 Use of the stick and playing equipment.

a. play the ball intentionally with the back of the stick.

b. take part in or interfere with the game unless thay have their stick in their hand.

c. play the ball above shoulder height with any part of the stick.

d. lift their sticks over the heads of players.

e. raise their sticks in a mannner that is dangerous, intimidating or hampering to other players when approaching, attempting to play or playing the ball.

f. play the ball dangerously or in such a way as to be likely

to lead to dangerous play. A ball is dangerous when it causes legitimate evasive action by players.

g. hit, hook, charge, kick, shove, trip, strike at or personally handle another player or their stick or clothing.

h. throw any object or piece of playing equipment on to the field, at the ball, at another player, or at an umpire.

13.1.2 Use of body, hands, feet

a. stop or catch the ball with the hand.

There is nothing to prevent players using their hands to protect themselves from dangerously raised balls.

b. intentionally stop, kick, propel, pick up, throw or carry the ball with any part of their bodies.

It is not an offence if the ball hits the foot or body of a player unless that player:
-has moved into the path of the ball, or
-made no effort to avoid being hit, or
-was positioned with the clear intention of stopping the ball, or
-gains undue benefit.
Players should not be penalised when the ball is played at them from a short distance.

c. use the foot or leg to support the stick in a tackle.
Mandatory Experiment

d. intentionally enter their opponents' goal, or stand on their opponents' goal-line.

e. intentionally run behind either goal.

13.1.3 Raised ball

a. intentionally raise the ball from a hit except for a shot at goal.

b. intentionally raise the ball so that it lands directly in the circle.

Not every ball entering the circle off the ground is forbidden. A ball which bounces into or lands in the circle after a short distance

must be judged solely on the intent or danger.

A ball raised over a player's stick or body when on the ground, even in the circle, must be judged solely on danger.

c. approach within 5 yds of a player receiving a falling raised ball until it has been played and is on the ground.

d. raise the ball at another player.

13.1.4 Obstruction
obstruct an opponent from attempting to play the ball by:
- moving or interposing themselves or their sticks.
- shielding the ball with their sticks or any part of their bodies.
- physically interfering with the sticks or bodies of opponents.

13.1.5 Time-wasting
delay play by time-wasting.
13.2 Goalkeepers may, when the ball is inside their own circle:

a. use their stick, kickers or pads to propel the ball, or any part of their bodies including the hands to stop but not propel or lie on the ball, provided such action is not dangerous or likely to lead to dangerous play.

A goalkeeper lying on the ball should be considered under the obstruction rule.

b. stop or deflect the ball with the stick above their shoulder unless dangerous or likely to lead to dangerous play.

c. deflect the ball over the cross-bar or around the goal-posts with the face of the stick or off any part of the body.
13.3 If the ball.

a. strikes an umpire or any loose object on the field, including any piece of playing equipment dropped unintentionally, the game shall continue.

14. Penalties

Advantage: a penalty shall be awarded only when a player or team has been clearly disadvantaged by an opponent's offence.
14.1 A free hit shall be awarded for:

a. an offence by an attacker within the opponents' 25-yards area.

b. an unintentional offence by the defence outside their circle within their own 25

Player (2) is playing the ball. Player (1) is offside on three counts.

➡ *page 68*

SKILLS

Players in a team are allocated (in variable numbers) to one of four positions - forward, midfielder, defender and one goalkeeper - although these roles are flexible enough to meet the demands of whatever team strategy is chosen. All players require stick control and co-ordination to be able to

Swivel stick
The ball can only be played with the left face of the stick so players must be adept at turning the stick to hit a ball on their left-hand side.

Dribble masters
Asian players used to dazzle opponents with their dribbling skills on grass pitches. But long dribbles are relatively rare on modern artificial surfaces.

receive the ball, bring it under control and then pass or dribble it quickly and accurately.

Forwards must be able to shoot well - and quickly - to take advantage of any opportunity to score. Midfielders are very much team players, supporting both the attack and the defence as needed. They must constantly be aware of other players' positions throughout the field. Stamina, anticipation and passing skills are all important. Defenders remain largely towards the back of their end of the field. Marking

(hanging close to an opponent and hampering his efforts to play the ball) and tackling are the basic elements of defensive play. The goalkeeper requires particular skills of his own. Any part of the body or the stick may be used to stop the ball, so this player needs to be extremely agile, quick and to have a high level of concentration at all times. The goalkeeper is also responsible for co-ordinating the team's defence, surveying the game and calling instructions out to the defence players in front of him.

TACTICS

There are two systems commonly used to position players strategically across the field. The 5-3-2-1 configuration (5 forwards, 3 midfielders, 2 defenders and a goalkeeper) is one. Another is the 'sweeper' variation, which uses the following configuration: 3-3-3-1, with one of the defenders positioned behind the other two (but in front of the goalkeeper) to 'sweep' up any balls or opponents that get through the defence.

Lay down
One way of robbing an opponent of the ball is to slam down your stick in front of him. But such a tackle can be hard on the knuckles.

Left-hand dribble
Skilful players can often carry the ball past a defender by reversing the stick.

Jab tackle
A jab tackle is made when your opponent is still in front of you. The idea is to surprise your opponent by twisting your stick so that the back faces the ground and jab it on to the ball.

Grey areas

Penalties for fouls can vary greatly, depending not only on where they are committed, but also whether they are committed intentionally or not. An umpire is responsible, therefore, for making an often difficult distinction in an instant.

In an attempt to help the flow of the game, the governing bodies are experimenting with doing away with the offside rule.

Getting some stick
The sheer speed of hockey and the force with which the sticks are often swung around means that injuries are frequent.. The problem for the umpire is to decide whether a blow was deliberate or not.

Reverse-side tackle
Tackling an opponent from the left side can be really awkward but if it has to be done, hold the stick in your left hand and twist the grip to point the toe downwards. Then use the toe to drag the ball away.

Open-side tackle
An open-side tackle is a conventional tackle. Often the best technique is to run with the dribbler until he makes an error.

Touchdown
With the reverse-side tackle, the idea is to trap the ball against the turf so that the attacker's momentum carries him on and past the ball.

Pushover
One of the most dynamic passing strokes is the 'slap push'. This involves a long swing at the ball with the right hand some way down the stick.

Dangerous play

Charging

Tripping

continued from page 65

yards area.

c. any offence by any player between the 25-yards lines.

14.2 A penalty corner shall be awarded for:

a. an intentional offence by the defence within their 25-yards area but outside the circle.

b. an intentional offence by a defender in the circle which neither prevents a goal being scored nor deprives an attacker of actual or likely possession of the ball.

c. an unintentional offence by the defence in their circle that does not prevent the probable scoring of a goal

d. the defence intentionally playing the ball over their

back-line.

14.3 A penalty stroke shall be awarded for:

a. an intentional offence by a defender in the circle to prevent a goal being scored or to deprive an attacker of actual or likely possession of the ball.

b. an unintentional offence by a defender in the circle that prevents the probable scoring of a goal.

c. persistent early breaking off the back-line by defenders at penalty corners.

14.4 If there is another offence before the awarded penalty has been taken, the penalty may be progressed up to 10 yds (9 m), upgraded and/or dealt with as misconduct or reversed if committed by the previously benefiting team.

15. Procedures for Penalties
15.1 Free hit

a. more than 5 yds (4.5 m) from the circle: close to where the offence occurred. 'Close to' allows the free hit to be taken within playing distance of where the offence occurred. It is intended that no undue advantage be gained but the flow of the game maintained.

b. outside the circle: to the defence within 16 yds (14.6 m) of the back-line up to 16 yds from the back-line in line with the offence, parallel to the side-line.

c. inside the circle: to the defence: anywhere within the circle or, outside it, up to 16 yds (14.6 m) from the back-line in line with the offence, parallel to the side-line.

d. within 5 yds (4.5 m) of the circle: to the attack: close to where the offence occurred: all players of both teams other

than the taker to be at least 5 yds from the ball.

e. the ball must be stationary.

f. the striker shall push or hit the ball: it must move at least a yard before another player of the same team is allowed to play the ball.

g. the ball shall not be raised intentionally or in such a way as to be dangerous or likely to lead to dangerous play.

h. after playing the ball, the striker may not play the ball again or approach within playing distance of it until it has been played by another player.

i. no player of the opposing team shall be within 5 yds (4.5 m) of the ball.

If a player is standing within 5 yds of the ball in order to gain an advantage, the free hit need not be delayed.

Mandatory Experiment

i. no player of either team, other than the taker, shall be within 5 yds (4.5 m) of the ball for free hits taken inside the 25-yards area; no player of the opposing team shall be within 5 yds of the ball for free hits taken between the 25-yards lines.

15.2 Penalty corner:
15.2.1

a. an attacker shall push or hit the ball, without intentionally raising it, from a spot on the back-line 10 yds (9 m) from the goal-post on whichever side the attacking team prefers.

b. the player taking the hit must have at least one foot outside the field.

c. no other player shall be within 5 yds of the ball.

d. the remaining attackers shall be on the field with sticks, hands and feet not touching the ground inside the circle.

e. not more than five defenders including the goalkeeper shall be behind the back-line with their sticks, hands and feet not touching the ground inside the circle.

f. the remaining defenders shall be beyond the centre-line.

g. until the ball has been played, no attacker other than the one taking the hit may enter the circle, nor may a defender cross the centre-line or back-line.

h. the attacker taking the hit may not play the ball again nor remain or approach within playing distance of it until it has been played by another player.

i. no shot at goal shall be made until the ball be stopped or come to rest on the ground outside the circle.

j. the ball may be passed or deflected by the attackers but if it remains within 5 yds of the circle must be stopped or come to rest on the ground outside the circle before a shot at goal is made.

k. if the first shot at goal is a hit, the ball must cross the goal-line at a height of not more than 18 in (45 cm) (the height of the backboard) for a goal to be scored, unless it touches the stick or body of a defender during its travel towards goal.

l. for flicks, deflections and scoops, and second and subsequent hits at goal, the ball may be raised to any height subject to there being no danger.

m. the attacker putting the ball into play may not score directly even if the ball is played into goal by a defender.

n. if the ball travels more than 5 yds (4.5 m) from the circle, the penalty corner rules no longer apply.

15.2.2 The penalty corner may be given again when:

a. defenders stand with feet, hands and/or sticks touching the ground inside the circle.

b. defenders are within 5 yds of the ball before it is played.

c. defenders cross the back-

Free hit
During a free hit no opponent may be within 5 yds (4.5 m) of the ball.

line or centre-line before the ball is played.

Attackers entering the circle before the ball is played should be penalized by a free hit.

Mandatory experiment 15.2.3
At half-time and full-time the game shall be prolonged to permit completion of a penalty corner. For this purpose the penalty corner shall be considered completed when:

a. a goal is scored

b. an attacker breaches any rule

c. a defender commits a breach of a rule except that if another penalty corner or penalty stroke is awarded the game shall be prolonged again to permit completion of the penalty

d. the ball travels more than 5 yards from the circle

e. the ball is played out of the circle over the back-line by an attacker or unintentionally by a defender

f. the ball goes out of the circle over the circle line again (that is, for the second time after the initial injection from the back-line)

15.3 Penalty stroke
15.3.1 Taking:
a. time shall be stopped when a penalty stroke is signalled and re-started when the whistle is blown for resumption of play.

b. the player taking the stroke shall stand close to and behind the ball prior to commencing the stroke.

c. all players, other than the defending goalkeeper, shall stand beyond the nearer 25-yards line, on the field, and shall not influence the situation.

d. the defending goalkeeper shall continue to wear protective headgear.

e. the defending goalkeeper shall stand with both feet on the goal-line and shall not leave the goal-line or move

either foot until the ball has been played.

f. the player may not take the stroke until the controlling umpire confirms that both the stroke taker and the goalkeeper are ready and has blown the whistle.

g. the ball may be pushed, flicked or scooped from the penalty spot.

h. the ball may be raised to any height.

i. the player may touch the ball only once and subsequently shall not approach either the ball or the goalkeeper.

j. in the process of taking the stroke, the player may take one step forward but the rear foot may not pass the front one until the ball has been played.

k. the player may not feint at playing the ball.

l. the defending goalkeeper shall not remove unnecessarily any protective equipment in order solely to gain time.

m. a penalty goal may be awarded by the umpire without the ball crossing the goal-line when a goalkeeper breaches the rules to prevent a goal being scored.

15.3.2 Ending:
a. a goal is scored or awarded.

b. the ball comes to rest inside the circle, lodges in the goalkeeper's pad, is caught by the goalkeeper, passes outside the circle or the stroke-taker breaches the rules and a goal is not scored or awarded.

15.3.3 Re-starting the game after a penalty stroke:
a. if a goal was scored or awarded: by a centre pass.

b. if a goal was not scored or awarded: a push or a hit by a defender 16 yds (14.6 m) in front of the centre of the goal-line.

15.3.4 Penalties:
a. free hit: for an offence by the stroke-taker, taken 16 yds (14.6

m) in front of the centre of the goal-line.

b. goal awarded: for a breach of the rules by the goalkeeper that prevents a goal being scored.

c. penalty stroke: may be taken again for an offence by any player of either team.

15.4 Personal penalties:
a. for rough or dangerous play, misconduct, or any intentional offence, the umpire may award the appropriate penalty and may:
- caution the offending player.
- warn the offending player: green card.
- temporarily suspend the offending player for a minimum of 5 minutes of playing time: yellow card.
- permanently suspend the offending player: red card.

b. temporarily suspended players shall remain in a designated place until permitted by the umpire who suspended them to resume play.

c. temporarily suspended

players may rejoin their team at half-time, then return to the designated place to complete their suspension.

d. permanently suspended players shall not remain within the playing facility or its surrounds.

16. Accidents/Injuries
a. if a goal is scored before the game is stopped it shall be allowed if it would have been scored had the accident not occurred.

b. if a player is incapacitated, the umpire may stop the game.

c. an injured or bleeding player should leave the field as soon as it is safe to do so and receive treatment off the field unless medical reasons prevent this.

d. players shall not return to the field until their wounds have been dressed and no player remain on, enter or re-enter the field wearing blood stained clothing.

e. if an umpire is incapacitated, the game shall be stopped; if injured and cannot continue, should be replaced.

f. the game shall be re-started with a bully, with the appropriate penalty or with a centre pass if a goal was scored.

Reprinted by permission of the International Hockey Federation. For a complete copy of the Rules of Hockey, including Appendices A-E, contact your national governing body.

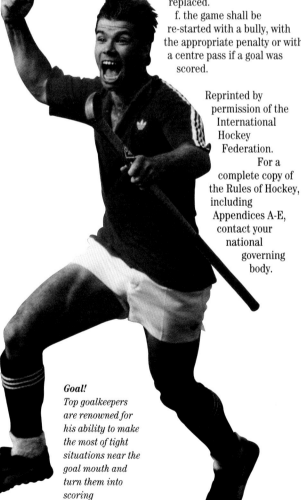

Goal!
Top goalkeepers are renowned for his ability to make the most of tight situations near the goal mouth and turn them into scoring opportunities.

Ice hockey
Essentials

With the puck being hit at speeds of up to 160 kph (146 ft/s), this is reputed to be the fastest game in the world. Players sport an amour of protective equipment to protect themselves against the puck as well as when they crash into other players, the boards or fall on the ice.

The rink

200 ft by 85 ft (61 m by 26 m), with corners rounded in the arc of a circle of radius 28 feet (8.5 m). Surrounded by the 'boards' (a white wooden or fibreglass fence), 40 – 48 in (1–1.2 m) in height above the ice surface.

Divided in half by a red line (centre line) and into three different zones by two blue lines.

Face-off spots are marked A.

Ice zones
An ice hockey rink is divided into three zones: the defending zone in front of your goal; the attacking zone in front of your opponents' goal; and the neutral zone in the middle. The ice hockey goal mouth is painted red so that it is clearly visible against the white ice.

Safety glass
The puck in ice hockey is hard and travels at incredible speeds, so spectators at ice hockey games are protected by a high wall of shatterproof glass or perspex on top of the boards.

The sticks

Wood or other approved material. Maximum length 63 in (1.6 m) from the heel to the end of the shaft, 12 ½ in (32 cm) from the heel to the end of the blade. The blade must be 2–3 in (5 – 7.5 cm) in width, with bevelled edges. The goal-keeper's stick is larger. It has a maximum width of 3 ½–4 ½ in (9 – 11 cm) at the heel and maximum length of 15 ½ in (29 cm) from heel to blade end.

The puck

Vulcanized rubber or other approved material. 1 in (2.5 cm) thick, 3 in (7.5 cm) in diameter and 5 ½–6 oz (156–170g) ounces in weight. Kept in a frozen condition during a game.

Outfield player's stick — 63 in (1.6 m)

12½ in (32 cm)

2–3 in (5–7.5 cm)

Goaltender's stick — 63 in (1.6 m)

Maximum width 3½ in–4½ (9–11 cm)

15½ in (39 4cm)

The goals

Positioned 11 ft (3.4 m) from each end of the rink and in the centre of a red line 2 in (5 cm) wide, drawn across the width of the ice and continued up the sides of the boards (the 'goal line'). Red goalposts are set 6 ft (1.8 m) apart, extend 4 ft (1.2 m) above the ice surface and are joined by a cross bar (also red). A white nylon net is attached to each goal frame.

Dress

Must be uniform throughout a team. Sweaters, short pants, stockings and skates. Sweaters feature individual identifying numbers and players' surnames. All players must wear a protective helmet. All other protective equipment, except gloves and goalkeepers' leg guards, must be worn under the uniform.

Keeping your head
With the puck moving at the speed of a racing car head protection is absolutely vital, so all players wear a helmet and player born after 1974 must wear a perspex visor.

Skates

Ice hockey skates have blades ⅙ in (42 mm) wide – thicker than on speed or figure skating skates. They are shorter, too.

Officials

A referee, two linesmen, game timekeeper, penalty timekeeper, official scorer and two goal judges.

Side by side

Ice hockey is a robust game and players are quite at liberty to shove an opponent off the ball. However, they are not allowed to 'check' an opponent, which means throwing them violently into the sideboards, or 'charge' them, which means basically running, jumping or charging into an opponent.

Face-off

Play starts with a face-off when the referee 'faces' the puck by dropping it on the ice between the sticks of two opposing centres.

How to play

Each team attempts to score goals by hitting the puck into their opponents' goal. Players use their sticks to pass or dribble the puck across the ice. It may also be kicked, but not in order to score a goal.

See Rule 70 (page 76).

Starting

The home team chooses an end to defend and the game is then started with a face-off in the centre of the rink. Two players (one from each team) stand facing each other with the blades of their sticks on the ice, each player facing his opponent's goal. All other players must remain outside the centre face-off area until the puck has been played. The referee or a linesman drops the puck on the ice between the two starting players, who each try to gain possession of it with their sticks.

Face spots

Face-offs occur either at the centre of the rink or in one of the end zone face-off spots – or at the point where an infringement occurred. The player of the attacking team must place his blade on the ice first if he is in his attacking zone

The players

Two teams of six players on the ice at a time. Not more than 18 players, excluding goalkeepers, are permitted per team.

Playing line-up

1 goalkeeper   4 centre
2 right defence   5 right wing
3 left defence   6 left wing

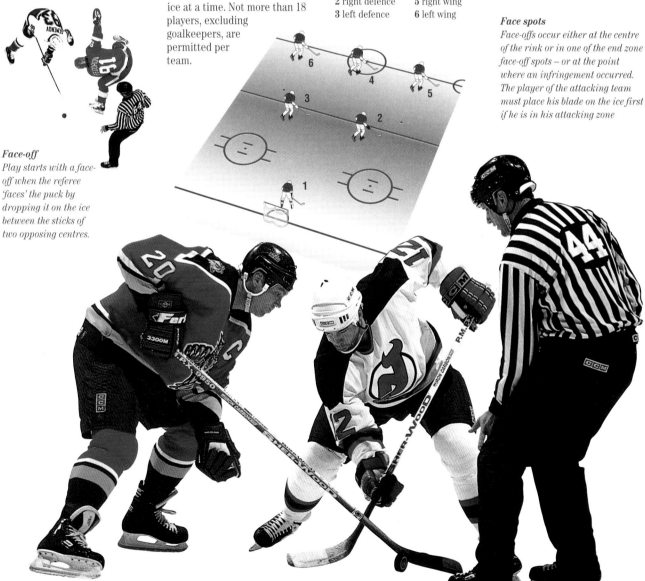

RULES OF ICE HOCKEY

These rules are abridged and summarized. Changes from the official rules are indicated in italics.

SECTION ONE – THE RINK
Rules 1 – 12
See page 70.

SECTION TWO – TEAMS
Rules 13 – 18
See page 71.

SECTION THREE – EQUIPMENT
Rules 19 – 24
See page 70.

SECTION FOUR – PENALTIES
Rules 25 – 33B

Penalties shall be actual playing time and shall be divided into the following classes:

1. Minor penalty – the offending player (excluding the goalkeeper) is ruled off the ice for two minutes. No substitutes are allowed during this time.

2. Bench minor penalty – as above, but may be served by any player of the offending team, apart from the goalkeeper.

3. Major penalty – as above, but the player is sent off for five minutes. A third major penalty results in the player being sent off for the remainder of the game.

4. Misconduct penalty – the player (excluding the goalkeeper) is sent off for ten minutes. A substitute is permitted.

5. Match penalty – suspension for the remainder of the game. A substitute is permitted after five minutes have elapsed.

6. Penalty shot – the Referee places the puck on the centre face-off spot for the player taking the shot at goal. Only the opposing goalkeeper may defend against the shot. All other players must withdraw to the sides of the rink.

If a goalkeeper incurs a minor penalty, major penalty, or misconduct penalty, the penalty is served by another member of his team. However, if he incurs three major penalties in one game, a game misconduct penalty or a match penalty, he is removed

from the game and replaced by a substitute.

SECTION FIVE – OFFICIALS
Rules 34 – 40A

(Deal with officials. *See also page 71.*)

SECTION SIX – PLAYING RULES

Rule 41 Abuse of Officials and other Misconduct

a) A misconduct penalty shall be imposed on any player who uses obscene, profane or abusive language to any person or who intentionally knocks or shoots the puck out of the reach of an Official who is retrieving it or who deliberately throws any equipment out of the playing area.

b) A minor penalty shall be assessed to any player who challenges or disputes the rulings of any Official during a game. If the player persists in such challenge or dispute, he shall be assessed a misconduct penalty and any further dispute will result in a game misconduct penalty being assessed to the offending player.

Rule 42 Adjustment to Clothing or Equipment

a) Play shall not be stopped nor the game delayed by reasons of adjustments to clothing, equipment, skates or sticks.

For an infringement of this Rule, a minor penalty shall be given.

Rule 43 Attempt to Injure

a) A match penalty shall be imposed on any player who deliberately attempts to injure an opponent A substitute for the penalized player shall be permitted at the end of the fifth minute.

b) A game misconduct penalty shall be imposed on any player who deliberately attempts to injure an Official, Manager, Coach or Trainer in any manner.

Rule 44 Board Checking

a) A minor or major penalty, at the discretion of the Referee, based upon the degree of violence of the impact with the boards, shall

be imposed on any player who checks an opponent in such a manner that causes the opponent to be thrown violently in the boards.

b) When a major penalty is imposed under this Rule for a foul resulting in an injury to the face or head of an opponent, a game misconduct shall be imposed.

Rule 45 Broken Stick

(a) A player without a stick may participate in the game. A player whose stick is broken may participate in the game provided he drops the broken stick. A minor penalty shall be imposed for an infraction of this Rule.

(b) A goalkeeper may continue to play with a broken stick until a stoppage of play or until he has been legally provided with a stick.

(c) A player who has lost or broken his stick may only receive a stick at his own players' bench or be handed one from a team-mate on the ice, and may not receive a stick thrown on the ice from any part of the rink. A minor penalty shall be imposed for an infraction of this Rule.

Rule 46 Butt-Ending

(NOTE) Butt-ending shall mean using the end of the shaft of the stick in a jabbing motion.

(a) A double-minor penalty will be imposed on a player who attempts to butt-end an opponent.

(b) A major penalty and a game misconduct shall be imposed on a player who butt-ends an opponent.

(c) A match penalty shall be imposed on a player who injures an opponent as a result of a butt-end.

Rule 47 Charging

Charging shall mean the actions of a player who, as a result of distance travelled, shall violently check an opponent in any manner. A charge may be the result of a check into the boards, into the goal from or in open ice.

(a) A minor or major penalty shall be imposed on a player who skates or jumps into, or charges an opponent in any manner.

Rule 48 Checking from Behind

A check from behind is a check delivered on a player who is not aware of the impending hit, therefore UNABLE TO DEFEND HIMSELF, and contact is made on the back part of the body. When a player intentionally turns his body to create contact with his back, no penalty shall be assessed.

(a) Any player who cross-checks, pushes or charges from behind an opponent who is unable to defend himself shall be assessed a major and a game misconduct. This penalty applies anywhere on the playing surface.

Rule 49 Clipping

Clipping is the act of throwing the body, from any direction, across or below the knees of an opponent.

(a) A player may not deliver a check in a clipping manner, nor lower his own body position to deliver a check on or below an opponent's knees.

Official crash
Players hurtle around the rink so fast that even the referee can get involved in collisions.

Rule 50 Cross-Checking

(NOTE) A cross-check shall mean a check rendered with both hands on the stick, and the extending of the arms, while the check is being delivered.

(a) A minor or major penalty, at the discretion of the Referee, shall be imposed on a player who cross-checks an opponent.

When a major penalty is assessed for cross-checking, an automatic game misconduct penalty shall be imposed on the offending player.

Rule 51 Delaying the Game

(a) A minor penalty shall be imposed on any player or goalkeeper who delays the game by deliberately shooting or batting the puck with his stick outside the playing area.

Rule 52 Deliberate Injury of Opponents

(a) A match penalty shall be imposed on a player who deliberately injures an opponent in any manner.

Rule 53 Elbowing

Elbowing shall mean the use of an extended elbow in a manner that may or may not cause injury.

(a) A minor or major penalty, at the discretion of the Referee, shall be imposed on any player who uses his elbow to foul an opponent.

(b) When a major penalty is imposed under this Rule for a foul resulting in an injury to the face or head of an opponent, a game misconduct shall be imposed.

Rule 54 Face-Offs
See page 71.

Rule 55 Falling on Puck

(a) A minor penalty shall be imposed on a player other than the goalkeeper who deliberately falls on or gathers the puck into his body.

Rule 56 Fisticuffs

An instigator of an altercation shall be a player who by his actions or demeanour demonstrates any/some of the following criteria: distance travelled; gloves off first; first punch thrown; menacing attitude or posture; verbal instigation or threats; conduct in retaliation to a prior game incident.

An altercation is a situation involving two players, with at least one to be penalised.

(a) A major penalty shall be imposed on any player who engages in fisticuffs. In addition, a minor, major and a game misconduct, at the discretion of the Referee, shall be imposed on any player involved in fisticuffs.

Rule 57 Goals and Assists
See page 74.

Rule 58 Gross Misconduct

The Referee may impose a "GROSS MISCONDUCT" penalty on any player, Manager, Coach or Trainer who is guilty of gross misconduct of any kind. Any person incurring a gross misconduct penalty shall be suspended for the balance of the game.

Rule 59 Handling Puck with Hands

(a) If a player, except a goalkeeper, closes his hand on the puck, the play shall be stopped and a minor penalty shall be imposed on him. A goalkeeper who holds the puck for longer than three seconds shall be given a minor penalty unless he is actually being checked by an opponent.

Rule 60 Head-Butting

(a) A double minor penalty shall be imposed on a player who attempts to head-butt an opponent.

(b) A major and a game misconduct penalty shall be imposed on a player who head-butts an opponent.

Rule 61 High Sticks

A high stick is one which is carried above the height of the opponent's shoulders. A player is permitted accidental contact on an opponent if the act is committed as a normal follow through of a shooting action.

(a) Any contact made by a stick on an opponent on an opponent above the shoulders is prohibited and a minor shall be imposed subject to section (b) of this Rule.

(b) When a player carries or holds any part of his stick above the shoulders of the opponent so that injury results, the Referee shall:

(i) Assess a double minor penalty for all contact that causes an injury, whether accidental or careless, in the opinion of the Referee.

(ii) Assess a match penalty to a player who, in the opinion

➡ *page 76*

Rule 53

High sticks

Foul play
Ice hockey rules specify over 14 different types of foul, including high sticks and hooking.

Hands off
Players are allowed to use their arms to block an opponent but they are not allowed to grab them or hold on to them with hands arms or legs.

Shooting for goal

Goals in ice hockey are usually scored from fairly close to the goal. Long- distance goals are rare. The best shooting position is from a small area directly in front of the goal called the 'slot'. Typically an attacker will pick up the puck in the slot and attempt a wrist shot in which the stick is swept along the ice until the player makes contact with the puck with a quick snap of the wrist. Often players will aim into the top and bottom corners of the goal where the goalkeeper is at his most vulnerable.

How to win

Goals are scored when the puck is put into the goal with the use of a stick. A player may not bat it across the goal-line with any part of his body and if the puck is deflected off another player into the net, no goal is scored. When a player scores a goal, an assist is credited to the player(s) who took part in the play immediately preceeding the goal. The team with the most goals wins.

KEY RULES
. . . .

• A game consists of three 20-minute periods with intervals of 15 minutes between each. Teams change ends after each period. If the score is tied at the end of the game an additional period of five minutes is played, with the first team to score winning the game.

• Six players only are allowed on the rink at one time, but a coach may make as many substitutions as he likes during a game.

• The puck may be passed among team-mates within any one of the three zones. A player must not pass it forward to a team-mate in another zone while his team is in attack or an off-side penalty is incurred. However, players of a defending team may make and take forward passes within their half of the rink (i.e. up to the centre line) without incurring the same penalty.
   (This is the Passing Rule.)

• (A player is off-side when both his skates are beyond the line bounding a particular zone.)

• Icing the puck means shooting it from behind the centre line right down to beyond the opposition's goal-line. If it enters the net a goal is scored, otherwise play is stopped and restarted with a face-off from the offending team's half.

See Rule 48 (page 72).

A penalty is incurred if a player commits an offence such as charging into an opponent *(Rule 47)*, carrying his stick above shoulder height *(Rule 61)*, falling on the puck *(Rule 55)*, engaging in fisticuffs *(Rule 56)* or butt-ending, cross-checking, hooking or spearing an opponent with his stick *(Rules 46, 50, 64 and 86).*

Icing the puck

Off the wall
When an attacker is under pressure from a defender, he will often play the puck off the boards at an angle either to get around his opponent or to pass the puck on to a team-mate who may be able to set up an attack.

SKILLS AND TACTICS

• A player must be adept at controlling the fast-moving puck with his stick (or feet), passing, receiving and shooting it swiftly and accurately. The pace of the game also demands excellent skating skills. Top players have the ability to travel at high speeds as well as start, stop or change direction in a matter of seconds.

• A *break-out play* involves setting up an attack once a team has gained possession of the puck in their defensive zone, with the defence players passing it and moving it up towards the forward players, often rebounding it off the boards to evade checkers (tacklers). Shots for goal are best made from the slot – the area directly in front of goal.

Hogging the goal
The ice hockey goal may be small but so, too, is the puck and it can quite easily shoot into the small gaps left. So goalkeepers spread themselves out to block off as much of the goal mouth as possible. But the frequency with which they are hit by fast moving pucks means they have to be made even bigger by heavy padding.

Splits
Ice is very slippery and the goalkeeper can frequently get into all kinds of contortions in his attempts to block the goal mouth.

continued from page 73

of the Referee, attempted to injure an opponent.

(iii) Assess a match penalty to a player who, in the opinion of the Referee, deliberately injured an opponent.

Batting the puck above the normal height of the shoulders with a stick is also prohibited.

Rule 62 Holding an Opponent

A minor penalty shall be imposed on a player who holds an opponent by using his hands, arms or legs.

(NOTE) A player is permitted to use his arm in a strength move, by blocking his opponent, provided he has body position and is not using his hands in a holding manner, when doing so.

Rule 63 Holding an Opponent's Stick

A player is not permitted to hold an opponent's stick. A minor penalty shall be assessed to a player who holds an opponent's stick.

Rule 64 Hooking

Hooking is the act of using the stick in a manner that enables a player to restrain an opponent.

(a) A minor penalty shall be imposed on a player who impedes the progress of an opponent by hooking with his stick.

(b) A major penalty and a game misconduct

shall be imposed on any player who injures an opponent by hooking.

Rule 65 Icing the Puck

(a) For the purpose of this Rule, the centre red line will divide the ice into halves. Should any player of a Team, equal or superior in numerical strength to the opposing Team, shoot, bat or deflect the puck from his own half of the ice beyond the goal line of the opposing Team, play shall be stopped and the puck faced-off at the end face-off spot of the offending Team, unless, on the play, the puck shall have entered the net of the opposing Team, in which case the goal shall be allowed.

For the purpose of this Rule, the point of last contact with the puck by the Team in possession shall be used to determine whether icing has occurred or not.

Rule 66 Illegal Puck

If at any time while play is in

progress, a puck other than the one legally in play shall appear on the playing surface, the play shall not be stopped but shall continue with the legal puck until the play then in progress is completed by change of possession.

Rule 67 Interference

A minor penalty shall be imposed, for example, on a player who interferes with or impedes the progress of an opponent who is not in possession of the puck, restrains an opponent who is attempting to forecheck, causes an opponent who is not in possession to be forced off-side or deliberately knocks a stick out of an opponent's hand.

Rule 68 Interference by/with Spectators

The referee shall stop play if a spectator interferes with a player (unless he is in possession, in which case the play is completed first). A player who interferes with a spectator incurs a gross misconduct penalty.

Rule 69 Kicking a Player

A match penalty shall be imposed on any player who kicks or attempts to kick another player.

Whether or not an injury occurs, the Referee will impose a five minute time penalty.

Rule 70 Kicking the Puck

(a) Kicking the puck shall be permitted in all zones. A goal cannot be scored by an attacking player who uses a distinct kicking motion to propel the puck into the net. A goal cannot be scored by an attacking player who kicks a puck that deflects into the net off any player, goalkeeper or Official.

(b) A puck that deflects into the net off an attacking player who does not use a distinct kicking motion, is a legitimate goal.

Rule 71 Kneeing

Kneeing is the act of a player making a distinct movement of his knee.

A minor, major or match penalty shall be imposed on any player who fouls an opponent by kneeing.

Close encounter
Ice hockey is a physical sport and tackles are frequently robust. The important point, though, is that each player is aiming for the puck with his stick – not his opponent.

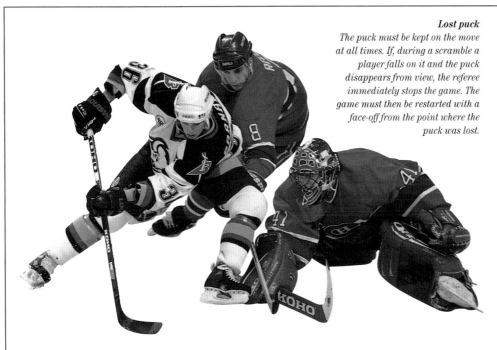

Lost puck
The puck must be kept on the move at all times. If, during a scramble a player falls on it and the puck disappears from view, the referee immediately stops the game. The game must then be restarted with a face-off from the point where the puck was lost.

Rule 72 Leaving Players' or Penalty Bench

A game misconduct penalty shall be imposed on the player who was the first or second player to leave the players' or penalty bench from either or both teams during an altercation or for the purpose of starting one.

Rule 73 Obscene or Profane Language or Gestures

A player incurs a game misconduct penalty for using obscene gestures and a misconduct penalty for using profane language anywhere on the rink.

Rule 74 Off-Sides

A player is off-side when both skates (but not his stick) are completely over the outer edge of the determining centre line or blue line involved in the play when the puck crosses the outer edge of this line. For an intentional off-side, the puck is faced-off at the end face-off spot in the offending team's defending zone.

Rule 75 Passes

See page 75

Rule 76 Physical Abuse of Officials

Players are suspended for 20, 10 or three games, depending on the degree of the offence.

Rule 77 Preceding Puck into Attacking Zone

(a) Players of the attacking team must not precede the puck into the attacking zone.

(b) For violation of this Rule, the play is stopped and the puck shall be faced-off in the neutral zone at the face-off spot nearest the attacking zone of the offending Team.

(NOTE) A player actually controlling the puck who shall cross the line ahead of the puck shall not be considered off-side.

Rule 78 Protection of Goalkeeper

(a) A minor penalty for interference shall be imposed on a player who, by means of his stick or his body, interferes with or impedes the movements of the goalkeeper by actual physical contact.

Rule 79 Puck Must Be Kept in Motion

(a) The puck must be kept in motion at all times.

(b) A minor penalty shall be imposed on any player, including the goalkeeper, who holds, freezes or plays the puck with his stick, skates or body in such a manner as deliberately to cause a stoppage of play.

(NOTE) With regard to a goalkeeper, this Rule applies outside of his goal crease area.

Rule 80 Puck Out of Bounds or Unplayable

When a puck goes outside the playing area, strikes any obstacles apart from the boards or glass, becomes lodged in the netting of a goal or is 'frozen' between opposing players, it shall be faced-off from a suitable spot.

Rule 81 Puck Out of Sight

Should a scramble take place or a player accidentally fall on the puck and the puck be out of sight of the Referee, he shall immediately blow his whistle and stop the play. The puck shall then be faced-off at the point where the play was stopped unless otherwise provided for in the Rules.

Rule 82 Puck Striking Official

(a) Play shall not be stopped if the puck touches an Official anywhere on the rink, regardless of whether a Team is shorthanded or not.

Rule 83 Refusing to Start Play

If a team refuses to start play when ordered to, the Referee shall impose a two minute penalty on a player of the offending team. Continued refusal incurs a fine of $200/£120 for the Manager or Coach of the team, followed by a forfeit to the non-offending team if refusal still persists.

Rule 84 Roughing

A minor altercation not worthy of a major penalty.

A minor penalty shall be imposed on a player who strikes an opponent.

Rule 85 Slashing

(a) A minor or major and a game misconduct penalty, at the discretion of the Referee, shall be imposed on any player who impedes the progress of an opponent by slashing (*swinging*) with his stick.

(b) A major and a game misconduct penalty shall be imposed on any player who injures an opponent by slashing.

Rule 86 Spearing

(a) A double minor penalty will be imposed on a player who spears (*stabs an opponent with the point of the stick blade*) an opponent and does not make contact.

(b) A major and a game misconduct shall be imposed on a player who spears an opponent.

Rule 87 Start of Game and Periods

See page 71.

Rule 88 Throwing Stick

If a defending player deliberately throws his stick at the puck or puck carrier in his defending zone and no goal is scored, a penalty shot is awarded to the attacking team. If the opposing goalkeeper has been removed and this act prevents the puck carrier from scoring, a goal is awarded to the attacking team. Otherwise, a player who throws his stick anywhere on the ice incurs a minor penalty.

Rule 89 Tied Game

See page 74.

Rule 90 Time of Match

See page 74.

Rule 91 Tripping

(a) A minor penalty shall be imposed on any player who shall place his stick or any portion of his body in such a manner that it shall cause his opponent to trip and fall.

Rule 92 Time-Outs

Each Team shall be permitted to take one thirty-second time-out during the course of any game. This time-out must be taken during a normal stoppage of play.

Rule 93 Video Goal Judge

Details the situations subject to review by the Video Goal Judge.

These rules are reprinted by permission of the National Hockey League. A complete copy of the rules is available from the League.

Men's lacrosse
Essentials

The Iroquois believe that lacrosse is a sacred game, a gift from The Creator, and that when a lacrosse match is to take place, The Great Spirit passes over the ground on which it is to be played and blesses the participants and their lacrosse sticks. The modern men's game is a full-contact sport in which players, armed with crosses and an array of protective gear, battle it out to gain possession of the ball. Not for the faint-hearted.

End lines
Goal
Goal crease
Goal area
Goal area line
110 yds
10 yds
20 yds
Centre line
10 yds
10 yds
Special substitution area
Side lines
6 yds
60 yds (54.86 m)

The field

A rectangular pitch, 110 yds (100.58 m) long and 60 yds (54.86 m) wide, with lines marked in white. Soft flexible cones are placed at each corner, at each end of the substitution gate and at the end of the halfway line which is opposite the bench area.

The goals

Two vertical posts joined by a crossbar, painted orange and fitted with a pyramidal shaped cord netting. The posts are 6 ft (1.83 m) apart and the crossbar is six feet from the ground. Each goal is 15 yds (13.72 m) from each end line and inside a circle (the goal crease) of radius 9 feet (2.74 m).

6 ft
6 ft

Crosse – net allows the ball to lodge.

The crosse

There are different lengths and head sizes. A short crosse is 40–42 in (101.6–106.68 cm), a long crosse is 52–72 in (132.08–182.88 cm). Apart from the goalkeeper's crosse, only four long crosses per team are allowed at a time. The head of the crosse must measure between 4 and 10 in (10.16–25.4 cm) at its widest point. The head of the goalkeeper's crosse may measure up to 15 in (38.1 cm). This stick may be any length.

The teams

Ten players a side – a goalkeeper, three defenders, three midfielders and three attackers – and up to 13 substitutes.

Officials

One head referee, two additional referees, a chief bench official, a timekeeper, two penalty timekeepers for each team and a scorer for each team.

Dress

All players must wear protective gloves and a helmet with a face mask and chinstrap. Jerseys are the same colour for the whole team and feature players' individual numbers (8 in/ 20.32 cm minimum height) on both front and back.

The ball

White or orange rubber, 7.75–8 in (19.69–20.32 cm) in circumference and 5–5.25 oz in weight.

Fast and free Despite their heavily armoured upper bodies, men's lacrosse players usually wear no protection whatsoever on their legs – for lacrosse is an extremely fast moving game with the ball travelling at high speeds and players need to be able to move free from any encumbrance.

Armed for the game Men's lacrosse has developed into the toughest of all ball and stick sports – a tough game in which protective gloves, helmet and arm pads are absolutely essential.

Getting some stick
Men's lacrosse is certainly a brutal sport but some interchanges are simply not allowed. It is not allowed, for instance, to hit your opponent over the head with your crosse.

HOW TO PLAY

Each team attempts to score by getting the ball into the opposition's goal. The ball is carried, thrown or batted with the crosse and only the goalkeeper, while within his own goal crease, can touch it with his hands.

Starting

A toss determines the choice of goals. Play is then started with a face-off. The referee places the ball on the ground at the centre of the field and one player from each team stands facing the other on his own side of the line. They then assume their face-off positions. Both crosses rest on the centre line, parallel to each other, on either side of the ball. Once these positions have been assumed, the referee calls "set" and, upon the whistle, either player may attempt to play the ball with his crosse.

How to win

Each goal scores one point. The team with the most points wins.

KEY RULES

A match is divided into four periods of 20 minutes; the intervals are of two, ten and, finally, three minutes. At the end of each quarter the teams change ends.

• In the event of a tie, two periods of four-minutes overtime are played, after which, if the scores are still even, the match is decided with the 'sudden death' procedure four-minute periods are played, with teams changing ends after each, until a goal is scored.

• Body-checking (take-outs) are permitted, but the opponent must be in possession of the ball or within 9 feet (2.74 m) of a loose ball (not in anyone's possession) or a ball in flight. Body-checks between players must be made from the front or side, below the neck but no lower than the hip.

• Less serious offences are penalized by possession of the ball being awarded to the opposition at the place where the foul occurred. If the opposition already has possession, the offending player is sent off for 30 seconds. Technical fouls include handling the ball, pushing or holding an opponent or his

GREY AREA

The avoidable body-check of an opponent after he has passed or shot the ball is an offence but, with the ball being propelled at speeds of up to 120 mph (193 kph), it can be difficult for a referee to judge the status of the ball at impact.

Where was the ball?
This kind of body-check is legal if the player is within 2.74 m of a ball in flight. But with the ball travelling as fast as an express train there is constant dispute over just how close the ball was.

crosse, delaying the game and being offside. More serious offences are termed 'personal fouls' and incur a penalty of suspension from the game for one to three minutes and loss of possession if applicable. *These fouls are detailed in Section 10, Personal Fouls (page 80).*

SKILLS AND TACTICS

All players need strength, resilience and courage to keep up with the demands of this invasive game. *Attackers* need to excel in the art of shooting. *Midfielders* must be versatile players, skilled at passing, catching and

running with the ball, as well as scooping it up from the ground. The main task of the *defenders* is to 'check' (tackle) opponents. To counteract the fact that an advanced player can evade opponents effectively by running with the ball, defenders play with longer crosses. Top level players are expert at dislodging the ball with a blow to an opponent's gloved hand or crosse.

Men's lacrosse is quite a coach-led game, with a variety of offensive formations. Tactics have a lot in common with those used in basketball, such as the fast break and zone defence.
See Basketball (page 143).

Passing away
The best midfield players are fast on their feet, very good at running with the ball and good at passing. This midfielder has managed to get the ball clean away just in time before he is tackled – and all this while running at high speed.

MEN'S LACROSSE
• • • • • • • • • • • • • •

The rules of men's lacrosse are extremely detailed, and here we can only give a basic outline of the major rules.

Italics have been used to indicate rules that have been edited.

Sections 1 to 8
– Refer to topics covered in pages 78-9.

Section 9 Technical Fouls
Rule 50 The Penalty for Technical Fouls

50.1 The penalty for a technical foul shall be as follows:
i)If the offending team has possession of the ball, or if the ball is loose at the time a technical foul is committed, then possession shall be awarded to the opposing team at the point where the ball was when the foul occurred.
ii)If the opponents of the offending team have possession of the ball at the time a technical foul is committed, then the penalty shall be suspension from the field of play for 30 seconds for the player committing the foul.
50.2 If a technical foul occurs prior to the start of the game, or after the scoring of a goal or the end of a period, then the opponents are awarded the ball.

Rule 51 The Nature of a Technical Foul

51.1 Technical fouls are those of a less serious kind.
Any breach of the rules of play as set forth in this section shall be a technical foul unless that breach is specifically listed as a personal or expulsion foul in Sections 10 or 11.

Rules 52-67 are examples of technical fouls.

Rule 52 Interference

A player may not interfere in any manner with an opponent in an attempt to keep him from a loose ball, except when both are within 9 ft (2.7 m) of a loose ball.

Rule 53 Pushing

53.1 A player may not push an opponent with his crosse.
53.2 A player may not push an opponent unless the opponent has possession of the ball or the opponent is within 3 yds (2.7 m) of a loose ball.
53.3 A player may not push an opponent from the rear.

The face-off
To start the game the ball is placed on the ground in the centre of the pitch between the backs of the crosses of two opponents. The crosses have to lie along the ground with the heads an inch apart. As soon as the referee blows his whistle the players can go for the ball with crosse or feet.

Pushing from the rear is defined as exerting enough pressure to force an opponent to move in a direction other than that in which he intends to go or, if in the direction he intends to go, then at a greater speed than he intends.

Rule 54 Illegal Pick

54.1 No offensive player shall move into and make contact with a defensive player with the purpose of blocking that defensive player from the man he is marking.
Before any contact is made the offensive player must be stationary and motionless, and he must be standing in his normal stance.
54.2 No offensive player shall hold his crosse rigid or extend his crosse rigid to impede the normal movement of a defender.

Rule 55 Holding

55.1 A player shall not *normally* hold an opponent or an opponent's crosse.

Rule 56 Kicking an Opponent's Crosse

56.1 A player may not deliberately step on or kick the crosse of an opponent.

Rule 57 Handling the Ball

57.1 A player shall not touch the ball with his hand(s) while it is in play, except the goalkeeper in his crease.

Rule 58 Withholding the Ball from Play

A player shall not withhold the ball from play in any manner.
A player shall not lie on a loose ball on the ground.
A player shall not trap a loose ball on the ground with his stick longer than is necessary for him to control the ball and pick it up in one continuous motion.

Rule 59 Illegal Actions with the Crosse

59.1 A player shall not throw his crosse under any circumstances.
59.2 A player shall not take part in the play of the game in any manner unless he is grasping his crosse with at least one hand.
A broken crosse is considered no crosse.
59.3 During the play of the game, a player may not exchange his crosse for another except to replace a broken crosse, but players who are legally on the playing field may exchange crosses.

Rule 61 Illegal Procedure

61.1 Any action by a player or a substitute of a technical nature which is not in conformity with the rules and regulations governing the play of the game shall be termed illegal procedure.
Illegal procedures include: Leaving the penalty box before being authorized to do so by the penalty timekeeper (this constitutes a foul). Delaying the

Take-out
Tackling in men's lacrosse is a fairly bruising business. It involves simply charging at your opponent with your shoulder and knocking him over. This is called the take-out.

game. Failure to be at least 10 yds (9.14 m) from a face-off at the time the whistle is blown. Failure to be at least 5 yds (4.57 m) from an opponent having a free play.

Rule 62 Stalling

62.1 Any deliberate action on the part of a team in possession of the ball to maintain possession of the ball outside the attack goal area by holding or passing the ball without reasonable effort to attack its opponents' goal is a technical foul known as 'stalling'. *There is a procedure for ensuring that the stalling side do not delay the game.*

Rule 65 Offside

65.1 A team is offside, provided that the ball is in play, when:
i) it has fewer than three men in its attack half of the field between the centre line and the end line;
ii) it has fewer than four men in its defensive half of the field between the centre line and the end line.

Section 10 Personal Fouls

Rule 68 The Penalty for a Personal Foul

68.1 The penalty for a personal foul shall be suspension from the game for a period of one to three minutes, depending upon the referees' diagnosis of the severity and intention of the foul. The ball shall normally be given to the team which has been fouled. If the foul occurs prior to the start of the game, or after the scoring of a goal or the end of a period, then the ball shall be awarded to the opponents of the offending team at the centre of the field.

Rule 69 The Nature of a Personal Foul

Personal fouls include illegal bodychecking (such as an opponent who is not in possession of the ball), slashing (swinging the crosse recklessly), cross-checking (checking an opponent with the crosse handle), tripping, unneccessary roughness and unsportsmanlike conduct.

Rule 76 Player Committing Five Personal Fouls

76.1 Any player committing five personal fouls shall be 'fouled out' of the game, and shall not be allowed to take any further part in it.
76.2 A substitute for such a player shall be allowed to enter the game at such a time as the fouled-out player would have been permitted to re-enter the game had he not committed five personal fouls.

Section 11 Expulsion Fouls

Rule 77 The Penalty for an Expulsion Foul

77.1 The penalty for an expulsion foul shall be suspension for the remainder of the game.
77.2 In the case of an expulsion foul against a player or a substitute, a substitution may be made after a lapse of three minutes.
77.3 In the case of an expulsion foul against a coach, non-playing member of a squad, or someone officially connected with a team, the In-home (a pre-nominated player) of the offending team shall be suspended from the game for three minutes, and he must remain in the penalty box for the entire three minutes.

Rule 78 The Nature of an Expulsion Foul

78.1 The act of deliberately striking or attempting to strike an opponent, a non-playing member of the opponents' squad, a coach or anyone controlling the play of the game with the hand, crosse, ball or

otherwise by a player, a substitute, a non-playing member of a squad, a coach or anyone officially connected with a team may be an expulsion foul.
78.2 Where a fight occurs on the field of play, and the officials have 'frozen' the benches, by indicating to the team personnel who are on the benches that they should remain there, then any team personnel pushing past an official in order to join in a fight may be expelled from the game.
78.3 Where two players from competing teams are fighting and a third participant enters the altercation, then the third man into the altercation shall be expelled from the game.
78.4 Refusal to accept the authority of the officials, or the use of foul or abusive language may be an expulsion foul.

Section 12 Execution of Penalties

Rule 79 Player Committing Foul

79.1 A player who has been sent out of the game by a referee shall report immediately to the timer's table. He must remain in the penalty box, subject to the rules below, until released by the penalty timekeeper.
79.2 In the case of a time penalty, the time refers to the time for which the player will be off the field and out of the game. The timing of a penalty will begin when the penalized player sits down on one of the seats in the penalty box, or when the whistle blows to restart play, whichever is the later. If there are no empty seats left in the relevant penalty box, then the penalized player should kneel on one knee beside the seats.

Rule 80 Restarting Play After a Penalty

80.1 When a penalty occurs in the offended team's defensive half of the field and penalty time is to be served, the ball shall be awarded to any player of the offended team on the offensive side of the centre line.
80.2 In *nearly* all other cases, the ball shall be awarded to any player of the offended team at the point where the ball was when play was suspended.

Rule 81 Simultaneous Fouls

81.1 When a member of a team commits a foul, and then a member of the opposing

team commits a foul, then the fouls shall be considered simultaneous fouls, provided that the fouls are not separated by a whistle which has restarted play, or by the scoring of a goal.
81.2 When simultaneous fouls have been committed and they are all technical, the fouls cancel, *and the team in possession retains possession where the ball was when the whistle sounded. If no team is in possession, the ball is faced where it was when the whistle sounded. But if at least one of the fouls was a personal, then all fouls are time served, the team with less penalty time will be awarded the ball.*

Rule 82 The Slow Whistle Technique

82.1 If a defending player commits a foul, and the attacking team has possession of the ball at the time that the foul occurs, and, in the opinion of the referees, a scoring play is imminent, and the act of fouling does not cause the attacking player who is in possession to lose the ball, then the referee will throw a signal flag and withhold his whistle until such time as the scoring play has been completed.

Shooting stars
Attackers who can catch the ball in the air and quickly make a shot – hurling the ball fast and accurately – into the tiny goal are matchwinners.

Rule 83 The Play-On Technique

83.1 Where a player commits a loose-ball technical foul, and the offended team may be disadvantaged by the immediate suspension of play, then the referee shall visually and verbally signal 'Play-on', and he shall withhold his whistle until such time as the situation involving the potential advantage has been completed.

These rules are reprinted by permission of the International Lacrosse Federation.

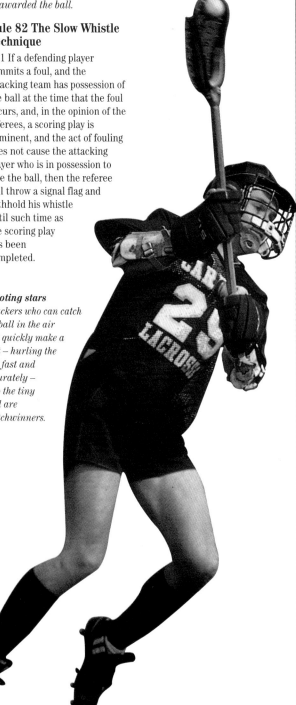

Women's lacrosse
Essentials

Unlike the men's game, this is a non-contact version of lacrosse in which only the goalkeepers wear protective clothing. Another major difference is the size of the pitch, which for this game has no set boundaries.

Goal line
Goal circle
15-m fan
Centre line
18 m
3 m
82-92 m
Centre circle
5.2 m
1.83 m

The field

The playing area has no measured boundaries, although an area of 110 m by 60 m (120 yds by 66 yds) is desirable. There is a goal circle (2.6 m/ 3 yds radius) at each end of the field and a centre circle (9 m/ 10 m radius) in the middle of the field, with a 3 m (3½ yds) centre line marked in the middle of this, parallel to the goal lines.

The keeper's pads
Only the goalkeeper may wear protective clothing. She can catch the ball with her hand, but must then put it in her stick and clear the ball within ten seconds.

The goals

Through the centre of each goal circle is a goal line, marked parallel to the width of the field and 1.83 m (2 yds) in length. The posts of each goal are placed at either end of the goal lines and are joined by a crossbar, 1.83 m (2 yds) above the ground. The posts and crossbars are 5 cm (2 in) square or in diameter, constructed of wood or metal and painted white. A goal net is attached to the frame and also to the ground at a point 1.83 m (2 yds) behind the centre of the goal line.

Dress

Shirt, kilt/shorts and composition or rubber-soled boots/shoes. Shirts are numbered front and back. All field players must wear mouthguards, but NOT head-gear or face masks. The goal-keeper must wear a helmet with face mask, a chest or body pad, a throat protector, padded gloves, arm pads and leg pads. Captains wear a distinctive arm band.

Officials

Up to three umpires, a scorer and a timer.

The teams

Two teams of 12 players each.

1.83 m
1.83 m
2.6 m

The ball

Rubber, of any solid colour, with a circumference of 20 – 20.3 cm (approx 8 in) and a weight of 142 – 149 g (approx 5 oz). It must bounce between 1.1 m and 1.3 m (approx 3½ ft) when dropped from 1.8m onto concrete at a temperature of 18 – 23°C.

The crosse (the stick)

Wood, plastic, fibreglass, nylon, leather and/or gut. Only the handle may be constructed of aluminium or graphite.
Field player's crosse: a total length of .9 – 1.1 m (approx 1 yd) and weight of no more than 567 g (20 oz). The crosse head must be 18 – 23 cm (approx 10 – 12 in) in width and 25.4 – 30.5 cm (approx 7 – 9 in) in length. The depth of the pocket, with the ball, must not exceed 6.3 cm (2½ in), i.e. the diameter of the ball.
Goalkeeper's crosse: a total length of .9 – 1.22 m (approx 1 yd) and weight of no more than 773 g (27 oz). The crosse head must have a maximum inside measurement (width) of 30 cm (12 in) and a length of 40 cm (16 in). The depth of the pocket is unlimited.

Sticking with it
Women's lacrosse players can use their sticks to pass, throw, catch, or carry the ball.

HOW TO PLAY

The ball is propelled into goals at either end of the field to score goals. It may be carried, passed, thrown or caught with the crosse. It must not be touched with the hands other than by the goalkeeper.

Starting

Teams toss for a choice of ends and then two opponents start play with a *draw*. Both players stand with their backs to the goal they are defending and with one foot toeing the centre line. Their crosses are held back to back in the air, above hip level and parallel to and above the centre line. The umpire places the ball between the crosses, says "Ready" and then blows the whistle, upon which the players draw their crosses up and away. The ball must go higher than the heads of these two players. All other players must remain outside the centre circle until the whistle blows.

How to win

A goal is scored when the ball passes completely over the goal lines. Goals scored by attacking players must be made with the crosse only – not the body – and from outside the goal circle. The team with the most goals wins.

KEY RULES

• A game consists of two periods of 25 minutes each, with a half-time of ten minutes. Teams change ends at half-time.

If the game is stopped due to an irregular incident – if, for example, the ball goes out of bounds, becomes lodged in the umpire's clothing or two opponents foul simultaneously – then play starts again with a *throw*. Two opposing players stand 1 m (1 yd) apart, facing into play closest to the goal they are defending. The umpire then tosses the ball towards them and they both run in and try to catch it. Other players must remain at a distance of 4 m (4¹/₂ yds) until the throw has been completed.
See Rule 15, (page 84).

• Only the goalkeeper (or someone deputising for her) may enter the goal circle and if the ball enters the circle, only she may play it, although she must be inside the circle herself to do so. The ball must also not be allowed to remain inside the goal circle for longer than ten seconds.
See Rules 17 and 18, (page 84).

• All fouls are penalized with the award of a *free position*. The player who has been fouled places the ball in her crosse while all other players stand at least 4 metres (4¹/₂ yds) away from her. When the whistle

Crossed
Players carrying the ball can be tackled by tapping the stick to dislodge the ball.

blows, she is free to run with the ball, pass or shoot it.
See Rule 19, (page 84).
Misconduct, such as unsportsmanlike behaviour, dangerous play or persistent breaking of the rules results in the award of a free position to the non-offending player or team and, in addition, the umpire may also show the offending player a yellow card (a warning) or a red card (suspension). If a player has already been shown a yellow card once, then a second case of misconduct will automatically result in a red card being shown.
See Rule 22, (page 85).

SKILLS AND TACTICS

Lacrosse is a fast, flowing game that calls for stamina, speed and determination. When in possession of the ball, a player must not leave herself open to attack. In order to dodge opponents she must combine secure, flexible handling of the crosse with the ability to manoeuvre herself out of tight situations, changing pace and direction constantly to open up space for running or passing the ball safely to a team-mate.

GREY AREA

Because women's lacrosse is so fast moving there are rules to prevent dangerous moves. One of these concerns the **pick**. A pick is an attacking player who deliberately blocks the path of a defending opponent to prevent her tackling a team-mate who is carrying the ball. A pick is only safe and legal if she is within her opponent's field of vision so that the opponent can take evasive action, although this can often be difficult for an umpire to judge.

Defenders attempt to regain possession in a number of ways. They may try to intercept the ball as it is passed between members of the opposing team, they may *steer* (following an individual opponent closely, forcing her to change her speed or direction or to pass the ball while in a weak position) or they may tackle by *crosse checking* (controlled tapping of an opponent's crosse in order to try and dislodge the ball).

Double cross
When the ball is loose on the ground players swoop in to catch it in their sticks, lift it into the air and gain possession.

RULES OF WOMEN'S LACROSSE
• • • • • • •

These rules are abridged and summarised. Changes to the official rules are indicated in italics. Rules 1 – 13 are covered on pages 82 – 83.

14. Ball outside field of play

When the ball crosses the boundary, it is deemed outside the field of play, and the umpire must blow the whistle.

A. If the ball is deliberately directed, carried or propelled out-of-bounds it is a minor foul.

B. If the ball is accidentally carried or propelled out-of-bounds, the player nearest the ball places the ball in her crosse and stands 4 m (4$\frac{1}{2}$ yds) inside the boundary from the spot where the ball went out of play. Play resumes on the umpire's whistle and arm signal.

1) All players shall maintain their relative field position at the time the whistle was blown. No player may be closer to the boundary than the player awarded the ball.

2) The player with the ball must be given 1 m (1 yd) clear space by her opponent(s).

3) A Throw is taken when the two opposing players closest to the ball are equidistant.

C. Play is not to be resumed within 11 m (12 yds) of the centre of the goal line.

15. The throw

Two opposing players stand with their feet and crosses at least 1 m apart. Each is nearer the goal she is defending and is facing in towards the game. The Throw must be taken at least 11 m from the centre of the Goal Line. The umpire stands between 4 m and 8 m (9 yds) from the players, and as the whistle is blown, throws the balls with a short high arc toward the players so they catch it as they move in towards the game. No other player may be within 4 m of the players taking the Throw. If the Throw is inaccurate or is not touched by either player, it must be taken again. The Throw is taken when:

A. the ball goes into the goal off a non-player. The Throw should be taken to the side of the goal by two opponents nearest the goal.

B. the ball goes out-of-bounds and two opposing players are equally near the ball.

C. there is an incident unrelated to the ball, and players are equidistant from the ball.

D. a ball lodges in the clothing of a field player or umpire.

E. two opponents foul simultaneously (major/major or minor/minor).

F. the game is restarted after an incident related to the ball when neither team had possession and two opposing players are equally near the ball, unless the accident has been caused by a foul.

G. the game is stopped for any reason not specified in the rules.

H. the attack fouls (major or minor) during a raised flag.

16. Conduct of play

A. A violation of any rule is a foul. The penalty for a foul is a Free Position.

B. All players must Stand when the whistle is blown. The umpire will indicate where the player taking the Free Position is to stand and where the offending player is to stand.

1) No player or her crosse is allowed within 4 m (4$\frac{1}{2}$ yds) of the player taking the Free Position.

2) A Free Position must not be taken within 11 m (12 yds) of the centre of the Goal Line.

3) The player awarded the Free Position places the ball in her crosse, and on the umpire's whistle and visual arm signal she may run, pass or shoot.

4) If two opposing players foul simultaneously and the fouls are equivalent (minor/minor or major/major), a Throw is taken. If the fouls are not equivalent, the team committing the major foul is penalized.

C. Advantage call

An umpire may refrain from enforcing any rule when it would penalize the non-offending team. If a player retains possession of the ball, even though she has been fouled, the umpire will indicate that she has seen the foul by extending her arm in the direction the player is attacking.

17. Goal circle rules

A. Only one player, either the goalkeeper or the person deputizing for her is allowed in the Goal Circle at any one time. No other player is allowed to enter or have any part of her body or crosse on or over the Goal Circle line at any time. A ball resting on the Goal Circle line is the goalkeeper's.

B. The goalkeeper, while within the Goal Circle:

1) must clear the ball within ten seconds after it has entered the Goal Circle.

2) may stop the ball with either hand and/or body as well as her crosse. If she catches the ball with her hand she must put it in her crosse and proceed with the game.

3) must remove a ball lodged in the goal netting or her clothing or pads, place it in her crosse and proceed with the game.

4) may reach out her crosse and bring the ball back into the Goal Circle provided no part of her body is grounded outside the Goal Circle.

C. When the goalkeeper or anyone deputizing for her is outside the Goal Circle: she loses all her goalkeeping privileges; she may only re-enter the Goal Circle without the ball; she may propel the ball into the Goal Circle and then follow it in; and she must return to the Goal Circle to play the ball if it is inside the circle.

D. An unprotected field player: may only enter or remain in the Goal Circle when her team has possession of the ball; must immediately leave the Goal Circle when her team loses possession of the ball; may go into the Goal Circle to play a rolling ball; while within the Goal Circle, must clear the ball within ten seconds after it has entered the Goal Circle and while within the Goal Circle, must remove a ball lodged in her clothing or crosse, place it in her crosse and proceed with the game.

18. Goal circle fouls and penalties

A. Goal Circle Fouls

1) A player must not follow through over the Goal Circle line with any part of her body or crosse at any time unless she is deputizing for the goalkeeper.

2) The goalkeeper or another player must not: allow the ball to remain within the Goal Circle for longer than ten seconds; when inside the Goal Circle, reach beyond the Goal Circle to play the ball with any part of her body; draw the ball into her Goal Circle when any part of her is grounded outside the Goal Circle; when outside the Goal Circle, step inside the Goal Circle with the ball; or throw any of her equipment to another player.

B. Penalties for Goal Circle Fouls

1) For all Goal Circle fouls, EXCEPT an unprotected field player illegally in the Goal Circle, the Free Position is taken

the Goal Circle.

2) may stop the ball with either hand and/or body as well as her crosse. If she catches the ball with her hand she must put it in her crosse and proceed with the game.

3) must remove a ball lodged in the goal netting or her clothing or pads, place it in her crosse and proceed with the game.

15 m (16$\frac{1}{2}$ yds) out from either side and level with the Goal Line.

2) An unprotected field player illegally in the Goal Circle is a major foul. The Free Position will be awarded at the centre hash mark on the 11 m line to the attack player nearest this mark. The offending player is placed 4 m (4$\frac{1}{2}$ yds) behind and the Penalty Line cleared. The goalkeeper must not return to the Goal Circle until play has restarted.

19. Minor foul rules and penalties

A. Minor Foul Rules

A player commits a minor foul if she, for example: covers a ground ball with her crosse or body so denying an opponent an opportunity to play the ball; touches the ball with her hand; checks/tackles the crosse of an opponent who is trying to gain possession of the ball; throws her crosse; draws illegally after one caution; enters the Centre Circle during the Draw prior to the Umpire's whistle; intentionally delays the game; adjusts the thongs of her crosse after an Umpire's request to inspect it; deliberately directs, propels or carries the ball out of bounds or fails to strike her crosse on the ground immediately if the ball becomes lodged in it. A goalkeeper must not be beyond 15 m (16$\frac{1}{2}$ yds) of her Goal Line during a Draw or score a goal for her team or proceed beyond the Centre Line at any time.

B. Minor Foul Penalties

1) For a minor foul, the offender is placed 4 m (4$\frac{1}{2}$ yds) from the player taking the Free Position, in the same direction from which she fouled. When the defence commits a minor foul within 15 m (16$\frac{1}{2}$ yds) of goal, the Free Position shall be taken on the 15-m Fan on a line which passes from the centre of the Goal Line through the point where the foul occurred.

2) Repeated minor fouls shall be penalized as major fouls.

20. Major foul rules and penalties

A. Major Foul Rules

A player commits a major foul if she, for example: roughly or recklessly checks/tackles an opponent's crosse; strikes an opponent with her crosse; holds her crosse within a field crosse width of an opponent's head or neck; reaches across the opponent's body; makes a legal check impossible by holding her crosse near her own or a team-mate's face or body while in possession; charges, blocks, barges, shoulders or pushes into an opponent with the hand or back; propels the ball or shoots dangerously or without control; prevents the attacking team from shooting safely by blocking the goal with her body; detains an opponent by holding, tagging, pressing or pushing with an arm, leg, body or crosse; trips or swipes at an opponent; violates the three second rule (i.e. remains in the 11 m area at the front of the goal circle for longer than three seconds, unless marking an opponent within a stick's length).

B. Major Foul Penalties

1) For a major foul, the offender is placed 4 m (4½ yds) behind the player taking the Free Position. The Free Position is set up at the spot of the foul, but never closer than 11 m (12 yds) to the centre of the Goal Line. If the foul occurs within the 11 m area, the Free Position is set up at the closest hash mark.

2) All players must clear the Penalty Lane of crosses and any part of their bodies when a Free Position is awarded for a major foul occurring within 11 m in front of the goal.

3) If the foul prevented an almost certain goal, the umpire may move any players positioned between the Free Position and the goal.

4) If any defender is in the Free Space to Goal when a Free Position is set, she should not be penalized for blocking the Free Space To Goal unless she does not immediately move out of this space after the umpire restarts play.

21. Advantage flag

A. Advantage Flag is raised instead of blowing a whistle for a major foul by defence when the attacking team is on a Scoring Play within 15 m (16½ yds) of goal. This includes the 15 m Fan and the playing area behind goal, which runs 9 m (10 yds) deep and 15 m to each side of the centre of the goal Line.

B. A yellow flag is raised by the umpire when an attack player, with or without the ball, is fouled on a Scoring Play.

(A Scoring Play is a continuous effort by the attacking team to move the ball toward the goal and complete a shot on goal.)

C. The Scoring Play is over when:

Foul play
Women's lacrosse is a minimum contact sport. Holding a player down is a major illegal check – see Rule 20A

a shot is taken, the attacking team passes or carries the ball behind the level of the Goal Line **and fails** to continue the initial momentum to score a goal, the attacking team stops its continuous effort to complete a shot on goal, the attacking team fouls, the defence commits a subsequent foul which requires the game to be stopped or the attacking team loses possession of the ball.

The Umpire must stop the Scoring Play immediately for a Free Space to Goal violation or for an unprotected player illegally in the Goal Circle.

D. Following the Advantage Flag:

1) If a shot on goal is successful, the goal counts.

2) If the attacking team chooses to shoot, the advantage indicated by the flag is complete and play continues.

3) If the Scoring Play ends without a further foul or shot on goal, a Free Position will be awarded to the attack player **who was fouled** and the penalized defender will be placed 4 m (4½ yds) behind.

For a foul:

a) between 11 m – 15 m (12 – 16½ yds) in front of goal, the Free Position is awarded where the foul occurred.

b) within 11 m in front of goal, the Free Position is awarded on the closest hash mark and the Penalty Lane cleared.

c) behind goal, the Free Position is awarded on the 11 m mark on the Goal Line extension.

4) If any additional fouls by the defence end the Scoring Play, the Free Position is awarded to the attack player who was fouled at the 11 m hash mark nearest the most recent foul. The defender who fouled will be placed 4 m behind and the Penalty Lane cleared.

5) If the attacking team fouls (major or minor), a Throw will be taken beyond 15 m, level with the Goal Line extension.

6) Whenever the Penalty Lane is cleared and the goalkeeper is outside her Goal Circle and has not fouled, she may return to her Goal Circle.

22. Misconduct and suspensions

A. Misconduct and Suspensions

A player must not: conduct herself in a rough, dangerous or unsportsmanlike manner; persistently cause infringement of the rules; deliberately endanger the safety of an opposing player or exhibit any type of behaviour which in the umpire's opinion amounts to misconduct.

B. Penalties

1) Misconduct and/or Suspension are treated as major fouls.

2) In addition to awarding the appropriate penalty, the Umpire may:

a) give a verbal caution.

b) warn the offending player with a Yellow Card.

c) suspend the offending layer by showing a Red Card.

d) show a Red Card to suspend from further

participation in the game and/or send from the field without previous warning, a player, coach or team/bench personnel guilty of dissent, misconduct, abusive language, flagrant or repeated violations of the rules.

e) If a player, coach or team/bench personnel is warned or suspended, the game is restarted within 30 seconds with a Free Position to the opponent nearest the ball when play was stopped.

23. Team fouls and penalties

A. Team Fouls

1) Delay of game.

2) Persistent fouling.

B. Team Foul Penalties

1) Delay of Game

a) On the first delay of game, the Umpire shall show the team's Captain a Green Card and award the appropriate penalty.

b) On the next delay of game, the umpire will show a Green and Yellow Card to the offending player and award the appropriate penalty. All subsequent offenders on that team shall receive a Green and Red Card suspension along with the appropriate penalty. The suspended player may return to the field on the next stoppage of play after a three minute lapse of playing time.

2) Persistent Fouls

a) For persistent team fouls, the umpire shall show a Green Card to the team's captain and award the appropriate penalty (if applicable). On the next similar offence by that team, the umpire will show the offender a Green and Yellow Card. Regardless of the act, the offence will be penalized as a major foul.

b) The next player from the carded team who commits a subsequent Team Foul will receive a Green and Red Card suspension in addition to the penalty for a major foul. The suspended player may return to the field on the next stoppage of play after a three minute lapse of playing time.

These rules are reprinted by permission of the International Federation of Women's Lacrosse Associations. For a complete copy of the rules, including Arm Signals for Umpires, Definitions and Tournament Rules and Overtime Procedures, contact the IFWLA or your national association.

Cricket
Essentials

The laws of cricket were compiled as early as 1744, although the game itself, in some form, is thought to date back to the 13th Century. The name of cricket has always been synonymous with the notion of fair play and this reputation still persists, alongside its growing high-profile, commercial appeal.

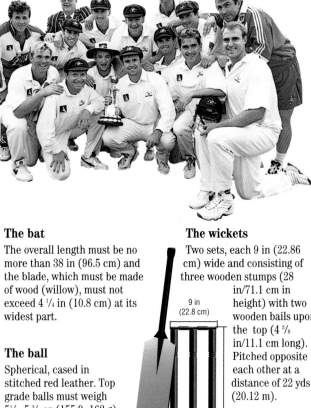

Above, fielding positions for a right handed batsman and their names

The players

Two sides of 11 players. Substitutes are allowed but they may not bat, bowl or act as wicketkeeper.

The playing field

Turf or non-turf. No specific size, although boundaries must be marked.

Officials

Two umpires.

The creases

The *bowling crease* is marked in line with the stumps. 8 ft 8 in (2.64 m) in length, with the stumps at the centre.

The *popping crease* is parallel to this. It is marked 4 ft (1.22 m) from the centre of the stumps and extends at least 6 ft (1.83 m) on either side of the line of the wicket. (The batsman must stands on this line as he awaits a delivery.)

The *return crease* is at right angles to the bowling crease. Marked to at least 4 ft (1.22 m) behind the wicket it must be considered to be of unlimited length.

The pitch

The area between the bowling creases. A width of 10 ft (3.04 m), with the centre line being that which joins the two middle stumps. (For a non-turf pitch the dimensions are minimum length 58 ft/17.68 m and minimum width 6 ft/1.83 m, with the same distance between the stumps, i.e. 22 yds/20.12 m.)

Below, test match crowd.

The bat

The overall length must be no more than 38 in (96.5 cm) and the blade, which must be made of wood (willow), must not exceed 4 ¼ in (10.8 cm) at its widest part.

The ball

Spherical, cased in stitched red leather. Top grade balls must weigh 5½–5 ¾ oz (155.9–163 g) and have a circumference of 18¹³/₁₆–19 in (22.4–22.9 cm).

The wickets

Two sets, each 9 in (22.86 cm) wide and consisting of three wooden stumps (28 in/71.1 cm in height) with two wooden bails upon the top (4 ³/₈ in/11.1 cm long). Pitched opposite each other at a distance of 22 yds (20.12 m).

HOW TO PLAY

Each team has its turn as the batting side. This side sends in two of its players at a time to face the bowlers of the opposing team at the wickets and to score runs by running simultaneously between the wickets as successfully hit balls are fielded.

The fielding side attempts to get them out and nominates bowlers to deliver balls at each wicket alternately in 'overs' – six at a time, not including wides or no-balls. When ten of the players of the batting side have been dismissed, this team starts its own batting innings.

Starting

The captains toss for the choice of innings (i.e. to bat or bowl/field first). When the umpire has called "play", the fielding team position themselves across the ground while the two opening batsmen from the opposite team take their places in front of each wicket.

How to win

The team with the highest run total at the end of the match wins. Once the ball has been hit, the batsmen will judge whether or not they each have time to run the length of the pitch once (one run), or more than once, while the ball is being retrieved. If the ball crosses the boundary line, four runs are automatically scored. If it is hit so that it crosses this line without first touching the ground, six runs are scored. In either case the batsmen need not run.

Single runs may also be earned as a result of penalties. *See Laws 24, 25 and 26.* Each batsman's runs are totalled individually and the team's score is the sum of these.

Willow and leather
Cricket relies on traditional materials for both equipment and clothing. Cricketers dress in cotton and wool whites and hit a leather ball with a bat of willow.

Head gear
The only non-traditional item in the professional cricketer's dress is a helmet and face guard, often worn as protection from fast or dangerous balls.

Dress

All-white trousers, shirt, shoes and sweaters (with team colours as a trim) for test matches, coloured outfits for one-day matches. The wicketkeeper must wear leg pads and protective gloves and batsmen must wear leg pads, gloves and protective helmets.

Sight-screens

Special screens are used to give batsmen a clear view of the bowler and are positioned behind each wicket and outside the playing area, but close to the boundary line. Sizes vary.

KEY RULES

• Test matches run for five days, with a maximum of 30 hours play and two innings for each side. If the team batting second is all out more than 200 runs behind, they may be asked to bat again by the opposing team.

• Shorter matches, such as the one-day matches for the World Cup, are limited-over competitions in which both teams have only one innings each. In these, a team attempts to score as many runs as it can before it runs out of overs or batsmen, whichever comes first.

• The captains are responsible at all times for ensuring that play is conducted within the spirit of the game as well as within the Laws.

• A batsman can be got out in a number of ways:

He is *bowled* if the bowler's ball knocks one of the bails off the stumps that he is guarding. *See Law 30, (page 89).*

He is *caught* if he hits the ball and it is caught by a member of the fielding side before it hits the ground. *See Law 32, (page 92).*

Leg before wicket (L.B.W.) occurs when his leg or any part of his body prevents the ball from hitting the stumps. *See Law 36, (page 93).* If he is running towards a wicket but fails to make it in time to touch the ground between the popping and bowling creases with his bat before an opponent puts the wicket down, he is *run out. See Law 38, (page 93).*

If he is standing close to his wicket but is out of his ground, the wicketkeeper may take advantage of this lapse to knock the bails off the stumps with the ball, in which case he is *stumped. See Law 39, (page 93).*

• Before an umpire will announce that a batsman is out, the fielding side must appeal to him with the words "how's that?" ("howzat") before the bowler begins his next run-up. *See Law 27, (page 89).*

M.D.C.C

CORNHILL CORNHILL CORNHILL

THE LAWS OF CRICKET
• • • • • • • • • • • • • • •

Laws 1–4

Deal with players and substitutes. *See pages 86–87.*

Laws 5–11

Deal with equipment and the playing field. *See pages 86–87.*

Laws 12–17

Deal with match procedure. *See pages 86–87*

Laws 18 and 19

Deal with scoring.

Law 20 Lost Ball

Law 21 The Result

Law 22 The Over

Law 23 Dead Ball

Law 24 No-Ball

1. Mode of Delivery

The umpire shall indicate to the striker whether the bowler intends to bowl over or round the wicket, overarm or underarm,or right- or left-handed. Failure on the part of the bowler to indicate in advance a change in his mode of delivery is unfair and the umpire shall call and signal "no-ball".

2. Fair Delivery – The Arm

For a delivery to be fair the ball must be bowled not thrown – see Note (a) below. If either umpire is not entirely satisfied with the absolute fairness of a delivery in this respect he shall call and signal "no-ball" instantly upon delivery.

Wide

3. Fair Delivery – The Feet

The umpire at the bowler's wicket shall call and signal "no-ball" if he is not satisfied that in the delivery stride:-
(a) the bowler's back foot has landed within and not touching the return crease or its forward extension or
(b) some part of the front foot whether grounded or raised was behind the popping crease.

4. Bowler Throwing at Striker's Wicket before Delivery

If the bowler, before delivering the ball, throws it at the striker's wicket in an attempt to run him out, the umpire shall call and signal "no-ball".
See Law 42 and Law 38.

5. Bowler Attempting to Run Out Non-Striker Before Delivery

If the bowler, before delivering the ball, attempts to run out the non-striker, any runs which result shall be allowed and shall be scored as no-balls. Such an attempt shall not count as a ball in the over. The umpire shall not call "no-ball". See Law 42.12.

6. Infringement of the Laws by a Wicketkeeper or a Fieldsman

The umpire shall call and signal "no-ball" in the event of the wicketkeeper infringing Law 40.1 or a Fieldsman infringing Law 41.2 or Law 41.3.

7. Revoking a Call

An umpire shall revoke the call "no-ball" if the ball does not leave the bowler's hand for any reason. See Law 23.2.

8. Penalty

A penalty of one run for a no-ball shall be scored if no runs are made otherwise.

9. Runs From a No-Ball

The striker may hit a no-ball and whatever runs result shall be added to his score. Runs made otherwise from a no-ball shall be scored no-balls.

10. Out From a No-Ball

The striker shall be out from a no ball if he breaks Law 34 and either batsman may be run out or shall be given out if either breaks Law 33 or Law 37.

11. Batsman Given Out Off a No-Ball

Should a batsman be given out off a no-ball the penalty for bowling it shall stand unless runs are otherwise scored.
Notes
(a) Definition of a Throw
A ball shall be deemed to have been thrown if, in the opinion of either umpire, the process of straightening the bowling arm, whether it be partial or complete, takes place during that part of the delivery swing which directly precedes the ball leaving the hand. This definition shall not debar a bowler from the use of the wrist in the delivery swing.
(b) No-Ball not Counting in Over
A no-ball shall not be reckoned as one of the over. See Law 22.3.

Law 25 Wide Ball

1. Judging a Wide

If the bowler bowls the ball so high over or so wide of the wicket that in the opinion of the umpire it passes out of reach of the striker, standing in a normal guard position, the umpire shall call and signal "wide ball" as soon as it has passed the line of the striker's wicket.

The umpire shall not adjudge a ball as being wide if:
(a) The striker, by moving from his guard position, causes the ball to pass out of his reach.
(b) The striker moves and thus brings the ball within his reach.

2. Penalty

A penalty of one run for a wide shall be scored if no runs are made otherwise.

3. Ball Coming to Rest in Front of the Striker

If a ball which the umpire considers to have been delivered comes to rest in front of the line

Wides

Wides are called when a ball is too wide or too high for the batsman to reach.

The ball is a 'wide' if it passes outside the return crease, providing the batsman does not move towards it.

A ball is a 'wide' if it passes high over the batsman's head.

of the striker's wicket, "wide" shall not be called. The striker has a right, without interference from the fielding side, to make one attempt to hit the ball. If the fielding side interfere, the umpire shall replace the ball where it came to rest and order the fieldsmen to resume the places they occupied in the field before the ball was delivered. The umpire shall call and signal "dead ball" as soon as it is clear that the striker does not intend to hit the ball, or after the striker has made one unsuccessful attempt to hit the ball.

4. Revoking a Call

The umpire shall revoke the call if the striker hits a ball which has been called "wide".

5. Ball Not Dead

The ball does not become dead on the call of "wide ball"– see Law 23.4.

6. Runs Resulting from a Wide

All runs which are run or result from a wide ball which is not a no-ball shall be scored wide balls, or if no runs are made one shall be scored.

7. Out from a Wide

The striker shall be out from a wide if he breaks Law 35 or Law 39. Either batsman may be run out and shall be out if he breaks Law 33 or Law 37.

8. Batsman Given Out Off a Wide

Should a batsman be given out off

No balls
The most common bowling faults are foot faults.

It is a 'no-ball' if, during delivery, the bowler's front foot ends up beyond the popping crease.

It is a 'no-ball' if, during delivery, the bowler's back foot is outside the return crease.

Byes

Byes are runs made without the batsman hitting the ball.

A 'leg bye' is a run taken when the ball deflects off any part of the batsman's body but his hands.

a wide, the penalty for bowling it shall stand unless runs are otherwise made.

Notes

(a) Wide Ball not Counting in Over

A wide ball shall not be reckoned as one of the over – see Law 22.3.

Law 26 Bye and Leg-Bye

1. Byes

If the ball, not having been called "wide" or "no ball" passes the striker without touching his bat or person, and any runs are obtained, the umpire shall signal "bye" and the run or runs shall be credited as such to the batting side.

2. Leg-Byes

If the ball, not having been called "wide" or "no-ball" is unintentionally deflected by the striker's dress or person, except a hand holding the bat, and any runs are obtained the umpire shall signal "leg-bye" and the run or runs scored shall be credited as such to the batting side.

Such leg-byes shall only be scored if, in the opinion of the umpire, the striker has:

(a) attempted to play the ball with his bat, or

(b) tried to avoid being hit by the ball.

3. Disallowance of Leg-Byes

In the case of a deflection by the striker's person, other than in 2(a) and (b) above the umpire shall call and signal "dead ball" as soon as one run has been completed or when it is clear that a run is not being attempted or the ball has reached the boundary. On the call and signal of "dead ball" the batsmen shall return to their original ends and no runs shall be allowed.

Law 27 Appeals

1. Time of Appeals

The umpires shall not give a batsman out unless appealed to by the other side which shall be done prior to the bowler beginning his run-up or bowling action to deliver the next ball. Under Law 23.1(g) the ball is dead on "over" being called; this does not, however, invalidate an appeal made prior to the first ball of the following over provided "time" has not been called. See Law 17.1.

2. An Appeal "How's That?"

An appeal "How's that?" shall cover all ways of being out.

3. Answering Appeals

The umpire at the bowler's wicket shall answer appeals before the other umpire in all cases except those arising out of Law 35 or Law 39 or Law 38 when this occurs at the striker's wicket.

When either umpire has given a batsman not out, the other umpire shall, within his jurisdiction, answer the appeal or a further appeal, provided it is made in time in accordance with 1. above.

4. Consultation by Umpires

An umpire may consult with the other umpire on a point of fact which the latter may have been in a better position to see and shall then give his decision. If, after consultation, there is still doubt remaining the decision shall be in favour of the batsman.

5. Batsman Leaving his Wicket under a Misapprehension

The umpires shall intervene if satisfied that a batsman, not having been given out, has left his wicket under a misapprehension that he has been dismissed.

6. Umpire's Decision

The umpire's decision is final. He may alter his decision, provided that such alteration is made promptly.

7. Withdrawal of an Appeal

In exceptional circumstances the captain of the fielding side may seek permission of the umpire to withdraw an appeal providing the outgoing batsman has not left the playing area. If this is allowed, the umpire shall cancel his decision.

Law 28 The Wicket is Down

1. Wicket Down

The wicket is down if:

(a) Either the ball or the striker's bat or person completely removes either bail from the top of the stumps. A disturbance of a bail, whether temporary or not, shall not constitute a complete removal, but the wicket is down if a bail in falling lodges between two of the stumps.

(b) Any player completely removes with his hand or arm a bail from the top of the stumps, providing that the ball is held in that hand or in the hand of the arm so used.

(c) When both bails are off, a stump is struck out of the ground by the ball or a player strikes or pulls a stump out of the ground, providing that the ball is held in the hand(s) or in the hand of the arm so used.

2. One Bail Off

If one bail is off, it shall be sufficient for the purpose of putting the wicket down to remove the remaining bail, or to strike or pull any of the three stumps out of the ground in any way of the ways stated in 1. above.

3. All the Stumps Out of the Ground

If all the stumps are out of the ground, the fielding side shall be allowed to put back one or more stumps in order to have an opportunity of putting the wicket down.

4. Dispensing with Bails

If owing to the strength of the wind, it has been agreed to dispense with the bails in accordance with Law 8 Note (a) the decision as to when the wicket is down is one for the umpires to decide on the facts before them. In such circumstances and if the umpires so decide the wicket shall be held to be down even though a stump has not been struck out of the ground.

Notes

(a) Remaking the Wicket

If the wicket is broken while the ball is in play, it is not the umpire's duty to remake the wicket until the ball has become dead – see Law 23. A member of the fielding side, however, may remake the wicket in such circumstances.

Law 29 Batsman out of his Ground

1. When out of his Ground

A batsman shall be considered to be out of his ground unless some part of his bat in his hand or of his person is grounded behind the line of the popping crease.

Law 30 Bowled

1. Out Bowled

The striker shall be out bowled if:

(a) His wicket is bowled down, even if the ball first touches his bat or person.

Clean cut

A square cut is one of the most exciting strokes to watch. It is made when an underpitched ball gives the batsman plenty of time to strike the ball with the bat almost horizontal to send it shooting towards the boundary.

➧ page 92

Twister

Instead of relying on pace and power to beat the batsman, spin bowlers rely on fooling him with the flight of the ball. A leg spin bowler holds the ball with his first three fingers well spaced apart, with the tips around the seam of the ball. The effect is to send the ball spinning towards the batsman's leg side.

SKILLS AND TACTICS

Batsmen will meet the ball with a combination of defensive and attacking shots so as to hold on to their wicket while also scoring as many runs as possible. Defensive strokes play the ball safely down to the ground, away from the wicket. Attacking strokes such as the drive are used to hit the ball some distance away from the pitch, to either side or straight ahead, to gain time for runs.

Bowlers have to develop their own pace and style. Most fall into two categories – fast and spin bowlers.

Although there are top all-rounders, most players will specialize as bowlers or batsmen.

All players must be good *fieldsmen*, however – constantly on the alert, ready to retrieve and return the ball quickly, or even catch it to get a batsman out. They must be able to judge in an instant which wicket is the more vulnerable and, therefore, which colleague to pass to. In some instances, a quick-thinking fieldsman will take aim at the wicket himself to save time if he thinks he has a chance of putting it down.

Speed merchants

The fastest bowlers hurl the ball towards the batsman at a ferocious pace. The sight of such a bowler building up his pace on his run-up, is often enough to disconcert the unfortunate batsman standing at the wicket.

Above, standard field positions for an off-spin bowler

Below, standard field positions for a right-handed outswing bowler

Umpire's hand signals

Boundary: six

Dead ball

Boundary: four

Leg-bye

Bye

Wide

No-ball

Out

Short run

Hand signals
Umpires give a variety of signals so that the scorers and everyone on the field understand his decision instantly.

Howzat!
A batsman is not given out unless a player on the opposing team appeals immediately. So games are often interrupted by loud cries of "howzat!".

GREY AREAS

Of all the ways a player can be out, L.B.W. is the one that causes most dispute and discussion. The problems arise either over whether the ball was on target or whether the player was genuinely attempting a stroke. The fact is the umpire's decision is paramount in all cases.

Disputes also arise because cricket boards and authorities sometimes introduce special playing conditions, such as for the Wide law, for particular kinds of match (e.g. one-day matches). This often leads to misunderstanding amongst players who are familiar with the normal conditions.

Out L.B.W.

Not out

Leg before wicket
L.B.W. decisions often cause dispute but a batsman whose leg blocks a ball heading for the wicket after pitching on the offside or straight before the wicket (left) is usually given out. A batsman whose leg obstructs a ball pitched outside the leg stump or hits the ball first with his bat (right) is usually not out.

continued from page 89

(b) He breaks his wicket by hitting or kicking the ball on to it before the completion of a stroke, or as a result of attempting to guard his wicket. See Law 34.1.

Notes

(a) Out Bowled – Not L.B.W.

The striker is out bowled if the ball is deflected on to his wicket even though a decision against him would be justified under Law 36.

Law 31 Timed Out

1. Out Timed Out

An incoming batsman shall be out timed out if he wilfully takes more than two minutes to come in – the two minutes being timed from the moment a wicket falls until the new batsman steps on to the field of play.

If this is not complied with and if the umpire is satisfied that the delay was wilful and if an appeal is made, the new batsman shall be given out by the umpire at the bowler's end.

2. Time to be Added

The time taken by the umpire to investigate the cause of the delay shall be added at the normal close of play.

Notes

Batsmen Crossing on Field of Play

It is an essential duty of the captains to ensure that the ingoing batsman passes the out-going one before the latter leaves the field of play.

Law 32 Caught

1. Out Caught

The striker shall be out caught if the ball touches his bat or if it touches below the wrist his hand or glove, holding the bat, and is subsequently held by a fieldsman before it touches the ground.

2. A Fair Catch

A catch shall be considered to have been fairly made if:

(a) The fieldsman is within the field of play throughout the act of making the catch.

(i) The act of making the catch shall start from the time when the fieldsman first handles the ball and shall end when he both retains complete control over the further disposal of the ball and remains within the field of play.

(ii) In order to be within the

field of play, the fieldsman may not touch or ground any part of his person on or over a boundary line. When the boundary is marked by a fence or board the fieldsman may not ground any part of his person over the boundary fence or board, but may touch or lean over the boundary fence or board in completing the catch.

(b) The ball is hugged to the body of the catcher or accidentally lodges in his dress or, in the case of the wicket-keeper, in his pads. However, a striker may not be caught if a ball lodges in a protective helmet worn by a fieldsman, in which case the umpire shall call and signal "dead ball". See Law 23.

(c) The ball does not touch the ground even though a hand holding it does so in effecting the catch.

(d) A fieldsman catches the ball, after it has been lawfully played a second time by the striker, but only if the ball has not touched the ground since being first struck.

(e) A fieldsman catches the ball after it has touched an umpire, another fieldsman or the other batsman. However a striker may not be caught if a ball has touched a protective helmet worn by a fieldsman.

(f) The ball is caught off an obstruction within the boundary provided it has not previously been agreed to regard the obstruction as a boundary.

3. Scoring of Runs

If a striker is caught, no runs shall be scored.

Notes

(a) Scoring from an Attempted Catch

When a fieldsman carrying the ball touches or grounds any part of his person on or over a boundary marked by a line,

six runs shall be scored.

(b) Ball Still in Play

When a fieldsman releases the ball before he crosses the boundary, the ball will be considered to be still in play and it may be caught by another fieldsman. However, if the original fieldsman returns to the field of play and handles the ball, a catch may not be made.

Law 33 Handled the Ball

1. Out Handled the Ball

Either batsman on appeal shall be out 'handled the ball' if he wilfully touches the ball while in play with his hand not holding the bat unless he does so with the consent of the opposite side.

Law 34 Hit the Ball Twice

1. Out Hit the Ball Twice

The striker, on appeal, shall be out 'hit the ball twice' if, after the ball is struck or is stopped by any part of his person, he wilfully strikes it again with his bat or person except for the sole purpose of guarding his wicket: this he may do with his bat or any part of his person other than his hands, but see law 37.2.

For the purpose of this law, a hand holding the bat shall be regarded as part of the bat.

2. Returning the Ball to a Fieldsman

The striker, on appeal, shall be out under this law, if, without the consent of the opposite side, he uses his bat or person to return the ball to any of the fielding side.

3. Runs from Ball Lawfully Struck Twice

No runs except those which result from an overthrow or penalty, see Law 41, shall be scored from a ball lawfully struck twice.

Law 35 Hit Wicket

1. Out Hit Wicket

The striker shall be out 'hit wicket' if, while the ball is in play:

(a) His wicket is broken with any part of his person, dress, or equipment as a result of any action taken by him in preparing to receive or in receiving a delivery, or in setting off for his first run, immediately after playing, or playing at, the ball.

(b) He hits down his wicket whilst lawfully making a second stroke for the purpose of guarding his wicket within the provisions of Law 34.1.

Notes

(a) Not Out Hit Wicket

A batsman is not out under this

Cricketing colours
Although traditional cricket whites are still worn for most test matches, players taking part in the one day knock-out series usually dress in highly colourful strips.

law should his wicket be broken in any of the ways referred to in 1(a) above if:

(i) It occurs while he is in the act of running, other than in setting off for his first run immediately after playing at the ball, or while he is avoiding being run out or stumped.

(ii) The bowler after starting his run-up or bowling action does not deliver the ball; in which case the umpire shall immediately call and signal "dead ball".

(iii) It occurs whilst he is avoiding a throw-in at any time.

Law 36 Leg before Wicket

1. Out L.B.W.

The striker shall be out L.B.W. in the circumstances set out below:

(a) Striker Attempting to Play the Ball

The striker shall be out L.B.W. if he first intercepts with any part of his person, dress or equipment a fair ball which would have hit the wicket and which has not previously touched his bat or a hand holding the bat, provided that:

(i) The ball pitched, in a straight line between wicket and wicket or on the off side of the striker's wicket, or was intercepted full pitch.
and

(ii) the point of impact is in a straight line between wicket and wicket, even if above the level of the bails.

(b) Striker Making No Attempt to Play the Ball

The striker shall be out L.B.W. even if the ball is intercepted outside the line of the off-stump, if, in the opinion of the umpire, he has made no genuine attempt to play the ball with his bat, but has intercepted the ball with some part of his person and if the other circumstances set out in (a) above apply.

Law 37 Obstructing the Field

1. Wilful Obstruction

Either batsman, on appeal, shall be out obstructing the field if he wilfully obstructs the opposite side by word or action.

2. Obstructing a Ball from Being Caught

The striker, on appeal, shall be out should wilful obstruction by either batsman prevent a catch being made.

This shall apply even though the striker causes the obstruction in lawfully guarding his wicket under the provisions of Law 34. See Law 34.1.

Law 38 Run Out

1. Out Run Out

Either batsman shall be out run out if in running or at any time while the ball is in play – except in the circumstances described in Law 39 – he is out of his ground and his wicket is put down by the opposite side. If, however, a batsman in running makes good his ground he shall not be out run out, if he subsequently leaves his ground, in order to avoid injury, and the wicket is put down.

2. "No-Ball" Called

If a no-ball is called, the striker shall not be given run out unless he attempts to run.

3. Which Batsman is Out

If the batsmen have crossed in running, he who runs for the wicket which is put down shall be out; if they have not crossed, he who has left the wicket which is put down shall be out. If a batsman remains in his ground or returns to his ground and the other batsman joins him there, the latter shall be out if his wicket is put down.

4. Scoring of Runs

If a batsman is run out, only that run which is being attempted shall not be scored. If however an injured striker himself is run out, no runs shall be scored. See Law 2.7.

Notes

(a) Ball Played on to Opposite Wicket

If the ball is played on to the opposite wicket neither batsman is liable to be run out unless the ball has been touched by a fieldsman before the wicket is broken.

(c) Run Out off a Fieldsman's Helmet

If, having been played by a batsman, or having come off his person, the ball rebounds directly from a fieldsman's helmet on to the stumps, with either batsman out of his ground, the batsman shall be "Not out".

Law 39 Stumped

1. Out Stumped

The striker shall be out stumped if, in receiving the ball, not being a no-ball, he is out of his ground otherwise than in attempting a run and the wicket is put down by the wicketkeeper without the intervention of another fieldsman.

2. Action by the Wicketkeeper

The wicketkeeper may take the ball in front of the wicket in an attempt to stump the striker only

if the ball has touched the bat or the person of the striker.

Law 40 The Wicketkeeper

1. Position of the Wicketkeeper

The Wicketkeeper shall remain wholly behind the wicket until a ball delivered by the bowler touches the bat or person of the striker, or passes the wicket, or until the striker attempts a run. In the event of the wicketkeeper contravening this law, the umpire at the striker's end shall call and signal "no-ball" at the instant of delivery or as soon as possible thereafter.

2. Restriction on Actions of the Wicketkeeper

If the wicketkeeper interferes with the striker's right to play the ball and to guard his wicket, the striker shall not be out, except under Laws 33, 34, 37 and 38.

3. Interference with the Wicketkeeper by the Striker

If in the legitimate defence of his wicket, the striker interferes with the wicketkeeper, he shall not be out, except as provided for in Law 37.2.

Law 41 The Fieldsman

1. Fielding the Ball

The fieldsman may stop the ball with any part of his person, but if he wilfully stops it otherwise, five runs shall be added to the run or runs already scored; if no runs have been scored five penalty runs shall be awarded. The run in progress shall count provided that the

batsmen have crossed at the instant of the act. If the ball has been struck, the penalty shall be added to the score of the striker, but otherwise to the score of byes, leg-byes, no-balls or wides as the case may be.

2. Limitation of On-Side Fieldsmen

The number of onside fieldsmen behind the popping crease at the instant of the bowler's delivery shall not exceed two. In the event of infringement by the fielding side the umpire at the striker's end shall call and signal "no-ball" at the instant of delivery or as soon as possible thereafter.

3. Position of Fieldsmen

Whilst the ball is in play and until the ball has made contact with the bat or the striker's person or has passed his bat, no fieldsman, other than the bowler, may stand on or have any part of his person extended over the pitch (measuring 22 yds/20.12 m by 10 ft/3.05 m). In the event of a fieldsman contravening this law, the umpire at the bowler's end shall call and signal "no-ball" at the instant of delivery or as soon as possible thereafter. See Law 40.1.

4. Fieldsmen's Protective Helmets

Protective helmets, when not in use by members of the fielding side, shall only be placed, if above the surface, on the ground behind the wicketkeeper. In the event of the ball, when in play, striking a helmet whilst in this position, five penalty runs shall be awarded, as laid down in Law 41.1 and Note (a).

Law 42 Unfair Play

These laws are reprinted by permission of the Marylebone Cricket Club. Contact the MCC for a complete copy of the Laws of Cricket.

Bouncer
Bouncers are fast, short pitched balls that bounce up sharply towards the batsman's head. They are not actually illegal but they are considered unfair against tail-enders.

Baseball
Essentials

This is the national summer sport of the United States, although its popularity is now firmly established in countries as far afield as Japan, Australia and the Netherlands. Its roots are generally traced back to the 1700s, when the similar game of rounders was introduced by English settlers to the American colonies.

The field

Grass or artificial turf. Consists of an outfield and a diamond – a 90-ft (27-m) square, with 90 ft being the distance between each base. Home base is marked by a five-sided slab of whitened rubber; first, second and third bases are marked by 15 in (38 cm) square white canvas bags, attached to the ground. The pitcher's plate is a rectangular slab of whitened rubber, 24 by 6 in (61 by 15 cm). The distance between the pitcher's plate and home base is 60 ft, 6 in (18.4 m).

Dress

Uniform throughout a team. All players' uniforms feature 6 in (15 cm) numbers on their backs.

Leagues may require teams to always wear one distinctive uniform or they may allow two sets – a white one for home games and a different colour for away games. Uniforms must not feature glass buttons, polished metal or any patterns that might suggest the shape of a baseball. The catcher may wear a leather mitt (not more than 38 in (96.5 cm) in circumference and 15½ in (39 cm) in length), the first baseman may wear a leather glove or mitt (not more than 12 in (30 cm) in length). All other fielders may wear a leather glove. The pitcher's glove must not be white or grey. The catcher must wear a catcher's protective helmet and all players, while at bat, must use some type of protective helmet.

A run-out

The catcher

Players

Two teams of nine players each. When fielding, team members assume the following positions on the field:

❶ pitcher
❷ catcher
❸ first baseman
❹ second baseman
❺ third baseman
❻ shortstop
❼ left fielder
❽ center fielder
❾ right fielder

*Field diagram labels:*
3rd base
Coaches' box
Next batter's box
Pitcher's plate
Home base plate
1st base
2nd base
Grass line – 95 ft from pitcher's plate
60½ ft
90 ft
Foul line
Fence 60 ft from base or foul line

Officials

One or more umpires. If there are two or more, one is designated the umpire-in-chief and the others, field umpires.

The bat

A smooth, round stick; one piece of solid wood. Not more than 42 in (107 cm) in length and not more than 2¾ in (7 cm) in diameter at the thickest part.

The ball

Spherical, a core of cork, rubber or similar material, wound with yarn and covered with white horsehide or cowhide. A weight of 5–5¼ oz (approx 142 g) and circumference of 9–9¼ in (approx 23 cm).

HOW TO PLAY

The object of the game is to strike the ball and then complete the circuit of first, second, third and back to home base, touching each on the way, to score a run. Teams take it in turns to bat. The fielding side must put three players of the batting side out in order to end their opponents' half of the inning and begin their own batting period.

Starting

Once both teams have established their batting order (given to the umpire-in-chief five minutes before the game), the home team takes the field and the visiting team prepares to bat first.

How to win

The team which scores the most runs wins. One run is scored each time a runner completes the circuit of bases. If the ball is hit far enough, this may be completed in one go for a home run. A home run is also scored if a fly ball (one not touching the ground) passes over a fence or into the stands, at least 250 ft (76 m) away from home base. When a home run is hit, all the runners on the field may run back to home base, touching all other bases on the way. In this way, a home run will score as many runs as there are runners in the field at the time (maximum four).

KEY RULES

• A game consists of nine innings, unless it is extended to resolve a tied score. The game ends at the end of the ninth inning if the visiting team are in the lead. However, if the home team scores the winning point in its half of the ninth inning, the game ends at this moment.

• The *strike zone* is an area directly above the home plate. In terms of height, this zone begins at a line level to the bottom of the batter's kneecap and ends level to his armpits (or more specifically, at the midpoint between the top of his trousers and the top of his shoulders) as he assumes a batting stance. A ball that does not keep to this zone is called a *'ball'* and after four balls, a batter is allowed to walk to first base. If the delivery of a pitcher is legal (within the strike zone) and the batter fails to hit it, a *strike* is called. After three strikes a batter is out.

• A batter can also be out if the ball is caught before it touches the ground or if he or first base is *tagged* (touched by a fielder who has possession of the ball) before he makes it to first base. When the batter hits a fair ball into *fair territory* (the area bounded by the first and third baselines, from home base to the bottom of the playing field fence, including the foul lines) he may start running to first base, or further if he has time.
See Rule 6, The Batter (page 96).

• A runner making his way around the bases can also be put out. He can be tagged by a fielder, or if a fielder manages to reach a base he is running towards before he does and, with the ball in his possession, stands with one foot on the base, then the runner cannot occupy it and is out.

• Runners must not deviate too far from the direct line between bases simply to avoid being tagged. If they do, they are out, unless they stray from this line so as not to interfere with a fielder's play. If wilful interference does occur in any way, the offending runner and/or batter-runner will be called out. (Likewise, interference on the part of the fielding team is also penalized.)

• Only one runner can occupy a base at a time and runners must proceed around the circuit in the order that they batted. A *force play* is when a batter becomes a runner and runs towards first base, forcing the player already occupying this base to proceed onto the next one (as well as any runners ahead of him in turn).
See Rule 7, The Runner (page 98).

• The pitcher mostly throws overarm, with a bent arm and he must keep one foot on the pitcher's plate until he has delivered the ball. When a new pitcher takes over (or at the start of an inning) he is allowed up to eight practice pitches to his catcher. He may make his pitch from either the wind-up position or the set position.
See Rule 8.01 (page 101).

• A *balk* occurs when there is a runner on a base and the pitcher commits an illegal act. This may be one of many things, such as feinting (making a movement to imply he is about to pitch or throw the ball and then failing to go through with it), delivering the ball while not facing the batter or dropping the ball while touching his plate. A balk entitles all the runners to advance one base each.
See Rule 8.05 (page 102).

• The *designated hitter* rule is used by some leagues and involves using a substitute player for a pitcher when it is his turn to bat. The designated hitter, though, does not participate when his team is fielding.
See Rule 7, The Runner (pages 98 – 101).

SKILLS AND TACTICS

A good eye and a powerful swing are two basic skills a *batter* requires. However, judgement is also vital. He must be able to make the snap decision to leave any pitch that looks like it may be a 'ball', since he has so few chances to strike the ball. When he does hit the ball, he must calculate its distance and direction accurately enough to be able to make it safely to first base. He may 'tap' the ball carefully (a bunt) to place it somewhere within the infield, in which case the pressure is on him to get to first base extremely quickly. Alternatively, a ball hit high and hard may score a home run, but it also runs the risk of being caught by a fielder. Runners must be equally aware of the positioning of the ball and fielders.

To match the speed of runners progressing from base to base, *fielders* must be expert at retrieving and passing the ball, while the basemen cannot afford to fumble a catch when the difference between them catching the ball and a runner sliding into base may be a split second.

The role of the *pitcher* is arguably the most difficult one in the field. With the ball often travelling at speeds of around 90 mph (145 kph), it requires an enormous amount of intelligence, concentration and skill to deliver a series of pitches designed to make the batter's job as difficult as possible. A fast ball, as the name implies, relies on sheer speed, while a curve ball veers away from the batter and a slider uses spin to swerve towards or away from the batter late in its journey. *See Rule 8, The Pitcher (page 101).*

Big swing
A baseball is difficult to hit well so scoring is low. The key for the batter is keeping a low, even swing.

Strike zone
For a strike the ball must be within the strike zone, which depends on the batter's stance and lies between the midriff and the knees.

BASEBALL THE RULES

This is an abridged version of the
official rules of baseball.

1 Objectives of the Game
See How to win (page 94).

2 Definitions of Terms

3 Game Preliminaries

**4.00 Starting and Ending a
Game**
*See Starting (page 94) and Key
rules (page 95).*

**5.00 Putting the Ball in Play.
Live Ball**
5.01 At the time set for
beginning the game the umpire
shall call "Play".
5.02 After the umpire calls "Play"
the ball is alive and in play and
remains alive and in play until for
legal cause, or at the umpire's
call of "Time" suspending play,
the ball becomes dead. While the
ball is dead no player may be put
out, no bases may be run and no
runs may be scored, except that
runners may advance one or
more bases as the result of acts
which occurred while the ball
was alive (such as, but not
limited to a balk, an overthrow,
interference, or a home run or
other fair ball hit out of the
playing field).
5.03 The pitcher shall deliver the
pitch to the batter who may elect
to strike the ball, or who may not
offer at it, as he chooses.
5.04 The offensive team's
objective is to have its batter
become a runner, and its runners
advance.
5.05 The defensive team's
objective is to prevent offensive
players from becoming runners,
and to prevent their advance
around the bases.
5.06 When a batter becomes a
runner and touches all bases
legally he shall score one run for
his team.
5.07 When three offensive
players are legally put out, that
team takes the field and the
opposing team becomes the
offensive team.
5.08 If a thrown ball accidentally
touches a base coach, or a
pitched or thrown ball touches an
umpire, the ball is alive and in
play. However, if the coach
interferes with a thrown ball, the
runner is out.
5.09 The ball becomes dead and
runners advance one base, or
return to their bases, without
liability to be put out, when:
(a) A pitched ball touches a

batter, or his clothing, while in
his legal batting position;
runners, if forced, advance.
(b) The plate umpire
interferes with the catcher's
throw; runners may not advance.
Note: The interference shall be
disregarded if the catcher's throw
retires the runner.
(c) A balk is committed;
runners advance; (See Penalty
8.05).
(d) A ball is illegally batted;
runners return.
(e) A foul ball is not caught;
runners return. The umpire shall
not put the ball in play until all
runners have retouched their
bases.
(f) A fair ball touches a runner
or an umpire on fair territory
before it touches an infielder
including the pitcher, or touches
an umpire before it has passed an
infielder other than the pitcher.
If a fair ball goes through, or
by, an infielder, and touches a
runner immediately back of him,
or touches a runner after being
deflected by an infielder, the ball
is in play and the umpire shall
not declare the runner out. In
making such decision the umpire
must be convinced that the ball
passed through, or by, the
infielder and that no other
infielder had the chance to make
a play on the ball; runners
advance, if forced.
(g) A pitched ball lodges in the
umpire's or catcher's mask or
paraphernalia, and remains out
of play, runners advance one
base.
(h) Any legal pitch touches a
runner trying to score; runners
advance.
5.10 The ball becomes dead
when an umpire calls "Time". The
umpire-in-chief shall call "Time":
(a) When in his judgement
weather, darkness or similar
conditions make immediate
further play impossible.
(b) When light failure makes it
difficult or impossible for the
umpires to follow the play.
(c) When an accident
incapacitates a player or an
umpire.
(1) If an accident to a runner
is such as to prevent him from
proceeding to a base to which he
is entitled, as on a home run hit
out of the playing field, or an
award of one or more bases, a
substitute runner shall be
permitted to complete the play.
(d) When a manager requests
"Time" for a substitution, or for a
conference with one of his
players.
(e) When the umpire wishes to

examine the ball, to consult with
either manager, or for any similar
cause.
(f) When a fielder, after
catching a fly ball, falls into a
bench or stand, or falls across
ropes into a crowd when
spectators are on the field. As
pertains to runners, the
provisions of 7.04 (c) shall
prevail. If a fielder after making a
catch steps into a bench, but
does not fall, the ball is in play
and runners may advance at their
own peril.
(g) When an umpire orders a
player or any other person
removed from the playing field.
(h) Except in the cases stated
in paragraphs (b) and (c) (1) of
this rule, no umpire shall call
"Time" while a play is in progress.
5.11 After the ball is dead, play
shall be resumed when the
pitcher takes his place on the
pitcher's plate with a new ball or
the same ball in his possession
and the plate umpire calls "Play".
The plate umpire shall call "Play"
as soon as the pitcher takes his
place on his plate with the ball in
his possession.

6 The Batter
6.01 (a) Each player of the
offensive team shall bat in the
order that his name appears in
his team's batting order.
(b) The first batter in each
inning after the first inning shall
be the player whose name follows
that of the last player who legally
completed his time at bat in the
preceding inning.
6.02 (a) The batter shall take his
position in the batter's box
promptly when it is his time at
bat.
(b) The batter shall not leave
his position in the batter's box
after the pitcher comes to set
position, or starts his wind-up.
Penalty: If the pitcher pitches,
the umpire shall call "Ball" or
"Strike", as the case may be.
(c) If the batter refuses to take
his position in the batter's box
during his time at bat, the umpire
shall order the pitcher to pitch,
and shall call "Strike" on each
such pitch. The batter may take
his proper position after any such
pitch, and the regular ball and
strike count shall continue, but if
he does not take his proper
position before three strikes are
called, he shall be declared out.
6.03 The batter's legal position
shall be with both feet within the
batter's box.
Approved Ruling: The lines
defining the box are within the
batter's box.

6.04 A batter has legally
completed his time at bat when
he is put out or becomes a
runner.
6.05 A batter is out when:
(a) His fair or foul fly ball
(other than a foul tip) is legally
caught by a fielder.
(b) A third strike is legally
caught by the catcher.
(c) A third strike is not caught
by the catcher when first base is
occupied before two are out.
(d) He bunts foul on third
strike.
(e) An infield fly is declared.
(f) He attempts to hit a third
strike and the ball touches him.
(g) His fair ball touches him
before touching a fielder.
(h) After hitting or bunting a
fair ball, his bat hits the ball a
second time in fair territory. The
ball is dead and no runners may
advance. If the batter-runner
drops his bat and the ball rolls
against the bat in fair territory
and, in the umpire's judgement,
there was no intention to
interfere with the course of the
ball, the ball is alive and in play.
(i) After hitting or bunting a
foul ball, he intentionally deflects
the course of the ball in any
manner while running to first
base. The ball is dead and no
runners may advance.
(j) After a third strike or after
he hits a fair ball, he or first base
is tagged before he touches first
base.
(k) In running the last half of
the distance from home base to
first base, while the ball is being
fielded to first base, he runs
outside (to the right of) the 3-ft
line, or inside (to the left of) the
foul line, and in the umpire's
judgment in so doing interferes
with the fielder taking the throw
at first base; except that he may
run outside (to the right of) the
3-ft line or inside (to the left of)
the foul line to avoid a fielder
attempting to field a batted ball.
(l) An infielder intentionally
drops a fair fly ball or line drive,
with first, first and second, first
and third, or first, second and
third base occupied before two
are out. The ball is dead and
runner or runners shall return to
their original base or bases.
Approved Ruling: In this
situation, the batter is not out if
the infielder permits the ball to
drop untouched to the ground,
except when the infield fly rule
applies.
(m) A preceding runner shall,
in the umpire's judgement,
intentionally interfere with a
fielder who is attempting to catch

a thrown ball or to throw a ball in an attempt to complete any play.

(n) With two out, a runner on third base, and two strikes on the batter, the runner attempts to steal home base on a legal pitch and the ball touches the runner in the batter's strike zone. The umpire shall call "Strike three", the batter is out and the run shall not count; before two are out, the umpire shall call "Strike three", the ball is dead, and the run counts.

6.06 A batter is out for illegal action when:

(a) He hits a ball with one or both feet on the ground entirely outside the batter's box.

(b) He steps from one batter's box to the other while the pitcher is in position ready to pitch.

(c) He interferes with the catcher's fielding or throwing by stepping out of the batter's box or making any other movement that hinders the catcher's play at home base. Exception:

Batter is not out if any runner attempting to advance is put out, or if runner trying to score is called out for batter's interference.

(d) He uses or attempts to use a bat that, in the umpire's judgement, has been altered or tampered with in such a way to improve the distance factor or cause an unusual reaction on the baseball. This includes bats that are filled, flat-surfaced, nailed, hollowed, grooved or covered with a substance such as paraffin, wax, etc. No advancement on the bases will be allowed and any out or outs made during a play shall stand.

In addition to being called out, the player shall be ejected from the game and may be subject to additional penalties as determined by his league president.

6.07 Batting out of Turn

(a) A batter shall be called out, on appeal, when he fails to bat in his proper turn, and another batter completes a time at bat in his place.

(1) The proper batter may take his place in the batter's box at any time before the improper batter becomes a runner or is put out, and any balls and strikes shall be counted in the proper batter's time at bat.

(b) When an improper batter becomes a runner or is put out, and the defensive team appeals to the umpire before the first pitch to the next batter of either team, or before any play or attempted play, the umpire shall

(1) declare the proper batter out; and (2) nullify any advance or score made because of a ball batted by the improper batter or because of the improper batter's advance to first base on a hit, an error, a base on balls, a hit batter or otherwise.

Note: If a runner advances, while the improper batter is at bat, on a stolen base, balk, wild pitch or passed ball, such advance is legal.

(c) When an improper batter becomes a runner or is put out, and a pitch is made to the next batter of either team before an appeal is made, the improper batter thereby becomes the proper batter, and the results of his time at bat become legal.

(d) (1) When the proper batter is called out because he has failed to bat in turn, the next batter shall be the batter whose name follows that of the proper batter thus called out; (2) When an improper batter becomes a proper batter because no appeal is made before the next pitch, the next batter shall be the batter whose name follows that of such legalized improper batter. The instant an improper batter's actions are legalized, the batting order picks up with the name following that of the legalized improper batter.

6.08 The batter becomes a runner and is entitled to first base without liability to be put out (provided he advances to and touches first base) when:

(a) Four "balls" have been called by the umpire.

(b) He is touched by a pitched ball which he is not attempting to hit unless (1) The ball is in the strike zone when it touches the batter, or (2) The batter makes no attempt to avoid being touched by the ball.

If the ball is in the strike zone when it touches the batter, it shall be called a

strike, whether or not the batter tries to avoid the ball. If the ball is outside the strike zone when it touches the batter, it shall be called a ball if he makes no attempt to avoid being touched. Approved Ruling: When the batter is touched by a pitched ball which does not entitle him to first base, the ball is dead and no runner may advance.

(c) The catcher or any fielder interferes with him. If a play follows the interference, the manager of the offense may advise the plate umpire that he elects to decline the interference penalty and accept the play. Such election shall be made immediately at the end of the play. However, if the batter reaches first base on a hit, an error, a base on balls, a hit baseman, or otherwise, and all other runners advance at least one base, the play proceeds without reference to the interference.

(d) A fair ball touches an umpire or a runner on fair territory before touching a fielder. If a fair ball touches an umpire after having passed a fielder other than the pitcher, or having touched a fielder, including the pitcher, the ball is in play.

6.09 The batter becomes a runner when:

(a) He hits a fair ball.

(b) The third strike called by the umpire is not caught, providing (1) first base is unoccupied, or (2) first base is occupied with two out.

(c) A fair ball, after having passed a fielder other than the pitcher, or after having been touched by a fielder, including the pitcher, shall touch an umpire or runner on fair territory.

(d) A fair ball passes over a fence or into the stands at a distance from home base of 250 ft (76 m) or more. Such hit entitles the batter to a home run when he shall have touched all bases legally. A fair fly ball that passes out of the playing field at a point less than 250 ft (76 m) from home base shall entitle the batter to advance to second base only.

(e) A fair ball, after touching the ground, bounds into the stands, or passes through, over or under a fence, or through or under a scoreboard, or through or under shrubbery, or vines on the fence, in which case the batter and the runners shall be entitled to advance two bases.

(f) Any fair ball which, either before or after touching the ground, passes through or under a fence, or through or under a scoreboard, or through any opening in the fence or scoreboard, or through or under shrubbery, or vines on the fence, or which sticks in a fence or scoreboard, in which case the batter and the runners shall be entitled to two bases.

(g) Any bounding fair ball is deflected by the fielder into the stands, or over or under a

➡ *page 98*

Winning strike
A straight swing and a strong follow-through are needed to send the ball far into the outfield without sending it into the air (fly ball) and risking a catch.

Throwback
*For fielders in the outfield a good return
throw is vital. The fielder must be able
to make a strong accurate throw ahead
of the runners to stop them moving on.
Typically they will aim the ball for a
'cut off' man in the infield who will
target the base.*

continued from page 97

fence on fair or foul territory, in
which case the batter and all
runners shall be entitled to
advance two bases.

(h) Any fair fly ball is deflected
by the fielder into the stands, or
over the fence into foul territory,
in which case the batter shall be
entitled to advance to second
base; but if deflected into the
stands or over the fence in fair
territory, the batter shall be
entitled to a home run. However,
should such a fair fly be deflected
at a point less than 250 ft (76 m)
from home plate, the batter shall
be entitled to two bases only.
6.10 Any league may elect to use
the Designated Hitter Rule.

(a) In the event of inter-league
competition between clubs of
leagues using the Designated
Hitter Rule and clubs of the
leagues not using the Designated
Hitter Rule, the rule will be used
as follows:

1. In World Series or exhibition
games, the rule will be used or
not used as is the practice of the
home team.

2. In All-Star games, the rule
will only be used if both teams
and both Leagues so agree.

(b) The Rule provides as
follows:

A hitter may be designated to
bat for the starting pitcher and
all subsequent pitchers in any
game without otherwise affecting
the status of the pitcher(s) in the
game. A designated hitter for the
pitcher must be selected prior to
the game and must be included in
the line-up cards presented to the
umpire-in-chief. The designated
hitter named in the starting line-
up must come to bat at least one
time, unless the opposing club
changes pitchers. It is not
mandatory that a club designate
a hitter for the pitcher, but
failure to do so prior to the game
precludes the used of a
designated hitter for that game.
Pinch hitters for a designated
hitter may be used. Any
substitute hitter for a designated
hitter becomes the designated
hitter. A replaced designated
hitter shall not re-enter the game
in any capacity. The designated
hitter may be used defensively,
continuing to bat in the same
position in the batting order, but
the pitcher must then bat in the
place of the substituted defensive
player, unless more than one
substitution is made, and the
manager then must designate
their spots in the batting order. A
runner may be substituted for the
designated hitter and the runner

assumes the role of designated
hitter. A designated hitter may
not pinch run. A designated
hitter is 'locked' into the batting
order. No multiple substitutions
may be made that will alter the
batting rotation of the designated
hitter.

Once the game pitcher is
switched from the mound to a
defensive position this move shall
terminate the designated hitter
rule for the remainder of the
game. Once a pinch hitter bats
for any player in the batting order
and then enters the game to
pitch, this move shall terminate
the designated hitter role for the
remainder of the game. Once the
game pitcher bats for the
designated hitter this move shall
terminate the designated hitter
role for the remainder of the
game. (The game pitcher may
only pinch-hit for the designated
hitter.) Once a designated hitter
assumes a defensive position this
move shall terminate the
designated hitter role for the
remainder of the game. A
substitute for the designated
hitter need not be announced
until it is the designated hitter's
turn to bat.

7 The Runner.
7.01 A runner acquires the right

to an unoccupied base when he
touches it before he is out. He is
then entitled to it until he is put
out, or forced to vacate it for
another runner legally entitled to
that base.
7.02 In advancing, a runner shall
touch first, second, third and
home base in order. If forced to
return, he shall retouch all bases
in reverse order, unless the ball is
dead under any provision of Rule
5.09. In such cases, the runner
may go directly to his original
base.
7.03 Two runners may not occupy
a base, but if, while the ball is
alive, two runners are touching a
base, the following runner shall
be out when tagged. The
preceding runner is entitled to
the base.
7.04 Each runner, other than the
batter, may without liability to be
put out, advance one base when:

(a) There is a balk.

(b) The batter's advance
without liability to be put out
forces the runner to vacate his
base, or when the batter hits a
fair ball that touches another
runner or the umpire before such
ball has been touched by, or has
passed a fielder, if the runner is
forced to advance.

(c) A fielder, after catching a
fly ball, falls into a bench or

Run out
Most players are actually dismissed by being run out. Typically when a fielder throws the ball to a baseman so quickly that a runner forced to run is beaten.

Tagged out
Occasionally runners are put out when a fielder 'tags' (touches) him with the ball when he is running between bases.

stand, or falls across ropes into a crowd when spectators are on the field.

(d) While he is attempting to steal a base, the batter is interfered with by the catcher or any other fielder.

Note: When a runner is entitled to a base without liability to be put out, while the ball is in play, or under any rule in which the ball is in play after the runner reaches the base to which he is entitled, and the runner fails to touch the base to which he is entitled before attempting to advance to the next base, the runner shall forfeit his exemption from liability to be put out, and he may be put out by tagging the base or by tagging the runner before he returns to the missed base.

7.05 Each runner including the batter-runner may, without liability to be put out, advance:

(a) To home base, scoring a run, if a fair ball goes out of the playing field in flight and he touched all bases legally; or if a fair ball which, in the umpire's judgement, would have gone out of the playing field in flight, is deflected by the act of a fielder in throwing his glove, cap, or any article of his apparel.

(b) Three bases, if a fielder

deliberately touches a fair ball with his cap, mask or any part of his uniform detached from its proper place on his person. The ball is in play and the batter may advance to home base at his peril.

(c) Three bases, if a fielder deliberately throws his glove at and touches a fair ball. The ball is in play and the batter may advance to home base at his peril.

(d) Two bases, if a fielder deliberately touches a thrown ball with his cap, mask or any part of his uniform detached from its proper place on his person. The ball is in play.

(e) Two bases, if a fielder deliberately throw his glove at and touches a thrown ball. The ball is in play.

(f) Two bases, if a fair ball bounces or is deflected into the stands outside the first or third base foul lines; or if it goes through or under a field fence, or through or under a scoreboard, or through or under shrubbery or vines on the fence; or if it sticks in such fence, scoreboard, shrubbery or vines.

(g) Two bases when, with no spectators on the playing field, a thrown ball goes into the stands, or into a bench (whether or not the ball rebounds into the field), or over or under or through a

field fence or on a slanting part of the screen above the backstop, or remains in the meshes of a wire screen protecting spectators. The ball is dead. When such wild throw is the first play by an infielder, the umpire, in awarding such bases, shall be governed by the position of the runners at the time the ball was pitched; in all other cases the umpire shall be governed by the position of the runners at the time the wild throw was made.

Approved Ruling: If all runners, including the batter-runner, have advanced at least one base when an infielder makes a wild throw on the first play after the pitch, the award shall be governed by the position of the runners when the wild throw was made.

(h) One base, if a ball, pitched to the batter, or thrown by the pitcher from his position on the pitcher's plate to a base to catch a runner, goes into a stand or a bench, or over or through a field fence or backstop. The ball is dead;

Approved Ruling: When a wild pitch or passed ball goes through or by the catcher, or deflects off the catcher, and goes directly into the dugout, stands, above the break, or any area where the ball

is dead, the awarding of bases shall be one base. One base shall also be awarded if the pitcher while in contact with the rubber, throws to a base, and the throw goes directly into the stands or into any area where the ball is dead.

If, however, the pitched or thrown ball goes through or by the catcher or through the fielder, and remains on the playing field, and is subsequently kicked or deflected into the dugout, stands or other area where the ball is dead, the awarding of bases shall be two bases from position of runners at the time of the pitch or throw.

(i) One base, if the batter becomes a runner on Ball Four or Strike Three, when the pitch passes the catcher and lodges in the umpire's mask or paraphernalia. If the batter becomes a runner on a wild pitch which entitles the runners to advance one base, the batter-runner shall be entitled to first base only.

7.06 When obstruction occurs, the umpire shall call or signal "Obstruction".

(a) If a play is being made on the obstructed runner, or if the

➡ *page 100*

continued from page 99

batter-runner is obstructed before he touches first base, the ball is dead and all runners shall advance, without liability to be put out, to the bases they would have reached, in the umpire's judgement, if there had been no obstruction. The obstructed runner shall be awarded at least one base beyond the base he has last legally touched before the obstruction. Any preceding runners, forced to advance by the award of bases as the penalty for obstruction, shall advance without liability to be put out.

(b) If no play is being made on the obstructed runner, the play shall proceed until no further action is possible. The umpire shall then call "Time" and impose such penalties, if any, as in his judgement will nullify the act of obstruction.

7.07 If, with a runner on third base and trying to score by means of a squeeze play or a steal, the catcher or any other fielder steps on, or in front of home base without possession of the ball, or touches the batter or his bat, the pitcher shall be charged with a balk, the batter shall be awarded first base on the interference and the ball is dead.

7.08 Any runner is out when:

(a) (1) He runs more than 3 ft (0.9 m) away from a direct line between bases to avoid being tagged unless his action is to avoid interference with a fielder fielding a batted ball; or (2) after touching first base, he leaves the baseline, obviously abandoning his effort to touch the next base. Approved Ruling: When a batter becomes a runner on third strike not caught, and starts for his bench or position, he may advance to first base at any time before he enters the bench. To put him out, the defense must tag him or first base before he touches first base.

(b) He intentionally interferes with a thrown ball; or hinders a fielder attempting to make a play on a batted ball.

(c) He is tagged, when the ball is alive, while off his base. Exception: A batter-runner cannot be tagged out after overrunning or oversliding first base if he returns immediately to the base.

Approved Ruling: (1) If the impact of a runner breaks a base loose from its position, no play can be made on that runner at that base if he had reached the base safely.

Approved Ruling: (2) If a base is dislodged from its position during a play, any following runner on the same play shall be considered as touching or occupying the base if, in the umpire's judgement, he touches or occupies the point marked by the dislodged bag.

(d) He fails to retouch his base after a fair or foul ball is legally caught before he, or his base, is tagged by a fielder. He shall not be called out for failure to retouch his base after the first following pitch, or any play or attempted play. This is an appeal play.

(e) He fails to reach the next base before a fielder tags him or the base, after he has been forced to advance by reason of the batter becoming a runner. However, if a following runner is put out on a force play, the force is removed and the runner must be tagged to be put out. The force is removed as soon as the runner touches the base to which he is forced to advance, and if he overslides or overruns the base, the runner must be tagged to be put out. However, if the forced runner, after touching the next base, retreats for any reason towards the base he has ;just occupied, the force play is reinstated, and he can again be put out if the defense tags the base to which he is forced.

(f) He is touched by a fair ball in fair territory before the ball has touched or passed an infielder. The ball is dead and no runner may score, nor runners advance, except runners forced to advance. Exception: If a runner is touching his base when touched by an infield fly, he is not out although the batter is out. If runner is touched by an infield fly when he is not touching his base, both runner and batter are out.

(g) He attempts to score on a play in which the batter interferes with the play at home base before two are out. With two out, the interference puts the batter out and no score counts.

(h) He passes a preceding runner before such runner is out.

(i) After he has acquired legal possession of a base, he runs the bases in reverse order for the purpose of confusing the defense or making a travesty of the game. The umpire shall immediately call "Time" and declare the runner out.

(j) He fails to return at once to first base after overrunning or oversliding that base. If he attempts to run to second he is

out when tagged. If, after overrunning or oversliding first base he starts toward the dugout, or toward his position, and fails to return to first base at once, he is out, on appeal, when he or the base is tagged.

(k) In running or sliding for home base, he fails to touch home base and makes no attempt to return to the base, when a fielder holds the ball in his hand, while touching home base, and appeals to the umpire for the decision.

7.09 It is interference by a batter or a runner when:

(a) After a third strike he hinders the catcher in his attempt to field the ball.

(b) After hitting or bunting a fair ball, his bat hits the ball a second time in fair territory. The ball is dead and no runners may advance. If the batter-runner drops his bat and the ball rolls against the bat in fair territory and, in the umpire's judgement, there was no intention to interfere with the course of the ball, the ball is alive and in play.

(c) He intentionally deflects the course of a foul ball in any manner.

(d) Before two are out and a runner on third base, the batter hinders a fielder in making a play at home base; the runner is out.

(e) Any member or members of the offensive team stand or gather around any base to which a runner is advancing, to confuse, hinder or add to the difficulty of the fielders. Such runner shall be declared out for the interference of his team-mate or team-mates;

(f) Any batter or runner who has just been put out hinders or impedes any following play being made on a runner. Such runner shall be declared out for the interference of his team-mate.

(g) If, in the judgement of the umpire, a base runner wilfully and deliberately interferes with a batted ball or a fielder in the act of fielding a batted ball with the obvious intent to break up a double play, the ball is dead. The umpire shall call the runner out for interference and also call out the batter-runner because of the action of his team-mate. In no event may bases be run or runs scored because of such action by a runner.

(h) If, in the judgement of the umpire, a batter-runner wilfully and deliberately interferes with a batted ball or a fielder in the act of fielding a batted ball, with the obvious intent to break up a double play, the ball is dead; the

umpire shall call the batter-runner out for interference and shall also call out the runner who had advanced closest to the home plate regardless where the double play might have been possible. In no event shall bases be run because of such interference.

(i) In the judgement of the umpire, the base coach at third base, or first base, by touching or holding the runner, physically assists him in returning to or leaving third base or first base.

(j) With a runner on third base, the base coach leaves his box and acts in any manner to draw a throw by a fielder.

(k) In running the last half of the distance from home base to first base while the ball is being fielded to first base, he runs outside (to the right of) the 3-ft line, or inside (to the left of) the foul line and, in the umpire's judgement, interferes with the fielder taking the throw at first base, or attempting to field a batted ball.

(l) He fails to avoid a fielder who is attempting to field a batted ball, or intentionally interferes with a thrown ball, provided that if two or more fielders attempt to field a batted ball, and the runner comes in contact with line or more of them, the umpire shall determine which fielder is entitled to the benefit of this rule, and shall not declare the runner out for coming in contact with a fielder other than the one the umpire determines to be entitled to field such a ball.

(m) A fair ball touches him on fair territory before touching a fielder. If a fair ball goes through, or by, an infielder, and touches a runner immediately back of him, or touches the runner after having been deflected by a fielder, the umpire shall not declare the runner out for being touched by a batted ball. In making such decision the umpire must be convinced that the ball passed through, or by, the fielder, and that no other infielder had the chance to make a play on the ball. If, in the judgement of the umpire, the runner deliberately and intentionally kicks such a batted ball on which the infielder has missed a play, then the runner shall be called out of interference.

Penalty for Interference: The runner is out and the ball is dead.

7.10 Any runner shall be called out, on appeal, when:

(a) After a fly ball is caught, he

fails to retouch his original base before he or his original base is tagged.

(b) With the ball in play, while advancing or returning to a base, he fails to touch each base in order before he, or a missed base, is tagged.

Approved Ruling: (1) No runner may return to touch a missed base after a following runner has scored. (2) When the ball is dead, no runner may return to touch a missed base or one he has left after he has advanced to and touched a base beyond the missed base.

(c) He overruns or overslides first base and fails to return to the base immediately, and he or the base is tagged.

(d) He fails to touch home base and makes no attempt to return to that base, and home base is tagged.

Any appeal under this rule must be made before the next pitch, or any play or attempted play, If the violation occurs during a play which ends a half-inning, the appeal must be made before the defensive team leaves the field. An appeal is not to be interpreted as a play or attempted play. Successive appeals may not be made on a runner at the same base. If the defensive team on its first appeal errs, a request for a second appeal on the same runner at the same base shall not be allowed by the umpire. (Intended meaning of the word 'err' is that the defensive team in making an appeal threw the ball out of play. For example, if the pitcher threw to first base to appeal and threw the ball into the stands, no second appeal would be allowed.) Appeal plays may require an umpire to recognize an apparent 'fourth out'. If the third out is made during a play in which an appeal play is sustained on another runner, the appeal play decision takes precedence in determining the out. If there is more than one appeal during a play that ends a half-inning, the defense may elect to take the out that gives it the advantage. For the purpose of this rule, the defensive team has 'left the field' when the pitcher

and all infielders have left fair territory on their way to the bench or clubhouse.

7.11 The players, coaches or any member of an offensive team shall vacate any space (including both dugouts) needed by a fielder who is attempting to field a batted or thrown ball. Penalty: Interference shall be called and the batter or runner on whom the play is being made shall be declared out.

7.12 Unless two are out, the status of a following runner is not affected by a preceding runner's failure to touch or retouch a base. If, upon appeal, the preceding runner is third out, no runners following him shall score. If such third out is the result of a force play, neither preceding nor following runners shall score.

interruption or alteration. He shall not raise either foot from the ground, except that in his actual delivery of the ball to the batter, he may take one step backward, and one step forward with his free foot. When a pitcher holds the ball with both hands in front of his body, with his entire pivot foot on, or in front of and touching but not off the end of the pitcher's plate, and his other foot free, he will be considered in the wind-up position.

(b) The Set Position. Set position shall be indicated by the pitcher when he stands facing the batter with his entire pivot foot on, or in front of, and in contact with, and not off the end of the pitcher's plate, and his other foot in front of the pitcher's

8 The Pitcher
8.01 Legal pitching delivery. There are two legal pitching positions, the wind-up position and the set position, and either position may be used at any time. Pitchers shall take signs from the catcher while standing on the rubber.

(a) The Wind-up Position. The pitcher shall stand facing the batter, his entire pivot foot on, or in front of and touching and not off the end of the pitcher's plate, and the other foot free. From this position any natural movement associated with his delivery of the ball to the batter commits him to the pitch without

Outfield throw

plate, holding the ball in both hands in front of his body and coming to a complete stop. From such set position he may deliver the ball to the batter, throw to a base or step backward off the pitcher's plate with his pivot foot. Before assuming set position, the pitcher may elect to make any natural preliminary motion such as that known as 'the stretch'. But if he so elects, he shall come to set position before delivering the ball to the batter. After assuming set position, any natural motion associated with his delivery of the ball to the

batter commits him to the pitch without alteration or interruption.

Preparatory to coming to a set position, the pitcher shall have one hand on his side; from this position he shall go to his set position as defined in Rule 8.01 (b) without interruption and in one continuous motion. The whole width of the foot in contact with the rubber must be on the rubber. A pitcher cannot pitch from off the end of the rubber with just the side of his foot touching the rubber. The pitcher, following his stretch, must (a) hold the ball in both hands in front of his body and (b) come to a complete stop. This must be enforced. Umpires should watch this closely. Pitchers are constantly attempting to 'beat the rule' in their efforts to hold runners on bases and in cases where the pitcher fails to make a complete 'stop' called for in the rules, the umpire should immediately call a "Balk".

(c) At any time during the pitcher's preliminary movements and until his natural pitching motion commits him to the pitch, he may throw to any base provided he steps directly toward such base before making the throw.

(d) If the pitcher makes an illegal pitch with the bases unoccupied, it shall be called a ball unless the batter reaches first base on a hit, an error, a base on balls, a hit batter or otherwise.

(e) If the pitcher removes his pivot foot from contact with the pitcher's plate by stepping backward with that foot, he thereby becomes an infielder and if he makes a wild throw from that position, it shall be considered the same as a wild throw by any other infielder.

8.02 The pitcher shall not:
(a) (1) Bring his pitching hand in contact with his mouth or lips while in the 18 ft circle surrounding the pitching rubber. Exception: Provided it is agreed

➡ *page 102*

continued from page 101

to by both managers, the umpire prior to the start of a game played in cold weather, may permit the pitcher to blow on his hand.

Penalty: For violation of this part of this rule the umpires shall immediately call a ball. However, if the pitch is made and a batter reaches first base on a hit, an error, a hit batsman or otherwise, and no runner is put out before advancing at least one base, the play shall proceed without reference to the violation. Repeated offenders shall be subject to a fine by the league president.

(2) Apply a foreign substance of any kind to the ball;

(3) expectorate on the ball, either hand or his glove;

(4) rub the ball on his glove, person or clothing;

(5) deface the ball in any manner;

(6) deliver what is called the 'shine' ball, 'spit' ball, 'mud' ball or 'emery' ball. The pitcher, of course, is allowed to rub the ball between his bare hands.

Penalty: For violation of any part of this rule 8.02(a) (2 to 6) the umpire shall:

(a) Call the pitch a ball, warn the pitcher and have announced on the public address system the reason for the action.

(b) In the case of a second offense by the same pitcher in the same game, the pitcher shall be disqualified from the game.

(c) If a play follows the violation called by the umpire, the manager of the offense may advise the plate umpire that he elects to accept the play. Such election shall be made immediately at the end of the play. However, if the batter reaches first base on a hit, an error, a base on balls, a hit batsman, or otherwise, and no other runner is put out before advancing at least one base, the play shall proceed without reference to the violation.

(d) Even though the offense elects to take the play, the violation shall be recognized and the penalties in (a) and (b) will still be in effect.

(e) The umpire shall be the sole judge on whether any portion of this rule has been violated.

(b) Have on his person, or in his possession, any foreign substance. For such infraction of this section (b) the penalty shall be immediate ejection from the game.

(c) Intentionally delay the game by throwing the ball to players other than the catcher, when the batter is in position, except in an attempt to retire a runner.

Penalty: If, after warning by the umpire, such delaying action is repeated, the pitcher shall be removed from the game.

(d) Intentionally pitch at the batter.

If, in the umpire's judgement, such a violation occurs, the umpire may elect either to:

1. Expel the pitcher, or the manager and the pitcher, from the game, or

2. may warn the pitcher and the manager of both teams that

Landslide
All good base runners can finish their run to the base with a slide which lands them on the base.

another such pitch will result in the immediate expulsion of that pitcher (or a replacement) and the manager.

If, in the umpire's judgement, circumstances warrant, both teams may be officially 'warned' prior to the game or at any time during the game.

8.03 When a pitcher takes his position at the beginning of each inning, or when he relieves another pitcher, he shall be permitted to pitch not to exceed eight preparatory pitches to his catcher during which play shall be suspended. A league by its own action may limit the number of preparatory pitches to less than eight preparatory pitches. Such preparatory pitches shall not consume more than one minute of time. If a sudden emergency causes a pitcher to be summoned into the game without any opportunity to warm up, the umpire-in-chief shall allow him as many pitches as the umpire deems necessary.

8.04 When the bases are unoccupied, the pitcher shall deliver the ball to the batter within 20 seconds after he receives the ball. Each time the pitcher delays the game by violating this rule, the umpire shall call "Ball". The intent of this

rule is to avoid unnecessary delays. The umpire shall insist that the catcher return the ball promptly to the pitcher, and that the pitcher take his position on the rubber promptly. Obvious delay by the pitcher should instantly be penalized by the umpire.

8.05 If there is a runner, or runners, it is a balk when:

(a) The pitcher, while touching his plate, makes any motion naturally associated with his pitch and fails to make such delivery.

(b) The pitcher, while touching his plate, feints a throw to first base and fails to complete the throw.

(c) The pitcher, while touching his plate, fails to step directly toward a base before throwing to that base.

(d) The pitcher, while touching his plate, throws, or feints a throw to an unoccupied base, except for the purpose of making a play.

(e) The pitcher makes an illegal pitch.

(f) The pitcher delivers the ball to the batter while he is not facing the batter.

(g) The pitcher makes any motion naturally associated with his pitch while he is not touching the pitcher's plate.

(h) The pitcher unnecessarily delays the game.

(i) The pitcher, without having the ball, stands on or astride the pitcher's plate or while off the plate, he feints a pitch.

(j) The pitcher, after coming to a legal pitching position, removes one hand from the ball other than in an actual pitch, or in throwing to a base.

(k) The pitcher, while touching his plate, accidentally or intentionally drops the ball.

(l) The pitcher, while giving an intentional base on balls, pitches when the catcher is not in the catcher's box.

(m) The pitcher delivers the

pitch from set position without coming to a stop.

Penalty: The ball is dead, and each runner shall advance one base without liability to be put out, unless the batter reaches first on a hit, an error, a base on balls, a hit batter, or otherwise, and all other runners advance at least one base, in which case the play proceeds without reference to the balk.

Approved Ruling: In cases where a pitcher balks and throws wild, either to a base or to a home plate, a runner or runners may advance beyond the base to which he is entitled at his own risk.

Approved Ruling: A runner who misses the first base to which he is advancing and who is called out on appeal shall be considered as having advanced one base for the purpose of this rule.

8.06 A professional league shall adopt the following rule pertaining to the visit of the manager or coach to the pitcher:

(a) This rule limits the number of trips a manager of coach may make to any one pitcher in any one inning.

(b) A second trip to the same pitcher in the same inning will cause this pitcher's automatic removal.

(c) The manager or coach is prohibited from making a second visit to the mound while the same batter is at bat, but

(d) if a pinch-hitter is substituted for this batter, the manager or coach may make a second visit to the mound, but must remove the pitcher. A manager or coach is considered to have concluded his visit to the mound when he leaves the 18-ft circle surrounding the pitcher's rubber.

9 The Umpire

10.00 The Official Scorer

The Official Major League Baseball Rules are copyrighted works owned by the Office of the Commissioner of Baseball and are used with permission of Major League Baseball Properties, Inc.

A copy of the complete rules, including various explanations to the rules, as well as the rules of scoring, is available from the League.

Softball
Essentials

Originally established as an indoor version of baseball, softball featured at the Olympic Games for the first time in 1996. Softball is played on a smaller pitch than baseball and pitching is underarm. However there are two versions – fast pitch, in which the pitcher winds up to pitch the ball hard and fast, and slow pitch. Here the focus is on the fast pitch game.

Fence

3rd base

See distance table on pg104

See distance table on pg104

Pitcher's plate

2nd base

Batter's box

Home plate

same length as the diamond

16 ft

Home plate

Pitching distance See distance table on pg104

1st base

Back to basics
Softball may be played on a properly marked out pitch, but more often than not it is played on any open grass area with just four bases and the pitcher's plate marked out.

Softball team
The fielding positons in softball are given names, but only pitchers and catchers have to stand in their prescribed positions when fieldng.

The field
Bases are 60 ft (approx 18 m) apart and the outfield fences are set at a radius of 225 ft (68 m) (men) or 200 ft (61 m) (women) from the home plate. The pitching distance from the pitching rubber to the home plate is 46 ft (14 m) (men) or 40 ft (12 m) (women). A pitching circle of radius 8 ft (2.4 m).

Casual dress
In the slow pitch game popular with amateurs almost anything goes as regards dress.

The bat
Generally made of aluminium alloy (although metal, bamboo, fibreglass or other International Softball Federation approved materials may be used). No longer than 34 in (86 cm) and weighing no more than 38 oz ((approx 1 kg). A safety grip is required on softball bats due to the short distances and the closeness of the infielders.

The ball
White, spherical. A circumference of 12 in (30 cm) and a weight of 6 1/4–7 oz (approx 184 g). The ball must be of flat seam style with no less than 88 stitches in each cover.

Players

Nine players per team.
The positions are:
pitcher (F1)
catcher (F2)
first baseman (F3)
second baseman (F4)
third baseman (F5)
shortstop (F6)
left fielder (F7)
center fielder (F8)
right fielder (F9).

Strong arm
Fielders have to be agile and fast: able to catch and throw the ball quickly and accurately back to the baseman.

Base to base
A player may begin to run between the bases as soon as the ball leaves the pitcher's hand and may continue to run as long as the ball is in play.

Dress

Uniform in colour and style throughout a team. All catchers must wear a mask, throat protector, helmet, body protector and shin-guards. All offensive players must wear helmets while batting and baserunning. Shoes may feature soft or hard rubber cleats. Spikes on the sole or heel must not exceed ³/₄ in (1.9 cm).

Officials

A plate umpire (who stands behind the catcher to judge balls and strikes) and a base umpire (to judge base decisions).

HOW TO PLAY

Each team takes it in turns to bat and field. The batting side sends one of its players to strike at the ball and then run around to each of the bases and back to the home plate in order to score runs. The fielding side must put out three of the batters in order to bring the innings to a close and become the batting side themselves.

Starting

Teams toss a coin to decide who will bat first.

How to win

One run is scored each time a runner gets back to the home plate after touching the first, second and third bases in turn. Players run around this circuit in the order in which they batted and the team with the most runs at the end of the game wins.

Distance table

Game	Division	Bases	Pitching	Fences
Adult				
Fast pitch	Female	60 ft (18.29 m)	40 ft (12.2m)	200 ft (60.96 m)
	male	60 ft (18.29 m)	46 ft (14.0 m)	225 ft (68.58m) – 250 ft (76.20 m)
Modified	Female	60 ft (18.29 m)	40 ft (12.2m)	200 ft (60.96 m)
	male	60 ft (18.29 m)	46 ft (14.0 m)	265 ft (80.80 m)
Slow pitch	Female	65 ft (19.81 m)	46 ft (14.0 m)	250 ft (76.20 m)
	Male	65 ft (19.81 m)	46 ft (14.0 m)	275 ft (83.82 m)
	Co-ed	65 ft (19.81 m)	46 ft (14.0 m)	275 ft (83.82 m)
	Super	65 ft (19.81 m)	46 ft (14.0 m)	300 ft (91.44 m m)
Youth				
Fast pitch	Girls under 10	55 ft (16.76 m)	35 ft (10.67 m)	150 ft (45.72 m) – 175 ft (53.34 m)
	Boys under 10	55 ft (16.76 m)	35 ft (10.67 m)	150 ft (45.72 m) – 175 ft (53.34 m)
	Girls under 12	60 ft (18.29 m)	35 ft (10.67 m)	175 ft (53.34 m) – 200 ft (60.96 m)
	Boys under 12	60 ft (18.29 m)	40 ft (12.2 m)	175 ft (53.34 m) – 200 ft (60.96 m)
	Girls under 15	60 ft (18.29 m)	40 ft (12.2 m)	175 ft (53.34 m) – 200 ft (60.96 m)
	Boys under 15	60 ft (18.29 m)	46 ft (14.0 m)	175 ft (53.34 m) – 200 ft (60.96 m)
	Girls under 19	60 ft (18.29 m)	40 ft (12.2 m)	200 ft (60.96 m) – 225 ft (68.58m)
	Boys under 19	60 ft (18.29 m)	46 ft (14.0 m)	200 ft (60.96 m) – 225 ft (68.58m)
Fast pitch	Girls under 10	55 ft (16.76 m)	35 ft (10.67 m)	150 ft (45.72 m) – 175 ft (53.34 m)
	Boys under 10	55 ft (16.76 m)	35 ft (10.67 m)	150 ft (45.72 m) – 175 ft (53.34 m)
	Girls under 12	60 ft (18.29 m)	40 ft (12.2 m)	175 ft (53.34 m) – 200 ft (60.96 m)
	Boys under 12	60 ft (18.29 m)	40 ft (12.2 m)	175 ft (53.34 m) – 200 ft (60.96 m)
	Girls under 15	65 ft (19.81 m)	46 ft (14.0 m)	225 ft (68.58m) – 250 ft (76.20 m)
	Boys under 15	60 ft (18.29 m)	46 ft (14.0 m)	250 ft (76.20 m) – 275 ft (83.82 m)
	Girls under 19	65 ft (19.81 m)	46 ft (14.0 m)	225 ft (68.58m) – 250 ft (76.20 m)
	Boys under 19	65 ft (19.81 m)	46 ft (14.0 m)	275 ft (83.82 m) – 300 ft (91.44 m m)

KEY RULES

• A game consists of seven innings.

• The *pitcher's delivery* is made underarm and must begin with both feet in contact with the pitching rubber and the ball held with both hands in front of the body. The pitch itself begins when one hand is taken off the ball.

A pivot foot is used to maintain contact with the rubber or to push off from it. For a delivery to be legal, the ball must be pitched into the strike zone. This is the space over any part of the home plate, no higher than the batter's arm pit and no lower than his knee when he assumes his natural batting stance. If the ball deviates from the strike zone it is a no-ball (called a 'ball').

• A *batter* has three chances to strike the ball. He becomes a 'batter-runner' as soon as he hits a *fair ball* – a legally batted ball. The ball must keep within the angle between first and third base (*fair territory*). It may pass out of the playing field and up to the outfield fence as long as it remains within this angle. The batter may also run after four balls.

• The other *runners* in the field may advance to their next base as soon as the ball leaves the pitcher's hand and while it continues to be in play. They must return to the base they legally occupied at the time the ball was pitched if the ball is caught, if it is batted illegally or if interference occurs on either side.

• There are several ways in which a *batter* can be *out*. He is caught out if a fielder catches the ball after it has been struck and before it touches the ground (a *'fly ball'*). He is run out if the ball reaches the base he is running towards before he gets there. (The fielder receiving the ball must have at least one foot on the base.)

A *strike* occurs when the ball is pitched into the strike zone but the batter does not attempt to hit it or does make the attempt and misses. A player is allowed three strikes, after which he is out. He is also out if he is touched with the ball before he touches first base, or, while off any base during a live ball, he is touched with the ball.

• *Runners* are declared *out* if they are touched with the ball in the hand of a fielder while they are not in contact with a base, if they deviate too much from the direct line between bases in order to avoid being touched by a fielder in possession of the ball, if they overtake the runner in front of them, if they are hit by a fair ball or if the ball reaches the fielder at the base ahead of them before they do, i.e. run out. A *'force out'* occurs when a runner is forced to advance due to the batter becoming a runner.

• Violations by a player – any form of unsportsmanlike conduct – are penalized with removal of the offender from the game.

SKILLS

The main skills in softball are throwing, catching and batting.

Fielders have to be very good at catching a hard, fast moving ball with their gloved hand and transferring it quickly to their throwing arm. They also have to be strong, accurate throwers to throw it back precisely to the baseman who has to catch the ball without leaving his base.

Pitchers: the underarm throw typically used by the pitcher in softball looks easy but it is surprisingly difficult to pitch fast and accurate in this style, so good pitchers are highly valued. A good fast pitch pitcher can throw a 'rise ball', a 'drop', a 'curve ball', a 'change-up' and a straight fast ball. The use of these various type pitches makes it more difficult for the batter to hit the ball.

Slow pitch softball
This popular recreational game requires an underhand delivery with an arc of between six and 12 ft. There are four outfielders rather than the three for fast pitch, the bases are 65 ft apart and pitching for men and women is at 50 ft. Scores are much higher in slow pitch as it is considered a hitter's game, whereas the fast pitch game tends to be pitcher controlled.

Batters: hitting a softball well is more about timing than strength. Good batting is not only belting the ball far into the outfield for a home run, but also about making short but highly controlled shots to gain a few vital bases.

Free hand
Despite its name, the ball in softball is very far from soft and a glove is almost essential hand protection for anyone fielding. A right-handed fielder wears a glove on her left hand for catching so that her right hand is free for returning the ball.

Rounders
Essentials

This game was one of the origins of baseball. Simple to understand and organize, it is popular with teams of both sexes and all ages.

The pitch

May be grass, gravel, asphalt or any surface suitable for running on, although mixed surfaces are not permitted. Marked out with four vertical posts, 1.2 m (4 ft) high and supported in bases heavy enough to keep them upright in wind.

2nd post

1.2 m

3rd post

Bowling square

12 m

2.5 m

1st post

4th post

2 m

Batting square

Pipped at the post
Unlike baseball, in which bases are flat, rounders players run between posts with heavy rubber bases.

Family game
Rounders can be played with just a bat and ball and as few as six players on either team.

46 cm (18 in)

The bat

Round, made of wood, aluminium or plastic. Ideally one for each member of the batting team. No more than 46 cm (18 in) in length. It must not measure more than 17 cm (6½ in) round its thickest part.

The ball

Leather, with a weight of 70–85 g (2½–3 oz) and a circumference of 18–20 cm (7–8 in). Only white N.R.A.-approved balls are used for matches.

The players

Two teams with a minimum of six and a maximum of 15 players each, although there may be no more than nine in the field at a time. No more than five male players are allowed in mixed teams.

Dress

All players must be clearly numbered. Spiked footwear is prohibited, although studs 30 mm (1¼ in) in circumference at the base, 12 mm (½ in) maximum length) are allowed.

Officials

Two umpires.

HOW TO PLAY

One team is the batting side, the other fields. Players from the batting side take it in turns to hit the ball, then run round the track to the fourth post – in one go or in stages during their 'live' go – to score 'rounders'. The fielding side attempts to get as many batters out as possible.

Starting

The captain winning the toss has the choice of innings. The fielding team positions itself across the pitch, while the batting players wait in the backward area for their turn to bat. The first batter takes up position in the batting square to meet the ball of the first bowler.

How to win

If a batter hits the ball successfully and manages to touch the fourth post, one *rounder* is scored. A *half rounder* is scored by completing the track in the same way, but without hitting the ball. A *penalty half* rounder is scored if the bowler delivers two consecutive no-balls to a batter, or if a fielder obstructs a batter. *See Rule 7, Scoring (page 109)*.

The team with the most rounders wins.

KEY RULES

A match consists of two innings. A team which is five or more rounders behind after the first innings bats again and, if it fails to exceed the other team's total after its second innings, the game is declared over.

• Each batter is entitled to one good ball only (three for the last remaining batter). Having hit the ball, attempted to hit it or let it pass, the batter must run to at least the first post, carrying the bat. Only one batter can stay at a post at a time, so if one batter needs to run to the next post, the batter in front must also run forwards. *See Rule 4, Batting (page 108)*.

• A *'no-ball'* occurs when a ball is higher than the batter's head or lower than the batter's knee, is wide on the hitting side of the batter, is aimed at the batter's body , is aimed at the non-hitting side of the batter, is not

delivered with a smooth and continuous action or if the bowler does not have both feet within the bowling square until the ball is released. *See Rule 5, Bowling (page 109)*.

• Batters have right of way when running round the track. If obstruction does occur, a half rounder is awarded to the batting team. Likewise, a batter must not obstruct a fielder by deviating from the track. The penalty is a half rounder to the fielding side. *See Rule 4b, Obstruction–*

Batting Side (page 108), and Rule 6c, Fielding Side Obstruction (page 109).

• A batter is out if he fails to keep both feet within the batting square until the ball has been hit or passed, if a fielder touches the post ahead of him with the ball (or hand holding the ball) or if he runs to the inside of a post. *See Rule 4c, Batter Out (page 108)*.

Running out
A batter is run out if a fielder touches a post, towards which the batter is running, with the ball or with the hand holding the ball, before the batter can touch it. A really quick post fielder may be able to run out the batter running towards her post, then throw it on to another post fielder to run out a second batter.

SKILLS

Batters need a good sense of timing and coordination. They must be able to strike a ball with one fluid movement, sending it deep into the field, allowing time to complete the track. Good *bowlers* are adept at using speed and spin to make an otherwise straightforward, underarm delivery difficult to hit. *Fielders* must be quick, accurate and constantly aware of the state of play.

ROUNDERS THE RULES
• • • • • • • •

Rule 1 Equipment
See page 106.

Rule 2 The Pitch
See The pitch (page 106).

Rule 3 The Game
See How to play (page 107).

Rule 4 Batting

(A) A Batter

(a) whilst waiting for his/her turn to bat shall be in the backward area, well away from the fourth post and batting square.

(b) shall stand with both feet within the batting square and shall not cross the front or back line of the square during hitting, or in the course of attempting to hit a good ball or until the ball has passed him/her.

NB This does not prevent a batter from leaving the batting square whilst the fielding side adjust its fielding positions, or during a break in play.

(c) shall have only one good ball bowled to him/her and shall also be deemed to have hit the ball if s/he strikes the ball with the bat or the hand holding the bat.

(d) must run to first post after having hit, attempted to hit, or let pass the first good ball delivered by the bowler.

(e) who hits a ball so that it pitches in the backward area shall have made a 'backward hit' (this does not refer to balls that drop in the forward area and afterwards go behind).

(f) may, at his/her own discretion, take a 'No-Ball' and score in the usual way; s/he shall have been considered to have taken the ball if s/he has come within reach of, made contact with or passed first post.

(g) shall be entitled, if s/he is the only batter left in on entering the square:

(i) to have the option of 3 good balls but shall forfeit the right to any remaining balls if s/he is caught or takes the ball. (S/he shall be considered to have taken the ball if s/he has come within reach of, made contact with or passed the first post). S/he can be put out in any of the usual ways or when the ball has been thrown full pitch or placed in the batting square.

(ii) to a rest of one minute after each rounder s/he may score.

(B) Obstruction–Batting Side

(a) While waiting to bat or after being given out, shall stand behind the marked line in the backward area out of the way of the backstop and fourth post fielders.

Penalty: The umpire shall award a half rounder to the fielding side in the event of obstruction.

(b) A batter shall be considered to have obstructed if s/he:

(i) impedes the player who is fielding the ball by deviating from the running track;

(ii) intentionally deflects the course of the ball;

(iii) verbally misleads the other team.

Penalty: The umpire shall declare the batter out and any rounder scored due to the obstruction shall be declared void.

(c) Whilst running round the track within the rules, a batter shall have right of way.

(d) A non-striking batter causing an obstruction and a rounder being scored by the striking batter on his ball, the rounder would be declared void, but the striking batter would remain in. (The obstructing batter would be declared out.)

(C) Batter Out

A batter shall be declared out:

(i) if the ball be caught from bat or hand holding the bat except on a no-ball.

(ii) if his/her foot projects over the front or back line of the batting square before s/he has hit the ball or it has passed him/her, except on a no-ball.

(iii) if s/he runs to the inside of a post, unless prevented from reaching it by an obstructing fielder.

(iv) if a fielder touches the post immediately ahead with the ball or the hand holding the ball while the batter is running to the post and before the batter has touched the post, except for first post in the case of a no-ball.

NB If any post and/or base(s) should be moved either accidentally or deliberately from the correct position(s):

(a) if any part of the base is in contact with the base spot then contact should be made with the base.

(b) if both the post and the base are moved out of position then contact should be made with the ground marking indicating the correct position of the posts(s).

(v) if s/he obstructs a fielder or intentionally deflects the course of the ball.

(vi) if s/he overtakes another batter.

(vii) if s/he loses contact or runs at any time when the bowler has the ball and is in his/her square (except an overrun or unless ordered to do so by an umpire).

(viii) if s/he loses contact with the post during the bowler's action but before s/he releases the ball.

(ix) if after having been ordered to make contact with a post a batter has not done so.

(x) if s/he drops or throws his/her bat deliberately.

(D) Side Out

(a) Where there is no batter awaiting his/her turn to bat, all the batters on the running track can be put out simultaneously, by the ball being thrown full pitch or placed by any fielder into the batting square before any batter has reached and touched fourth post.

(b) Where there is no batter waiting his/her turn to bat and the bowler has possession of the ball in the bowling square so that no batter can leave a post the side shall be declared out.

(E) Procedure of Game

Whilst waiting at a post a member of the batting team shall have the advantage of running on if a no-ball is bowled and not taken by the batter. S/he can, at his/her discretion, continue to run round the track in the normal way.

Similarly a batter need not run for every ball bowled unless the next batter immediately behind him/her is obliged to run. More than one batter may be put out between the delivery of consecutive balls.

(F) Running Round the Track

A batter:

(a) shall run round the track carrying his/her bat in an attempt to reach fourth post having passed outside each post or the correct position of the post(s) if any has been displaced. Posts must be passed in the order first, second, third, fourth and a batter is permitted to halt at one or more posts if s/he chooses. On reaching fourth post s/he shall rejoin the waiting batters. A batter who drops the bat accidentally will be allowed to continue to run round the track until the bowler has

possession of the ball in the bowling square. The bat shall then be returned to the batter.

Penalty: The umpire shall declare the player out if s/he runs deliberately inside a post or deliberately drops or throws his/her bat. (When trying to make contact with a post, a batter who goes inside the post owing to obstruction by the fielder is not out)

(b) shall not run beyond the first post after a backward hit until the ball returns or has been returned to the forward area.

Penalty: The umpire shall order him/her back to the first post.

(c) shall not wait between posts.

Penalty: The umpire shall order him/her to continue and make contact with the next post.

(d) stopping (even temporarily) within reach of a post shall make and maintain contact with it using his/her hand or bat except that s/he may run on whenever the bowler is not in possession of the ball and in his/her square.

Penalty:

(1) If s/he does not make contact, the umpire shall order him/her to do so, and if s/he does not, the umpire shall declare him/her out.

(2) If s/he loses contact or runs at any time when the bowler has the ball and is in his/her square (except an overrun) or unless ordered to do so by an umpire or during the bowler's action but before s/he releases the ball, the umpire shall declare him/her out.

(e) shall continue his/her run to the next post if s/he loses contact between posts when the bowler becomes in possession of the ball and is in his/her square but may not run past the post.

Penalty: The umpire shall order the player back to the post s/he passes.

(f) may not remain at the same post as another batter.

Penalty: The umpire shall order the player who batted first to run on and s/he may be put out in the usual ways.

(g) shall not return to a post unless s/he is ordered to do so by the umpire, or unless in the umpire's opinion s/he has overrun a post.

Penalty: The umpire shall order him/her on to the next post and s/he may be put out in the usual ways. A batter may return to fourth post to make contact before the next ball is bowled.

(h) when completing the track, shall not overtake any batter who is running ahead.

Penalty: The umpire shall declare the batter who overtakes to be out.

(i) must touch fourth post with his/her hand or bat.

Penalty: The umpire shall declare him/her out if the fourth post is touched with the ball or with the hand holding the ball by the fielding side provided that another ball has not been bowled.

Rule 5 Bowling

(A) The Bowler

(a) The bowler shall deliver one good ball to each incoming batter, except the last remaining incoming batter who is entitled to have the option of three good balls.

(b) A bowler may leave the bowling square to field the ball.

(c) A bowler may not deliver two consecutive no-balls to the same batter.

Penalty: half rounder to the batting team.

(d) A dummy throw or bowl is not allowed. The ball must be delivered in the direction of the batting square. A player losing contact through a dummy ball will be allowed to return to his/her original position.

(B) No-Ball

(a) Decisions on height are based on the actual height of the batter. Decisions on direction are based on the position of the batter when the bowler releases the ball.

(b) A no-ball is one that:

(i) is higher than the top of the head or lower than the knee when it reaches the batter.

(ii) hits the ground on the way to the batter.

(iii) would hit the batter.

(iv) is on the non hitting side of the batter.

(v) is wide on the hitting side of the batter.

(vi) is not delivered with a continuous and smooth underarm pendulum action (this does not prevent spin).

(vii) is bowled when the bowler fails to keep both feet within the bowling square until the ball is released (the lines of the square are considered to be part of the square and the bowler should be penalized only when part of his/her foot projects over the line).

(C) Bowling Substitutes
See 3. The Game.

Rule 6 Fielding

(A) The Fielder

(a) If a fielder touches the post immediately ahead with the ball or the hand holding the ball, whilst the batter is running to that post and before the batter has touched the post the batter shall be declared out, excepting first post in the event of a no-ball.

(b) A fielder may put a batter out if s/he catches the ball directly from the bat or the hand holding the bat, except in the case of a no-ball.

(c) A fielder may prevent a 'live' batter who is at or within reach of a post from scoring by touching the next post with the ball or the hand holding the ball. This does not prevent the batter continuing his/her run. The 'live' batter is defined as the batter to whom the most recent ball was bowled irrespective of whether the ball was a no-ball or not.

(B) Side Out

(i) where there is no batter waiting his/her turn to bat, all the batters on the running track may be put out simultaneously, by the ball being thrown full pitch or placed by a fielder into the batting square before any batter has reached and touched fourth post.

(ii) Where there is no batter waiting his/her turn to bat and the bowler has possession of the ball in the bowling square so that no batter can leave a post, the side shall be declared out.

(C) Fielding Side Obstruction
Obstruction of the batter occurs if, in the opinion of the umpire, the batter was impeded whilst running round the track or during his/her batting action or was verbally misled.
Penalty: The umpire shall award half a rounder to the batting team and the batter shall be allowed to make contact with the post to which s/he is running.

Rule 7 Scoring

(A) One Rounder

(a) One rounder only may be scored from any one hit. In the case of a no-ball which is hit and caught, the batter may still score in the usual way.

(b) One rounder shall be scored if, after hitting the ball, the batter succeeds in running round the track and touches fourth post, or from first post when the ball returns or has been returned by a fielder to the

forward area after a backward hit, provided that:

(i) s/he has not overtaken any other batter.

(ii) the bowler has not delivered another ball.

(iii) whilst s/he was waiting at a post, the post immediately ahead was not touched by a fielder with the ball or the hand holding the ball.

(B) Half Rounder
Half a rounder shall be scored by the batter if s/he completes the track fulfilling the same conditions as for scoring one rounder but without hitting the ball.

(C) Penalty Half Rounder
A penalty half rounder shall be awarded to the batting team when:

(a) the bowler delivers two consecutive no-balls to the same batter. After a penalty half rounder has been awarded for two consecutive no-balls the previous

no-balls are cancelled and the count starts again.

(b) a fielder obstructs a batter.

(D) One Rounder and Penalty Half Rounders
It should be noted that the rounder may be scored with the addition of the award:

(a) One penalty half rounder if the ball that is hit is the second consecutive no-ball to that batter.

(b) One penalty half rounder if the batter is obstructed.

(c) Two penalty half rounders if both (a) and (b) apply.

These rules are reprinted by permission of the National Rounders Association. A complete set of the Rules of Rounders, including Hints to umpires, can be obtained from the Association.

Big swing
The rounders bat is small and held in one hand. To hit the ball well, a batter has to give a strong flick of the wrist and turn the hand over at the same time as turning the shoulders to follow through.

Tennis
Essentials

Originating from the old indoor game of real tennis, its proper name is lawn tennis, although the only major tournament in the world still to use grass courts today is that held at Wimbledon.

Officials

For high level matches, an umpire, referee and assistants. *See Rule 29, Role of Court Officials (page 120).*

The court

Rectangular, 78 ft (23.77 m) long and 27 ft (8.23 m) wide for singles, 78 ft long and 36 ft (10.97 m) wide for doubles. Divided into two courts by a net across the centre and then into two service courts and a back court on either side of this by lines on the ground. Surfaces may be grass, clay, plastic, wood or concrete.

Server

Centre mark

Service court

Central service line

Service line

Singles court sideline

Doubles court sideline

Net-cord judge

Umpire

Receiver

Baseline

The players

One a side for singles, two for doubles. Men or women or mixed.

Dress

A shirt and shorts or skirt. Clothing is usually white, although colours are also permitted. Shoes should be fairly lightweight with a reasonable amount of grip.

The racket

Aluminium, graphite or composite, various different weights, with a single layer of strings of uniform pattern. The frame must not exceed 29 inches (73.66 cm) in overall length for professional play. Its overall width must be no more than 12 1/2 in (31.75 cm).

Below, clay court.

The net

Mesh, suspended from a cord or metal cable attached to the tops of two posts which are positioned three ft (.914 m) outside each sideline at the centre of the court. The top of the net must be three ft (.914 m) above the ground at its centre, at which point the net is also held taut by a vertical white strap.

The ball

Yellow or white, with a fabric cover. Between 2 1/2 and 2 5/8 in (6.350–6.668 cm) in diameter and between 2 and 2 1/16 oz (56.7–58.5 g) in weight. The ball must rebound to a height of 53-58 in (134.62–147.32 cm) when dropped from a height of 100 in (254 cm).

White out

Tennis used to be played strictly in all white – a shirt and shorts for men, and shirt and skirts for women. In recent years however a much broader range of colours has started to be used.

HOW TO PLAY

Two or four players hit the ball alternately with rackets so that it passes over the net and into the opponent's court. When a player loses a rally, his opponent is awarded a point.

Starting

The winner of the toss decides to accept a choice of ends or the right to serve or receive first. The player taking the first serve stands with his feet behind the base line on the right-hand side of his court. His feet must remain behind the base line and within the imaginary extensions of the centre-mark and the side lines until the ball is played. The ball is then thrown into the air and struck with the racket before it hits the ground. It must land in the receiver's right-hand court to be 'in'. The server has two chances to make a good service, after which the point is lost ('double fault').

How to win

Players must win points, games and, then, sets in order to win a match. When a player loses his first point, his score remains 'love' (nil) while his opponent's becomes '15'. The second point is called '30', the third '40' and the fourth point is the one needed to win the game. If the score is 40-all, a 'deuce' is called. Either player must now score two additional points in succession to win. When the first one is scored, the umpire will call 'Advantage server/receiver' (depending on which player scored), but if this player fails to win a second point, the score reverts back to deuce.

The first player to win six games wins a set. However, if the score reaches five games all, the winner is the first to win two additional games. A match has a maximum of five sets for men, three for women.

KEY RULES

• The ball is allowed to bounce only once in a player's court before it must be returned. It must bounce once following a service, but during a rally it need not bounce at all, i.e. if a player returns it with a volley shot.

• It is a 'let' if, following a serve, the ball hits the net before landing in the receiver's court. The point is replayed in this case.

• Play is continuous. Service alternates between players

with each game and ends are changed at the end of the first, third and every subsequent alternate game of a set. *See Rule 16 (page 117).* After the third set (men) or second set (women) in professional matches, players are allowed a ten-minute break. *See Rule 30, Continuous Play and Rest Periods (page 120).*

• To prevent excessively long sets, a tie-break game may be played to determine the winner of a set in the case of a six-all score. In singles tie-break games, the first player to reach seven points wins the game (and the set). The player who is due to serve does so first, then after this the service alternates with every two points scored. In doubles, each player serves for two points in rotation, following the sequence already established for the set.
See Rule 27, (page 120).

High speed service
New light, tough racket materials have made tennis a very fast, demanding game. Men's services frequently cross the net at speeds of over 130 mph. Even women's services have been timed at over 110 mph.

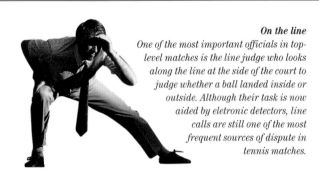

RULES OF TENNIS

The Singles Game

1. The court

The court shall be a rectangle 78 ft (23.77 m) long and 27 ft (8.23 m) wide. It shall be divided across the middle by a net suspended from a cord or metal cable of a maximum diameter of one-third of an inch (0.8 cm), the ends of which shall be attached to, or pass over, the tops of the two posts, which shall be not be more than 6 in (15 cm) square or 6 in (15 cm) in diameter. These posts shall not be higher than 1 in (2.5 cm) above the top of the net cord. The centres of the posts shall be 3 ft (.914 m) outside the court on each side and the height of the posts shall be such that the top of the cord or metal cable shall be 3 ft 6 in (1.07 m) above the ground.

When a combined doubles (see Rule 34) and singles court with a doubles net is used for singles, the net must be supported to a height of 3 ft 6 in (1.07 m) by means of two posts, called "singles sticks", which shall be not more than 3 inches (7.5 cm) square or 3 in (7.5 cm) in diameter. The centres of the singles sticks shall be 3 ft (.914 m) outside the singles court on each side.

The net shall be extended fully so that it fills completely the space between the two posts and shall be of sufficiently small mesh to prevent the ball passing through. The height of the net shall be 3 ft (.914 m) at the centre, where it shall be held down taut by a strap not more than 2 in (5 cm) wide and completely white in colour. There shall be a band covering the cord or metal cable and the top of the net of not less than 2 in (5 cm) nor more than 2 ½ in (6.35 cm) in depth on each side and completely white in colour.

There shall be no advertisement on the net, strap band or singles sticks.

The lines bounding the ends and sides of the court shall respectively be called the base-lines and the side-lines. On each side of the net, at a distance of 21 ft (6.40 m) from it and parallel with it, shall be drawn the service-lines. The space on each side of the net between the service-line and the side-lines shall be divided into two equal parts called the service-courts by the centre service-line, which must be 2 in (5 cm) in width, drawn half-way between, and parallel with, the side-line. Each base-line shall be bisected by an imaginary continuation of the centre service-line to a line 4 in (10 cm) in length and 2 in (5 cm) in width called "the centre mark" drawn inside the court, at right angles to and in contact with such base-lines. All other lines shall be not less than 1 inch (2.5 cm) nor more than 2 in (5 cm) in width, except the base-line which may be not more than 4 in (10 cm) in width, and all measurements shall be made to the outside of the lines. All lines shall be of uniform colour. If advertising or any other material is placed at the back of the court, it may not contain white, or yellow. A light colour may only be used if this does not interfere with the vision of the players.

If advertisements are placed on the chairs of the linesmen sitting at the back of the court, they may not contain white or yellow. A light colour may only be used if this does not interfere with the vision of the players.

Note 1: In the case of the Davis Cup or other Official Championships of the International Tennis Federation, there shall be a space behind each base-line of not less than 21 ft (6.4 m), and at the sides of not less than 12 ft (3.66 m). The chairs of linesmen may be placed at the back of a court within 21 ft (6.4m) or at the side of the court within the 12 ft (3.66 m), provided they do not protrude into that area more than 3 ft (.914 m).

Note 2: In the case of the stadium courts in the Davis Cup World Group and the Fed Cup Main Draw there should be space behind each baseline of not less than 27 ft (8.23 m) and at the sides of not less than 15 ft (4.57 m).

Note 3: At club or recreational level, the space behind each baseline should be not less than 18 ft (5.5 m) and at the sides not less than 10 ft (3.05 m).

Below, indoor court.

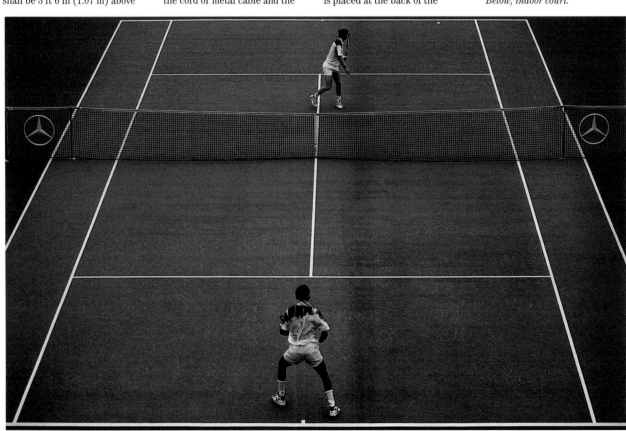

2. Permanent fixtures

The permanent fixtures of the court shall include not only the net, posts, singles sticks, cord or metal cable, strap and band, but also, where there are any such, the back and side stops, the stands, fixed or movable seats and chairs round the court, and their occupants, all other fixtures around and above the court, and the Umpire, Net-cord Judge, Foot-fault Judge, Linesmen and Ball Boys when in their respective places.

3. The ball

The ball shall have a uniform outer surface consisting of a fabric cover and shall be white or yellow in colour. If there are any seams they shall be stitchless. The ball shall be more than $2\frac{1}{2}$ in (6.350 cm) and less than $2\frac{5}{8}$ in (6.668 cm) in diameter, and more than 2 oz (56.7 g) and less than $2\frac{1}{16}$ oz (58.5 g) in weight. The ball shall have a bound of more than 53 in (134.62 cm) and less than 58 in (147.32 cm) when dropped 100 in (254.00 cm) upon a concrete base. The ball shall have a forward deformation of more than .220 in (.559 cm) and less than .290 in (.737 cm) and return deformation of more than .315 in (.800 cm) and less than .425 in (1.080 cm) at 18 lb (8.165 kg) load. The two deformation figures shall be the averages of three individual readings along three axes of the ball and no two individual readings shall differ by more than .030 in (.076 cm) in each case. For play above 4, 000 ft (1219 m) in altitude above sea level, two additional types of ball may be used. The first type is identical to those described above except that the bound shall be more than 48 in (121.92 cm) and less than 53 in (134.62 cm) and shall have an internal pressure that is greater than the external pressure. This type of tennis ball is commonly known as a pressurised ball. The second type is identical to those described above except that it shall have a bound of more than 53 in (134.62 cm) and less than 58 in (147.32 cm) and shall have an internal pressure that is approximately equal to the external pressure and have been acclimatised for 60 days or more at the altitude of the specific tournament. This type of tennis ball is commonly known as a zero-pressure or non-pressurised ball. All tests for bound, size and deformation shall be made in accordance with the regulations in Appendix 1. The International Tennis Federation shall rule on the question of whether any ball or prototype complies with the above specifications or is otherwise approved for play. Such ruling may be taken on its own initiative, or upon application by any party with a bona fide interest therein, including any player, equipment manufacturer or National Association or members thereof. Such rulings and applications shall be made in accordance with the applicable review and hearing procedures of the International Tennis Federation, copies of which may be obtained from the Federation.

4. The racket

Rackets failing to comply with the following specifications are not approved for play under the Rules of Tennis:
(a) The hitting surface of the racket shall be flat and consist of a pattern of crossed strings connected to a frame and alternately interlaced or bonded where they cross; and the stringing pattern shall be generally uniform, and in particular not less dense in the centre than in any other area. The strings shall be free of attached objects and protrusions other than those utilised solely and specifically to limit or prevent wear and tear or vibration, and which are reasonable in size and placement for such purposes.
(b) For professional play, the frame of the racket shall not exceed 29 in (73.66 cm) in overall length, including the handle, as from 1st January 1997. For non-professional play, the frame of the racket shall not exceed 29 in (73.66cm) in overall length, including the handle, as from 1st January 2000. The frame of the racket shall not exceed $12\frac{1}{2}$ in (31.75 cm) in overall width. The strung surface shall not exceed $15\frac{1}{2}$ in (39.37 cm) in overall length, and $11\frac{1}{2}$ in (29.21 cm) in overall width.
(c) The frame, including the handle, shall be free of attached objects and devices other than those utilised solely and specifically to limit or prevent wear and tear or vibration, or to distribute weight. Any objects and devices must be reasonable in size and placement for such purposes.
(d) The frame, including the handle, and the strings, shall be free of any device which makes it possible to change materially the shape of the racket, or to change the weight distribution in the direction of the longitudinal axis of the racket which would alter the swing moment of inertia, during the playing of a point.
The International Tennis Federation shall rule on the question of whether any racket or prototype complies with the above specifications or is otherwise approved, or not approved, for play. Such ruling may be undertaken on its own initiative, or upon application by any party with a bona fide interest therein, including any player, equipment manufacturer or National Association or

➡ *page 116*

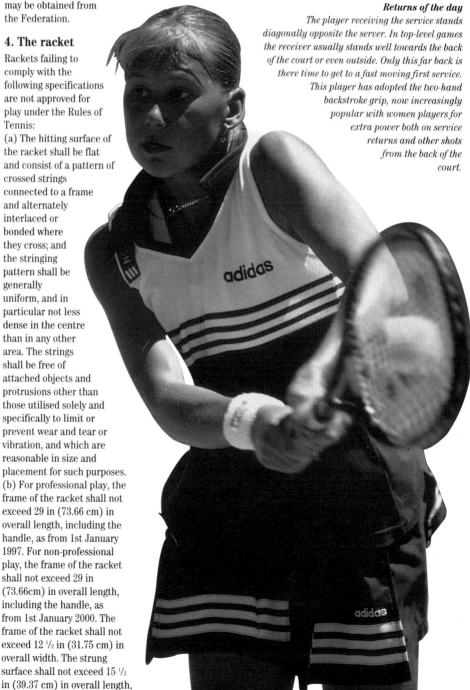

Returns of the day
The player receiving the service stands diagonally opposite the server. In top-level games the receiver usually stands well towards the back of the court or even outside. Only this far back is there time to get to a fast moving first service. This player has adopted the two-hand backstroke grip, now increasingly popular with women players for extra power both on service returns and other shots from the back of the court.

SKILLS

Tennis requires the same mobility, ball control and strategic thinking as most racket sports. Players also need to be able to combine powerful, robust shots with a high degree of accuracy.

The *service* is an essential stroke to get right. Because the server has complete control of the ball this is an opportunity to score points and quickly gain the upper hand. A strong player will be able to serve the ball hard and fast, making sure that it lands in, yet, at the same time, placing it so deep into the corners of the receiver's court that it is impossible to return. This is called an 'ace'.

The forehand and backhand drive are basic *ground-strokes*. They are strong shots, usually played from near the base-line and travelling the length of the court. Players turn sideways to the net and 'follow through' on the swing of the racket as the ball is struck to give it power and momentum. For backhand drives, many players achieve greater control and force by gripping the racket with both hands.

The *volley* is an aggressive shot, played before the ball has bounced in a player's court. It involves 'punching' the ball with a short, quick movement. A well-judged volley will allow an opponent very little time to respond, particularly if it is aimed at an unguarded area close to the net.

An overhead *smash* is another potential point-scoring stroke. The action is similar to that used for the service.

The addition of spin – topspin or underspin (slice) – is a relatively complex skill. By tilting the face of the racket, the behaviour of the ball in the air or as it rebounds in the receiver's court can be made unpredictable for an opponent. Topspin will cause it to bounce to a much lower height than anticipated, while slice can be used to make it swerve through the air.

Forehand drive

Below, Tim Henman prepares for a forehand drive – he has a full backswing and will hit the ball with the face of the racket square to the ball – his swing will 'follow through' for maximum power.

Service power

The tennis serve is a dramatic overhead smash that involves the player's whole body as well as just the racket arm. To accelerate the ball from a standstill to cannonball speed requires the player to effectively to throw the head of the racket at the ball. The movement begins at the ankles then moves rapidly up through the body as the server twists to throw maximum weight behind the ball.

Aerial combat
Playing backhanded and off the ground, the competitive John McEnroe is still able to return his opponent's shot.

Backhander
Below and right, the backhand stroke is made with the racket up across the body and so is usually much weaker than the forehand. However, a skilled player can more than make up for the lack of power with highly accurate placing and clever disguise of their shot.

Ground control
Left, the forehand volley is an attacking stroke played from the front of the court with a short 'punching' action.

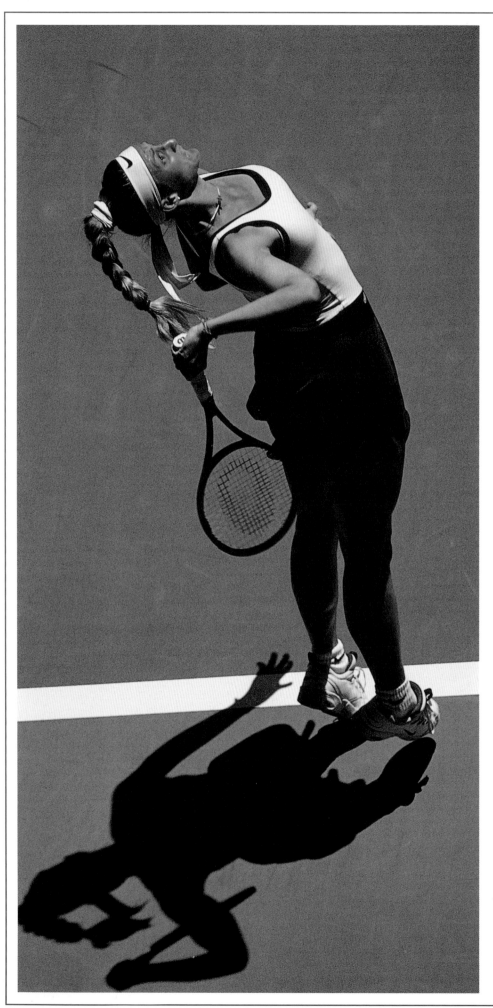

continued from page 113

members thereof. Such rulings and applications shall be made in accordance with the applicable Review and Hearing Procedures of the International Tennis Federation, copies of which may be obtained from the Federation.

5. Server and receiver

The players shall stand on opposite sides of the net; the player who first delivers the ball shall be called the server, and the other the receiver.

6. Choice of ends and service

The choice of ends and the right to be server or receiver in the first game shall be decided by toss. The player winning the toss may choose or require his opponent to choose:-

(a) The right to be Server or receiver, in which case the other player shall choose the end; or

(b) The end, in which case the other player shall choose the right to be server or receiver.

7. The service

The service shall be delivered in the following manner. Immediately before commencing to serve, the Server shall stand with both ft at rest behind (i.e. further from the net than) the base-line, and within the imaginary continuations of the centre-mark and side-line. The server shall then project the ball by hand into the air in any direction and before it hits the ground strike it with his racket, and the delivery shall be deemed to have been completed at the moment of the impact of the racket and the ball. A player with the use of only one arm may utilise his racket for the projection.

8. Foot fault

The server shall throughout the delivery of the Service:-
a) Not change his position by walking or running. The Server shall not by slight movements of the feet which do not materially affect the location originally taken up by him, be deemed "to change his position by walking or running".
b) Not touch, with either foot, any area other than that behind

Line judgement
Left, Mary Pierce arches back preparing for a powerful serve, but is careful not to overstep the base-line, so making a foot fault.

the base-line within the imaginary extension of the centre-mark and side-lines.

9. Delivery of service

(a) In delivering the service, the Server shall stand alternately behind the right and left halves of the court beginning from the right in every game. If service from a wrong half of the court occurs and is undetected, all play resulting from such wrong service or services shall stand, but the inaccuracy of station shall be corrected immediately it is discovered.

(b) The ball served shall pass over the net and hit the ground within the service court which is diagonally opposite, or upon any line bounding such court, before the receiver returns it.

10. Service fault

The service is a fault:
(a) If the Server commits any breach of Rules 7, 8 or 9(b);
(b) If he misses the ball in attempting to strike it;
(c) If the ball served touches a permanent fixture (other than the net, strap or band) before it hits the ground.

11. Second service

After a fault (if it is the first fault) the Server shall serve again from behind the same half of the court from which he served that fault, unless the service was from the wrong half, when in accordance with Rule 9, the Server shall be entitled to one service only from behind the other half.

12. When to serve

The Server shall not serve until the receiver is ready. If the latter attempts to return the service, he shall be deemed ready. If however, the receiver signifies that he is not ready, he may not claim a fault because the ball does not hit the ground within the limits fixed for the service.

13. The let

In all cases where a let has to be called under the rules, or to provide for an interruption to play, it shall have the following interpretations:-
(a) When called solely in respect of a service that one service only shall be replayed.
(b) When called under any other circumstance, the point shall be replayed.

14. The 'let' in service

The service is a let:-

(a) If the ball served touches the net, strap or band, and is otherwise good, or, after touching the net, strap or band, touches the receiver or anything he wears or carries before hitting the ground.
(b) If a service or a fault is delivered when the receiver is not ready (see Rule 12).
    In case of a let, that particular service shall not count, and the server shall serve again, but a service let does not annul a previous fault.

15. Order of service

At the end of the first game the receiver shall become server, and the server receiver; and so on alternately in all the subsequent games of a match. If a player serves out of turn, the player who ought to have served shall serve as soon as the mistake is discovered, but all points scored before such discovery shall stand. A fault served before such discovery shall not stand. If a game shall have been completed before such discovery, the order of service shall remain as altered.

16. When players change ends

The players shall change ends at the end of the first, third and every subsequent alternate game of each set, and at the end of each set unless the total number of games in such set is even, in which case the change is not made until the end of the first game of the next set.

    If a mistake is made and the correct sequence is not followed, the players must take up their correct station as soon as the discovery is made and follow their original sequence.

17. The ball in play

A ball is in play from the moment at which it is delivered in service. Unless a fault or a let is called it remains in play until the point is decided.

18. Server wins point

The Server wins the Point:-
(a) If the ball served, not being a let under Rule 14, touches the receiver or anything he wears or carries, before it hits the ground;
(b) If the receiver otherwise loses the point as provided by Rule 20.

19. Receiver wins point

The receiver wins the point:-
(a) If the Server serves two

consecutive faults;
(b) If the Server otherwise loses the point as provided by Rule 20.

20. Player loses point

A player loses the point if:-
(a) He fails, before the ball in play has hit the ground twice consecutively, to return it directly over the net (except as provided in Rule 24 (a) or (c)); or
(b) He returns the ball in play so that it hits the ground, a permanent fixture, or other object, outside any of the lines which bound his opponent's court; or
(c) He volleys the ball and fails to make a good return even when standing outside the court; or
(d) In playing the ball he deliberately carries or catches it on his racket or deliberately touches it with his racket more than once; or
(e) He or his racket (in his hand or otherwise) or anything which he wears or carries touches the net, posts, singles sticks, cord or metal cable, strap or band, or the ground within his opponent's court at any time while the ball is in play; or
(f) He volleys the ball before it has passed the net or
(g) The ball in play touches him or anything he wears or carries, except his racket in his hand or hands; or
(h) He throws his racket at and hits the ball; or
(i) He deliberately and materially changes the shape of his racket during the playing of the point.

21. Player hinders opponent

If a player commits any act which hinders his opponent in making a stroke, then, if this is deliberate, he shall lose the point or if involuntary, the point shall be replayed.

22. Ball falls on line

A ball falling on a line is regarded as falling in the court bounded by that line.

23. Ball touches Permanent fixtures

If the ball in play touches a permanent fixture (other than the net, posts, singles sticks, cord or metal cable, strap or band) after it has hit the ground, the player who struck it wins the point; if before it hits the ground, his opponent wins the point.

24. A good return

It is a good return:-
(a) If the ball touches the net, posts, singles sticks, cord or metal cable, strap or band, provided that it passes over any of them and hits the ground within the court; or
(b) If the ball, served or returned, hits the ground within the proper court and rebounds

➡ *page 120*

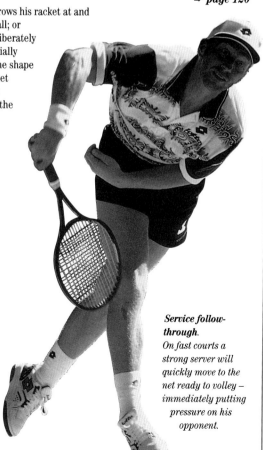

Service follow-through.
On fast courts a strong server will quickly move to the net ready to volley – immediately putting pressure on his opponent.

TACTICS

Top players tend to be one of two types. The *serve-and-volley* player excels on a fast court (e.g. grass). He will try to begin with a powerful serve and then follow up by moving quickly to the net to meet his opponent's weak return with a volley or a smash.

Base-line players do better on slow courts. Their tactic is to play mostly from the back of their court, maintaining rallies until a winning shot can be made, or until their opponent makes a mistake.

GREY AREA

Q. If, following a service, the racket flies from the server's hand and hits the net before the ball lands, is this a fault or does he lose the point?

A. He loses the point, according to Rule 20 e). His racket touched the net whilst the ball was still in play.

Forehand slice
A player can achieve tremendous power with the racket hitting the ball square on, but many winning shots involve slicing the racket against the ball to set it spinning. This player, above, has given his forehand return a little backspin by slicing under the ball. Backspin lofts the ball slightly higher in the air, so the shot has to be aimed slightly lower than for a straight drive.

Top spin
Jeremy Bates, right, prepares to return the ball with a top spin – slicing over the top of the ball with the racket causing the ball to spin forwards so that it travels fast and stays low off the bounce.

Fast return
Left, Steffi Graf chases across court, preparing to hit the ball square for a fast fore-hand return.

continued from page 117

or is blown back over the net, and the player whose turn it is to strike reaches over the net and plays the ball, provided that he does not contravene Rule 20 (e); or

(**c**) If the ball is returned outside the posts, or singles sticks, either above or below the level of the top to the net, even though it touches the posts or singles sticks, provided that it hits the ground within the proper court; or

(**d**) If a player's racket passes over the net after he has returned the ball, provided the ball passes the net before being played and is properly returned; or

(**e**) If a player succeeds in returning the ball, served or in play, which strikes a ball lying in the court.

25. Hinderance of a player

In case a player is hindered in making a stroke by anything not within his control, except a permanent fixture of the court, or except as provided for in Rule 21, a let shall be called.

26. Score in a game

If a player wins his first point, the score is called 15 for that player; on winning his second point, the score is called 30 for that player; on winning his third point, the score is called 40 for that player, and the fourth point won by a player is scored game for that player except as below:-

If both players have won three points, the score is called deuce; and the next point won by a player is scored advantage for that player. If the same player wins the next point, he wins the game; if the other player wins the next point the score is again called deuce; and so on, until a player wins the two points immediately following the score at

deuce, when the game is scored for that player.

27. Score in a set

(**a**) A player (or players) who first wins six games wins a set; except that he must win by a margin of two games over his opponent and where necessary a set shall be extended until this margin is achieved.

(**b**) The tie-break system of scoring may be adopted as an alternative to the advantage set system in paragraph (a) of this Rule provided the decision is announced in advance of the match.

In this case, the following Rules shall be effective:

The tie-break shall operate when the score reaches six games all in any set except the third or fifth set of a three set or five set match, when an ordinary advantage set shall be played, unless otherwise decided and announced in advance of the match.

The following system shall be used in a tie-break game:

Singles

(i) A player who first wins seven points shall win the game and the set provided he leads by a margin of two points. If the score reaches six points all, the game shall be extended until this margin has been achieved. Numerical scoring shall be used throughout the tie-break game.

(ii) The player whose turn it is to serve shall be the server for the first point. His opponent shall be the server

for the second and third points and thereafter each player shall serve alternately for two consecutive points until the winner of the game and set has been decided.

(iii) From the first point, each service shall be delivered alternately from the right and left courts, beginning from the right court. If service from a wrong half of the court occurs and is undetected, all play resulting from such wrong service or services shall stand, but the inaccuracy of the station shall be corrected immediately it is discovered.

(iv) Players shall change ends after every six points and at the conclusion of the tie-break game.

(v) The tie-break game shall count as one game for the ball change, except that, if the balls are due to be changed at the beginning of the tie-break, the change shall be delayed until the second game of the following set.

Doubles

In doubles the procedure for singles shall apply. The player whose turn it is to serve shall be the server for the first point. Thereafter each player shall serve in rotation for two points, in the same order previously in that set, until the winners of the game and set have been decided.

Rotation of Service

The player (or pair in the case of doubles) whose turn it was to serve first in the tie-break game shall receive service in the first game of the following set.

28. Maximum number of sets

The maximum number of sets in a match shall be 5, or, where women take part, 3.

29. Role of court officials

In matches where an umpire is appointed, his decision shall be final; but where a referee is appointed, an appeal shall lie to him from the decision of an umpire on a question of law, and in all such cases the decision of the referee shall be final. In matches where assistants to the umpire are appointed (Linespersons, Net-cord Judges, Foot-fault Judges) their decisions shall be final on questions of fact except that if in the opinion of an umpire a clear

mistake has been made he shall have the right to change the decision of an assistant or order a let to be played. When such an assistant is unable to give a decision he shall indicate this immediately to the umpire who shall give a decision. When an umpire is unable to give a decision on a question of fact he shall order a let to be played. In Davis Cup matches or other team competitions where a referee is on court, any decision can be changed by the referee, who may also instruct an umpire to order a let to be played.

The referee, in his discretion, may at any time postpone a match on account of darkness or the condition of the ground or the weather. In any case of postponement the previous score and previous occupancy of courts shall hold good, unless the referee and the players unanimously agree otherwise.

30. Continuous play and rest periods

Play shall be continuous from the first service until the match is concluded, in accordance with the following provisions:

(**a**) If the first service is a fault, the second service must be struck by the server without delay.

The receiver must play to the reasonable pace of the server and must be ready to receive when the server is ready to serve. When changing ends a maximum of one minute thirty seconds shall elapse from the moment the ball goes out of play at the end of the game to the time the ball is struck for the first point of the next game.

The umpire shall use his discretion when there is interference which makes it impracticable for play to be continuous. The organisers of international circuits and team events recognised by the ITF may determine the time allowed between points, which shall not at any time exceed twenty (20) seconds from the moment the ball goes out of play at the end of one point to the time the ball is struck for the next point.

(**b**) Play shall never be suspended, delayed or interfered with for the purpose of enabling a player to recover his strength, breath, or physical condition. However, in the case of accidental injury, the umpire may allow a one-time three-minute suspension for that injury.

Smash hit
Agassi jumps to produce maximum power for this overhead drive.

(c) If, through circumstance outside the control of the player, his clothing, footwear or equipment (excluding racket) becomes out of adjustment in such a way that it is impossible or undesirable for him to play on, the umpire may suspend play while the maladjustment is rectified.

(d) The umpire may suspend or delay play at any time as may be necessary and appropriate.

(e) After the third set, or when women take part the second set, either player shall be entitled to a rest, which shall not exceed 10 minutes, or in countries situated between latitude 15 degrees north and latitude 15 degrees south, 45 minutes and furthermore, when necessitated by circumstances not within the control of the players, the umpire may suspend play for such a period as he may consider necessary. If play is suspended and is not resumed until a later day, the rest may be taken only after the third set (or when women take part the second set) of play on such a later day, completion of an unfinished set being counted as one set. If play is suspended and is not resumed until 10 minutes have elapsed in the same day the rest may be taken only after three consecutive sets have been played without interruption (or when women take part two sets), completion of an unfinished set being counted as one set.

Any nation and/or committee organising a tournament, match or competition, is at liberty to modify this provision or omit it from its regulations provided this is announced before the event commences. With respect to the *Davis Cup* and Fed Cup, only the International Tennis Federation may modify this provision or omit it from its Regulations.

(f) A tournament committee has the discretion to decide the time allowed for a warm-up period prior to a match but this may not exceed five minutes and must be announced before the event commences.

(g) When approved point penalty and non-accumulative point penalty systems are in operation, the umpire shall make his decisions within the terms of those systems.

(h) Upon violation of the principle that play shall be continuous the umpire may, after giving due warning, disqualify the offender.

31. Coaching
During the playing of a match in a team competition, a player may receive coaching from a captain who is sitting on the court only when he changes ends at the end of a game, but not when he changes ends during a tie-break game.

A player may not receive coaching during the playing of any other match. The provisions of this rule must be strictly construed.

After due warning an offending player may be disqualified. When an approved point penalty system is in operation, the umpire shall impose penalties according to that system.

32. Ball change
In cases where balls are to be changed after a specified number of games, if the balls were not changed in the correct sequence, the mistake shall be corrected when the player, or pair in the case of doubles, who should have served with new balls is next due to serve. Thereafter the balls shall be changed so that the number of games between changes shall be that originally agreed.

THE DOUBLES GAME

33. The Doubles game
The above Rules shall apply to the Doubles Game except as below.

34. The doubles court
For the doubles court, the court shall be 36 ft (10.97 m) in width, i.e. 4 $\frac{1}{2}$ ft (1.37 m) wider on each side than the Court for the Singles Game, and those portions of the singles side-lines which lie between the two service-lines shall be called the service side-lines. In other respects, the court shall be similar to that described in Rule 1, but the portions of the singles side lines between the base line and service line on each side of the net may be omitted if desired.

35. Order of service in doubles
The order of serving shall be decided at the beginning of each set as follows:-

The pair who have to serve in the first game of each set shall decide which partner shall do so and the opposing pair shall decide similarly for the second game. The partner of the player who served in the first game shall serve in the third; the partner of the player who served in the second game shall serve in the fourth, and so on in the same order in all the subsequent games of a set.

36. Order of receiving in doubles
The order of receiving the service shall be decided at the beginning of each set as follows:-

The pair who have to receive the service in the first game shall decide which partner shall receive the first service, and that partner shall continue to receive the first service in every odd game throughout that set. The opposing pair shall likewise decide which partner shall receive the first service in the second game and that partner shall continue to receive the first service in every even game throughout that set. Partners shall receive the service alternately throughout each game.

37. Service out of turn in doubles
If a partner serves out of his turn, the partner who ought to have served shall serve as soon as the mistake is discovered, but all points scored, and any faults served before such discovery, shall be reckoned. If a game shall have been completed before such discovery, the order of service remains as altered.

38. Error in order of receiving in doubles
If during a game the order of receiving the service is changed by the receivers it shall remain as altered until the end of the game in which the mistake is discovered, but the partners shall resume their original order of receiving in the next game of that set in which they are receivers of the service.

39. Service fault in doubles
The service is a fault as provided for by Rule 10, or if the ball touches the server's partner or anything which he wears or carries; but if the ball served touches the partner of the receiver, or anything which he wears or carries, not being a let under Rule 14 (a) before it hits the ground, the server wins the point.

40. Playing the ball in doubles
The ball shall be struck alternately by one or other player of the opposing pairs, and if a player touches the ball in play with his racket in contravention of this Rule, his opponents win the point.

Note: Except where otherwise stated, every reference in these Rules to the masculine includes the feminine gender.

AMENDMENT TO THE RULES OF TENNIS
International Tennis Federation Rule 69
The official and decisive text to the Rules of Tennis shall be for ever in the English language and no alteration or interpretation of such Rules shall be made except at an Annual General Meeting of the Council, nor unless notice of the resolution embodying such alteration shall have been received by the Federation in accordance with Rule 21 (Notice of Resolutions) and such resolution or one having the like effect shall be carried by a majority of two-thirds of the votes recorded in respect of the same.

Any alteration so made shall take effect as from the first day of January following unless the Meeting shall by the like majority decide otherwise.

The Committee of Management shall have power, however, to settle all urgent questions of interpretation subject to confirmation at the General Meeting next following.

This Rule shall not be altered at any time without the unanimous consent of a General Meeting of the Council.

These Rules are reprinted by permission of the International Tennis Federation.

The complete Rules of Tennis, including Appendix I (Regulations for making tests), Appendix II (Rules of Wheelchair Tennis) and Suggestions on How to Mark out a court are available from the Federation.

Badminton
Essentials

A game requiring both stamina and strategy, badminton evolved from a children's game called battledore and shuttlecock. The original rules for badminton were set in 1877 by British officers in India.

The players
One player on each side for singles, two on each side for doubles.

Officials
An umpire and, in some events, a referee.

Dress
There are no strict rules. For a man, shorts and a lightweight shirt are practical, while a woman may replace the shorts with a skirt. Clothing must allow ease of movement.

The court
Must be rectangular. Lines generally mark out a court which can be used for both singles and doubles, although a singles-only court is possible.

The net
Ideally hung from two posts, both 1.55 m (approx 5 ft) in height from the court's surface and positioned on the doubles sidelines. The net itself must be 760 mm (30 in) in depth, of dark colour and with a mesh of between 15 and 20 mm (approx 0.7 in). The top of the net must be edged with a 75 mm (3 in) white tape and must measure 1.524 m (5 ft) from the court's surface at the centre and 1.55 m (approx 5 ft) over the doubles sidelines.

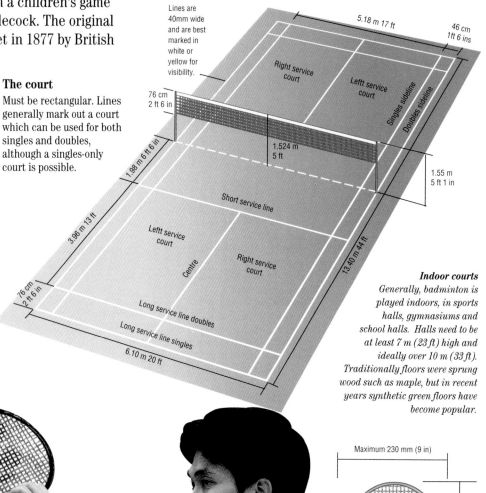

Lines are 40mm wide and are best marked in white or yellow for visibility.

76 cm 2 ft 6 in

Right service court

Leftt service court

Singles sideline

Doubles sideline

5.18 m 17 ft

46 cm 1ft 6 ins

1.524 m 5 ft

1.98 m 6 ft 6 in

1.55 m 5 ft 1 in

Short service line

3.96 m 13 ft

Leftt service court

Centre

Right service court

13.40 m 44 ft

76 cm 2 ft 6 in

Long service line doubles

Long service line singles

6.10 m 20 ft

Indoor courts
Generally, badminton is played indoors, in sports halls, gymnasiums and school halls. Halls need to be at least 7 m (23 ft) high and ideally over 10 m (33 ft). Traditionally floors were sprung wood such as maple, but in recent years synthetic green floors have become popular.

Maximum 230 mm (9 in)

Maximum 680 mm (27 in)

Shuttle
This feathered shuttle is the type used at the highest level: 16 feathers, ideally goose feathers.

The shuttle
Can be the original feathered or the newer synthetic model. Both must have a rounded base of 25–8 mm (approx 1 in) diameter and a total weight of between 4.74 and 5.50 g (approx 0.2 oz). The speed of the shuttle depends on its weight. (Manufacturers produce a variety of different speeds.)

Testing a shuttle
Occasionally it is worth checking that the shuttle is in playing condition. To do this, hold the shuttle over the baseline and use an underarm stroke to hit it at an upwards angle, straight to the other back boundary line. If the speed is correct it will land no less than 530 mm (21 in) and no more than 990 mm (39 in) short of the opposite line.

The racket
The frame must be no more than 680 mm (27 in) in overall length and 230 mm (9 in) in overall width. The stringed area must be flat and of a uniform pattern. Frames are generally made of graphite or aluminium, while natural gut gives the best performance for the strings.

HOW TO PLAY

Singles

Two players compete for the opportunity to serve and then, hopefully, score points. If the player serving wins a rally they also win a point. If the server loses a rally (see Law 15, Faults, page 125), the serve passes to the opponent. If the player loses another fault while his opponent is the server, a point goes to the opponent.

Doubles

As above, except the serve is passed on from one player to their partner before it can be 'lost' to the receiving side.

Starting

The winner of a toss decides whether to pick an end or to choose between serving or receiving first (in which case, the opponent picks an end). The first serve is an underarm shot from the right service court to the receiver in the court diagonally opposite.

How to win

Points may only be scored when serving. Generally a match consists of three games, each won by the first side to reach 15 points. Ladies' singles are won by the first to win 11 points. *For points in 'set' games, see Law 9, Scoring (page 124).*

KEY RULES

Players must change ends after the first game and then again before commencing a third game. *See Law 10, Change of Ends (page 124).*

• Any one of a number of faults will mean the loss of the right to serve or a point to the opposition. Obviously if a player misses the shuttle altogether it will be deemed a fault. But if the shuttle gets caught in the net, lands outside the boundaries of the court or even touches the clothing of a player, the umpire will also call a fault. *See Law 15, Faults (page 125).*

• Strict rules also govern how a correct service is made. Both the server and the receiver must have part of both feet on the court. The shuttle must also be hit while it is below the waist of the server and the head of the racket must be below the server's hand holding the racket. *See Law 11, Service (page 124).*

High serve
One of the first serves that beginners learn in badminton is the high serve. This loops the shuttle high over the net to force opponents far back in the court and weaken their attack.

Drop shot
Because a shuttle, unlike a tennis ball, decelerates very rapidly, the drop shot which delicately places the shuttle just over the net is a common attacking shot in badminton.

• Circumstances may sometimes require a 'let' to be called by the umpire, or by a player in the absence of an umpire. This halts play temporarily and is necessary if, for example, the shuttle disintegrates during play, or gets caught in the mesh of the net. *See Law 16, Lets (page 125).*

SKILLS

A successful player needs to be extremely fit and alert in order to keep up with the quick-fire rallies that characterize badminton. Although control of the racket with the arm and wrist is all-important, balance, speed and clever footwork are also vital if a player is to use stroke skills anywhere inside the court at a moment's notice.

Back breaker
The backhand drive is an attacking shot often used in doubles to hit the shuttle hard and fast down the sidelines.

The grip

Because the racket is so light, it needs to be held firmly but not tightly. The basic forehand grip, assumed by 'shaking hands' with the racket with the stringed area at right angles to the ground, allows flexibility, enabling both power strokes

and delicate shots to be played. Two other variations for specific shots are the backhand and the flat grip.

Strokes

Forehand and backhand drives are made by hitting the shuttle flat and low over the net, generally from the middle or back of the court. They are fast, attacking shots requiring control and power. The player must have both feet firmly placed and be able to pivot the body to follow through on the stroke.

The smash is an aggressive overhead stroke which, if used at the right moment, can instantly weaken an opponent's game and is often used to score points. Ideally the shuttle travels steeply and quickly downwards, catching an opponent off guard and causing them to play a weak return or to miss the shot altogether.

Net shots are neat, effective shots played close to the net. The aim is to gently tap the shuttle just over the net with a flick of the wrist so that the opposition is taken by surprise and is unable to reach it in time.

TACTICS

In any game, the aim is to make any combination of these and other strokes as unpredictable as possible in order to wear down opponents and weaken their defence until a well-timed attack shot can be employed to end a rally and score a point.

With doubles, more complex tactics may come into play, depending on the strengths and weaknesses of either partner. Generally the stronger of the two will choose to cover the middle to back of the court, while his partner protects the area close to the net. In mixed doubles the woman invariably takes the latter position.

GREY AREA

Q. Since the lines form part of the court, would it be a fault if a player stood on a line?

A. Yes it could be. Although a shuttle hitting a line is always 'in', a player, when **serving** or **receiving**, is outside the court if either foot so much as touches the line.

Service position

BADMINTON
• • • • • • • • •

The Laws
1. The Court
See The court (page 122).
2. Posts
3. Net
See The net (page 122).
4. Shuttle
See The shuttle (page 122).
5. Racket
See The racket (page 122).
6. Approved Equipment
For specifications and rulings contact the International Badminton Federation.
7. Players
See (page 123).
8. Toss
See Starting (page 123).

9. Scoring
9.1 The opposing sides shall play the best of three games unless otherwise arranged.
9.2 Only the serving side can add a point to its score.
9.3 In doubles and men's singles a game is won by the first side to score 15 points, except as provided in Law 9.6.
9.4 In ladies' singles a game is won by the first side to score 11 points, except as provided in Law 9.6.
9.5.1 If the score becomes 13-all or 14-all (9-all or 10-all in ladies' singles), the side which first scored 13 or 14 (9 or 10) shall have the choice of 'setting' or 'not setting' the game (Law 9.6).
9.5.2 This choice can only be made when the score is first reached and must be made before the next service is delivered.
9.5.3 The relevant side (Law 9.5.1) is given the opportunity to set at 14-all (10-all in ladies' singles) despite any previous

decision not to set by that side or the opposing side at 13-all (9-all in ladies' singles).
9.6 If the game has been set, the score is called 'Love-all' and the side first scoring the set number of points (Law 9.6.1 to 9.6.4) wins the game.
  9.6.1 13-all setting to 5 points.
  9.6.2 14-all setting to 3 points.
  9.6.3 9-all setting to 3 points.
    9.6.4 10-all setting to 2 points.
    9.7 The side winning a game serves first in the next game.

10. Change of Ends
10.1 Players shall change ends:
  10.1.1 At the end of the first game;
  10.1.2 Prior to the beginning of the third game (if any); and
  10.1.3 In the third game, or in a one-game match, when the leading score reaches:
-6 in a game of 11 points
-8 in a game of 15 points
10.2 When players omit to change ends as indicated by Law 10.1, they shall do so immediately the mistake is discovered and the existing score shall stand.

11. Service
11.1 In a correct service:
  11.1.1 Neither side shall cause undue delay to the delivery of the service;
  11.1.2 The server and receiver shall stand within diagonally opposite service courts without touching the boundary lines of these service courts; some part of both feet of the server and receiver must remain in contact with the surface of the court in a stationary position until the service is delivered (Law 11.4);
  11.1.3 The server's racket shall initially hit the base of the shuttle while the whole of the shuttle is below the server's waist;
  11.1.4 The shaft of the server's racket at the instant of hitting the shuttle shall be pointing in a downward direction to such an extent that the whole of the head of the racket is discernibly below the whole of the server's hand holding the racket;
  11.1.5 The movement of the server's racket must continue forwards after the start of the service (Law 11.2) until the service is delivered; and
  11.1.6 The flight of the shuttle shall be upwards from the server's racket to pass over the net, so that, if not intercepted, it falls in the receiver's service court.

11.2 Once the players have taken their positions, the first forward movement of the server's racket head is the start of the service.
11.3 The server shall not serve before the receiver is ready, but the receiver shall be considered to have been ready if a return of service is attempted.
11.4 The service is delivered when, once started (Law 11.2), the shuttle is hit by the server's racket or the shuttle lands on the floor.
11.5 In doubles, the partners may take up any positions which do not unsight the opposing server or receiver.

12. Singles
12.1 The players shall serve from, and receive in, their respective right service courts when the server has not scored or has scored an even number of points in that game.
12.2 The players shall serve from, and receive in, their respective left service courts when the server has scored an odd number of points in that game.
12.3 If a game is set, the total points scored by the server in that game shall be used to apply Laws 12.1 and 12.2.
12.4 The shuttle is hit alternately by the server and the receiver until a 'fault' is made or the shuttle ceases to be in play.
12.5.1 If the receiver makes a 'fault' or the shuttle ceases to be in play because it touches the surface of the court inside the receiver's court, the server scores a point. The server then serves again from the alternate service court.
12.5.2 If the server makes a 'fault' or the shuttle ceases to be in play because it touches the surface of the court inside the server's court, the server loses the right to continue serving, and the receiver then becomes the server, with no point scored by either player.

13. Doubles
13.1 At the start of a game, and each time a side gains the right to serve, the service shall be delivered from the right service court.
13.2 Only the receiver shall return the service: should the shuttle touch or be hit by the receiver's partner, the serving side scores a point.
13.3.1 After the service is returned, the shuttle is hit by either player of the serving side and then by either player of the receiving side, and so on, until

the shuttle ceases to be in play.
13.3.2 After the service is returned, a player may hit the shuttle from any position on that player's side of the net.
13.4.1 If the receiving side makes a 'fault' or the shuttle ceases to be in play because it touches the surface of the court inside the receiving side's court, the serving side scores a point, and the server serves again.
13.4.2 If the serving side makes a 'fault' or the shuttle ceases to be in play because it touches the surface of the court inside the serving side's court, the server loses the right to continue serving, with no point scored by either side.
13.5.1 The player who serves at the start of any game shall serve from, or receive in, the right service court when that player's side has not scored or has scored an even number of points in that game, and the left service court otherwise.
13.5.2 The player who receives at the start of any game shall receive in, or serve from, the right service court when that player's side has not scored or has scored an even number of points in that game, and the left service court otherwise.
13.5.3 The reverse pattern applies to the partners.
13.5.4 If a game is set, the total points scored by a side in that game shall be used to apply Laws 13.5.1 to 13.5.3.
13.6 Service in any turn of serving shall be delivered from the alternate service courts, except as provided in Laws 14 and 16.
13.7 The right to serve passes consecutively from the initial server in any game to the initial receiver in that game, and then consecutively from that player to that player's partner and then to one of the opponents and then the opponent's partner, and so on.
13.8 No player shall serve out of turn, receive out of turn, or receive two consecutive services in the same game, except as provided in Laws 14 and 16.
13.9 Either player of the winning side may serve first in the next game and either player of the losing side may receive.

14. Service-Court Errors
14.1 A service-court error has been made when a player:
  14.1.1 Has served out of turn;
  14.1.2 Has served from the wrong service court; or
  14.1.3 Standing in the wrong service court, was prepared to

receive the service and it has been delivered.

14.2 When a service-court error has been made, then:

14.2.1 If the error is discovered before the next service is delivered, it is a 'let' unless only one side was at fault and lost the rally, in which case the error shall not be corrected.

14.2.2 If the error is not discovered before the next service is delivered, the error shall not be corrected.

14.3 If there is a 'let' because of a service-court error, the rally is replayed and the error corrected.

14.4 If a service-court error is not to be corrected, play in that game shall proceed without changing the player's new service courts (nor, when relevant, the new order of serving).

15. Faults

It is a 'fault':

15.1 If a service is not correct (Law 11.1).

15.2 If the server, in attempting to serve, misses the shuttle.

15.3 If, on service, the shuttle is caught on the net and remains suspended on top or, on service, after passing over the net is caught in the net.

15.4 If in play, the shuttle:

15.4.1 Lands outside the boundaries of the court;

15.4.2 Passes through or under the net;

15.4.3 Fails to pass the net;

15.4.4 Touches the roof, ceiling, or side walls;

15.4.5 Touches the person or dress of a player; or

15.4.6 Touches any other object or person outside the immediate surroundings of the court;

(Where necessary, on account of the structure of the building, the local badminton authority may, subject to the right of veto of its National Organization, make by-laws dealing with cases in which a shuttle touches an obstruction.)

15.5 If, when in play, the initial point of contact with the shuttle is not on the striker's side of the net. (The striker may, however, follow the shuttle over the net with the racket in the course of a stroke.)

15.6 If, when the shuttle is in play, a player:

15.6.1 Touches the net or its supports with racket, person or dress;

15.6.2 Invades an opponent's court with racket or person in any degree except as permitted

in Law 15.5; or

15.6.3 Invades an opponent's court under the net with racket or person such that an opponent is obstructed or distracted;

15.6.4 Obstructs an opponent, i.e. prevents an opponent from making a legal stroke where the shuttle is followed over the net.

15.7 If, in play, a player deliberately distracts an opponent by any action such as shouting or making gestures.

15.8 If, in play, the shuttle:

15.8.1 Be caught and held on the racket and then slung during the execution of a stroke;

15.8.2 Be hit twice in succession by the same player with two strokes;

15.8.3 Be hit by a player and the player's partner successively; or

15.8.4 Touches a player's racket and continues towards the back of that player's court.

15.9 If a player is guilty of flagrant, repeated or persistent offences under Law 18.

16. Lets

"Let" is called by the umpire, or by a player (if there is no umpire) to halt play.

16.1 A 'let' may be given for any unforeseen or accidental occurrence.

16.2 If a shuttle is caught on the net and remains suspended on top, or after passing over the net is caught in the net, it is a 'let' except during service.

16.3 If during service, the receiver and server are both faulted at the same time, it shall be a 'let'.

16.4 If the server serves before the receiver is ready. it shall be a 'let'.

16.5 If during play, the shuttle disintegrates and the base completely separates from the rest of the shuttle, it shall be a 'let'.

16.6 If a line judge is unsighted and the umpire is unable to make a decision, it shall be a 'let'.

16.7 When a 'let' occurs, the play since the last service shall not count, and the player who served shall serve again, except when Law 14 is applicable.

17. Shuttle not in Play

A shuttle is not in play when:

17.1 It strikes the net and remains attached there or suspended on top;

17.2 It strikes the net or post and starts to fall towards the surface of the court on the striker's side of the net;

17.3 It hits the surface of the court; or

17.4 A 'fault' or 'let' has occurred.

18. Continuous Play, Misconduct, Penalties

18.1 Play shall be continuous from the first service until the match is concluded, except as allowed in Laws 18.2 and 18.3.

18.2 An interval not exceeding five minutes is allowed between the second and third games of all matches in all of the following situations:

18.2.1 In international competitive events;

18.2.2 In International Badminton Federation (IBF) sanctioned events; and

18.2.3 In all other matches (unless the National Organization has previously published a decision not to allow such an interval).

(Note: Badminton Association of England Limited has resolved that, except in international events, there will be no interval of five minutes between the second and third games of matches in England unless prior approval of Badminton Association of England Limited has been obtained.)

18.3 When necessitated by circumstances not within the control of the players, the umpire may suspend play for such a period as the umpire may consider necessary, If play be suspended, the existing score shall stand and play be resumed from that point.

18.4 Under no circumstances shall play be suspended to enable a player to recover his strength or wind, or to receive instruction or advice.

18.5.1 Except in the intervals provided in Laws 18.2 and 18.3, no player shall be permitted to receive advice during a match.

18.5.2 Except during the interval described in Law 18.2, no player shall leave the

court during a match without the umpire's consent.

18.6 The umpire shall be sole judge of any suspension of play.

18.7 A player shall not:

18.7.1 Deliberately cause suspension of play;

18.7.2 Deliberately interfere with the speed of the shuttle;

18.7.3 Behave in an offensive manner; or

18.7.4 Be guilty of misconduct not otherwise covered by the Laws of Badminton.

18.8 The umpire shall administer any breach of Law 18.4, 18.5, or 18.7 by:

18.8.1 Issuing a warning to the offending side;

18.8.2 Faulting the offending side, if previously warned; or

18.8.3 In cases of flagrant offence or persistent offences, faulting the offending side and reporting the offending side immediately to the referee, who shall have the power to disqualify.

18.9 Where a referee has not been appointed, the responsible official shall have the power to disqualify.

19. Officials and Appeals

For details contact the International Badminton Federation.

Space does not permit the inclusion of Appendixes 1 to 5 or the Recommendations to Court Officials, which can be obtained, together with the complete Laws of Badminton, from the IBF.

Lunge time
Badminton is a game that involves rapid movements across the court to reach the shuttle and running forward to the net usually ends in a long lunge.

Squash
Essentials

As much a test of endurance as a game of skill and strategy, squash is an intense and physically demanding game. It originated as 'squash rackets', first played at Harrow School in England in the 19th Century.

The court
A rectangular box with a level floor and four vertical walls of varying height. The glass/perspex court, an innovation developed for televised matches, allows an audience to see in but prevents the players from seeing out. Below the 'board' is an area at the base of the front wall, usually surfaced with metal and known as the 'tin'. *See Key rules.*

Rackets
Preferably made of graphite with two layers of strings woven into a uniform pattern. Strings may be gut, nylon or a substitute material.

The racket
Squash rackets have a smaller, rounder head than tennis rackets and a long shaft which is sometimes hollowed out to reduce vibration. Maximum weight 255 gm.

Players
Two players. (A game of doubles is also possible, but this has an entirely different set of rules and court dimensions.)

Dress
A light shirt with shorts or a skirt. Proper squash shoes are advisable as these feature a heel and grip sole designed for the game.

Officials
A marker and a referee.

Front wall line

Front wall

Services must hit above this line

Board

Tin

1780mm

430mm

4570mm

11665mm for doubles

12,375mm for doubles

50mm

5400mm

Side wall line

9750mm

Back wall line

Service box

1600mm

1600mm

2130mm

Service 'in' area

Service 'in' area

Service box

6400mm
7260mm for doubles

The ball
Must have a diameter of 39.5–40.5 mm (1.5–1.6 in) and weigh 23–24 g (0.8–0.84 oz). Balls come in a range of different speeds – indicated by the colour of the dot they bear. A blue dot is the fastest (used by beginners). A yellow dot is the super-slow ball used for matches.

Hard and fast
Squash is demanding because the ball travels very fast, not just off the front wall, but off all the other walls. Sometimes a player has to hit the ball off the back wall so hard that it reaches the front wall above the board, as this player is doing here. Such shots demand tremendous power.

HOW TO PLAY

Two players attempt to outlast each other in rallies, taking it in turns to strike the ball down the court and back again, making sure the ball hits the front wall on the way, without first touching the floor or either of the players.

Starting

Before play begins, the players are given five minutes to warm up the ball. This allows the air inside the ball to expand and provide extra bounce. The right to serve first is then decided by spinning a racket. (For each game after this, the winner of the previous game serves first.) The server then elects a box to serve from, alternating boxes with each point until the service is lost.

How to win

A match is the best of three or five games. The first player to score nine points wins the game, but at eight-all the receiver may elect to play on to nine points ('set one') or ten points ('set two'). Points may only be scored by the server. If the server loses a stroke, the service passes to the opponent. The new server must now win a stroke to score a point.

KEY RULES

Play is continuous, as far as possible, with intervals of 90 seconds between the warm up and the first game, and then between all following games. *See Rule 7, Continuity of Play (page 128).*

The ball must always strike the front wall above the board. It may do this via another wall or walls, but before the ball bounces on the floor or touches any part of a player. *See Rule 6, Good Return (page 128).*

A player may allow the ball to bounce only once before being returned, otherwise a 'down' or 'not up' is called and the rally is lost.

Many of the rules of squash arise from the fact that the game is played in such a confined space. If a striker's return is heading straight for the front wall but is blocked by the opponent, the striker wins the stroke. Wherever possible, players must allow their opponent direct access to the ball and the freedom to hit it to any part of the front wall. *For details see Rule 9, Hitting an Opponent with the Ball (page 129)*

If a striker faces interference or is afraid of injuring an opponent, a let must be requested with the words "Let please" – before the shot is played. If a let is awarded, the rally starts again. *See Rule 12 (page 132).*

The service
The service in squash is relatively tame compared with a tennis service, but it is the best chance a player gets to select where the ball will land in relation to his or her opponent. Points can only be won off service so a skilful service is crucial to a player's armoury.

The grip
The most popular grip in squash is called the 'shake hands' grip. The idea is to "shake hands" with the racket so that the top edge of the shaft goes into the V between the thumb and forefinger with the forefinger slightly separated from the other three.

Jansher Khan, *World Champion in the late 1980s.*

Shoes for squash have to be well padded to avoid jarring feet and ankles. They must also have rubber soles that provide sure grip but will not mark the floor.

RULES OF THE WORLD SINGLES GAME

1. The Game
See page 126.

2. The Score
See How to Win (page 127)

3. Points
See page 127.

4. The Service

4.1 Play commences with a service and the right to serve first is decided by the spin of a racket. Thereafter, the server continues to serve until losing a stroke, whereupon the opponent becomes the server, and this procedure continues throughout the match. At the commencement of the second and each subsequent game the winner of the previous game serves first.

4.2 At the beginning of each game and each hand the server has the choice of serving from either box and thereafter shall serve from alternate boxes while remaining the server. However, if a rally ends in a let, the server shall serve again from the same box.

4.3 When serving, a player shall drop or throw the ball from either a hand or the racket before striking it. Should the player, having dropped or thrown the ball, make no attempt to strike it, the ball shall be dropped or thrown again for that service.

4.4 A service is good when it does not result in the server serving the hand out. The server

serves the hand out and loses the stroke if:

4.4.1 The ball, after being dropped or thrown for service, touches a wall, the floor, ceiling or any object(s) suspended from the walls or ceiling before being served. – Called 'Fault'.

4.4.2 At the time of striking the ball the server fails to have part of one foot in contact with the floor within the service-box without any part of that foot touching the service-box line (part of that foot may project over this line provided that it does not touch the line). – Called 'Foot fault'.

4.4.3 The server makes one or more attempts to strike the ball, but fails to do so. – Called 'Not up'.

4.4.4 The ball is not struck correctly. – Called 'Not up'.

4.4.5 The ball is served out. – Called 'Out'.

4.4.6 the ball is served against any wall of the court before the front wall. – Called 'Fault'.

4.4.7 The ball is served onto the floor or onto or below the service line. – Called 'Fault' if above the board and 'Down' if on the floor or on or below the board.

4.4.8 The first bounce of the ball, unless volleyed by the receiver, is on the floor on or outside ten short or half court lines of the quarter court opposite to the server's box. – Called 'Fault'.

4.5 the server must not serve until the Marker has completed calling the score.

5. The Play
See page 127.

6. Good Return

6.1 A return is good if the ball, before it has bounced more than once upon the floor, is returned correctly by the striker onto the front wall above the board, either directly or via side wall(s) and/or back wall, without first touching the floor or any part of the striker's body or clothing, or the opponent's racket, body or clothing, provided the ball is not hit out.

6.2 It shall not be considered a good return if the ball touches the board before or after it hits the front wall and before it bounces on the floor, or if the

racket is not in the player's hand at the time the ball is struck.

7 Continuity of Play

After the first service is delivered play shall be continuous so far as is practical provided that:

7.1 At any time play may be

Sheer volley
In squash the ball is usually hit on the volley or half volley. It is very rarely allowed to bounce completely. The aim is typically to strike the ball just over the top of the board so that your opponent has very little time to get to the ball for the volley.

suspended, owing to bad light or other circumstances beyond the control of the players, for such period as the Referee shall decide. The score shall stand. If another court is available when the court originally in use remains unsuitable, the match may be transferred to it if both players agree or as directed by the Referee.

In the event of play being suspended for the day the score shall stand unless both players agree to start the match again.

7.2 An interval of 90 seconds shall be permitted between the end of the warm-up and the commencement of the first game and also between all games. Players may leave the court during such intervals but must

be ready to play prior to the expiry of the 90-second time interval.

By mutual consent of the payers play may commence or resume prior to the expiry of the 90-second time interval.

7.3 Provided a player satisfies the Referee that a change of equipment, clothing or footwear is necessary, the player may leave the court, but is required to effect the change as quickly as possible, and shall be allowed a period not exceeding ninety seconds for this purpose.

7.4 When 15 seconds of a permitted 90-second time interval remain the Referee shall call '15 seconds' to advise the players to be ready to resume play. At the end of this interval the Referee shall call 'Time'. The calls should be made in a loud voice. It is the responsibility of the players to be in a position to hear the calls of '15 seconds and 'Time'.

7.5 A player suffering illness or disability has the choice of continuing or resuming play without delay, conceding the game in progress, or conceding the match. If conceding the game, the player shall retain any points already scored and at the conclusion of the 90-second interval between games shall either resume play or concede the match.

However, if the illness or disability involves visible blood flow, a continuation or resumption of play is not permitted. The player shall leave the court but is not required at that time to concede the game in progress. If the player wishes to resume play, the illness or disability shall be dealt with by the Referee as a self-inflicted injury and the provisions of Rule 16.2 shall apply.

7.6 In the event of an injury to a player the Referee shall refer to the provisions of Rule 16.

7.7 The Referee shall apply the provisions of Rule 17 to a player who in the opinion of the Referee, delays play unreasonably. Such delay may be caused by:

7.7.1 Unduly slow preparation

Types of serve
In squash, the ball is often served with a hammer drive or a lob. A lob (1) serve sends the ball high into the middle of the front wall so that it loops back into the far court, hitting the side wall just below the out line; a drive(2) aims to power the ball staight back into the angle between the wall and the floor, making a return awkward.

to serve or to receive service.

7.7.2 Prolonged discussion with the Referee.

7.7.3 Delay in returning to the court, having left under the terms of Rule 7.2, 7.3 or 15.1.

7.8 If an object, other than a player's racket, falls to the floor of the court while a rally is in progress the requirements are:

7.8.1 The Referee, on becoming aware of a fallen object, shall stop play immediately.

7.8.2 A player becoming aware of a fallen object may stop play and appeal for a let.

7.8.3 If the object falls from a player, then that player shall lose the stroke unless Rule 7.8.5 applies or unless the cause is a collision with the opponent. In the latter case a let shall be allowed except that if an appeal for interference is made the Referee shall apply the provisions of Rule 12.

7.8.4 If the object falls from a source other than a player a let shall be allowed unless Rule 7.8.5 applies.

7.8.5 If a player has already made a clear winning return when the object falls to the floor of the court, then that player shall win the stroke.

7.9 If a player drops a racket, the Referee shall allow the rally to continue unless Rule 12, 13.1.1, 13.1.3 or 17 applies.

8. Strokes

A player wins a stroke:

8.1 Under Rule 4.4 when the player is the receiver.

8.2 If the opponent fails to make a good return of the ball when the opponent is the striker, unless a let is allowed or a stroke is awarded to the opponent.

8.3 If the ball touches the opponent (including anything worn or carried), without interference, when the opponent is the non-striker, except as is otherwise provided for in Rules 9 and 10. If interference occurs, then the provisions of Rule 12 apply. In all cases the Referee shall rule accordingly.

8.4 If a stroke is awarded to the player by the Referee as provided for in the rules.

9. Hitting an Opponent with the Ball

If the ball, before reaching the front wall, hits the striker's opponent (including anything worn or carried), the ball shall cease to be in play and:

9.1 Unless Rule 9.2 applies, the striker shall win the stroke if the return would have been good and the ball would have struck the front wall without first touching any other wall.

9.2 If the return would have been good, but the striker has either followed the ball round and turned or the ball has passed around the striker who, in either case, strikes the ball to the right of the body after the ball has passed to the left (or vice versa) then a let shall be allowed in all cases.

9.3 If the ball either had struck or would have struck any other wall and the return would have been good, a let shall be allowed unless, in the opinion of the Referee, a winning return has been prevented, in which case the striker shall win the stroke.

10. Further Attempts to Hit the Ball

If the striker strikes at and misses the ball, further attempts to strike it may be made. If, after being missed, the ball touches the opponent (including anything worn or carried) then, in the opinion of the Referee:

10.1 If the striker could otherwise have made a good return, a let shall be allowed, or

10.2 If the striker could not have made a good return, the striker shall lose the stroke.
If any such further attempt is successful but results in a good return being prevented from reaching the front wall by hitting the striker's opponent (including anything worn or carried), a let shall be allowed in all circumstances. If any such further attempt would not have resulted in a good return, the striker shall lose the stroke.

11. Appeals

The loser of a rally may appeal against any decision of the marker affecting that rally.
An appeal to the Referee under Rule 11 should be prefaced with the words 'Appeal please'. Play shall then cease until the Referee has given the decision.

If an appeal under Rule 11 is

➡ *page 132*

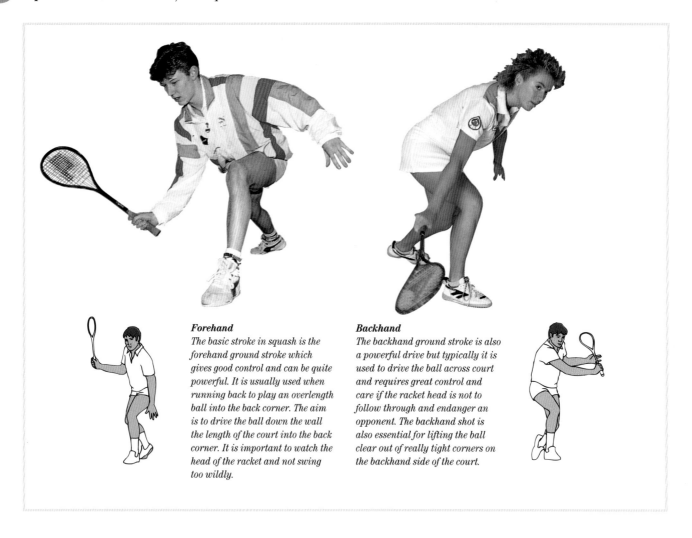

Forehand

The basic stroke in squash is the forehand ground stroke which gives good control and can be quite powerful. It is usually used when running back to play an overlength ball into the back corner. The aim is to drive the ball down the wall the length of the court into the back corner. It is important to watch the head of the racket and not swing too wildly.

Backhand

The backhand ground stroke is also a powerful drive but typically it is used to drive the ball across court and requires great control and care if the racket head is not to follow through and endanger an opponent. The backhand shot is also essential for lifting the ball clear out of really tight corners on the backhand side of the court.

SKILLS

Racket skills are all-important in the game of squash, but these must be combined with a high level of fitness. Although the court is relatively small, a player will cover this ground many times over in a game, often at great speed. A highly skilful player will also be able to deliver a constantly varied, unpredictable pace in order to wear down an opponent.

Strokes

A good, secure grip is necessary for precision and control, but it must also allow flexibility of the wrist. The basic *forehand ground stroke* can be used from anywhere along the length of the court. It is an easily controlled driving shot which can be quite powerful. The *backhand ground stroke* takes care of shots from the other ide of the court. In between strokes it is best to wait with the racket poised in front of the body, ready for backhand or

forehand strokes. The *volley* is a quick-response stroke, meeting the ball before it bounces on the floor. This is an effective attacking shot, often making it very difficult for an opponent to manage a return. The *drop* is another potential point-scoring stroke, particularly if the opponent is fooled into anticipating a driving shot and remains on the 'T' (the intersection of the short line and the half-court line). The ball is played near the tin or along the side wall, making it nearly impossible to reach and return in time. *Boast* shots are clever angle shots made by playing the ball on to a side wall so that it rebounds directly on to the front wall and on to the floor, or on to the

opposite side wall and then to the floor. A well-judged boast shot will disorientate the opponent if unexpected.

Blocked volley

In squash there is often no time to make a full swing at the ball. As a result, squash players often have to play a blocked volley.

Overhead volley or smash

The overhead volley is often used to cut off high cross-court lobs. The aim is to play the ball at a point in front of and above the racket shoulder.

1 The shot begins with the racket dropped down the back, the back arched and the racket arm held high with the wrist cocked.

TACTICS

Because a rally can be exhausting, both players will try to conserve energy by dominating the court from the T. This central position guarantees the shortest possible travelling distance to any area of the court and also enables whichever player occupies it to place shots that are difficult for their opponent to reach, thus tiring them out and weakening their defences.

Boasting

A boast shot is a shot that bounces off the side wall before hitting the front. One of the most effective is the 'tickle boast'. This is a delicate shot played near the front wall and designed to drop low into the front of the court. The player often disguises this stroke by shaping to play a drive then checking the downswing to cock his wrist and tickle the ball into the corner.

2 *The racket arm then swings over in a throwing action, with the arm at full length to give maximum leverage and a fast-moving racket head, to strike the ball downwards at the top of the swing.*

3 *As with all squash strokes, it is important to follow through. The player should aim to present the back of the non-racket shoulder to the ball at the beginning of the stroke and only turn full-face towards the end.*

Continued from page 129

disallowed, the Marker's decision
shall stand. If the Referee is uncertain, a let shall be allowed except where provided for in the Notes to Referees (see complete rules).

Appeals upheld or Referee intervention under Rule 20.4 are dealt with in each specific situation below.

11.1 Appeals on Service

11.1. If the Marker calls 'Fault', 'Foot fault', 'Not up', 'Down' or 'Out' to the service, the receiver may appeal, either immediately or at the end of the rally if the receiver has played or attempted to play the ball. If, in the opinion of the Referee, the service was not good, the Referee shall stop play immediately and award the stroke to the receiver.

11.2 Appeals on Play other than Service

11.2.1 If the Marker calls 'Not up' or 'Out' following a player's return, the player may appeal. If the appeal is upheld, the Referee shall allow a let except that if, in the opinion of the Referee:

The Marker's call has interrupted that player's winning return, the Referee shall award the stroke to the player.

The Marker's call has interrupted or prevented a winning return by the opponent, the Referee shall award the stroke to the opponent.

11.2.2 If the Marker fails to call 'Not up', 'Down' or 'Out' following a player's return, the opponent may appeal either immediately or at the end of the rally if the opponent has played or attempted to play the ball. If, in the opinion of the Referee, the return was not good, the Referee shall stop play immediately and award the stroke to the opponent.

12. Interference

12.1 The player whose turn it is

to play the ball is entitled to freedom from interference by the opponent.
12.2 To avoid interference the opponent must make every effort to provide the player with:
12.2.1 Unobstructed direct access to the ball.
12.2.2 A fair view of the ball.
12.2.3 Freedom to hit the ball.
12.2.4 Freedom to play the ball directly to any part of the front wall.

12.3 Interference occurs if the opponent fails to fulfil any of the requirements of Rule 12.2, irrespective of whether the opponent makes every effort to fulfil those requirements.

12.4 A player encountering possible interference has the choice of continuing with play or of stopping and appealing to the Referee.
12.4.1 The correct method of appeal, whether a let or a stroke is sought by a player, is with the words 'Let please'.
12.4.2 An appeal may be made only by the player (the person whose turn it is to play the ball). The appeal must be made either immediately the interference occurs or, where the player clearly does not continue with play beyond the point of interference, without undue delay.

12.5 The Referee shall decide on the appeal and shall announce the decision with the words 'No let', 'Yes let' or 'Stroke to...(name of appropriate player)'. In assessing the situation the only relevant opinion is that of the Referee and the decision of the Referee shall be final.

12.6 The Referee shall not allow a let and the player shall lose the rally if:
12.6.1 There has been no interference.
12.6.2 Interference has occurred but either player would

not have made a good return or the player has not made every effort to get to the ball.
12.6.3 The player has clearly accepted the interference and played on.
12.6.4 The player has created the interference in moving to the ball.

12.7 The Referee shall allow a let if there has been interference which the opponent has made every effort to avoid and the player would have made a good return.

12.8 The Referee shall award a stroke to the player if:
12.8.1 There has been interference which the opponent has not made every effort to avoid and the player would have made a good return.
12.8.2 There has been interference which the opponent has made every effort to avoid and the player would have made a winning return.
12.8.3 The player has refrained from hitting the ball which, if hit, would clearly have struck the opponent going directly to the front wall; or to a side wall, but in the latter case would have been a winning return (unless in either case turning, ball passing around player, or further attempt applies).

12.9 The Referee is also empowered to allow a let under Rule 12.7 or to award a stroke under Rule 12.8 without an appeal having been made, if necessary stopping play to do so.

12.10 The provisions of Rule 17, Conduct On Court, may be applied in interference situations. The Referee shall, stopping play if it has not already stopped, apply an appropriate penalty if:
12.10.1 The player has made unnecessary physical contact with the opponent or vice versa.
12.10.2 The player has

endangered the opponent with an excessive racket swing.

13. Lets

In addition to lets allowed under other rules, lets may or shall be allowed in certain other cases. Any request for a let should be prefaced by the words 'Let please'.

13.1 A let may be allowed:
13.1.1 If the ball in play touches any article lying on the floor.
13.1.2 If the striker refrains from hitting the ball owing to a reasonable fear of injuring the opponent.
13.1.3 If, in the opinion of the Referee, either player is distracted by an occurrence on or off the court.
13.1.4 If, in the opinion of the Referee, a change in court conditions has affected the result of the rally.

13.2 A let shall be allowed:
13.2.1 If the receiver is not ready and does not attempt to return the service.
13.2.2 If the ball breaks during play.
13.2.3 If the Referee is asked to decide an appeal and is unable to do so.
13.2.4 If an otherwise good return has been made but the ball either lodges in any part of the playing surface of the court, preventing it from bouncing more than once upon the floor, or the ball goes out on its first bounce.

13.3 If the striker appeals for a let under Rules 13.1 (1 to 4), in order for a let to be allowed the striker must have been able to make a good return. For a non-striker appeal under Rules 13.1.1, 13.1.3 and 13.1.4 this is not a requirement.

13.4 No let shall be allowed under Rules 13.1.2 and 13.2.1 if the player attempts to play the ball but may be allowed under Rules 13.1.1, 13.1.3, 13.1.4, 13.2.2, 13.2.3 and 13.2.4.

13.5 The appeals requirements of Rule 13 are:
13.5.1 An appeal by the player is necessary for a let to be allowed under Rules 13.1.2 (striker only), 13.1.3, 13.2.1 (striker only) and 13.2.3.
13.5.2 An appeal by the player or Referee intervention without appeal is applicable to Rules 13.1.1, 13.1.4, 13.2.2 and 13.2.4.

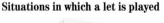

Situations in which a let is played

1. When the ball hits an opponent, when it would have hit the front wall.

2. When the player is unable to hit the ball without being in danger of hitting his opponent.

3. If the striker's shot hits his opponent unwittingly after a follow through.

14. The Ball

14.1 At any time, when the ball is not in actual play, another ball may be substituted by mutual consent of the players, or on appeal by either player at the discretion of the Referee.

14.2 If a ball breaks during play, it shall be replaced promptly by another ball.

14.3 If a ball has broken during play but this has not been established, a let for the rally in which the ball broke shall be allowed if the server appeals prior to the next service or if the receiver appeals prior to attempting to return that service.

14.4 The provisions of Rule 14.3 do not apply to the final rally of a game. An appeal in this case must be immediately after the rally.

14.5 If a player stops during a rally to appeal that the ball is broken only to find subsequently that the ball is not broken, then that player shall lose the stroke.

14.6 Between games the ball shall remain within the court unless removal is permitted by the Referee.

15. Warm-Up

15.1 Immediately preceding the start of play the two players together shall be allowed on the court of play a period of five minutes for the purpose of warming up the ball to be used for the match.

After two and a half minutes of the warm-up, the Referee shall call "Half time" and ensure that the players change sides unless they mutually agree otherwise. The Referee shall also advise when the warm-up period is complete with the call of "Time".

15.2 Where a ball has been substituted under Rule 14 or when the match is being resumed after considerable delay, the Referee shall allow the ball to be warmed up to playing condition. Play shall then resume on the direction of the Referee, or upon mutual consent of the players, whichever is the earlier.

15.3 The ball may be warmed up by either player between the end of the five-minute warm-up and start of play, between games and

when the opponent is changing equipment.

16. Injury

16.1 In the event of an injury to a player the Referee shall decide whether the injury category is:

16.1.1 Self-inflicted (where the injury to the player was not contributed to by the opponent).

16.1.2 Contributed (where the injury was accidentally contributed to, or accidentally caused by, the opponent).

16.1.3 Opponent-inflicted (where the injury was caused by the opponent's dangerous play, or by a deliberate or dangerous action).

16.2 For a self-inflicted injury the Referee shall allow the injured player three minutes to recover from the injury. This time interval may be extended at the discretion of the Referee only if the injury involves visible blood flow. The Referee shall call "Time" at the end of the three-minute period and at the end of any additional period permitted. If the injured player has not returned to court when "Time" is called the Referee shall award the match to the opponent.

If additional recovery time is needed by the player beyond the total time permitted by the Referee, the Referee shall require the injured player to resume play; or concede one game, accept the time interval available and then either resume play or concede the match.

16.3 For a contributed injury (Rule 16.1.2) the Referee shall allow one hour for the injured player to recover, or such additional time as is provided for in the time schedule of the competition.The injured player must, by the end of this period of time, resume play or concede the match. If play is resumed the score at the conclusion of the rally in which the injury occurred shall stand, except that if play is resumed on another day the match may start again if both players agree.

16.4 For an opponent-inflicted injury (Rule 16.1.3) the Referee shall apply an appropriate Rule 17 penalty, except that if the injured player requires time to recover the Referee shall award the match to the injured player.

16.5 Irrespective of the category

of injury, or of illness or disability, a player shall not resume play while a wound which is bleeding remains uncovered, or blood flow is visible from a covered wound or on any part of the player's body, or with blood-stained clothing.

16.6 An injured player, having been granted a period of recovery time, may resume play prior to the expiry of that period of time provided that the opponent is also ready to resume play.

16.7 If a player resumes play, having treated bleeding that resulted from a contributed injury, and that wound again begins to bleed, the Referee shall then consider this under the category of a self-inflicted injury, and the provisions of Rule 16.2 shall apply.

16.8 If a player resumes play, having treated bleeding that resulted from a self-inflicted injury, and that wound again begins to bleed, the Referee shall require the player to concede the match; or concede one game, accept the time interval available, and then either resume

play or concede the match.

16.9 If a player claims injury and the Referee is not satisfied that an injury has occurred, the Referee shall require the player to resume play; or concede one game, accept the time interval available and then either resume play or concede the match.

17. Conduct on Court

If the Referee considers that the

behaviour of a player on court could be intimidating or offensive to an opponent, official or spectator, or could in any way bring the game into disrepute, the player shall be penalized.

Offences which should be dealt with under this rule include audible and visible obscenities, verbal and physical abuse, dissent to Marker or Referee, abuse of racket, ball or court, and coaching, other than during the interval between games. Other offences include unnecessary physical contact and excessive racket swing, unfair warm-up. late back on court, dangerous play or action and time wasting.

For these and any other offences which, in the opinion of the Referee, justify the application of this rule, one of the following penalty provisions shall be applied.

Warning by the Referee (called a Conduct Warning).

Stroke awarded to opponent (called a Conduct Stroke).

Game awarded to opponent (called a Conduct Game).

Match awarded to opponent (called a Conduct Match).

18. Control of a Match
19. Duties of a Marker
20. Duties of a Referee

These rules are reprinted by permission of the World Squash Federation. For a complete copy of the Rules, including notes to Referees and Appendices 1 – 11, contact the WSF.

High ball
High balls such as this are generally a gift to an opponent, allowing her to smash the ball low and hard down towards the board, in the direction she chooses.

Table tennis
Essentials

The simplicity and accessibilty of table tennis, also known as ping pong, make it one of the most widely played sports in the world. Yet its reputation as a fun pastime for all ages and abilities belies the fact that at competition level players have amazing skills.

1,525m

2.74m

76cm

The net
A net suspended from a cord attached to two posts, each 6 in (15.25cm) high and joined to the table with clamps. The bottom of the net must be as close to the playing surface as possible. The top of the net must measure 6 in (15.25 cm) above the playing surface.

The bat
May be of any size, shape or weight, but must have a flat blade of even thickness. The blade must consist of 85 per cent natural wood and be covered with pimpled or sandwich rubber on the striking side or sides. The pimples may face inwards or outwards.

The table
Rectangular, with a dark coloured, matt playing surface which yields a uniform bounce of about 23 cm (9 in) when a standard ball is dropped on to it from a height of 30 cm (11.8 in). Divided into two equal courts by a net assembly across the middle.

Officials
An umpire and an assistant umpire.

Players
Two for singles, four for doubles.

Dress
A short-sleeved shirt, and shorts or a skirt. The main colour must be clearly different to that of the ball, and the shirts of opposing players must be different from each other.

Service
To start a rally in table tennis one player serves by throwing the ball up from the palm of his hand at least 16 cm and then striking the ball with the bat as it falls.

The ball
Matt, spherical, with a diameter of 38 mm (1.5 in) and a weight of 2.5 g (0.08 oz). May be white, yellow or orange and made of celluloid or similar plastics material.

HOW TO PLAY

In singles, two players take it in turns to strike the ball after it has bounced once in their court so that it passes over (or around) the net and into their opponent's court. Points are scored by winning rallies. In doubles there is a set striking order to follow. The service is received by one opponent. The ball must then be struck by the server's partner and then, finally, by the receiver's partner. This sequence is maintained throughout a rally.

Starting

Players may practise for up to two minutes on the table before a match. The winner of the toss has the choice of ends or the option of serving or receiving first. Whoever serves first must strike the ball so that it bounces once on their side of the net before it enters the opponent's court. After every five serves the service passes to the opposing side. *See Rule 2.6, A Good Service (page 136).*

How to win

The first player or pair to score 21 points wins the game. If there is a score of 20-all, the first to score two points more than the opponent wins. (Service alternates in this situation.) A match is the best of three or five games.

Stance
A table tennis player needs a good stance to enable him to spring quickly around the table. A good stance invovles starting with your feet about as wide apart as your shoulders, your knees slightly bent in a crouching position so that your chin is directly above your knees. The playing arm is held out in front with the elbow bent.

KEY RULES

When serving, the ball must be thrown up into the air to a height of at least 6 in (16 cm), with the palm – not the fingers – of the server's free hand. It may be struck only once it has begun to fall. It must be struck while it is behind the server's end line, but no further back from the table than the part of the server's body other than the arm, head or leg, which is farthest from his end line. *See Rule 2.6, A Good Service (page 136).*

A white line down the centre of the table divides each court into two for doubles games. Services must be made from

the right hand court and land in the opposite right-hand court. As with the striking sequence, the service passes from the first server to the first receiver, then to the first server's partner and then to the first receiver's partner.

Players or pairs swap ends after each game. In the last game ends are changed as soon

as either side reaches ten points. *See Rule 2.13, The Choice of Serving, Receiving and Ends (page 136).*

If, after 15 minutes, a game is still unfinished and neither side has scored at least 19 points, the Expedite System comes into play. For the remainder of the game, service alternates after each point scored. If the receiver makes 13 successive good returns he scores a point.
See Rule 2.15, The Expedite System (page 137).

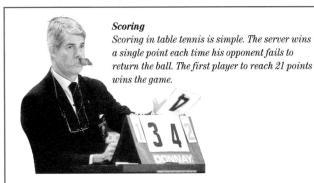

Scoring

Scoring in table tennis is simple. The server wins a single point each time his opponent fails to return the ball. The first player to reach 21 points wins the game.

LAWS OF TABLE TENNIS

(The masculine gender is used throughout but may refer to men or women.)

2.1 The Table
See The Table (page 134).

2.2 The Net Assembly
See The Net (page 1340).

2.3 The Ball
See The Ball (page 134).

2.4 The Bat
See The Bat (page 134).

2.5 Definitions
2.5.1 A *rally* is the period during which the ball is in play.

2.5.2 The *ball* is in play from the last moment at which it is stationary on the palm of the free hand before being intentionally projected in service until the rally is decided as a let or a point.

2.5.3 A *let* is a rally of which the result is not scored.

2.5.4 A *point* is a rally of which the result is scored.

2.5.5 The *racket hand* is the hand carrying the racket.

2.5.6 The *free hand* is the hand not carrying the racket.

2.5.7 A player *strikes* the ball if he touches it in play with his racket, held in the hand, or with his racket hand below the wrist.

2.5.8 A player *obstructs* the ball if he, or anything he wears or carries, touches it in play when it has not passed over the playing surface or his end line, not having touched his court since last being struck by his opponent.

2.5.9 The *server* is the player due to strike the ball first in a rally.

2.5.10 The *receiver* is the player due to strike the ball second in a rally.

2.5.11 The *umpire* is the person appointed to control a match.

2.5.12 The *assistant umpire* is the person appointed to assist the umpire with certain decisions.

2.5.13 Anything that a player *wears or carries* includes anything that he was wearing or carrying at the start of the rally.

2.5.14 The ball shall be regarded as passing *over or around* the net assembly if it passes over, under or outside the projection of the net assembly outside the table or if, in a return, it is struck after it has bounced back over or around the net.

2.5.15 The *end line* shall be regarded as extending indefinitely in both directions.

2.6 A Good Service
2.6.1 At the start of service the ball shall be stationary, resting freely on the flat, open palm of the server's free hand, behind the end line and above the level of the playing surface.

2.6.2 The server shall then project the ball near vertically upwards, without imparting spin, so that it rises at least 6 in (16cm) after leaving the palm of the free hand and then falls without touching anything before being struck.

2.6.3 As the ball is falling the server shall strike it so that it touches first his court and then, after passing over or around the net assembly, touches directly the receiver's court; in doubles, the ball shall touch successively the right half court of server and receiver.

2.6.4 The ball and the racket shall be above the level of the playing surface from the last moment at which the ball is stationary before being projected until it is struck.

2.6.5 When the ball is struck it shall be behind the server's end line but not farther back than the part of the server's body, other than his arm, head or leg, which is farthest from his end line.

2.6.6 It is the responsibility of the player to serve so that the umpire or assistant umpire can see that he complies with the requirements for a good service.

2.6.6.1 If the umpire is doubtful of the legality of a service but neither he nor the assistant umpire is sure that it is illegal he may, on the first occasion in a match, warn the server without awarding a point.

2.6.6.2 If subsequently in the match the same player's service is of dubious legality, for the same or for any other reason, he shall not be given the benefit of the doubt and the receiver shall score a point.

2.6.6.3 Whenever there is a clear failure to comply with the requirements for a good service no warning shall be given, and the receiver shall score a point, on the first as on any other occasion.

2.6.7 Exceptionally, the umpire may relax the requirements for a good service where he is notified, before play begins, that compliance is prevented by physical disability.

2.7 A Good Return
See (page 135)

2.8 The Order of Play
See How to Play (page 135)

2.9 A Let
2.9.1 The rally shall be a let:

2.9.1.1 if in service the ball, in passing over or around the net assembly, touches it, provided the service is otherwise good or the ball is obstructed by the receiver or his partner;

2.9.1.2 if the service is delivered when the receiving player or pair is not ready, provided that neither the receiver nor his partner attempts to strike the ball;

2.9.1.3 if failure to make a good service or a good return or otherwise to comply with the Laws is due to a disturbance outside the control of the player;

2.9.1.4 if play is interrupted by the umpire or the assistant umpire;

2.9.1.5 if, in doubles, the wrong player serves or receives.

2.9.2 Play may be interrupted

2.9.2.1 to correct an error in the order of serving, receiving or ends;

2.9.2.2 to introduce the expedite system;

2.9.2.3 to warn or penalise a player;

2.9.2.4 because the conditions of play are disturbed in a way which could affect the outcome of the rally.

2.10 A Point
2.10.1 Unless the rally is a let, a player shall score a point:

2.10.1.1 if his opponent fails to make a good service;

2.10.1.2 if his opponent fails to make a good return;

2.10.1.3 if the ball, after he has made a good service or a good return, touches anything other than the net assembly before being struck by his opponent;

2.10.1.4 if the ball, after his opponent has struck it, passes over his end line without having touched his court;

2.10.1.5 if his opponent obstructs the ball;

2.10.1.6 if his opponent strikes the ball twice successively;

2.10.1.7 if his opponent strikes the ball with a side of the racket blade whose surface does not comply with the requirements of 2.4.3;

2.10.1.8 if his opponent, or anything his opponent wears or carries, moves the playing surface;

2.10.1.9 if his opponent, or anything his opponent wears or carries, touches the net assembly;

2.10.1.10 if his opponent's free hand touches the playing surface;

2.10.11 if a doubles opponent strikes the ball out of proper sequence;

2.10.1.12 if, under the expedite system, he makes, or he and his doubles partner make, 13 successive good returns, including the return of service.

2.11 A Game

2.12 A Match
See How to Win (page 135)

2.13 The Choice of Serving, Receiving and Ends
2.13.1 The right to choose the initial order of serving, receiving and ends shall be decided by lot and the winner may choose to serve or to receive first or to start at a particular end.

2.13.2 When one player or pair has chosen to serve or to receive first or to start at a particular end, the other player or pair shall have the other choice.

2.13.3 After each five points have been scored the receiving player or pair shall become the serving player or pair and so on until the end of the game, unless both players or pairs have scored 20 points or the expedite system is in operation, when the sequences of serving and receiving shall be the same but each player shall serve for only one point in turn.

2.13.4 In each game of a doubles match, the pair having the right to serve first shall choose which of them will do so and in the first game of a match the receiving pair shall decide which of them will receive first; in subsequent games of the match, the first server having been chosen, the first receiver shall be the player who served to him in the preceding game.

2.13.5 In doubles, at each change of service the previous receiver shall become the server and the partner of the previous server shall become the receiver.

2.13.6 The player or pair serving first in a game shall receive first in the next game of the match and in the last possible game of a doubles match the pair due to receive next shall change their order of receiving when first either pair scores ten points.

2.13.7 The player or pair starting at one end in a game shall start at the other end in the next game of the match and in the last possible game of a match the players or pairs shall change ends when first either player or pair scores ten points.

2.14 Out of Order of Serving, Receiving or Ends

2.14.1 If a player serves or receives out of turn, play shall be interrupted by the umpire as soon as the error is discovered and shall resume with those players serving and receiving who should be server and receiver respectively at the score that has been reached, according to the sequence established at the beginning of the match and, in doubles, to the order of serving chosen by

the pair having the right to serve first in the game during which the error is discovered.

2.14.2 If the players have not changed ends when they should have done so, play shall be interrupted by the umpire as soon as the error is discovered and shall resume with the players at the ends at which they should be at the score that has been reached, according to the sequence established at the beginning of the match.

2.14.3 In any circumstances, all points scored before the discovery of an error shall be reckoned.

2.15 The Expedite System

2.15.1 The expedite system shall come into operation if a game is unfinished after 15 minutes' play, unless both players or pairs have scored at least 19 points, or at any earlier time at the request of both players or pairs.

2.15.1.1 If the ball is in play when the time limit is reached, play shall be interrupted by the umpire and shall resume with service by the player who served in the rally that was interrupted.

2.15.1.2 If the ball is not in play when the time limit is reached, play shall resume with service by the player who received in the immediately preceding rally of the game.

2.15.2 Thereafter, each player shall serve for one point in turn until the end of the game and if the receiving player or pair makes 13 good returns the receiver shall score a point.

2.15.3 Once introduced, the expedite system shall remain in operation until the match's end.

Reprinted by permission of the International Table Tennis Federation.

To give a ball back-spin the player slices down sharply under the ball as he strikes it.

To give a ball topspin a player slices the bat over the top of the ball as he hits it.

SKILLS AND TACTICS

Good anticipation and reaction skills, stamina and coordination will improve any player's game.

Two basic *grips* are used. The first is similar to the 'shaking hands' grip used in many other racket games. The other is the 'penholder' grip – the handle is held close to the base of the blade, as if it were a pen. Although this grip allows a much faster recovery time, since only one side of the bat is ever used, it can make it difficult to return tricky

backhand or angle shots.

Imparting spin to the ball is an essential skill. Attacking players use *topspin* to force a weak return from an opponent. This causes the ball to dart forwards suddenly as it hits the playing surface. *Backspin* has the effect of 'holding back' the ball as it travels down the table. Both spins are acheived by angling the bat as it makes contact with the ball, brushing it rather than driving through it to set it spinning.

Players will often try to confuse opponents by turning the bat in their hands while waiting for a return - 'twiddling'. If the bat has two different surface materials the ball will rebound differently according to which one is used. The opponent will therefore not know what sort of return to expect until the last minute.

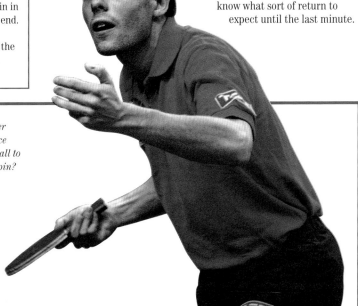

GREY AREA

The service law is frequently changed to maintain a fair balance between server and receiver, as players are continually seeking new ways to deceive their opponents. The main technique is to hide the ball as it is struck, so that the receiver cannot judge the spin. Some players struck the ball behind their backs until this was made illegal; others conceal it with their arms or even their legs.

Is this server going to slice under the ball to give it topspin?

Basketball
Essentials

Invented in 1891 by the Canadian, James Naismith, who hung peach baskets at either end of a gymnasium for players to throw a ball into, basketball is now the most widely played indoor sport in the world.

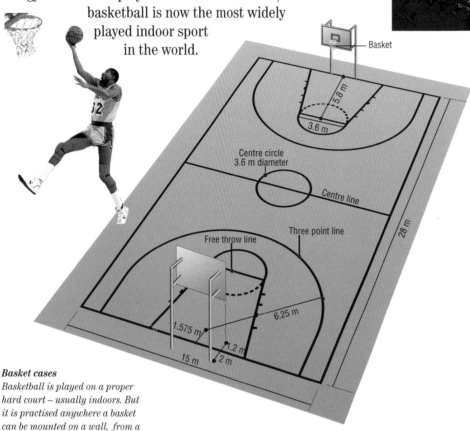

Basket

5.8 m

3.6 m

Centre circle
3.6 m diameter

Centre line

Three point line

28 m

Free throw line

6.25 m

1.575 m

1.2 m

2 m

15 m

Basket cases
Basketball is played on a proper hard court – usually indoors. But it is practised anywhere a basket can be mounted on a wall, from a backyard to an office.

The court
Usually indoors, rectangular 28 m x 15 m (31 x 16 yds) for official FIBA competitions, minimum 26 m x 14 m (28 x 15 yds for all other competitions) with a flat, hard surface. The height of the ceiling or the lowest obstruction must be at least 7 m (23 ft). Lines marking out the boundaries, centre line and centre circle, are all 5 cm (approx 2 in) wide and drawn in the same colour.

Technical equipment
A game clock to time periods of play, a stop-watch to time time-outs, a 30-second device (automatic, digital, indicating time in seconds) for the administration of the 30-second rule. *See Rule 5, Art 18 (page 140)*. And very loud signals for the timekeeper/scorer and 30-second operator.

Game for all
The simplicity of basketball has made it popular with people from all walks of life.

Equipment
Two rectangular backboards at each end of the court, made of 0.03 m (approx 1 in) thick hard wood (painted white) or transparent material: 1.80 m (6 ft) wide and 1.05 m (3½ ft) high, with the lower edges 2.90 m (1½ ft) from the floor. A basket is attached to each backboard. Its ring is made of solid iron, painted orange, with an inside diameter of 0.45 m (1½ ft). The net is made of white cord and is suspended from the ring. It is 40 – 45 cm (approx 17½ in) long and constructed so that it checks the ball momentarily as it passes through.

Officials
A referee and an umpire, assisted by a timekeeper, a scorer, assistant scorer and a 30-second operator.

Players
Two teams of ten for 2 by 20 minute games, twelve for 4 by 12 minute games or for tournaments in which a team has to play more than three games. For all games only five players are allowed on the court at a time.

The ball
Spherical, of an approved shade of orange. An outer surface of leather, rubber or synthetic material and a circumference of 74.9—78 cm (approx 30 in). It must weigh between 567g and 650 g (20–23 oz) and when dropped on to the playing surface from a height of 1.80 m (2 yds), must rebound to a height of 1.20–1.40 m (4 ft) approximately.

HOW TO PLAY

Each team scores points by throwing the ball into their opponents' basket, while preventing them from doing the same. The ball is passed, thrown, tapped, rolled or dribbled in any direction on the court as provided for in the rules.

Starting

The referee starts the game by stepping into the centre circle with the ball. Two opposing players take their places in the circle. The referee tosses the ball up into the air betwen them and, once it begins its descent, both players attempt to tap it to their team members. This is called a 'jump ball'. *See Rule 6, Art. 26 (page 141).* The game clock is started when the ball is tapped the first time, and until such time, all

other players must remain outside the centre circle.

How to win

A goal from a free throw is worth one point. Two points are awarded for a goal from the field and three points are awarded for a goal from the three-point field goal area (this is the entire floor area of the playing ground except for the area near the opponents' basket which is limited by and includes the three-point line). The team scoring the most points wins.

Dress

Shirts and shorts of the same dominant colour contrasting with the opponents' team, whereby the shorts may be a different colour from the shirts. The shirts must have a number on the front and the back. Only numbers from 4 to 15 are allowed. Socks and shoes.

KEY RULES

• A game usually consists of two halves of 20 minutes each, with a half time interval of 10–15 minutes. Teams change baskets for the second half. (It may also consist of four periods of 12 minutes each.) If the score is tied at the end of the second half, as many extra periods of five minutes as are necessary are played until there is a winner.

• The ball is played with the hands only. When a player receives the ball when standing, he must

not take more than one step, using the other foot as a pivot foot. If he is moving when he receives it, two steps are allowed. *See Rule 7, Art. 39, Travel Rule (page 145).*

• Once he has gained control of the ball he may dribble it by throwing, tapping or rolling it on the floor, but the dribble ends as soon as he touches the ball simultaneously with both hands. *See Rule 7, Art. 38, Dribbling Rule (page 144).*

• There are several different time rules in basketball to ensure a fast-moving game. *The 30-second rule* requires a team to

shoot at the basket for a goal within 30 seconds of gaining possession of the ball. *See Rule 5, Art. 18 (page 140).*

The ten-second rule (Art. 42) states that a team must cause the ball to go into its front court within ten seconds of gaining control of it. *The three-second rule* restricts a player to only three consecutive seconds in his opponents' restricted area while his team is in control of the ball. *See Rule 7, Art. (40 page 145).*

• Basketball is theoretically a no-contact sport and 'personal fouls' are committed when a player breaks this rule (or indulges in unsportsmanlike behaviour). One or more free throws are awarded to the opponents. 'Technical fouls' are those which do not involve contact and are penalized with two free throws to the opponents (or two free throws and possession to the opponents in the case of a technical foul by a coach). In two by 20 minute games, a player may commit up to five fouls, after which he must leave the court. (Six fouls in a four by 12 minute game.)

• Free throws are an opportunity to score one point, uncontested, from a position behind the free-throw line and inside the semi-circle. No other player is allowed into the restricted area while the throw is being taken.

• A team's coach may request 'time-outs' to advise his players. These last one minute each. *See Rule 5, Art. 19, Charged Time-out (page 140).*

Guardsmen
Every basketball team has its 'guards'. The guards are often fairly short but are fast on their feet and are good at dribbling quickly upfield to set up attacks.

Basketball can be played in trainers but most serious players wear basketball boots which provide good grip and ankle support.

BASKETBALL THE RULES

These rules are abridged and summarised. Where the official rules have been edited, this is shown in italics.

Rule 1

The Game
Art. 1 The Definition
See How to play (page 139).

Rule 2

Dimensions And Equipment
Arts 2-4
See The court and equipment (page 138).

Rule 3

Officials and Their Duties
Arts 5 – 11

Rule 4

Players, Substitutes and Coaches
Arts 12-15
See Players (page 138).

Rule 5

Timing Regulations
Art. 16 Playing Time
See Key rules (page 139).

Art. 17 Game Clock Operations
1. The game clock shall be started when:
    a. During a jump ball, the ball is legally tapped by a player(s) after having reached its highest point on a toss.
    b. After an unsuccessful free throw and the ball is to continue in play, the ball touches a player on the court.
    c. After a throw-in from out of bounds, the ball touches a player on the court.
2. The game clock shall be stopped when:
    a.Time expires at the end of a half or a period.
    b. An official blows his whistle.
    c. The 30-second signal is sounded.
    d. A field goal is scored against a team which has requested a charged time-out.

Art. 18 Thirty-second Rule
1. When a player gains control of a live ball on the court, a shot for goal must be attempted by his team within 30

Stopping the clock after a foul.

seconds.
2. Failure of the team in control of the ball to shoot for goal within 30 seconds will be indicated by the sounding of the 30-second signal.
3. The 30-second device shall be operated as follows:
    a. The 30-second device shall be started as soon as a player gains control of a live ball on the court.
    b. The device shall be stopped as soon as team control is ended (see Art. 28).
    c. The device shall be reset to 30 seconds and restarted only when a new 30-second period begins as player control is next established on the court.
    1. If the game is stopped because of an action(s) by an opponent(s) of the team in control of the ball, a new 30-second period shall be awarded to the team in control of the ball.
    2. The mere touching of the ball by an opponent does not start a new 30-second period if the same team remains in control of the ball.
    d. The 30-second

device shall be stopped but not reset when:
    1. The ball has gone out of bounds and the throw-in is to be taken by a player from the same team that was previously in control of the ball.
    2. The officials have suspended play to protect an injured player of the team in control of the ball.
    3. The game is stopped because of an action(s) by the team in control of the ball.
    The 30-second operator shall restart the device from the time it was stopped as soon as a player of the same team gains control of the ball on the court after the throw-in.
    e. For any other reason(s), a new 30-second period shall be awarded to the team in control of the ball, unless, in the judgement of the officials, the opponents have been placed at a disadvantage, in which case the officials shall not award a new 30-second period to the team in control of the ball.

Art. 19 Charged Time-out
A. Description
A time-out of one minute's duration shall be charged to a team under the following provisions:
1. For games played in 2x20 minutes, two charged time-outs may be granted to each team during each half of playing time and one charged time-out for each extra period.
2. For games played in 4x12 minutes, three charged time-outs may be granted to each team during each half (two periods) of playing time and one charged time-out for each extra period.
3. If the team responsible for the time-out is ready to play before the end of the charged time-out, the referee shall resume the game as soon as possible.
4. During the time-out, the players are permitted to leave the playing court and sit on the team bench.
B. Procedure
1. A coach or assistant coach has the right to request a charged time-out. He shall do so by going in person to the scorer and asking clearly for a "time-out", making the proper conventional sign with his hands.

Art. 20 Injury to Players or Officials
Art. 21 Tied Score and Extra Periods
See Key rules (page 139).

Rule 6
Playing Regulations
Art. 22 Decision of a Game
Art. 23 Beginning of the Game
See Starting (page 139).
Art. 24 Status of the Ball
1. The ball is in play (goes into play) when:
    a. An official with the ball enters the circle to administer a jump ball.
    b. An official enters the free-throw lane with or without the ball to administer a free throw.
    c. The ball is at the disposal of a player for a throw-in from out of bounds.
2. The ball becomes alive when:
    a. During a jump ball, it is legally tapped by a jumper(s) after having reached its highest point.
    b. An official places it at the disposal of a free-throw shooter.
    c. After a throw-in from out of bounds, it touches a player on the court.
3. The ball becomes dead when:
    a. Any goal is legally made.
    b. An official's whistle sounds while the ball is alive or in play.
    c. It is apparent that the ball will not go into the basket on a free throw for:
    1. A free throw which is to be followed by another free throw(s).
    2. A free throw which is to be followed by a further penalty.
    d. The 30-second operator's signal is sounded while the ball is alive.
    e. Time expires for a half or a period.
    f. The ball which is already in flight on a shot for goal is legally touched by a player of either team after time has expired for a half or a period, or after a foul has been called.
Art. 25 Location of a Player and of an Official
1. The location of a player is determined by where he is touching the floor. While he is in the air from a leap, he retains the same status as where he last touched the floor. This includes the boundary lines, the centre line, the three-point line, the free- throw line and the lines delimiting the free-throw lanes.
2. The location of an official is determined in the same manner as that of a player. When the ball touches an official, it is the same as touching the floor at the official's location.
Art. 26 Jump Ball
1. A jump ball takes place when an official tosses the ball between two opposing players.
2. For a jump ball to be legal, the

ball must be tapped with the hand(s) by one or both jumpers.
3. A jump ball shall take place at the nearest circle:

a. *When held ball* is called, that is, when one or more players of opposing teams have one or both hands firmly on the ball so that neither player could gain possession without undue roughness. If there are more than two players involved, the jump ball shall be between two opposing players of approximately the same height as designated by the official.

b. If the ball goes out-of-bounds and:

1. It was last touched simultaneously by two opponents, or

2. The official is in doubt as to who last touched the ball; or

3. If the officials disagree, the jump ball shall be between the two players involved.

c. Whenever a live ball lodges on the basket support: the jump ball shall be between any two opponents.

d. Whenever penalties of the same gravity are cancelled according to Art. 59 and the result is a jump ball: the jump ball shall be between any two opponents.

e. Whenever the ball accidentally enters the basket from below: the jump ball shall be between any two opponents.

4. The following conditions shall apply:

a. During a jump ball the two jumpers shall stand with their feet inside that half of the circle which is nearer to their own baskets, with one foot near the centre of the line that is between them.

b. The official shall then toss the ball upward (vertically) between the jumpers to a height greater than either of them can reach by jumping and such that it will drop between them.

c. The ball must be legally tapped by one or both of the

jumpers after it reaches its highest point.

d. Neither jumper shall leave his position until the ball has been legally tapped.

e. Neither jumper may catch the ball or touch it more than twice until it has touched one of the eight non-jumpers, the floor, the basket or the backboard. Under this provision four taps are possible, two by each jumper.

f. The other players shall remain outside the circle until the ball has been tapped.

g. If the ball is not tapped by one or both of the jumpers or if it touches the floor without being tapped by at least one of the jumpers, the jump ball shall be retaken.

h. Team-mates may not occupy adjacent positions around the circle if an opponent desires one of the positions. An infraction of conditions a., c., d., e., and f is a violation.

Art. 27 How the Ball is Played

1. In basketball, the ball is played with the hands. It is a violation to run with the ball, kick it or strike it with the fist.
2. Kicking the ball means striking it or blocking it with the knee, any part of the leg below the knee, or the foot. Such action is a violation only when it is done deliberately.
3. To accidentally contact or

Ball practice
Ball handling is such a central skill in basketball that players will spend hours every day practising.

touch the ball with the foot or leg is not a violation.

Art. 28 Control of the Ball

1. A player is in control when:

a. He is holding or dribbling a live ball.

b. The ball is at his disposal for a throw-in during an out of bounds situation.

2. A team is in control when:

a. A player of that team is in control.

b. The ball is being passed between team-mates.

3. Team control continues until:

a. An opponent secures control.

b. The ball becomes dead.

c. The ball is no longer in contact with the hand(s) of the shooter on a shot for goal.

Art. 29 Player in the Act of Shooting
Definitions:
Throw: to hold the ball in one or both hands and then project it through the air towards the basket.
Dunk: to force or attempt to force the ball downwards into the basket with one or both hands.
Tap: to strike the ball with the hand or hands towards the basket.

1. A player is in the act of shooting when, in the judgement of an official, he has started an attempt to score by throwing, dunking or tapping the opponents' basket and the attempt continues until the ball has left the

player's hand(s).

2. In the case of an airborne shooter, the act of shooting continues until the attempt is completed (the ball has left the hand(s) of the shooter) and both the player's feet return to the floor. Team control, however, ends when the ball is released.

3. For a foul to be considered to have been committed on a player in the act of shooting, the foul must occur, in the judgement of the official, after a player has started the continuous movement of his arm(s) in his attempt to shoot for goal. Continuous movement:

a. Begins when the ball comes to rest in the hand(s) of the player and the shooting motion, usually upward, has started.

b. May include arm(s) and/or body movement used by the player in his attempt to shoot for goal.

If the criteria regarding continuous movement are as stated above, then the player is considered to be in the act of shooting.

Note: There is no relationship between the number of steps taken and the act of shooting.

4. The goal shall count if made, even if the ball has left the player's hand after the whistle has blown.
This provision (number 4.) does not apply:

a. At the end of a period (see Art. 33).

b. When the 30-second signal sounds (see Art. 18).

5. The goal does not count if an entirely new effort (movement) is made after the whistle has blown.

6. A player who taps the ball towards the basket directly from a jump ball is not considered to be in the act of shooting.

Penalty
See Art. 47, Penalty 2.

Art. 30 Goal – When Made and its Value

1. A goal is made when a live ball enters the basket from above and remains within or passes through.

2. A goal from the field is credited to the team attacking the basket into which the ball is thrown as

➡ *page 144*

Some players make almost an art form of dribbling – great to watch.

SKILLS
• • • • •

In addition to the basics of passing and catching, *shooting* is a key skill for all players of a team. Because of the pace and pressure of a game, shots at the basket have to be attempted at every opportunity. Apart from when a free throw is used to score, shots at goal may be made from every angle, taken on the move or as the ball rebounds off the basket or backboard after an unsuccessful shot. A player can aim and throw the ball so that it soars up and over, or jump so that he is able to drop the ball in with a flick of the wrist from above the ring (the 'jump shot').

By handling the ball intermittently, a player can avoid the footwork restrictions otherwise placed on him. A player who has a good *dribbling* technique is able to gain possession of the ball, divert it and move it rapidly towards the basket, keeping it tightly under control with the fingers of just one hand at a time while also keeping an eye on his opponents.

High jump
Basketball forwards are frequently very tall. It is quite common to find players of well over 2.13 m (7 ft) tall. Height like this gives them an edge in reaching for the basket, ten feet off the floor. A player named Manute Bol in America's professional league was over 2.31 m (7 ft 7 in) tall.

Hold-up
The net in basketball is designed to slow the ball down momentarily after it passes through the hoop – so it is absolutely clear that a score has been made.

Shooting skills

Most basketball players shoot with one hand but they begin the shot with the other one on the ball to keep it steady as the ball is released. The ball should be kept close in front of the body, with the wrist and elbow of the shooting arm almost underneath.

As the shot is made the player straightens his arm upwards towards the basket. He then releases the ball with a powerful snap of the wrist, following through to ensure the ball's momentum.

Eyes up
When dribbling it is essential not to look at the ball all the time, but to look ahead to see where your team-mates and opponents are. Every player will therefore practise dribbling 'blind'.

High-speed dribble
Some players are so fast on their feet that they can use pure speed to beat a defender when dribbling. In a full speed dribble the player pushes the ball out in front of him rather than protecting it with his body because he is moving into an empty space.

Off the chest
The most common pass in basketball is the chest pass, which is used when the player has a clear path to his team-mate. The player throws the ball directly from his chest to a team-mate who is signalling. To make the pass he takes the ball very close in front of his chest. He grips the ball with his fingers and thumbs only – that is, not his palms – with the tips of the thumbs pointing upwards. He makes the pass by cocking his wrists and then stepping forward as he sharply extends his arms.

Protected dribble
When dribbling close to an opponent you have to shield the ball so that he cannot 'steal' it. The technique is to keep the ball on the side away from your opponent, bouncing it close to your foot on that side with your knees bent. Always keep your body between the ball and your opponent, and let your free shoulder hang loose to bar your opponent's way if he tries to steal it.

TACTICS

Players may move anywhere on the court, but the three basic positions are guard, forward and centre. The guard usually plays between the free-throw line and the halfway mark, backing up the players who are best at shooting goals. *Forwards* play around the sides of the court, often shooting from here, while the *centre*, who is usually a team's tallest player, stays near the basket and is responsible for most of the shooting.

A coach will follow the progress of a game and decide on the best formation to use, based on these positions.

The *fast break* – the aim is for a team to attack quickly once they have managed to gain control of the ball, giving the opposition no time to organize the defence of their goal.

Defensive tactics include *man-to-man defence*, (marking of individual players by their counterparts) and *zone defence* (players defend areas rather than players).

Free throw
For a free throw the thrower stands just below the free throw line while two opponents stand outside the lane opposite the basket.

continued from page 141

follows:

a. A goal from a free throw counts one point.

b. A goal from the field counts two points.

c. A goal from the three-point field goal area counts three points.

Art. 31 Throw-in

A. Following a field goal or a successful last free throw:

1. Any opponent of the team credited with the score shall be entitled to throw the ball in from any point out-of-bounds on or behind the endline at the end of the court where the goal was made.

2. He may pass it to a team-mate on or behind the endline, but the five second count starts the instant the ball is at the disposal of the first player out of bounds.

3. The official should not handle the ball unless by doing so the game can be resumed more quickly.

4. Opponents of the player making the throw-in shall not touch the ball after it passes through the basket. Allowances may be made for touching the ball accidentally or instinctively, but if the game is delayed by interfering with the ball, it is a technical foul.

B. Following an infraction or for any stoppage of play and the game is to be resumed by a throw-in (except after a valid free throw or field goal):

1. The player who is to throw the ball in, shall stand out of bounds as designated by the official, at the place nearest the point of the infraction or where the play was stopped, except directly

behind the backboard.

2. An official must hand the ball directly to, or place it at the disposal of the player making the throw-in.

3. The player who is to make the throw-in shall not take and complete more than one normal step laterally (approximately 1 m (3 ft) and in more than one direction from the place designated by the official before releasing the ball.

a. Several small steps in one direction are permitted provided the distance covered is not more than one normal step.

b. To move backwards and perpendicular to the line as far as the circumstances will allow is permitted.

C. A player making a throw-in shall not violate the following provisions:

1. Touch the ball in the court before it has touched another player.

2. Step on the court while releasing the ball.

3. Consume more than five seconds before releasing the ball.

4. Throw the ball over the backboard to another player on the court.

5. Cause the ball to touch out of bounds, or to lodge on the basket support or to enter the basket before contacting a player on the court following the release of the ball for the throw-in.

D. Any other player may not have any part of his body over the boundary line before the ball has been thrown across the line.

Personal foul
If a player makes contact with an opponent who is in the act of shooting he commits a 'personal foul' and is penalized.

An infraction of B.3., C and D is a violation.

Penalty

The ball is awarded to the opponents for a throw-in at the point of the original throw-in.

Art. 32 Substitutions

Art. 33 When a Period or a Game is Terminated

1. A period, a half or a game shall terminate at the sounding of the timekeeper's signal indicating the end of playing time.

2. When a foul is committed simultaneously with or just prior to the timekeeper's signal ending any half or any period, any eventual free throw(s) as a result of the foul shall be taken.

Art. 34 Game Lost by Forfeit

A team shall lose the game by forfeit if:

1. It refuses to play after being instructed to do so by the referee.

2. By its

actions it prevents the game from being played.

3. Fifteen minutes after the starting time, the team is not present or is not able to field five players.

Penalty

The game is awarded to the opponents and the score shall be 20 to zero. Further, the forfeiting team shall receive zero points in the classification.

Art. 35 Game Lost by Default

A team shall lose a game by default if, during the game, the number of players of that team on the court is less than two.

Penalty

If the team to which the game is awarded is ahead, the score at the time of the stoppage shall stand. If the team to which the game is awarded is not ahead, the score shall be recorded as two to zero in its favour.

Further, the defaulting team shall receive one point in the classification.

Rule 7
Violations
Art. 36 Violations

1. A violation is an infraction of the rules.

2. The penalty is the loss of the ball by the team that committed the violation.

3. The ball is awarded to the opponents for a throw-in from out of bounds at the closest point to the infraction, except directly behind the backboard.

Article 37 Player Out-of-Bounds and Ball Out-of-Bounds

1. A player is out of bounds when any part of his body is in contact with the floor or any object other than a player on, above or outside the boundary lines.

2. The ball is out of bounds when it touches:

a. A player or any other person who is out of bounds.

b. The floor or any object on, above or outside a boundary line.

c. The supports or the back of the backboards.

3. The ball is caused to go out of bounds by the last player to touch it or be touched by it before it goes out of bounds, even if the ball goes out of bounds by touching something other than a player.

Art. 38 Dribbling Rule

1. A dribble starts when a player, having gained control of the ball throws, taps or rolls it on the floor and touches it again before it touches another player.

2. The dribble is completed the instant the player touches the ball simultaneously with both hands or permits the ball to come to rest in one or both hands.

3. There is no limit to the number of steps a player may take when the ball is not in contact with his hand.

4. The following are not dribbles:

a. Successive shots for goal.

b. Accidentally losing and then regaining player control (fumble) at the beginning or at the end of a dribble.

c. Attempts to gain control of the ball by tapping it from the vicinity of other players striving for it.

d. Tapping the ball from the control of another player.

e. Blocking a pass and recovering the ball.

f. Tossing the ball from hand(s) to hand(s) and permitting it to come to rest before touching the floor, provided he does not commit a travelling violation (See Art. 39).

5. A player shall not dribble a second time after his first dribble has ended, unless it is after he has lost control because of:

a. A shot for goal;

b. A tap by an opponent; or

c. A pass or fumble that has then touched or been touched by another player.

6. A player shall not throw the ball against a backboard and touch it again before it touches another player unless, in the opinion of the official, it was a shot.

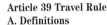

Article 39 Travel Rule
A. Definitions

1. A pivot takes place when a player who is holding a live ball steps once or more than once in any direction with the same foot, while the other foot, called the 'pivot' foot, is kept at its point of contact with the floor.

2. Travelling or progressing with the ball (inside the playing court), is the moving of one or both feet in any direction while holding the ball in excess of the limits outlined in this article.

B. Establishing a Pivot Foot

1. A player who catches the ball with both feet on the floor may use either foot as the pivot foot. The moment one foot is lifted, the other becomes the pivot foot.

2. A player who catches the ball while moving or dribbling may stop and establish a pivot foot as follows:

a. If one foot is touching the floor:

1. That foot becomes the pivot foot as soon as the other foot touches the floor.

2. The player may jump off that foot and simultaneously land on both feet, then neither foot can be the pivot foot.

b. If both feet are off the floor and the player:

1. Lands simultaneously on both feet, then either foot may be the pivot foot. The moment one foot is lifted, the other becomes the pivot foot.

2. Lands on one foot followed by the other foot, then the first foot to touch the floor is the pivot foot.

3. Lands on one foot, the player may jump off that foot and simultaneously land on **both** feet, then neither foot can be the pivot foot.

C. Progressing with the Ball

1. After having established a pivot foot:

a. On a pass or a try for a field goal, the pivot foot may be lifted but may not be returned to the floor before the ball is released from the hand(s),

b. To start a dribble, the pivot foot may not be lifted before **the** ball is released from the hand(s);

2. After coming to a stop when neither foot is the pivot foot:

a. On a pass or a try for a field goal, one or both feet may be lifted but may not be returned to the floor before the ball is released from the hand(s).

b. To start a dribble, neither foot may be lifted before the ball is released from the hand(s).

Art. 40 Three-second Rule

1. While his team is in control of the ball, a player shall not remain for more than three consecutive seconds in the opponents' restricted area.

2. The lines bounding the restricted area are part of the restricted area and a player touching one of these lines is in the area.

3. The three-second restriction is in force in all out of bounds situations. The count shall start at the moment the player making the throw-in is out of bounds and the ball is at his disposal (is in play).

4. The three-second restriction does not apply:

a. While the ball is in the air during a shot for goal.

b. During a rebound.

c. When the ball is dead.

5. Allowance must be made for a player who, having been in the restricted area for less than three seconds, dribbles in to shoot for goal.

Art. 41 Closely Guarded Player

A closely guarded player (within one normal step) who is holding the ball shall pass, shoot, roll or dribble the ball within five seconds.

Art. 42 Ten-second Rule

1. A team's front court consists of the opponents' basket, the inbounds part of the backboard and that part of the court limited by the endline behind the opponents' basket, the sidelines and the edge of the centre line nearer to the opponents' basket. The other part of the court, including the centre line and that team's basket, including the inbounds part of the backboard, is the team's back court.

2. When a player gains control of a live ball in his back court, his team must, within ten seconds, cause the ball to go back into its front court.

➡ *page 146*

Triple threat
The pivot is one of the most important skills in basketball. When a player receives the ball he should pivot at once to face his opponents' basket, holding the ball on his chest with his knees bent and elbows spread out. This is called the triple threat position because a player can shoot, pass or move into a dribble.

Behind hand
The 'behind the back' dribble is a real crowd pleaser and it is also a great way of changing hands and throwing off a defender – although it is very difficult to master.

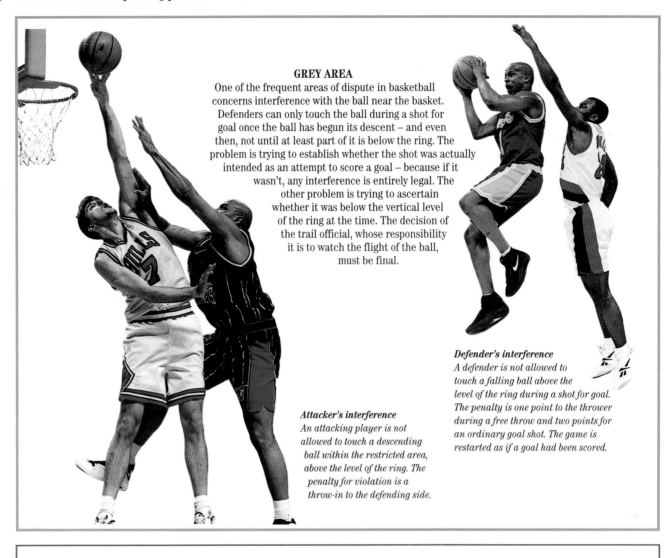

GREY AREA

One of the frequent areas of dispute in basketball concerns interference with the ball near the basket. Defenders can only touch the ball during a shot for goal once the ball has begun its descent – and even then, not until at least part of it is below the ring. The problem is trying to establish whether the shot was actually intended as an attempt to score a goal – because if it wasn't, any interference is entirely legal. The other problem is trying to ascertain whether it was below the vertical level of the ring at the time. The decision of the trail official, whose responsibility it is to watch the flight of the ball, must be final.

Defender's interference
A defender is not allowed to touch a falling ball above the level of the ring during a shot for goal. The penalty is one point to the thrower during a free throw and two points for an ordinary goal shot. The game is restarted as if a goal had been scored.

Attacker's interference
An attacking player is not allowed to touch a descending ball within the restricted area, above the level of the ring. The penalty for violation is a throw-in to the defending side.

continued from page 145

3. The ball goes into a team's front court when it touches the front court or touches a player who has part of his body in contact with the front court.

Art. 43 Ball Returned to the Back Court

1. A player whose team is in control of the ball which is in the front court may not cause the ball to go into his back court.
2. The ball is considered to have gone into the back court when a player of the team in control of the ball is:
   a. The last to touch the ball before it goes into the back court, and
   b. A player of that same team is the first to touch the ball after
   1. It has touched the back court; or
   2. If this player is in contact with the back court.
3. This restriction applies to all situations in a team's front court, including throw-ins from out of bounds.
4. It does not apply to throw-ins from the mid-point of a sideline.

Art. 44 Interference with the

Ball on Offence and Defence

During playing time:
1. An offensive or a defensive player may not touch the ball when it is in its downward flight and completely above the level of the ring during a shot for a field goal.
This restriction applies only until:
   a. The ball touches the ring.
   b. It is evident that it shall not touch the ring.
2. A defensive player shall not touch the ball or the basket while the ball is within the basket.
3. An offensive or a defensive player shall not touch the basket or the backboard while the ball is in contact with the ring during a shot for a field goal.

Penalty

A. The ball becomes dead when the violation is called by the official(s).
1. If the violation is by the offence:
No point can be scored and the ball is awarded to the opponents for a throw-in from out of bounds at the free-throw line extended.
2. If the violation is by the

defence:
The shooter is awarded two points, or three points if the field goal was attempted from the three-point field goal area.
The game is restarted from out of bounds behind the endline as though the shot for goal has been successful.
B. When a shot is taken near the end of playing time (for a period or a half) and the ball has left the player's hand and is in the air before time expired:
1. If the ball enters the basket directly, the goal shall count.
2. If the ball strikes the ring, rebounds and then enters the basket, the goals shall count.
3. If, after the ball has touched the ring, a player of either team touches the ball, the basket or the backboard, it is a violation.
   a. If a defensive player commits the violation, the goal shall count and either two or three points shall be awarded.
   b. If an offensive player commits the violation, the ball becomes dead and the goal, if scored, shall not count.
4. These provisions apply until it is evident that the shot will not

be successful.

Rule 8
Personal Fouls
Art. 45 Fouls

1. A foul is an infraction of the rules when personal contact with an opponent or unsportsmanlike behaviour is involved.
2. It is charged against the offender and consequently penalized according to the provisions of the relevant article of the rules.

Art. 46 Contact

1. Basketball is, theoretically, a no-contact game. Nevertheless, it is obvious that personal contact cannot be avoided entirely when ten players are moving with great speed over a limited space.
2. If the personal contact is incidental and such contact does not place the opponent who has been contacted at a disadvantage, the contact should not be penalized.

Art. 47 Personal Foul

1. A personal foul is a player foul which involves contact with an opposing player, whether the

ball is alive, in play or dead.
2. A player shall not block, hold, push, charge, trip, impede the progress of an opponent by extending his arm, shoulder, hip, knee,

or foot, nor by bending his body into other than a normal position, nor shall he use any rough tactics.

Definitions:

1. **Blocking:** is personal contact which impedes the progress of an opponent.

2. **Charging:** is personal contact, with or without the ball, by pushing or moving into an opponent's torso.

3. **Guarding from the Rear:** is personal contact with an opponent by a defensive player from behind the opponent. The mere fact that the defensive player is attempting to play the ball does not justify his making contact with an opponent.

4. **Handchecking:** is the action by a defensive player in a guarding situation where the hand(s) are used to contact an opponent to either impede his progress or to assist the defensive player in guarding his opponent.

5. **Holding:** is personal contact with an opponent that interferes with his freedom of movement. This contact (holding) can occur with any part of the body.

6. **Illegal Use of Hands:** occurs when a player contacts an opponent with his hand(s) in an attempt to play the ball. If such contact is only with the opponent's hand while it is on the ball, it shall be considered incidental.

7. **Pushing:** is personal contact with any part of the body that takes place when a player forcibly moves or attempts to move an opponent who has or does not have control of the ball.

8. **Illegal Screening:** is an attempt to illegally delay or prevent an opponent who does not control the ball from reaching a desired position on the playing court.

Penalty

A personal foul shall be charged to the offender in all cases. In addition:

1. If the foul is committed on a player who is not in the act of

shooting:

 a. The game shall be resumed by a throw-in by the non-offending team from out of

bounds nearest the place of the infraction.

 b. If the offending team was in the penalty, then Art. 58 will come into effect.

Laying up

The main shot for goal in basketball is a moving shot called the 'lay up'. In this you take two steps then jump from the left leg with your right knee raised to shoot with your right hand from the right-hand side of the basket.

[This stipulates that for games of 2x20 minutes, when a team has committed seven (personal or technical) player fouls in a half, all subsequent player personal fouls shall be penalized by the awarding of two free throws to the player offended against.

The same penalty applies when a team has committed four (personal or technical) player fouls in one period of a game of 4x12 minutes.)

2. If the foul is committed on a player who is in the act of shooting:

 a. If the goal is made, it shall count and one free throw shall be awarded.

 b. If the shot for goal for two points is unsuccessful, two free throws shall be awarded.

 c. If the shot for goal for three points is unsuccessful, three free throws shall be awarded.

3. If a foul is committed by a player while his team is in control of the ball:

 a. The game shall be resumed by a throw-in by the non-offending team from out of bounds nearest the place of the infraction.

Comments

A. Principle of Verticality

1. On the basktball court, each player has the right to a position on the floor and the space (cylinder) above him.

2. This principle protects the space on the floor which he occupies and the space above him.

3. As soon as the player leaves his vertical position (cylinder) and body contact occurs with an opponent who had already established his own vertical position (cylinder), the player who left his vertical position (cylinder) is responsible for the contact.

 a. The defender must not be penalized for leaving the floor vertically (within his cylinder) or having his hands and arms extended above him and within the cylinder,

 b. The offensive player, whether on the floor or airborne, shall not cause contact with the defensive player or use his arms to create additional space for himself (clear-out).

B. Legal Guarding Position

1. A defensive player has established a legal guarding position when:

 a. He is facing his opponent, and

 b. He has both feet on the floor in a normal straddle position. The distance between his feet in a normal straddle position is generally proportional to his height.

2. The legal guarding position extends vertically above him (cylinder). He may raise his arms above his head but he must maintain them in a vertical postion inside the imaginary cylinder.

C. Guarding a Player who Controls the Ball

1. In guarding a player who controls (he is holding or dribbling) the ball, the elements of time and distance do not apply.

2. The player with the ball must expect to be guarded and must be prepared to stop or change his direction whenever an opponent takes a legal guarding position in front of him, even if this is done within a fraction of a second.

3. The guarding (defensive) player must establish a legal guarding position without causing body contact prior to taking his position.

4. Once the defensive player has established a legal guarding position, he must maintain this position (see number 5. below), that is, he may not extend his arms, shoulders, hips or legs to prevent the dribbler from passing by him.

5. When judging a Block/Charge – player with the ball situation, an official shall use the following principles:

➡ *page 148*

continued from page 147

a. The defensive player must establish an initial legal guarding position by facing the player with the ball and having both feet on the floor.

b. The defensive player may remain stationary or move laterally or backwards in order to maintain the guarding position. In moving to maintain the guarding position, one or both feet may be off the floor for an instant, as long as the lateral or backwards movement is considered normal defensive movement.

c. The defensive player must be on the spot first and contact must occur on the torso. If the contact is on the torso, then the defensive player would be considered to have been on the spot first.

If the three items above are present, then the foul is caused by the player with the ball.

D. **The Player who is in the air**

1. A player who has jumped in the air from a spot on the court has the right to land again on the same spot.

2. He has the right to land on another spot on the court, provided that:

a. The landing spot is not already occupied by an opponent(s) at the time of the take-off.

b. The direct path between the take-off and landing spot is not already occupied by an opponent(s).

3. If a player has taken-off and landed but his momentum causes him to contact an opponent who has taken a legal guarding position near the landing spot, then the jumper is responsible for the contact.

4. A player may not move into the path of an opponent after the latter has jumped into the air.

5. Moving under a player who is in the air and contact occurs, is always an unsportsmanlike foul and in certain cases it may be a disqualifying foul.

E. **Guarding a Player who does NOT Control the Ball**

1. A player who does not control the ball is entitled to move freely on the court and take any position not already occupied by another player.

2. The elements of time and distance shall apply. This means that a defensive player cannot take a position:

a. So near to an opponent in motion that the latter does not have sufficient distance to either stop or change his direction.

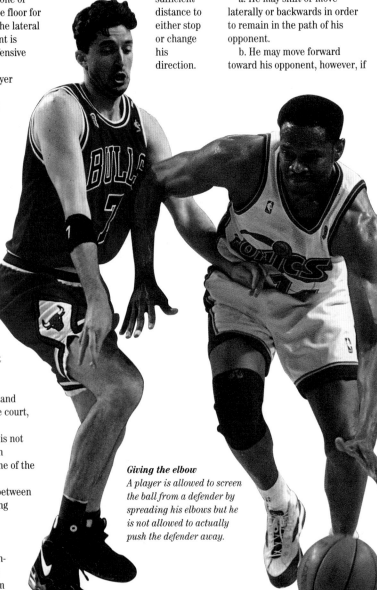

Giving the elbow
A player is allowed to screen the ball from a defender by spreading his elbows but he is not allowed to actually push the defender away.

b. So quickly in the path of a moving opponent that the latter does not have sufficient time or distance to either stop or change his direction. The distance is directly proportional to the speed of the opponent, never less than one and never more than two steps. If a player disregards the elements of time and distance in taking his position and body contact with an opponent occurs, he is

responsible for the contact.

3. Once a defensive player has taken a legal guarding position, he may not prevent his opponent from passing him by extending his arms, shoulders, hips or legs in his path. He may, however, turn or place his arm(s) in front of and close to his body to avoid injury.

4. Once a defensive player has taken a legal guarding position:

a. He may shift or move laterally or backwards in order to remain in the path of his opponent.

b. He may move forward toward his opponent, however, if

body contact occurs, he is responsible for it.

c. He must respect the element of space, that is, the distance between himself and his opponent as per 2.b. above.

F. **Screening – Legal and Illegal**

1. Screening occurs when a player attempts to delay or prevent an opponent who does not control the ball from reaching a desired position on the court.

2. Legal screening takes pace when the player who is screening an opponent is:

a. Stationary (inside his cylinder) when contact occurs.

b. Has both feet on the floor when contact occurs.

3. Illegal screening takes place when the player who is screening an opponent:

a. Was moving when contact occurred.

b. Did not give the appropriate distance in setting a screen outside the field of vision of a stationary opponent when contact occurred.

c. Did not respect the elements of time and distance on an opponent in motion when contact occurred.

4. If the screen is set within the field of vision of a stationary opponent (frontal or lateral), a player may establish the screen as close to him, short of contact, as he desires.

5. If the screen is set outside the field of vision of a stationary opponent, the screener must permit the opponent to take one normal step toward the screen without making contact.

6. If the opponent is in motion, the elements of time and distance shall apply. The screener must leave enough space so that the player who is being screened is able to avoid the screen by stopping or changing direction. The distance required is never less than one normal step but never more than two steps.

7. A player who is legally screened is responsible for any contact with the player who has set up the screen.

G. **Blocking**

1. A player who is attempting to screen is committing a blocking foul if contact occurs when he is moving and his opponent is stationary or retreating from him.

2. If a player disregards the ball, faces an opponent and shifts his position as the opponent shifts, he is primarily responsible for any contact that ensues, unless other factors are involved. The expression 'unless other factors are involved' refers to deliberate pushing, charging or holding of the player who is being screened.

3. It is legal for a player to extend his arm(s) or elbow(s) in taking position on the floor, but they must be lowered (inside the

cylinder) when an opponent attempts to go by. If a player fails to lower the arm(s) or elbow(s) and contact occurs, it is blocking or holding.

H. Touching Opponents with the Hands

1. The touching of an opponent with a hand or hands, in itself, is not necessarily an infraction. However, when the opponent is in the field of vision of a player, there is no justification in touching with the hands and such action could be considered illegal personal contact. The Officials must decide whether an advantage has been gained.
2. If the contact restricts in any way the freedom of movement of an opponent, such contact is a foul.
3. A dribbler may not use an extended forearm or hand to prevent an opponent from securing the ball. Situations of this nature can result in an advantage not intended by the rules and could lead to increased contact between opponents.

I. Post Play

1. The principle of verticality also applies to post play. The offensive player in the post position and the opponent guarding him must respect each other's vertical rights (cylinder).
2. The post player must not be allowed to shoulder or hip his opponent out of position, nor interfere with the latter's freedom of movement by the use of extended elbows or arms.
3. The defensive player must not be allowed to interfere with the post player's freedom of movement by the illegal use of arms, knees or other parts of the body.

Art. 48 Double Foul

A. A double foul is a situation in which two opposing players commit fouls against each other at approximately the same time.

Art. 49 Unsportsmanlike Foul

1. An unsportsmanlike foul is a personal foul on a player with or without the ball which, in the opinion of the official, was deliberately committed by a player against an opposing player.
2. The unsportsmanlike foul must be interpreted the same way at the beginning as well as near the end of the game, that is, throughout the whole game.
3. The official must judge only

the action.
4. To judge whether a foul is unsportsmanlike, the officials must apply the following principles:
   a. If a player commits a foul while making a legitimate effort to play the ball (normal basket ball play), it is not an unsportsmanlike foul.
   b. If, in the effort to play the ball, the player causes excessive contact (hard foul), then the contact shall be considered to be unsportsmanlike.
   c. Holding, hitting or pushing a player who is away from the ball is usually an unsportsmanlike foul.
5. A player who repeatedly commits unsportsmanlike fouls may be disqualified.

Penalty

1. An unsportsmanlike foul shall be charged to the offender.
2. Free throw(s) shall be awarded to the non-offending team, followed by possession of the ball.
3. The number of free throws to be awarded shall be as follows:
   a. If the foul is committed on a player not in the act of shooting, two free throws.
   b. If the foul is committed on a player who is in the act of shooting, the goal, if made, shall count and in addition one free throw.
   c. If the foul is committed on a player in the act of shooting who fails to score, two or three free throws, according to the place from where the shot for goal was attempted.
4. During the free throw(s) all other players shall remain behind the free-throw line extended and behind the three-point field goal line until the free throw(s) have been completed.
5. After the free throw(s), whether or not the last free-throw is successful, the ball shall be thrown in by any player of the free throw

Magic Johnson, player turned coach

shooter's team from out of bounds at mid-court on the sideline opposite the scorer's table.
6. The player taking the throw-in shall have one foot on either side of the extended centre line, and shall be entitled to pass the ball to a player at any point on the playing court.

Art. 50 Disqualifying Foul

Any flagrantly unsportsmanlike infraction of Art. 47, 49, 52 (technical foul by a player) or 53 (technical foul by coaches, substitutes or team followers) is a disqualifying foul.

Penalty

1. A disqualifying foul shall be charged to the offender.
2. He shall be disqualified and shall go to and remain in his team's dressing room for the duration of the game or, if he so chooses, he shall leave the building.
3. Free throw(s) shall be awarded to the non-offending team, followed by possession of the ball.
4. The number of free throws to be awarded shall be as follows:
   a. If the foul is committed on a player not in the act of shooting, two free throws.
   b. If the foul is committed on a player who is in the act of shooting, the goal, if made, shall count and in addition one free throw.
   c. If the foul is committed on a player in the act of shooting who fails to score, two or three free throws, according to the place from where the shot for goal was attempted.
5. During the free throw, all other players shall remain behind the free throw line extended and behind the three-point field goal line until the free throw(s) have been completed.
6. After the free throw(s), whether or not the last free throw is successful, the ball shall be thrown in by any player of the free throw shooter's team from out of bounds at mid-court on the sideline opposite the scorer's table.
7. The player taking the throw-in shall have one foot on either side of the extended centre line, and shall be entitled to pass the ball to a player at any point on the playing court.

Rule 9
Technical Fouls
Art. 51-55

These cover fouls which do not involve contact with an opponent, such as using offensive language, disrespectfully addressing an official, baiting an opponent or obstructing his vision by waving his hands near his eyes or grasping the ring in such a way that the weight of the player is supported by the ring. The penalty is two free throws to the opponents.

Rule 10
General Provisions

Covers the awarding of fouls.

These rules are reprinted by permission of the International Basketball Federation (FIBA). A complete copy of the rules, including Official Game Procedures, is available from FIBA.

Handball
Essentials

One of the oldest games of all – probably played in ancient Greece and now an Olympic sport since 1932. This version is the fast-moving team game (as opposed to court handball, which is played by two or four players in a court with four walls).

The court
Rectangular, 40 by 20 m, (44 by 22 yds) divided into two halves by a centre line.

40 m (44 yds)
Side line
Centre line
4.5 m
4.5 m
Substitution lines
Free throw line
Penalty or 7-metre line
Goal area line
Goalkeeper refraining line
4 m
20 m (22 yds)
Goal line

The players
12 players per team, with a maximum of seven on the court at any one time, including one goalkeeper.

The goals
One at either end, at the centre of each goal line. Each consists of two posts, 2 m (6½ ft) high and 3 m (10 ft) apart, joined by a crossbar. Both are made of wood, light metal or synthetic material and painted in two colours in alternate stripes. A net is attached to the goal.

The ball
Spherical, with an outer casing of leather or synthetic material. The outer case must not be too shiny or slippery. A weight of 425–475 g (15–16¾ oz) for women and juniors, 325 –400 g (11½–14 oz) and a circumference of 54–56 cm (21¼–22 in). Two balls must be available at the start of a game, although the one chosen is then used solely throughout.

A ball in the hand
Unlike in games such as basketball, the ball for handball is small enough for players to hold in one hand. It also has a matt surface so that it does not slip too easily from the grip. So shots for goal are usually made by hurling the ball at the net with a single hand.

Dress
All players in a team must be uniformly dressed, wearing sports shoes and their colours must be clearly distinguishable from the other team. Both goalkeepers should wear colours that distinguish them from all the other players and each other. Each captain wears a 4-cm (1.6-in)-wide armlet around the upper arm.

Officials
Two referees, a scorer and a timekeeper.

HOW TO PLAY

Teams score goals by getting the ball into their opponents' goal. Players may use their hands, arms, head, torso, thighs and knees. The ball can be passed or dribbled down the court.

Starting

The team winning the toss has the choice of ends or the option of beginning the game with a throw-off. The player taking it does so from the centre of the court. Once the referee has given a whistle signal, the player must execute the throw-off in any direction within three seconds. All other players must be in their own half of the court and the players of the non-starting team must be at least 3 m (10 ft) from the player taking the throw.

How to win

A goal is scored when the ball completely crosses the goal line and passes into a goal.
If it is prevented from doing so due, for example, to a spectator on the court, a goal is awarded if it would have been scored otherwise. The team with the most goals wins.

KEY RULES

• A game consists of two halves of 30 minutes each, with an interval of ten minutes and teams changing ends at half time. If there must be a winning team and the game results in a draw, two extra periods of four minutes are played.
• Players must not hold the ball for longer than three seconds, nor may they take more than three steps while in possession. They must also not intentionally touch the ball with any part of the leg below the knee. 'Passive play' occurs when possession of the ball is maintained without an attempt to move into attack or to score a goal. This is penalized by a free throw to the opposing team. *See Law 7 (page 152).*
• Infringements of the laws are penalized by a free throw – taken by a player of the non-offending team from the place where the infringement occurred – or a penalty throw 7 m (23 ft) – taken as a shot at goal from behind the 7 m line with all players other than the thrower remaining behind the nine metre line. *See Laws 13 and 14 (page 152).*
• Fouls or unsporting conduct by a player will result in a caution (the referee holds up a yellow card) and, if repeated, a two minute suspension. A third period of suspension brings instant disqualification, as does any extreme cause of misconduct.
See Law 17 (page 153).

SKILLS AND TACTICS

This is a rapid game of continuous action, requiring fitness and endurance as well as flexibility and balance. Good passing and catching skills enable a team to keep possession of the ball and thus go into the attack in order to score. The most frequently used pass is the *overhand pass*, made with an arm bent at the elbow and stretched up and back to give the ball momentum.
An alternative is the *wrist pass* – made with a quick flick of the wrist in situations where a quick response and direction, rather than force or distance, are needed.
Opportunities for shooting at goal occur frequently and players must be prepared to shoot on the move, from various angles or from a jump.
When not in attack, all the players of a team must play a rigorously defensive game, checking individual opponents and blocking the path of the ball wherever possible.

Ready to pass
Players are not allowed to hold the ball for longer than three seconds , nor may they take more than three steps while holding it – although they may run while bouncing the ball repeatedly. The game, therefore, depends on rapid passing from player to player.

GREY AREA
Rule 7.7 forbids players touching the ball twice – but there is an exception to this rule and this can cause dispute. The fact is that a player is allowed to touch the ball twice if he fumbles his catch. But he is not allowed to touch it again once he has caught it cleanly. It is the referee who must decide whether the ball is caught cleanly or not.

Interception
Since players have to pass the ball on quickly, defenders try to recapture the ball by blocking passes.

Going for the ball
Players can try to capture the ball from an opponent with their arms, palms and body. But they are not allowed to push, hold, run, jump into, trip or hit an opponent.

LAWS OF HANDBALL

These laws are abridged and summarized. Changes from the official laws are indicated in *italics*.

1. THE PLAYING COURT
2. DURATION OF PLAY
3. THE BALL
4. THE PLAYERS

See page 150.

5. THE GOALKEEPER

The goalkeeper may touch the ball with any part of his body in the act of defence but he may not use any part of his legs below the knee when the ball is stationary in the goal area or heading towards the playing area. He may leave the area while not in possession of the ball, but if he is in possession, this must only be in an attempt to control the ball in the act of defence. He may move without restriction inside the goal area, but the same restrictions as exist for all the other players apply as soon as he is outside it.

6. THE GOAL AREA

Court players (all apart from the goalkeeper) must not enter this area and if they do so they are penalized with a free throw (if they gain an advantage by doing so) or a penalty throw (if they gain an advantage over an attacking opponent in possession). If not in possession or no advantage is gained, a player does not incur a penalty. When the ball enters this area it belongs to the goalkeeper only.

7. PLAYING THE BALL

It is permitted:

7.1 to throw, catch, push or hit the ball using the hands (the hands may be open or closed), arms, head, torso, thighs and knees.

7.2 to hold the ball for a maximum of three seconds, even when it is lying on the floor.

7.3 to take a maximum of three steps, whilst in possession of the ball. One step is considered taken when:

a) A player who is standing with both feet in contact with the floor lifts one foot and puts it down again, or moves one foot from one position to another.

b) A player who is in contact with the floor with one foot only, catches the ball and then makes contact with the ground with the other foot.

c) A player, after a jump touches the floor with one foot only and

then hops on the same foot or touches the ground with the other foot.

d) A player after a jump touches the floor with both feet simultaneously and then lifts one and puts it down again, or, moves one foot from one place to another.

7.4 While standing or running

a) To bounce the ball once and catch it with both hands.

b) To bounce the ball or to roll the ball on the ground repeatedly, with one hand and thereafter catch or pick up the ball in one or both hands.

7.5 To place the ball from one hand to the other. (It is not allowed to throw the ball from one hand to the other).

7.6 To play the ball while kneeling, sitting or lying on the ground.

It is not permitted:

7.7 To touch the ball more than once unless it has first touched the ground or another player or any part of the goal. Where in the act of catching or stopping the ball, the player does not control the ball cleanly at the first attempt, and thereby fumbles in his/her efforts, such action shall not be penalized. However, where control of the ball has been established, the player must not touch it more than once after tapping or bouncing it.

7.8 To touch the ball with any part of the leg below the knee, except when the ball has been thrown against the legs of a player, by an opponent, and where the striking of the leg by the ball does not cause advantage to be gained by the player or his team.

7.9 To dive for the ball while it is lying or rolling on the ground.

7.10 To play the ball intentionally over the side line or the teams own outer goal line.

7.11 To keep the ball in the team's possession without making any recognizable attempt to attack or to score a goal.

Such action is considered to be **'passive play'** and is penalized by a free throw against the offending team. The throw is executed from that place where the ball was when the play was interrupted.

7.12 Where the ball makes contact with one of the referees, on the court, the play shall continue as the referee is,in this instance, considered to be part of the field of play.

8. APPROACH TO AN OPPONENT

A player may try to gain

possession of the ball using hands, arms, an open hand or the torso. However it is forbidden to : obstruct an opponent by means of arms, hands or legs; force an opponent into the goal area; hit or pull the ball from an opponent's hands; use a fist to dispossess him; throw the ball or feint with it in a dangerous manner towards an opponent; push, hold, run or jump into , trip or hit an opponent. The penalty incurred ranges from a free throw to the opposition to disqualification, depending on the degree of the offence.

9. SCORING

10. THROW-OFF

See Starting page 151.

11. THROW-IN

A throw-in is awarded against the team to last touch the ball if it completely crosses the sideline, on the ground or in the air. It is taken from the place where the ball crossed. A throw-in may also be awarded if a defender deflects the ball over the outer goal line, in which case it is taken from the intersection of this line and the side line.

12. GOALKEEPERS-THROW (GOAL THROW)

12.1 A goal-throw is awarded when the ball crosses the outer goal line, having last been touched by a member of the team attacking the goal or by the goalkeeper in the act of defending the goal.

12.2 The goal-throw is executed by means of the goalkeeper throwing the ball into the playing area, from a position inside the goal area. The throw is made without any whistle signal from the referee.The throw is considered taken when the ball has crossed the goal area line.

12.3 If the ball shall, on occasion, come to rest in the goal area, the goalkeeper shall bring the ball back into play by throwing the ball into the playing court.

12.4 Following the execution of a goal-throw, the goalkeeper is not allowed to make contact with the ball again until it has first touched another player.

13. FREE THROW

13.1 A free throw is awarded for incorrect substitution or for infringements:
by the goalkeeper, by court players in the goal area, when playing the ball, passive play,

approaching an opponent, a throw-off, a throw-in, a goalkeeper's throw, a free throw, a penalty throw, a referee's throw and a formal throw, unsporting conduct and assault. 13.2 –13.7 A free throw is taken without any whistle signal from the referee and from the place where he offence took place. Players of the attacking team must not cross or touch their opponents free-throw line until the throw has been taken. The referee will not award a free throw, if by so doing an advantage would be gained by the team causing the infringement and a disadvantage experienced by the team in possession of the ball. Where an infringement causes an attacking team to be placed at a disadvantage a free throw, at least, must be awarded. A free throw, at least, must be awarded if an infringement causes an attacking team to lose possession of the ball. A free throw must NOT be awarded if a player remains in full control of the ball in spite of the infringement.

If the game is interrupted, it shall be started by means of a free throw executed by the team having possession and from the place where the ball was at the time of the interruption. The free throw must be preceded by a whistle signal.

13.8 The ball **MUST** be put down **IMMEDIATELY** by a player in possession of the ball when a decision is made against him/her or his/her team.

14. PENALTY THROW (7-METRE THROW

14.1 **A 7-metre throw shall be awarded:**

a) When a clear chance of scoring a goal is prevented, by an infringement, in any part of the court, and even where the offender is a team official

b) When the goalkeeper enters the goal area in possession of the ball or when standing inside the goal are takes it into the goal area.

c) When a court player enters his/her own goal area to gain an advantage over an attacking opponent who is in possession of the ball.

d) When a court player deliberately plays the ball to his/her own goalkeeper inside the goal area and the goalkeeper touches the ball

e) When there is an unwarranted whistle signal which destroys a clear goal-scoring opportunity

f) When a clear goal-scoring opportunity is destroyed by interference of someone not authorized to be on the court

14.2 The penalty throw must be taken as a shot propelled towards the goal and within 3 seconds of the whistle signal given by the court referee.

14.3 The player taking the penalty throw must not touch or cross the 7 metre line before the ball has left the hand.

14.4 Once the penalty throw has been executed, the ball may not be played again until it has touched the goalkeeper or the goal.

14.5 While the penalty throw is being taken ALL players with the exception of the thrower must be positioned outside the free-throw line (9 metre line).

14.6 Players of the defending team must be at least 3 m (10 ft) from the 7 metre line, while a penalty throw is being taken. Where a defending player touches or crosses the 9 metre line or encroaches nearer than 3 m (10 ft) from the 7 metre line before the ball has left the thrower's hand, the referee shall decide as follows:
a) Goal if the ball goes into the goal
b) The retaking of the throw in all other cases

14.8 The referees shall not award a 7 metre throw for an infringement of the Rules by a defending team, if by doing so he/she causes a disadvantage to the attacking team.

A 7 metre throw, at least, must be awarded, if a clear goal scoring opportunity is destroyed and a goal does not result, due to an infringement of the Rules or an act of unsporting conduct, an unwarranted whistle signal, or by interference on the part of someone not authorized to be a part of the game. Where, in spite of an infringement, an attacking player retains full ball and body control, a penalty throw shall not be awarded.

15. REFEREE'S THROW

15.1 **A game shall be restarted by means of a Referee's Throw when:**
a) The Rules have been infringed simultaneously, on the court, by players of both teams
b) The ball has touched the roof or fixed equipment above the playing court
c) An interruption of the game is

caused through no infringement of the Rules and while neither side was in possession of the ball.

15.2 There shall always be a 'time out' when a referee's throw is awarded.

15.3 The execution of the referee's throw shall be from the centre of the court by the court referee throwing the ball vertically into the air, following a whistle signal.

15.4 With the exception of one player from each team all other players must be positioned at least 3 m (10 ft) from the referee whilst the referee's throw is being executed. The two competing players shall stand either side of the referee, each on that side which is nearer to their own goal. The referee shall throw the ball into the air and the two players shall jump to try and gain possession. However, the ball may only be played after it has reached its highest point.

16. EXECUTION OF FORMAL THROWS

16.1 All players must adopt the positions prescribed for the throw in question.

16.2 During the execution of the throw-off, throw-in, free throw and penalty throw, the thrower must keep at least a part of one foot in constant contact with the floor. It is permitted, however, for the player to repeatedly lift and put down the other foot.

16.4 A throw is considered to have been executed once the ball has left the hand of the thrower.

16.5 Once the player taking the throw has released the ball he/she is not allowed to play the ball again until it has first touched another player or the goal.

16.6 A goal may be scored directly from any throw.

16.7 When a throw-in or free throw is being taken, players of the team not in possession shall be at least 3 m (10 ft) from the thrower.

Free throw
On a free throw attackers must stay behind their opponents' free throw line until the throw is taken. The throw must be taken within three seconds of the referee blowing his whistle.

17. PUNISHMENTS

17.1 **A caution can be given for:**
a) Infringements concerning approach to an opponent.
A caution shall be given for:
b) infringements concerning the approach to an opponent and which are to be punished progressively.
c) Infringements of the Rules when an opponent is attempting to execute a throw.
d) Unsporting conduct by a player or official.

17.2 The referee shall indicate the decision to issue a caution to an offending player by holding up a yellow card.

17.3 **A suspension (2 minutes) shall be given:**
a) For an incorrect (faulty) substitution or for entering the court contrary to the Rules.
b) For repeated infringements of the Rules governing the approach to an opponent and which are to be punished progressively.
c) For repeated unsporting conduct by a player on the court.
d) When a player fails to place the ball down on to the floor, immediately, when a decision for an infringement has been made against an attacking team.
e) For repeatedly infringing the Rules when the opposing team are executing a formal throw.
f) In consequence of a disqualification of a player or team official.
In exceptional circumstances a suspension can be awarded without recourse to an initial caution.

17.4 The decision to suspend a player must be clearly indicated to the player concerned by the referee raising one arm in the air with two fingers extended.

17.5 **A disqualification shall be awarded:**
if a player who is not entitled to participate enters the court; for serious infringements relating to the approach to an opponent; for repeated unsporting conduct

by a team official or a player outside the court; for serious unsporting conduct by a player or team official; for a third period of suspension; or for an assault by a team official.

The disqualification of a player or a team official during the playing time shall always result in a period of suspension and the team's strength on the court being reduced by one.

17.6 When awarding a disqualification the referee shall indicate the punishment by the holding up of a red card. The disqualification of a player or official applies for the remainder of the playing time. The player or official must leave the court and the substitution area immediately. A disqualification reduces the number of players and/or officials available to the team. The team may, however, continue to play at full strength on the court following the expiry of the suspension time awarded against the disqualified player or official.

17.7 **An exclusion shall be given:** In the event of an assault, during the playing time both on and outside the court.

17.9 Any player having been given a period of suspension and who is guilty of another infringement, before the game is restarted shall be further punished by means of the most severe of the applicable punishments allowed for in the Rules.

17.10 In the event of a goalkeeper being suspended, disqualified or excluded, another player must take up the position of goalkeeper.

17.11 The referees must caution any player they deem guilty of unsporting conduct, irrespective of whether such takes place on or outside the court.

18. THE REFEREE
(Refers to referees).

These laws are reprinted by permission of the International Handball Federation. For a complete copy of the Laws of the Game, including various notes, Clarifications of the Rules and Regulations Governing the Substitution Area, contact the Federation.

Netball
Essentials

Traditionally played only by women, netball is fast becoming popular with both sexes and is often played by mixed teams, although games at the highest level are restricted to single-sex teams.

The pitch

Must have a firm surface. Lines divide the court into three equal parts, with a semicircle of radius 4.9 m (16 ft) in the centre third. Lines must not exceed 50 mm (2 in) in width.

Marking game

Since netball players are not allowed to move with the ball, attack depends on accurate passing and defence on close marking.

The teams

Two teams of seven players, with up to three substitutes. The playing positions are:
Goal Shooter (GS)
Goal Attack (GA)
Wing Attack (WA)
Centre (C)
Wing Defence (WD)
Goal Defence (GD)
Goalkeeper (GK)
See below right, page 155, for their positions on court.

Officials

Two umpires, two scorers and a timekeeper.

Dress

A shirt with shorts or a skirt. Initials of playing positions (150 mm/6 in high) must be worn both front and back above the waist. Shoes must not have spiked soles and no jewellery may be worn except a wedding ring, which must be taped.

Getaway

Attackers must try to get away from defenders by quick acceleration and changes of direction.

The goalposts

Two goalposts, 3.05 m (10 ft) high, at the mid-point of each goal line and preferably inserted into the ground for international matches. Each has a metal ring (internal diameter 380 mm/15 in) 150 mm (6 in) from the top. The attachment joining the ring and post must allow 150 mm (6 in) between the post and the near side of the ring.

The ball

Must be a netball or an association football size five. Between 690 mm (27 in) and 710 mm (28 in) in circumference and between 400 g (14 oz) and 450 g (16 oz) in weight.

HOW TO PLAY

A team scores points by passing the ball down the court and through the ring of the goal guarded by their opponents. Each player must keep to his or her designated playing area and pass the ball rather than travel with it.

Starting

The captain winning the toss chooses between taking the first centre pass or choosing an end. The centre of the team taking the first centre pass stands inside the centre circle in the middle of the court and upon the umpire's whistle, must pass within three seconds. Apart from the centre and the opposition's centre, all players must remain outside the centre third until the whistle blows. A centre pass is made after each goal is scored, taken alternately by the two centres.

How to win

Goals are scored by the goal shooter or goal attack sending the ball through the ring defended by their opponents, while standing within the goal circle. If a defending player deflects a shot and the ball goes through the ring, a goal is also scored.

See Rule 15, Scoring a Goal (page 156).

KEY RULES

• A game consists of four quarters of 15 minutes each. Teams change ends each quarter.

• The ball is out of the court when it touches the ground outside the court or if it touches an object, person or player in contact with the ground inside the court. (A player is not penalized for standing outside the court while not playing the ball.)

• A player may catch the ball with one or both hands or tip, bat or bounce it to another player, but once caught, the ball must be played within three seconds. A player is not allowed to bounce or throw the ball and then replay it, or to roll the ball to another player. It is also against the rules to deliberately kick the ball, grab it from an opponent or to play it while lying, sitting or kneeling on the ground.

See Rule 13, Playing the Ball (page 156).

• A player may not run with the ball. If the player lands on one foot when receiving the ball, the other foot may be used to regain balance or to change direction with any number of steps, pivoting on the landing foot. If the landing foot is lifted, the ball must be passed before the foot can be grounded again. If the player lands on both feet when receiving, either foot can be moved, but once it is, it becomes the stepping foot and the other becomes the landing foot and the rule applies as before.

See Rule 14, Footwork (page 156).

SKILLS

Catching

The ball should be caught with two hands whenever possible. Fingers and thumbs should be spread out widely to secure the catch safely. Balance is essential if a player is to intercept, secure and then pass the ball accurately within the few seconds allowed, whilst also obeying the footwork rule.

Throwing

Players must be able to throw firmly and swiftly, also anticipating the speed and direction of the receiver. A *shoulder pass,* made with one or both hands above the shoulder and slightly behind the body, gives the ball impetus for long distances. A *chest pass* is made from the chest with both hands and is mostly used for short, direct passes. A *low pass* can be achieved with the underarm pass, swinging the ball forward from below the waist with one hand, while the *bounce pass* allows the ball to neatly dodge an opponent, bouncing too low for them to intercept yet rebounding at an easy-to-catch height beyond them.

Shooting

An essential skill. Although the defending player must remain at least 0.9 m (3 ft) from the shooter, their presence can make it difficult to shoot at goal. An advanced player will be able to cope with interference and still shoot accurately, even in an off-balance position.

TACTICS

When a team is in attack, individual players must try to break free from their opponents and reach a clear, strategic point from which to receive the ball and form a link down the court. Deceptive 'trick' moves by the thrower and/or receiver are often used to confuse opponents.

Defence takes the form of zone defence (keeping guard over a particular area of the court and intercepting passes) or one-to-one marking (closely following individual counterparts to hamper their play).

GREY AREA

The rule that causes most dispute in netball is the 'contact' rule. The problem is that umpires interpret the phrase "which interferes" in different ways. The umpire must decide whether the contact interferes or not and decisions may vary according to whether the umpire thinks the player could cope successfully with the contact, the umpire's position at the time of the incident, his or her speed of judgement and so on.

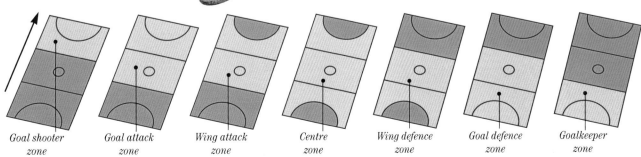

| Goal shooter zone | Goal attack zone | Wing attack zone | Centre zone | Wing defence zone | Goal defence zone | Goalkeeper zone |

NETBALL THE RULES

I. Organization of the Game
Rules 1 to 7

See How to play (page 155).

II. Areas of Play
Rules 8 to 10

See diagram (page 155).

III. Conduct of the Game
11. Positioning of Players for Start of Play

12. Start of Play

See Starting (page 155).

13. Playing the Ball

13.1 A player may:
(i) Catch the ball with one or both hands.
(ii) Gain or regain control of the ball if it rebounds from the goalpost.
(iii) Bat or bounce the ball to another player without first having possession of it.
(iv) Tip the ball in an uncontrolled manner once or more than once and then:
  a) Catch the ball; or
  b) Direct the ball to another player.
(v) Having batted the ball once, either catch the ball or direct the ball to another player.
(vii) Roll the ball to oneself to gain possession.
(viii) Fall while holding the ball but must regain footing and throw within three seconds of receiving the ball.
(ix) Lean on the ball to prevent going offside.
(x) Lean on the ball on court to gain balance.
(xi) Jump from a position in contact with the court and play the ball outside the court, provided that neither the player nor the ball makes contact with the ground, or any object or person outside the court while the ball is being played.
13.2 A player may not:
(i) Strike the ball with a fist.
(ii) Deliberately fall on the ball to get it.
(iii) Attempt to gain possession of the ball while lying, sitting or kneeling on the ground.
(iv) Throw the ball while lying, sitting or kneeling on the ground.
(v) Use the goalpost as a support in recovering the ball going out of the court.
(vi) Use the goalpost as a

means of regaining balance, or in any other way for any other purpose.
(vii) Deliberately kick the ball (if a ball is thrown and accidentally hits the leg of a player it is not a kick).
Penalty: Free pass to the opposing team where the infringement occurred.
13.3 A player who has caught or held the ball shall play it or shoot for goal within three seconds. To play the ball a player may:
(i) Throw it in any manner and in any direction to another player;
(ii) Bounce it with one or both hands in any direction to another player.
13.4 A player who has caught or held the ball may not:
(i) Roll the ball to another player.
(ii) Throw the ball and play it before it has been touched by another player.
(iii) Toss the ball into the air and replay it.
(iv) Drop the ball and replay it.
(v) Bounce the ball and replay it.
(vi) Replay the ball after an unsuccessful shot at goal unless it has touched some part of the goalpost.
Penalty: Free pass to the opposing team where the

infringement occurred.
13.5 Passing Distances
13.5.1 Short Pass
(i) On the court: at the moment the ball is passed there must be room for a third player to move between the hands of the thrower and those of the receiver.
(ii) At the throw-in: at the moment the ball is passed there must be room on the court between the hands of the thrower and those of the receiver for a third player to attempt an interception.
Penalty: Free pass to the opposing team where the ball is caught.
13.5.2 Over a Third
(i) The ball may not be thrown over a complete third without being touched or caught by a player who, at the time of touching or catching the ball, is wholly within that third or who lands in that third.
(ii) The player who lands with the first foot wholly within the correct third is judged to have received the ball in that third. The subsequent throw shall be considered to have been made from the third in which the player first landed.
(iii) The player who lands on both feet simultaneously with one foot wholly within the correct third and the other in the incorrect third shall be penalized.
Penalty: Free pass to the opposing team taken just beyond the second line that the ball has crossed, except where the ball thrown from the centre third passes out of the court over the goal-line, when a throw-in shall be taken.

Shooting circle
For a valid shot at goal a player must be inside the shooting circle.

14. Footwork

14.1 A player may receive the ball with one foot grounded or jump to catch and land on one foot and then:
(i) Step with the other foot in any

direction, lift the landing foot and throw or shoot before this foot is regrounded.
(ii) Step with the other foot in any direction any number of times, pivoting on the landing foot. The pivoting foot may be lifted but the player must throw or shoot before regrounding it.
(iii) Jump from the landing foot on to the other foot and jump again, but must throw the ball or shoot before regrounding either foot.
(iv) Step with the other foot and jump, but must throw the ball or shoot before regrounding either foot.
14.2 A player may receive the ball while both feet are grounded, or jump to catch and land on both feet simultaneously and then:
(i) Step with either foot in any direction, lift the other foot and throw or shoot before this foot is regrounded.
(ii) Step with either foot in any direction any number of times pivoting on the other. The pivoting foot may be lifted but the player must throw or shoot before regrounding it.
(iii) Jump from both feet on to either foot, but must throw or shoot before regrounding the other foot.
(iv) Step with either foot and jump but must throw the ball or shoot before regrounding either foot.
14.3 A player in possession of the ball may not:
(i) Drag or slide the landing foot.
(ii) Hop on either foot.
(iii) Jump from both feet and land on both feet unless the ball has been released before landing.
Penalty: A free pass to the opposing team where the infringement occurred.

15. Scoring a Goal

15.1 A goal is scored when the ball is thrown or batted over and completely through the ring by Goal Shooter or Goal Attack from any point within the goal circle including the lines bounding the goal circle:
(i) If another player throws the ball through the ring no goal is scored and play continues.
(ii) If a defending player deflects a shot for goal and the ball then passes over and completely through the ring a goal is scored.
(iii) Goal Shooter or Goal Attack may shoot for goal or pass if the

ball is won at a toss-up in the goal circle.

(iv) If the whistle for an interval or 'time' is blown before the ball has passed completely through the ring, no goal is scored.

(v) If the whistle for an interval or 'time' is blown after a penalty pass or shot has been awarded in the goal circle, the penalty pass or shot shall be taken.

15.2 In taking a shot for goal a player shall:

(i) Have no contact with the . ground outside the goal circle either during the catching of the ball or whilst holding it. It is not contact with the ground to lean on the ball, but if this happens behind the goal line the ball is considered to be out of court.

(ii) Shoot within three seconds of catching or holding the ball.

(iii) Obey the Footwork Rule.

Penalty: A free pass to the opposing team in the goal circle where the infringement occurred.

15.3 A defending player may not cause the goalpost to move so as to interfere with the shot at goal.

Penalty: Penalty pass or shot to the opposing team to be taken:

(i) From where the infringer was standing unless this places the non-offending team at a disadvantage.

(ii) If the infringer was out of court, on court near where the infringer was standing.

16. Obstruction

16.1 An attempt to intercept or defend the ball may be made by a defending player if the distance on the ground is not less than 0.9 m (3 ft) from a player in possession of the ball. When the ball is received, this distance is measured as follows:

(i) If the player's landing, grounded or pivoting foot remains on the ground, the distance is measured from that foot to the nearest foot of the defending player.

(ii) If the player's landing, grounded or pivoting foot is lifted, the distance is measured from the spot on the ground from which the foot was lifted, to the nearer foot of the defending player.

(iii) If the player is standing or lands on both feet simultaneously and remains grounded on both feet, the distance is measured from whichever is the nearer foot of that player to the nearer foot of the defending player.

(iv) If the player is standing or lands on both feet

simultaneously and either foot is lifted, the other foot is considered to be the grounded foot from which the 0.9 m (3 ft) distance is measured.

16.2 From the correct distance, a defending player may attempt to intercept or defend the ball:

(i) By jumping towards the player with the ball, but if the landing is within 0.9 m (3 ft) of that player and interferes with the throwing or shooting motion, obstruction occurs.

(ii) If the player with the ball steps forward to lessen the distance of 0.9 m (3 ft) between them.

16.3 A player may be within 0.9 m (3 ft) of an opponent in possession of the ball providing no effort is made to defend and there is no interference with that opponent's throwing or shooting action.

16.4 From the correct distance, a defending player may not attempt to intercept or defend the ball by stepping towards an opponent with the ball.

16.5 Obstruction of a player not in possession of the ball

16.5.1 A player is obstructing if within a distance of 0.9 m (3 ft) (measured on the ground) from an opponent without the ball, any movements are employed by that player (whether attacking or defending) which take the arms away from the body, other than those involved in natural body balance. Within this distance a player is not obstructing if the arms are outstretched:

(i) To catch, deflect or intercept a pass or feint pass.

(ii) To obtain a rebound from an unsuccessful shot at goal.

(iii) Momentarily to signal for a pass, or to indicate the intended direction of movement.

16.6 Obstruction by intimidation When a player with or without the ball intimidates an opponent it is obstruction.

Penalty for 16.1 to 16.6: Penalty pass or shot where the infringer is standing except where this places the non-offending team at a disadvantage, when the penalty shall be taken where the obstructed player was standing.

16.7 Defending a player who is out of court

16.7.1 A player may defend an opponent who has chosen to go out of court provided that the defending player does not leave the court or own playing area in

order to defend.

Penalty: A penalty pass or penalty pass or shot from the point where the infringer leaves the court.

16.7.2 A player who goes out of court to collect a ball, to take a throw-in, or for any other valid reason, must be allowed back into the area of play near to the

Physical contact is not allowed.

point at which the player left the court or took the throw-in. Any opponent attempting to prevent the player from re-entering the court is penalized.

Penalty: A penalty pass or penalty pass or shot on court immediately opposite the point where the infringer was standing.

16.8 Obstruction by a player from out of court

16.8.1 A player who is standing out of court may not attempt to defend a player who is on the court.

Penalty: A penalty pass or penalty pass or shot on the court opposite the point where the infringer was standing.

17. Contact

17.1 Personal Contact

17.1.1 No player shall come into personal contact with an opponent in such a manner as to interfere with the opponent's play either accidentally or deliberately.

17.1.2 In an effort to attack or defend or to play the ball a player shall not:

(i) push an opponent in any way;

(ii) bump or rush into an opponent;

(iii) trip or knock an opponent

in any way;

(iv) use any part of the body to interfere with an opponent's play;

(v) hold an opponent; this includes feeling to keep near an opponent;

(vi) charge an opponent, i.e. when jumping, bump against an opponent.

17.1.3 Whether attempting to attack or to defend, a player is responsible for any personal contact:-

(i) If taking up a position so near an opponent that contact cannot be avoided.

(ii) If moving so quickly into the path of a moving player that contact cannot be avoided.

17.1.4 A player shall not contact another on any occasion or in any other way in such a manner as to interfere with the opponent's play.

17.2 Contact with the ball

17.2.1 A player, while holding the ball, shall not touch or push an opposing player with it in such a manner as to interfere with that opponent's play.

17.2.2 A player shall not, either accidentally or deliberately, place a hand or hands on, or remove from an opponent's possession, a ball held by an opposing player.

17.2.3 Where 17.2.1 and 17.2.2 occur simultaneously a toss-up is taken between those two players.

Penalty for 17.1 to 17.2.2: Penalty pass or penalty pass or shot where the infringer is standing except where this places the non-offending team at a disadvantage, when the penalty shall be taken where the contacted player was standing.

IV. CONDUCTING PENALTIES

The penalties awarded for the breaking of the rules are:

Free Pass

Penalty Pass or Shot

Throw-in

Toss-up

V. DISCIPLINE

These rules are reprinted by permission of the All-England Netball Association. A complete copy of the rules, including Rules IV and V, plus two Appendices, are available from the AENA.

Volleyball
Essentials

From its humble beginnings in 1895 as 'minonette', a game devised for those not fit enough to play basketball, this has become a popular sport worldwide. It can be played as an informal, recreational game or a highly competitive, vigorous one at competition level.

The ball

Spherical, made of a flexible leather case containing a bladder made of rubber or similar material. A circumference of 65–67 cm (approx 26 in) , weight of 260–280 g (approx 9.5 oz) and an inside pressure of 0.30–0.325 kg/sq cm.

The net

9.5 m (31 ft) long and 1 m (3 ft) wide when hung taut. A height of 2.43 m (approx 8 ft) (men) or 2.24 m (approx 7 ft) (women). Made of 10 cm (approx 4 in) square black mesh, with a 5-cm (2-in) wide band of white canvas across the top and two 5-cm (2-in) wide/1 m (3 ft) long white side bands. Two flexible vertical antennae, 1.8 m (6 ft) long, are fastened at the outer edge of each side band to mark the boundaries that the ball must keep to when crossing the net.

Posts

Two rounded posts with a height of 2.55 m (8 ft). Fixed to the ground at a distance of 0.50–1 m (1½–3 ft) from each sideline.

Officials

A first referee, second referee, scorer and four (FIVB World Competitions) or two line judges.

The court

Various surfaces, although World Competitions always use wooden or synthetic surfaces only. (Beach Volleyball is now a separate Olympic sport using a sand court of the same dimensions.) A playing court measuring 18 m x 9 m (approx 59 x 30 ft), surrounded by a symmetrical rectangular free zone, minimum 3 m (10 ft) wide (wider for top level competitions). A minimum height of 7 m (23 ft) above the playing surface must be free from all obstructions. Indoor courts must generally be of a light colour.

Divided into two courts by a centre line. Each court is then divided into a front and back zone by the attack line.

Dress

Shirt, shorts and shoes, the same colour throughout a team. Players' shirts are numbered (numbers 1 to 18) front and back.

Warm and bright

For competition volleyball, warmth and adequate lighting are essential. The temperature on court must never drop below 16°C (61°F) nor rise higher than 25°C (77°F). The lighting should be between 1,000 and 1,500 lux.

Indoors or outdoors

Volleyball can be played indoors or outdoors, but most major tournaments are played indoors. The rules stipulate that indoor courts must be one colour.

Footwear

Most players wear light, pliable shoes without heels. However players may obtain permission from the officials to play barefoot.

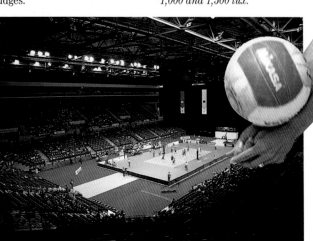

The players

Two teams of six players each, with up to six substitutes. (Beach Volleyball is usually two a side.)

HOW TO PLAY

Each team attempts to send the ball over the net to the opposite team by hitting it with their hands or arms. They are allowed to hit the ball three times before sending it back, but must not catch or hold it, or let it touch the ground in their own court.

Starting

The winner of the toss chooses the right to serve or receive, or a side of the court. All players except the server must be in their own court at the moment the ball is served, with each team arranged in two rows of three players – three front-row players (along the net) and three back-row players behind them. The ball is served by a player of the serving team standing behind the end line. The server hits the ball with one hand or arm, after which players are free to move about within their own court.

How to win

Teams must gain the right to serve before they can score points. If the receiving side fails to return the ball or commits a fault, one point is scored by the serving team. If the receiving team wins the rally they gain the right to serve and may go on to score points.

A set is won by the first team to score 15 points, with a lead of two points. If the score reaches 14-all, play continues until a two point lead is reached (although if the score reaches 16-all, one extra point is enough to win the set, in all but the deciding set).

A match is won by the team that wins three sets – the best of five. A deciding fifth set is played as a tie-break with the rally-point system, i.e., teams score points by winning rallies, regardless of whether they are the serving or receiving side.

KEY RULES

• Service and court ends alternate between teams after each set. Within a team players rotate in a clockwise direction from their initial starting positions so that each has a turn in each of the six court positions. However, the same player continues to serve from the baseline until the team loses a rally. When this occurs, each player of the opposing team moves around one place. A team's starting line-up is drawn up by each coach before a set to establish the order. Up to six substitutions may take place within a team in one set.

• The ball may be played with any part of a player's body and it must be clearly hit, not held. Unintentional contact with the ball counts as a hit and the same player must not hit the ball twice consecutively, except when blocking at the net or when making the first of the team's three hits. If two or three members of the same team touch the ball simultaneously this counts as two or three hits.
See Rule 14, Playing the Ball (page 160).

• Faults incur the loss of a rally or, if both teams commit faults simultaneously, the rally is replayed.

• A player must not touch the net whilst trying to play the ball. He also must not penetrate into his opponents' court with any part of his body (unless with his hands or feet, provided part of his hand(s) or foot (feet) remains in contact with, or above, the centre line).
See Rule 16, Player at the Net (page 161).

• Front-row players may attack (i.e. send over the net) the ball at any height, as well as block the ball (jump up to intercept or divert a ball from the opposition). Back-row players may only attack hit at any height whilst they are in the back zone. If they move to the front zone, all attacking hits must be made when at least part of the ball is below the level of the net. They may not block the ball.
See Rule 18, Attack-Hit (page 164).

SKILLS

The *serve* – a potentially dynamic start to a rally. The most basic is an underarm serve, although experienced players use a serve similar to that performed with a racket in tennis or the 'jump' serve – used at the top level of play, in which a server throws the ball both up and forwards and then runs to meet it, hitting it as he jumps into the air.

The *volley* – a basic two-handed overhead shot, used to keep the ball in play or pass it over the net.

The *dig* – is made with both arms extended out to the front of the body and both hands clasped. The ball is met with the forearms. This is used to take the speed out of a forceful delivery or to make contact with a low travelling ball. Hardly any movement is used on impact.

The *smash* or spike – made by striking the ball downwards rapidly into the opponents' court.

Service jump
To serve, a player tosses the ball into the air with either one or both hands and then knocks it over the net with one hand or part of the arm. Services include: the 'hook', made with the body sideways to the net; the 'tennis' serve, facing the net; and the 'underhand' serve. Some competition players jump high in the air when serving for extra penetration.

Serving around
Every member of a volleyball team serves in rotation. The ball is always served by the back right-hand player and the players move clockwise around the court one position at a time to take up the serve.

Server

VOLLEYBALL THE RULES
● ● ● ● ● ● ● ● ● ● ● ● ● ●

SECTION I: THE GAME

Chapter One: Facilities and Equipment
Rules 1–3
See page 158.

Chapter Two:
Participants
Rules 4–6
See The Players (page 158).

Chapter Three:
Point ,Set and Match Winner
Rule 7
See How to win (page 159).

Chapter Four:
Preparation of the Match: Structure of Play
Rules 8 and 9
See Starting (page 159).

10 Players' Positions and Rotation
10.1 Positions
10.1.1 At the moment the ball is hit by the server, each team must be within its own court (except the server) in two rows of three players. These rows may be broken.
10.1.2 The three players along the net are front-row players and occupy positions 4 (left), 3 (centre) and 2 (right).
The other three are back-row players and occupy positions 5 (left), 6 (centre) and 1 (right). Each back-row player must be positioned further back from the centre line than the corresponding front-row player.
10.1.3 The positions of players are determined and controlled according to the positions of their feet contacting the ground as follows:
a) Each front-row player must have at least part of one foot closer to the centre line than the feet of the corresponding back-row player.
b) Each right (left) side player must have at least part of one foot closer to the right (left) sideline than the feet of the centre player in the same row.
10.1.4 Once the ball has been served, the players may move around and occupy any position on their own court and in the free zone.
10.2 Rotation
When the receiving team has gained the right to serve, its players must rotate one position clockwise (player in position 2 rotates to position 1 to serve, player in 1 rotates to 6, etc.).
10.3 Positional Faults

Set for a smash
The best volleyball teams take advantage of the 'three touch' rule to set up a player for a smash. One player may volley the ball at the back of the court to a player near the net who sets it up for the smasher at the right height.

10.3.1 The players of a team commit a fault if they are not in their correct positions at the moment the ball is hit by the server.
10.3.2 If the server commits a serving fault at the moment of hitting the ball, this fault prevails over a positional fault and is thus penalized.
If, after the ball has been hit, the service becomes a fault, it is a positional fault that will be penalized.
10.3.3 A positional fault leads to the following consequences:
– the fault is penalized with the loss of a rally.
– the players are returned to their correct positions.
10.4 Rotation Faults
10.4.1 A rotation fault is committed when the service is not made according to the rotation order. This corresponds to a positional fault; the error must be corrected and the team at fault penalized according to Rule 10.3.3.
10.4.2 The scorer should determine the exact moment the fault was committed. All points scored subsequently by the team at fault must be cancelled. The opponents' points remain valid. If the points scored while the player was out of position or out of service order cannot be determined, a loss of rally is the only sanction.

11 Substitution of Players
11.1 Definition
A substitution is the act by which the referees authorize a player to leave the court and another player to occupy his position.
11.2 Limitations of Substitutions
11.2.1 Six substitutions is the maximum permitted per team

per set. One or more players may be substituted at the same time.
11.2.2 A player of the starting line-up may leave the game and re-enter, but only once in a set, and only to the player's previous position in the line-up.
11.2.3 A substitute player may enter the game only once per set, in place of a player of the starting line-up, and can be replaced only by the same player.
11.3 Exceptional Substitution
An injured player who cannot continue playing should be legally substituted. If this is not possible, the team is entitled to make an exceptional substitution, beyond the limits of Rule 11.2.
11.4 Substitution for Expulsion
An expelled or disqualified player must be replaced through a legal substitution. If that is not possible, the team is declared incomplete.
11.5 Illegal Substitution
11.5.1 A substitution is illegal if it exceeds the limitations indicated in Rule 11.2.
11.5.2 When a team makes an illegal substitution and the play is resumed, the following procedure shall apply:
– the fault is penalized with the loss of a rally.
– the substitution is rectified.
– the points scored by the team at fault, after the fault was committed, are cancelled. The opponents' points remain valid.

Chapter Five:
Playing Actions
12 States of Play
12.1 Ball 'In Play'
The first referee's whistle authorizes the service. The ball is 'in play' from the service hit.
12.2 Ball 'Out of Play'
The rally ends with the referee's

whistle. However, if the whistle is due to a fault made in play, the ball is 'out of play' the moment the fault was committed.
12.3 Ball 'In'
The ball is 'in' when it touches the floor of the playing court including the boundary lines (Rule 1.3.2).
12.4 Ball 'Out'
The ball is 'out' when:
a) the part of the ball which contacts the floor is completely outside the boundary lines,
b) it touches an object outside the court, the ceiling or a person out of play,
c) it touches the antennae, ropes, posts or the net itself outside the antennae/side bands,
d) it crosses completely underneath the vertical plane of the net.

13 Playing Faults
13.1 Definition
13.1.1 Any playing action contrary to the rules is a playing fault.
13.1.2 The referees judge the faults and determine the penalties according to these rules.
13.2 Consequences of a Fault
13.2.1 The consequence of a fault is the loss of a rally. The opponents of the team committing the fault win the rally according to Rule 7.3 in the first four sets or Rule 7.4 in the deciding set.
13.2.2 If two or more faults are committed successively, only the first one is counted.
13.2.3 If two or more faults are committed by opponents simultaneously, a double fault is counted and the rally is replayed.

14 Playing the Ball
14.1 Team Hits
14.1.1 The team is entitled to a maximum of three hits (in addition to blocking, Rule 19.2.1) for returning the ball over the net.
14.1.2 The hits of the team include not only intentional hits by the player, but also unintentional contacts with the ball.
14.1.3 A player may not hit the ball twice consecutively (except Rule 19.2.2 and 14.4.3).
14.2 Simultaneous Contact
14.2.1 Two or three players may touch the ball at the same moment.
14.2.2 When two (three) team-mates touch the ball simultaneously, it is counted as

two (three) hits (except at blocking). If two (three) team-mates reach for the ball but only one player touches it, one hit is counted. If players collide, no fault is committed.

14.2.3 If there are simultaneous contacts by opponents over the net and the ball remains in play, the team receiving the ball is entitled to another three hits. If such a ball goes 'out', it is the fault of the team on the opposite side. If simultaneous contacts by opponents lead to a 'held ball', it is a double fault (Rule 13.2.3) and the rally is replayed.

14.3 Assisted Hit

Within the playing area, a player is not permitted to take support from a team-mate or any structure or object in order to reach the ball. However, the player who is about to commit a fault (touch the net or cross the centre line etc.) may be stopped or held back by a team-mate.

14.4 Characteristics of the Hit

14.4.1 The ball may touch any part of the body.

14.4.2 The ball must be hit, not caught or thrown. It can rebound in any direction.

14.4.3 The ball may touch various parts of the body, provided that the contacts take place simultaneously.

Exceptions:

a) At blocking, consecutive contacts may occur with one or more blockers provided that the contacts occur during one action.

b) At the first hit of a team (19.2) the ball may touch various parts of the body consecutively, provided that this occurs during one action.

14.5 Faults Playing the Ball

a) Four Hits: a team hits the ball four times before returning it (Rule 14.1.1).

b) Assisted Hit: a player takes support from a team-mate or any structure or object in order to reach the ball within the playing area (Rule 14.3).

c) Held Ball: a player does not hit the ball cleanly, but catches or holds it (Rule 14.4.2).

d) Double Contact: a player hits the ball twice in succession or the ball contacts various parts of the body successively (Rules 14.1.3, 14.4.3).

15 Ball at the Net

15.1 Ball Crossing the Net

15.1.1. The ball sent to the opponents' court must go over the net within the crossing space. The crossing space is the part of the vertical plane of the net limited as follows:
– below, by the top of the net
– at the sides, by the antennae and their imaginary extension
– above, by the ceiling.

15.1.2 The ball that has crossed the net plane to the opponent's free zone (Rule 12) totally or partly outside of the crossing space, may be played back within the team hits provided that:
– the opponents' court is not touched by the player;
– the ball when played back crosses the net plane again outside the crossing space on the same side of the court.
The opposing team may not prevent such action.

15.1.3 The ball is 'out' when it crosses completely the lower space under the net.

15.2 Ball Touching the Net

When crossing the net (Rule 15.1.1) the ball may touch it, except during the service.

15.3 Ball in the Net (other than the service ball).

15.3.1 A ball driven into the net may be recovered within the limits of the three team hits.

15.3.2 If the ball rips the mesh of the net or tears it down, the rally is cancelled and replayed.

16 Player at the Net

16.1 Playing Area

16.1.1 Each team must play within its own playing area and space. The ball may, however, be retrieved from beyond the free zone.

16.2 Reaching Beyond the Net

16.2.1 In blocking, a blocker may touch the ball beyond the net, provided that there is no interference with the opponents' play before or during the latter's attack hit (Rule 19.3).

16.2.2 A player is permitted to pass a hand beyond the net after an attack hit, provided that the contact has been made within the player's own playing space.

16.3 Penetration Under the Net

16.3.1 It is permitted to penetrate into the opponents' space under the net, provided that this does not interfere with the opponents' play.

16.3.2 Penetration into the opponents' court:

a) to touch the opponents' court with a foot (feet) or hand(s) is permitted, provided that some part of the penetrating foot (feet) or hand(s) remains either in contact with or directly above the centre line.

b) to contact the opponents' court with any other part of the body is forbidden.

16.3.3 A player may enter the opponents' court after the ball is out of play (Rule 12.2). A player may penetrate into the opponents' free zone provided that there is no interference with the opponents' play.

16.4 Contact With the Net

16.4.1 Contact with the net is a fault, except when a player not attempting to play the ball accidentally touches the net.

16.4.2 Once a player has hit the ball, the player may touch the posts, ropes or any other object outside the total length of the net provided that it does not interfere with play.

16.4.3 When the ball is driven into the net and causes it to touch an opponent, no fault is committed.

16.5 Player's Faults at the Net

It is a fault if:

a) a player touches the ball in the opponents' space before or during the opponents' attack hit (Rule 16.2.1).

b) a player penetrates into the opponents' space under the net interfering with the latter's play (Rule 16.3.1).

c) a player penetrates into the opponents' court (Rule 16.3.2).

d) a player touches the net (Rule 16.4.1).

17 Service

17.1 Definition

The service is the act of putting the ball into play by the right back-row player, placed in the service zone, who hits the ball with one hand or arm.

17.2 First Service in a Set

17.2.1 The first service of sets one and five is executed by the team that has obtained the right to serve at the toss (Rule 8.1).

17.2.2 The other sets will be started with the service of the team that did not serve first in the previous set.

17.3 Service Order

17.3.1 The players must follow the service order recorded on the line-up sheet.

17.3.2 After the first service in a set, the player to serve is determined as follows:

a) when the serving team wins the rally, the player who served before, serves again.

b) when the receiving team wins the rally, it gains the right to serve and rotates. The player who moves from the right front-row position to the right back-row position will serve.

17.4 Authorization of the Service

The first referee authorizes the service after having checked that the server is in possession of the ball and that the teams are ready to play.

17.5 Execution of the Service

17.5.1 At the moment of the service hit or take-off for a jump service, the server must not touch the court (the end line included) nor the ground outside the service zone. After the service hit, the player may step or land outside the zone, or inside the court.

17.5.2 The server must hit the ball within five seconds after the first referee whistles for service.

17.5.3 A service executed before the referee's whistle is cancelled and repeated.

17.5.4 The ball shall be hit with one hand or any part of the arm after being tossed or released and before it touches the playing surface.

17.6 Service Attempt

17.6.1 If the ball, after having been tossed or released, lands without touching the server, it is considered a service attempt.

17.6.2 After the service attempt, the referee must authorize the service again, without any delay, and the server must execute it within the next three seconds.

17.6.3 One and only one service attempt is permitted for each service.

17.7 Screening

The players of the serving team must not prevent their opponents, through screening, from seeing the server and the path of the ball.

17.7.1 A player of the serving team who waves arms, jumps or moves sideways, etc., when the service is being executed, makes an individual screen, if the ball is served over the player.

17.7.2 A team makes a collective screen when the server is hidden behind a group of two or more team-mates, and the ball is served over them.

17.8 Serving Faults

The following faults lead to a change of service even if the opponents are out of position when the server:

a) violates the service order (Rule 17.3),

b) does not execute the service properly (Rule 17.5),

c) violates the rules of service attempt(Rule 17.6).

17.9 Serving Faults After Hitting the Ball

After the ball has been correctly hit, the service becomes a fault (unless a player is out of position) if the ball:

➡ *page 164*

Beach game?
Beach volleyball is not just a game for sunbathers, but a major spectator sport. This is the arena at Clearwater, Florida.

Hand tennis
Unlike indoor volleyball, beach volleyball involves just two players.

Tennis serve
The tennis serve, facing the net, can be made either from a standstill or by stepping into the serve for extra power. The ball is hit with the open hand and the arm completely straight. The service is followed through to carry the player forward on to the court and into play.

Hand to hand
Above, two beach volleyball players clash at the net in a quick interchange.

Service stations
In beach volleyball the underarm and tennis services tend to be the most popular. Players often try to give the ball a spin to fool their opponent.

Digging out
The dig is used by players receiving the ball from a service or to play a ball that is too low to volley.

The dig
With the dig, the two hands are kept close together and the ball is lofted with the forearms facing upwards

Just before receiving the ball the player bends his knees, then straightens them as he hits it.

TACTICS

The standard procedure for receiving and returning the ball is the dig-set-smash approach. The three hits permitted to a team are used to absorb the speed of a serve, pass it (setting it up for the smash) and then smash it to return it over the net, hopefully to score a point.

Up for the spike
The spike involves smashing the ball down into the opposition's court to complete a classic three touch move.

Plan B
The best volleyball teams exploit the three touch rule in a number of carefully planned dig, set and smash movements. This player is indicating a manoeuvre.

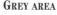

Smashing run
While team-mates are setting up the ball, the smasher runs in to gain maximum height and smash the ball right at the net.

GREY AREA
Traditionally volleyball was very strict about which parts of the body could be used to strike the ball, but in recent years the rules have been changed to allow other parts of the body to be used in order to make the game faster, flowing and more exciting for spectators. Rule changes have also allowed players more leniency when playing the ball, a move which has split players and coaches into those teaching the new skills and those who prefer a more traditional approach with a strict technical interpretation on the handling rules.

continued from page 161

a) touches a player of the serving team or fails to cross the vertical plane of the net,

b) touches the net (Rule 15.2),

c) goes "out" (Rule 12.4),

d) passes over an individual or collective screen (Rule 17.7).

18 Attack-Hit
18.1 Definition
18.1.1 All actions to direct the ball towards the opponent, except service and block, are considered attack-hits. During an attack-hit tipping is permitted if the contact is clean, and the ball is not accompanied by the hand.

18.1.2 An attack-hit is completed the moment the ball completely crosses the vertical plane of the net, or is touched by an opponent.

18.2 Front-Row Player's Attack-Hit
The front-row player may complete an attack-hit at any height provided that the contact with the ball has been made within the player's own playing space (except Rule 18.4d).

18.3 Restrictions to a Back-Row Player's Attack-Hit
18.3.1 A back-row player may complete an attack-hit at any height from behind the front zone. At take-off the player's foot (feet) must have neither touched nor crossed over the attack line.

After the hit a player may land within the front zone. (Rule 1.4.1).

18.3.2 A back-row player may also complete an attack-hit from the front zone, if at the moment of contact any part of the ball is below the top of the net.

18.4 Attack-Hit Faults
An attack-hit fault is committed when:

a) a player hits the ball within the playing space of the opposing team;

b) a player hits the ball 'out' (Rule 12.4);

c) a back-row player completes an attack-hit from the front zone, if at the moment of the hit the ball is entirely above the top of the net (Rules 18.1.2, 18.3.2);

d) a player completes an attack-hit on the opponents' service, when the ball is in the front zone and entirely above the top of the net.

19 Block
19.1 Definition
Blocking is the action of players close to the net to intercept the ball coming from the opponents

by reaching higher than the top of the net.

19.1.1 Block Attempt
A block attempt is the action of blocking without touching the ball.

19.1.2 Completed Block
A block is completed whenever the ball is touched by a blocker. Only front-row players are permitted to complete a block.

19.1.3 Collective Block
A collective block is executed by two or three players close to each other and is completed when one of them touches the ball.

19.2 Block and Team Hits
A block contact is not counted as a team hit (Rule 14.1.1).

19.2.1 After a block contact, a team is entitled to three hits to return the ball.

19.2.2 The first hit after the block may be executed by any player, including the one who has touched the ball at the block.

19.3 Blocking within the Opponents' Space
In blocking, the player may place hands and arms beyond the net, provided that the action does not interfere with the opponents' play. Thus, it is not permitted to touch the ball beyond the net until the opponent has executed an attack-hit.

19.4 Blocking Contact
19.4.1 Consecutive (quick and continuous) contacts may occur with one or more blockers, provided that the contacts are made during one action.

19.4.2 These contacts may occur with any part of the body.

19.5 Blocking Faults
a) The blocker touches the ball in the opponents' space either before or simultaneously with the opponents' action (Rule 19.3).

b) A back-row player completes a block or participates in a completed one (Rules 19.1.2, 19.1.3).

c) A player blocks the ball in the opponents' space from outside the antenna.

d) A player blocks the opponents' service.

e) The ball is sent 'out' off the block.

Chapter Six: Interruptions and Delays
20 Regular Game Interruptions
20.1 Categories
Regular game interruptions are for time-outs and player substitutions.

20.2 Number of Regular Interruptions
Each team is entitled to a maximum of two time-outs and

six player substitutions per set.

20.3 Request for Regular Interruptions
Interruptions may be requested only by the coach or the game captain, when the ball is out of play and before the whistle for service, by showing the correct hand-signal.

A request for substitution before the start of a set is permitted and should be recorded as a regular game interruption in that set.

20.4 Sequence of Interruptions
One or two time-outs and one request for player substitution by either team may follow one another, with no need to resume the game.

A team is not authorized to request consecutive interruptions for player substitutions unless the game has been resumed. However, two or more players may be substituted during the same interruption (Rule 20.6.2).

20.5 Time-out
20.5.1 A time-out lasts for 30 seconds.

20.5.2 During a time-out, the players in play must go to the free zone near their bench.

20.6 Player Substitution
20.6.1 A substitution shall last only the time needed for recording the substitution on the scoresheet, and allowing the entry and exit of players.

20.6.2 If the coach intends to make more than one substitution, the number must be signalled at the time of the request. In this case, substitutions must be made in succession, one pair of players after another.

20.6.3 At the moment of the request, the player(s) must be ready to enter, standing close to the coach (Rules 6.3.3). If that is not the case, the substitution is not granted and the team is sanctioned for a delay (Rules 21.2).

20.6.4 Substitutions must be carried out in the substitution zone (Rule 1.4.3).

20.7 Improper Requests
It is improper to request an interruption:

a) during a rally or at the moment of, or after, the whistle to serve (Rule 20.3);

b) by a non-authorised team member (Rule 20.3);

c) for player substitution before the game has been resumed from a previous substitution by the same team (Rule 20.4);

d) after having exhausted the authorized number of time-outs

or player substitutions (Rule 20.2);

Any improper request that does not delay the game shall be rejected without any sanction unless repeated in the same set (Rules 21.1 d).

21 Delays to the Game
21.1 Type of Delay
Any action of a team that defers resumption of the game is a delay and includes:

a) delaying a substitution;

b) prolonging other interruptions, after having been instructed to resume the game;

c) requesting an illegal substitution (Rule 11.2);

d) repeating an improper request in the same set (Rule 20.7);

e) delaying the game by a player in play.

21.2 Sanctions for Delays
21.2.1 The first delay by a team in a set is sanctioned with a delay warning.

The sanction of delay warning is a team sanction.

21.2.2 The second and subsequent delays of any type by any player or other member of the same team in the same set constitute a fault and are sanctioned with a delay penalty; loss of rally.

22 Exceptional Game Interruptions
22.1 Injury
22.1.1 Should a serious accident occur while the ball is in play, the referee must stop the game immediately. The rally is then replayed.

22.1.2 If an injured player cannot be substituted, legally or exceptionally (Rule 11.3), the player is given a three-minute recovery time, but not more than once for the same player in the match. If the player does not recover, the team is declared incomplete (Rules 9.2.2, 7.5.3).

22.2 External Interference
If there is any external interference during the game, play has to be stopped and the rally is replayed.

22.3 Prolonged Interruptions
If unforeseen circumstances interrupt the match, the first referee, the organiser and the control committee, if there is one, shall decide the measures to be taken to re-establish normal conditions.

22.3.1 Should one or several interruptions occur, not exceeding four hours in total, then:

a) If the match is resumed on

the same playing court, the interrupted set shall continue normally with the same score, players and positions. The sets already played will keep their scores.

b) If the match is resumed on another court, the interrupted set is cancelled and replayed with the same starting line-ups. The sets already played keep their scores.

22.3.2 Should one or several interruptions occur, exceeding four hours in total, the whole match shall be replayed.

23 Intervals and Change of Courts
23.1 Intervals
All intervals between sets, including the one between the fourth and fifth sets, last three minutes. During this period of time, the change of courts and line-up registration of the teams on the score sheets are made.
23.2 Change of Courts
23.2.1 After each set, the teams change courts, with the exception of the deciding set (Rule 8.1.2). Other team members change benches.
23.2.2 In the deciding set, once a team reaches eight points, the teams change courts without delay and the player positions remain the same. If the change is not made at the proper time, it will take place as soon as the error is noticed. The score at the time that the change is made remains the same.

Chapter Seven: Misconduct
24 Misconduct
Incorrect conduct by a team member towards officials, opponents, team-mates or spectators is classified in four categories according to the degree of the offence.
24.1 Categories
24.1.1 Unsportsmanlike conduct: arguing, intimidation, etc.
24.1.2 Rude conduct: acting contrary to good manners or moral principles, expressing contempt.
24.1.3 Offensive conduct: defamatory or insulting words or gestures.
24.1.4 Aggression: physical attack or intended aggression.
24.2 Sanctions
Depending on the degree of the incorrect conduct, according to the judgement of the first referee, the sanctions to be applied are:
24.2.1 Misconduct warning: For unsportsmanlike conduct, no penalty is given but:
a) the team member concerned is warned against repetition in the same match;
b) the warning is recorded on the score sheet
c) repeated unsportsmanlike conduct is sanctioned with loss of rally.
24.2.2 Misconduct Penalty: for rude conduct, the team is penalized with the loss of a rally which is recorded on the score sheet.

24.2.3 Expulsion: repeated rude conduct is sanctioned by expulsion. The team member who is sanctioned with expulsion must leave the playing area, the bench and the warm-up area for the rest of the set. The second expulsion of the same team member is regarded as a disqualification.
24.2.4 Disqualification: for offensive conduct and aggression, the player (or any

other team member) must leave the playing area, the team bench, and the warm-up area for the rest of the match.
24.3 Sanction Scale
The repetition of misconduct by the same person in the same set is sanctioned progressively as shown in the sanction scale below. Disqualification due to offensive conduct or aggression does not require a previous sanction.
24.4 Misconduct Before and Between Sets
Any misconduct

occurring before or between sets is sanctioned according to Rules 24.2 and sanctions apply in the following set.

SECTION II
Refers to referees.

These rules are reprinted by permission of the English Volleyball Association. A complete copy of the Volleyball International Rules can be obtained from the Association.

Misconduct sanctions scale

Catagories	Times	Sanction	Cards to follow	Consequences
1 Unsporting conduct	First	Warning	Yellow	Prevention, no penalty
	Second	Penalty	Red	Loss of rally
	Third	Expulsion	Both jointly	Expulsion from the playing area, warm-up area and the team bench for the set
2 Rude conduct	First	Penalty	Both jointly	Loss of rally
	Second	Expulsion	Both jointly	Expulsion from the playing area, warm-up area and the team bench for the set
3 Offensive conduct 4 Aggression	First	Disqualification	Both separately	Expulsion from the playing area, warm-up area and the team bench for the match

Korfball
Essentials

The name of this sport comes from the Dutch word, *korfbal*, meaning basketball. This is a no-contact game, played by two mixed teams on an indoor or outdoor pitch. The object of the game is to score by shooting the ball through the two baskets at either end of the pitch.

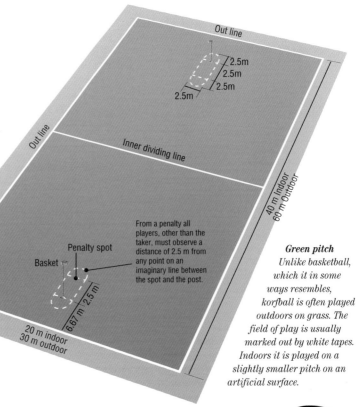

Out line

2.5m
2.5m
2.5m
2.5m

Out line

Inner dividing line

40 m Indoor
60 m Outdoor

Penalty spot

Basket

From a penalty all players, other than the taker, must observe a distance of 2.5 m from any point on an imaginary line between the spot and the post.

6.67 m 2.5 m

20 m indoor
30 m outdoor

The pitch

Indoor pitches are 40 m by 20 m (44 yds by 22 yds), outdoor (generally grass or artificial grass) are 60 m by 30 m (66 yds by 33 yds). Divided into two equal zones. The field of play is marked out by clearly visible lines or tapes, 3–5 cm wide (approx 1½ in). The free height of an indoor pitch must be no less than 7 m (23 ft).

Baskets

Cane, one colour, fitted to round posts which are set in each half, 6.66 m (22 ft) from each end. The basket is 25 cm (10 in) high, with an inner diameter of 39–41 cm (approx 16 in) and its top edge is 3.5 m (11 ft) above the ground.

Officials

A referee, a timekeeper and two linesmen.

Green pitch
Unlike basketball, which it in some ways resembles, korfball is often played outdoors on grass. The field of play is usually marked out by white tapes. Indoors it is played on a slightly smaller pitch on an artificial surface.

Mixed match
Korfball is one of the few games in which men and women play together on an equal footing. However, there are rules to prevent undue interference with players of the opposite sex.

The players

Two teams of four male and four female players each. Two men and two women are positioned in each zone. (Up to two substitutions are permitted, possibly more at the discretion of the referee in the case of injury.)

The ball

A number 5 ball, round, with a leather (or approved material) outer casing. Two-coloured for indoor games. It may, however, be a uniform colour for outdoor games. A circumference of 68–71 cm (approx 27 in) and a weight of 425–475 g (approx 16 oz) at the start of a match.

Dress

Uniform throughout a team and contrasting to that of the opposing team. Shoes must be worn. Players are not allowed to wear objects which may cause injuries during the game. The captain of each team must also wear a band on the upper part of the left arm.

Catching on the run
Players are not normally allowed to run with the bal. However, they may carry on running if they catch the ball on the run and combine it into a single throwing movement. It is up to the referee to decide whether the run on was legitimate.

HOW TO PLAY

Teams score goals by throwing the ball into their opponents' basket. The ball must be played only with the hands – not with a fist or with the legs or feet. Players are not allowed to run with the ball and they must pass it whenever possible.

Starting

The home team chooses a basket for the first half and both teams then arrange their players as attackers or defenders in the two zones. Play begins with a throw-off by an attackers from a point inside his zone, near the centre of the field. Each time two goals have been scored, players' roles change, i.e. attackers become defenders and vice versa. At half-time there is a change of ends, but players' roles do not change.

How to win

The winner is the team with the most goals.

KEY RULES

• A game consists of two halves of 30 minutes each (35 minutes for outdoor games), with a ten-minute rest. Teams also have the right to ask for up to two time-outs of 60 seconds each during the game.

• Players must not run with the ball, but they are allowed to pivot on one foot while in possession and in a stationary position. If the ball is caught whilst running, the player must either stop completely or pass it to another player straight away.

• It is against the rules to knock the ball out of an opponent's hand or to impede his progress with an arm or leg extended across his path. Intentional contact is not permitted and hindering an opponent must not involve actual physical obstruction.

• Shots at goal must not be made from a defended position, i.e., when a defender is within arm's length of the shooter, facing him and nearer to the post than him.
  See Infringement of the Rules, Rule 16 (page 168).

• Players must play the ball while in their own zones. The ball itself is out if it touches a boundary line or anything beyond it. An out-ball is penalized by a free pass against the offending team.
  See Rule 17, Out-Ball (page 169).

• A violation of the rules incurs a free pass taken from the spot where the infringement occurred.
  See Rule 19, Free Pass (page 169).

• An infringement which causes a team to lose a scoring opportunity is punished with a penalty to the non-offending team. This is taken from the penalty spot 2.5 m (8 ft) in front of the opposition's post and a goal may be scored directly from it. The attacking player taking the penalty must be allowed an unimpeded shot, all other players remaining at least 2.5 m (8 ft) from him until the ball is played.
  See Rule 20, penalty (page 169).

SKILLS AND TACTICS

Obviously agility and deft handling of the ball are important skills. However, defensive play is also a vital element of the game. Players must master the art of fair hindering – marking an opponent so that their moves and options with the ball are restricted as much as possible whilst respecting the ban on intentional physical contact.

The rules of korfball actively encourage tactical awareness and co-operation within a team. For example, rule 16e prevents a player from indulging in solo play and 16n (outlawing shooting from a defended position) is intended to make it necessary for players to work together and establish free positions on the pitch from which shots may be taken.

High scoring
The basket in korfball is much higher than in basketball and there is no possibility of even the tallest player being able to jump up and drop the ball in.

KORFBALL
THE RULES
INDOOR
• • • • • •

Chapter 1 Hall, Ground and Material: Rules 1–5

Chapter 2 Persons: Rules 6–10

See The players (page 166).

Chapter 3 The Game: Rules 11–15

See How to play (page 167).

16 Infringement of the Rules

During the game it is prohibited:
a) to touch the ball with leg or foot.
If the touching is unintentional and exerts no important influence upon the game it will not be punished.
b) to hit the ball with the fist
c) to take hold of the ball in a fallen position
d) to run with the ball
Running with the ball is contrary to the requirement of cooperation. Change of position with possession of the ball is therefore only permitted when otherwise it would be impossible to pass the ball fluently or to shoot or to stop with the ball.
In applying these principles three cases are to be distinguished.

1. When seizing the ball the player stands at rest.
In this case he may move one leg at will, provided the other one remains in its place. Turning on the latter is permitted.

2. When seizing the ball the player is running or jumping, first stops and afterwards throws the ball or shoots. The requirement is that, after seizing the ball, he has immediately and fully tried to come to a stop.
After coming to a stop, the same rules apply as mentioned under 1.

3. After seizing the ball while running or jumping the player throws the ball or shoots before he has come to a stop completely. In this case the player is not allowed to be still in possession of the ball at the moment that he places his foot on the ground for the third time after receiving the ball.
e) to avoid cooperation (solo-play)
Solo-play is not punishable:
1. when the player does not change his position appreciably.
2. when the avoidance of cooperation was not intentional.
f) to hand the ball to another of one's own team
g) to delay the game

h) to knock, take or run the ball out of an opponent's hand
i) to push, to cling to, or to hold off an opponent
This unlawful hindering of an opponent has to be punished no matter whether this opponent does or does not possess the ball even if the ball is in another zone. Every impediment of the free movement of an opponent is forbidden whether this is done deliberately or not.
This rule does not force a player to give way for another player, i.e. each player allowed to position himself just as he pleases. He will only be punished when he jumps so suddenly in the path of a moving opponent that a collision becomes inevitable.
j) to hinder an opponent excessively
This rule applies when the opponent has the ball in his possession.
The hindering player is allowed to hinder the throwing of the ball in the desired direction by actions which result in the ball being thrown against his hand or arm.
He is allowed to block the ball by bringing his arm in the path of the ball, but he must not:
1. hinder his opponent in the free use of his body by blocking the arm instead of the ball;
2. beat the ball or hit the throwing arm, i.e. the hindering arm or hand must not move towards the ball at the instant of contact.
Unexpected movements by an opponent will often cause a restriction in a player's freedom of movement. Such cases will not be punished, provided immediate action is taken by the opponent to restore the player's freedom of movement.
k) to hinder an opponent of the opposite sex in throwing the ball
l) to hinder an opponent who is already being hindered by another player
m) to play outside one's zone
n) to shoot from a defended position
The shot must be considered defended when the hindering defender satisfies each of the following three conditions:

1. he must be within arm's length of the attacker and must have his face turned towards him;
2. he must actually try to block the ball;
3. He must be nearer the post than the attacker, except when he and the attacker are near and on opposite sides of the post. In the latter case conditions 1 and 2 alone are sufficient.
o) to shoot after cutting past another attacker
Cutting occurs when a defender, who is within arm's length of his attacker, cannot follow this attacker because the attacker runs so close past another attacker that the defender collides with, or is likely to collide with, this attacker and is therefore forced to give up his position within arm's length.
p) to shoot from the defence zone, from a free pass or from a referee-throw (throw-up)
q) to shoot when one plays without a personal opponent
This occurs when the defence has only three players against an attack of four players. In that case the captain of the attacking side must inform the referee and the other captain, which of his attackers will not shoot.
The captain is entitled to change his decision during the match, but only after informing the referee and the other captain at a time when the ball is dead (i.e. the referee has blown for an infringement, a goal etc). This

change of an attacker is only allowed twice between a change of zones. A goal can be made from a penalty by an attacker without a personal opponent.
r) to influence a shot by moving the post
s) to take hold of the post when jumping, running or in order to move away quickly
t) to violate the conditions laid down for a free pass or a penalty
u) to play in a dangerous manner
For an attacker to force his defender, who is within arm's distance of the attacker, to collide at speed with another attacker.

17 Out-Ball

The ball is out as soon as it touches a boundary line of the field of play, the ground, a person or an object outside the field of play. The ball is also out when it touches the ceiling or an object above the field of play.
In the case of an out-ball a free pass is awarded against the side who touched the ball last.

18 Referee-Throw (throw-up)

When two opponents seize the ball simultaneously, the referee will stop play and will throw the ball up. The same applies when play must be restarted without one side being entitled to the ball. For this purpose the referee chooses two players from the zone concerned, who must be of

The right place
In korfball you are not allowed to move with the ball at all, so position is everything. Each player must not only be well positioned to receive passes from team-mates, but also well positioned to pass the ball on.

the same sex and if possible of about the same height. These two players may touch the ball after the ball has reached its highest point during the throw-up. The other players must observe a distance of 2.5 m (8 ft) and may only touch the ball after one of the two selected players has touched the ball or after the ball has been in contact with the ground. The attacker selected by the referee for the throw-up is not allowed to shoot directly from the throw-up.

19 Free Pass

a) when to award a free pass
A free pass is awarded to the opposing side after the referee has indicated that one of the rules (16 or 17) has been violated.

b) place of the free pass
The free pass is taken from the spot where the infringement was committed. If the infringement was committed against a certain person (16h, i, j, k, l and sometimes m), then the free pass is taken from the spot where this person was standing.

In the case of an out-ball or when 16 m (17.5 yds) has been violated on or outside the boundaries of the field of play, then the free pass is taken from outside the field near the boundary line where the ball or the offending player crossed the line.

When the ball is out because it touches the ceiling or an object above the field of play, the free pass is taken near one of the long boundaries and nearest to the spot where the ball touched the ceiling or the object.

c) how to take a free pass
At the moment that the player taking the free pass has, or can take the ball, in his hands the referee lifts one of his arms vertically and gives the signal with four fingers on his raised hand that he is going to whistle for the commencement of play within four seconds. Following the raising of the arm there are two possibilities (see A and B below).
A. 1. All the players are at a distance of at least 2.5 m (8 ft) from the taker of the free pass.
2. When the free pass is taken in the attack zone the players of the same team as the taker of the free pass are also at a distance of at least 2.5 m (8 ft) from each other.
As soon as the above situation exists within the four seconds preparation time the referee

shall blow his whistle to restart play. The player taking the free pass must bring the ball into play within no more than four seconds after the whistle has blown for the commencement of play (8c). If the taker of the free pass has not brought the ball into play within this period, then the referee shall blow his whistle and award a free pass to the other side. The players of the opposing team must remain meeting condition 1 until the taker of the free pass moves the ball or makes a clearly visible movement of an arm or leg.

The players of the same team as the taker of the free pass must remain meeting conditions 1 and 2 until the ball has been brought into play. The ball is brought into play when either 1. a player of the opposing team touches the ball or 2. a player of the same team as the player taking the free pass touches the ball whilst standing at least 2.5 m (8 ft) from the spot at which the pass has been taken or 3. the ball has travelled at least 2.5m (8 ft) from the place of the free pass (measured along the ground).

The player taking the free pass is not allowed to shoot directly from the free pass. He can only shoot when the ball has moved freely through the air and has been touched by another player. When the person taking the free pass touches a boundary line, or the playing area on the other side of the boundary line, after the referee has blown his whistle to indicate that the free pass can be taken and the ball has left his hands, then the referee awards a free pass to the opposing side on the other side of the boundary line.
B. When the players do not meet conditions 1 and 2 above

in A within four seconds of the referee raising his arm, he will whistle twice quickly in succession, the first time to re-start the game and the second time to stop play, and punish the infringing team with a free pass. If players from both teams are within 2.5 m (8 ft) then the referee will punish the player who is nearest to the taker of the free pass. If the referee considers players from both teams are at the same incorrect distance then the attacking team shall be penalized. When the defending team in the attacking zone makes this infringement for the second time at the same free pass the referee will give a penalty.

20 Penalty

a) when to award a penalty
Infringements which result in the loss of a scoring chance are punished by the award of a penalty to

the other side. A penalty can also be awarded for other infringements which repeatedly hinder the attack unfairly.

b) place of a penalty
The penalty must be taken from the penalty spot (see 2) which is 2.5 m (8ft) from the post as seen from the centre of the field.

c) how to take a penalty
It is permitted to score directly from a penalty. The person taking the penalty must not touch the ground between the post and the penalty spot with any part of his body before the ball has left his hands. The penalty must be retaken if it is taken before the referee has blown his whistle to indicate that the penalty may be taken.

All other players must observe a distance of 2.5 m (8 ft) (in all directions) from any point on the imaginary line between the spot and the post. They must refrain from any actions or comments which may disturb the person taking the penalty.

If necessary the first, as well as the second, half of the match will be prolonged for the taking of a penalty.

These rules are reprinted by permission of the International Korfball Federation. A complete copy of the rules, including Explanations to the rules and outdoor variations, is available from the Federation.

Block and tackle
Players can stand in the path of an attacker but may not use their arms to prevent them running past.

Bowls
Essentials

This is the traditional game of lawn bowls, also known as flat green bowls. Played both indoors and outdoors.

On the mat
At the start of his delivery the player must have both feet on the mat.

Bank 230 mm (9in) above green

37-40 m

37-40 m

5.5-5.8m

Rink

Ditch 200-380 mm (8–15 in) wide, 50–200 mm (2–8 in) deep

The green
Rectangular with a traditional grass or an artificial surface. Sides must measure 37–40 m (40–44 yds) for outdoor greens, 34–40 m for indoor greens. Surrounded by a ditch 200–380 mm (8–15 in) wide, 50–200 mm (2–8 in) deep. (End ditches only must comply with these specifications for indoor greens.) Also bounded by a bank, no less than 230 mm (9 in) above the level of the green.

The green is divided into several rinks, numbered consecutively, 5.5–5.8 m (18–19 ft) wide for outdoor greens and 4.6–5.8 m (15-19 ft) for indoor greens. White wooden pegs with green thread drawn tightly between them define the boundaries of each rink.

The mat
Black rubber, usually with a border of white, 600 mm (24 in) long and 360 mm (14 in) wide.

The jack
Spherical, white or yellow in colour. A diameter of 63–64 mm (approx 2.5 in) and weight of 225–285 g (8–10 oz) for outdoor games. Diameter of 63–67 mm, (approx 2.5 in) weight of 382–453 g (13–16 oz) for indoor games/synthetic greens.

Bowls
Wood (diameter 116–134 mm (4.5–5.3 in), maximum weight 1.59 kg (3.5 lb); rubber or composition (diameter 116–131 mm (4.5–5.2 in), maximum weight 1.59 kg (3.5 lb). Black, brown or other approved colour. Each bowl must have an approved bias (the degree to which it deviates from a straight line as it travels down the green) and an individual distinguishing mark on both sides for International Matches, World Bowls Championships and Commonwealth Games.

Smooth as a bowling green
Bowls is frequently played on an outdoor grass lawn. Such natural lawns need a huge amount of work to maintain their perfectly smooth manicured surface.

Crown green bowls
Crown green bowls is played mostly in the north of England, where it originated. Generally a game between two players, it uses a green which has a raised 'crown' at its centre.

Officials
An umpire and a marker.

Dress
Traditionally all white for both men and women. Footwear must be smooth-soled and heelless to protect the surface of the green.

Players
Two contending players in a singles game; two teams of two players in a pairs game; two teams of three players in a triples game; two teams of four players in a fours game; two teams of equal size in a side game.
Positions in order of playing are lead, second, third and skip.

White or not?
Traditionally bowlers wore all white with brown shoes. There is an increasing tendency among younger players and those playing the sport at high level to go for coloured tops and, illogically, white shoes.

Hard choice
Bowls come in different sizes, weights and colours and differences between makes can be so marked that experienced bowlers select their bowl to suit individual greens.

HOW TO PLAY

The object is for players get their bowls closer to the jack than their opponent's bowls. Players deliver bowls alternately and play every second end from the opposite 'end' of the rink.

Starting
Players or teams draw for rinks then toss to decide who plays first. The player who does so must 'place the mat' so that its centre line (lengthwise) lies on the centre line of the rink and its front edge is 2 m (6.5 ft) from the ditch. (It is picked up after each end and replaced prior to the next end.) With one foot within the confines of, or above, the mat, the player delivers the jack, making sure that it remains inside the rink, at least 2 m (6.5 ft) from the front ditch and at least 21 m (23 yds) from the front edge of the mat (23 m 25 yds) for indoor games). Now the player plays the first bowl.

Foot faults

A delivery is legal if the player keeps one foot on the mat.

A delivery is legal if one of the player's feet is above the mat, entirely within its confines.

A delivery is illegal if a player ends up with both feet entirely off the mat.

Holding the bowl
The best way to clasp a bowl is with an entirely natural grip with the fingers spread around the ball and the thumb giving it extra security on the far side. The fingers should be roughly parallel and the bowl should lie straight in your palm ready to roll out in the direction in which you intend to bowl it.

GREY AREA

Because bowls are played in parallel rinks there is always a danger of bowls straying in from neighbouring rinks. This is frequently a source of conflict. Traditionally players had lifted a bowl or jack to prevent it being knocked out of place by a stray bowl and in 1994 this practice was made legal (Law 37f), but there is still room for doubt over the way that this law is used. The point is that the bowl may only be lifted when doing so will not affect the play. It must be replaced in exactly the same place and at the same angle.

Stand and deliver
A delivery begins with the player standing with both feet firmly on the mat pointing in the right direction. He then swings back his bowling arm at the same time as stepping rapidly forward on the opposite leg. Then with his free hand on his bent knee to steady himself he swings his arm forward and releases the bowl.

ditch (unless it is a toucher) or goes out of the rink, it is called a dead bowl and is removed from the rink and placed on the bank straightaway.
See Law 35, Ball Accounted 'Dead' (page 172).

The jack becomes dead if it is driven away by a bowl so that it passes beyond the face of the bank, comes to rest beyond the side boundary or rebounds to within 18 m (35 yds) or 20 m (22 yds) for indoor games – of the front edge of the mat. A dead jack means that the end is also dead and must be replayed.
See Laws 40 and 41 (page 172).

How to win

The player or team with the bowl closest t o the jack wins the 'end'. However, shots are scored for each bowl that is closer to the jack than any of the opposition's bowls. The winner is the player or team with either the highest number of sets or winning ends.

KEY RULES

For top level matches:
Singles – Each player has four bowls per end, delivered alternately. The winner is the first to score 25 shots.
Pairs – Four bowls per player, played alternately. The game lasts for 21 ends.
Triples – Three bowls per player, played alternately. The game lasts for 18 ends.
Fours – Two bowls per player, played alternately. The game lasts for 21 ends.

A bowl must be 'live' in order to score, i.e. it must come to rest within the boundaries of the rink, no less than 14 m (15.3 ft) from the front edge of the mat. A bowl becomes a toucher if it touches the jack on its original course on the green. It is then marked with chalk. (Chalk marks are rubbed off at the close of each end.)
See Laws 31–33 (page 172).

If a bowl fails to travel at least 14 m (15.3 ft) from the front of the mat, ends up in a

Young or old
One of the attractions of bowls is that it can be played by anyone, no matter what their age or degree of fitness, with equal chance of success. Recently in Australia a man celebrated his 100th birthday with a marathon game of bowls.

SKILLS AND TACTICS

The *draw* is a basic shot, played both forehand and backhand and used to guide the bowl up to the jack. Players must be able to judge both length and line accurately – i.e. the distance the bowl must travel and the curving path it must take. The *trail* uses a slightly overweighted delivery to not only hit the jack but also to shift its position on the green. The *drive*, or firing shot, is a bowl which is delivered with extra speed or force in order to knock an opponent's bowls out of the way or to edge the jack out of position in order to break down an opponent's advantage.

The *skip* is in charge of the team and directs play. The *lead* establishes play with the first two bowls, trying to get them as close to the jack as possible and is followed by the *second*. The *third* acts generally as deputy to the skip. The third and skip in particular must be skilled all-rounders and are usually the most experienced members of the team.

THE LAWS OF BOWLS

Laws 1–30

Covered on pages 170–171.

Movement of Bowls

31. 'Live' Bowl

A bowl which, in its original course on the green, comes to rest within the boundaries of the rink, and not less than 14m (15.3 ft) from the front edge of the mat, shall be accounted as a 'Live' Bowl and shall be in play.

32. 'Touchers'

A bowl which, in its original course on the green touches the jack, even though such a bowl passes into the ditch within the boundaries of the rink, shall be counted as a 'live' bowl and shall be called a 'toucher'. If after having come to rest a bowl falls over and touches the jack before the next succeeding bowl is delivered, or if in the case of the last bowl of an end it falls and touches the jack within the period of 30 seconds invoked under Law 52, such a bowl shall also be a 'toucher'.

No bowl shall be accounted a 'toucher' by playing on to, or by coming into contact with, the jack while the jack is in the ditch. If a 'toucher' in the ditch cannot be seen from the mat its position shall be marked by a white or coloured indicator about 50 mm (2 in) broad placed upright on the top of the bank and immediately in line with the place where the 'toucher' rests.

33. Marking a 'Toucher'

A 'toucher' shall be clearly marked with a chalk mark by a member of the player's team. If, in the opinion of either skip, or opponent in singles, a 'toucher' or a wrongly chalked bowl comes to rest in such a position that the act of making a chalk mark, or of erasing it, is likely to move the bowl or to alter the head, the bowl shall not be marked or have its mark erased but shall be 'indicated' as a 'toucher' or 'non-toucher' as the case may be. If a bowl is not so marked or not so 'indicated' before the succeeding bowl comes to rest it ceases to be a 'toucher'. If both skips or opponents agree that any subsequent movement of the bowl eliminates the necessity for continuation of the 'indicated' provision the bowl shall thereupon be marked or have a chalk mark erased as the case may be. Care shall be taken to remove the 'toucher' marks from all bowls before they are played, but should a player fail to do so, and should the bowl not become a 'toucher' in the end in play, the marks shall be removed by the opposing skip or his deputy or marker immediately the bowl comes to rest unless the bowl is 'indicated' as a 'non-toucher' in circumstances governed by earlier provisions of this law.

34. Movement of 'Touchers'

A 'toucher' in play in the ditch may be moved by the impact of a jack in play or of another 'toucher' in play, and also by the impact of a 'non-toucher' which remains in play after the impact, and any movement of the 'toucher' by such incidents shall be valid. However, should the 'non-toucher' enter the ditch before the next succeeding bowl is delivered, it shall be dead, and the 'toucher' shall be deemed to have been displaced by a dead bowl and the provisions of Law 37(e) shall apply.

35. Bowl Accounted 'Dead'

(a) Without limiting the application of any other of these laws, a bowl shall be accounted dead if:
(i) not being a 'toucher' it comes to rest in the ditch or rebounds on to the playing surface of the rink after contact with the bank or with the jack or a 'toucher' in the ditch, or
(ii) after completing its original course, or after being moved as a result of play, it comes to rest wholly outside the boundaries of the playing surface of the rink, or within 14m (15.3 ft) of the front of the mat, or
(iii) in its original course, passes beyond a side boundary of the rink on a bias which would prevent its re-entering the rink. (A bowl is not rendered 'dead' by a player carrying it whilst inspecting the head.)
(b) Skips, or the opponents in singles, shall agree on the question as to whether or not a bowl is 'dead'. Any member of either team may request a decision from the skips, but no member shall remove any bowl prior to agreement by the skips. Once their attention has been drawn to the matter, the skips by agreement must make a decision. If they cannot reach agreement, the umpire must make an immediate decision.

36. Bowl Rebounding

Only 'touchers' rebounding from the face of the bank to the ditch or the rink shall remain in play.

37. Bowl Displacement

(a) Displacement by rebounding 'non-toucher' – bowl displaced by a 'non-toucher' rebounding from the bank shall be restored as near as possible to its original position, by a member of the opposing team or by the marker.
(b) Displacement by a participating player – if a bowl, while in motion or at rest on the green, or a 'toucher' in the ditch, be interfered with or displaced by one of the players, the opposing skip shall have the option of:
(i) restoring the bowl as near as possible to its original position;
(ii) letting it remain where it rests;
(iii) declaring the bowl 'dead';
(iv) or declaring the end 'dead'.
(c) Displacement by a neutral object or neutral person (other than as provided in Clause (d) hereof):
(i) of the bowl in its original course – if such a bowl be displaced within the boundaries of the rink of play without having disturbed the head, it shall be replayed. If it be displaced and has disturbed the head, the skips, or the opponents in singles, shall reach agreement on the final position of the displaced bowl and on the replacement of the head, otherwise the end shall be 'dead'.

These provisions shall also apply to a bowl in its original course displaced outside the boundaries of the rink of play provided such bowl was running on a bias which would have enabled it to re-enter the rink.
(ii) of a bowl at rest, or in motion as a result of play after being at rest – if such a bowl be displaced, the skips or opponents in singles, shall come to an agreement as to the position of the bowl and the replacement of any part of the head disturbed by the displaced bowl, otherwise the end shall be 'dead'.
(d) Displacement inadvertently produced – if a bowl be moved at the time of it being marked or measured it shall be restored to its former position by an opponent. If such displacement is caused by a marker or an umpire, the marker or umpire shall replace the bowl.
(e) Displacement by 'dead' bowl – if a 'touchers' in the ditch be displaced by a 'dead' bowl from the rink of play, it shall be restored to its original position by a player of the opposite team or by the marker.
(f) Displacement by a bowl from an adjoining rink – A bowl or jack at rest on the rink, if in danger of being moved by a bowl from an adjoining rink, may be lifted by the marker or any player at the head to allow the neutral bowl to pass, and then be replaced, provided such action would not influence the outcome of the head so moved.

38. 'Line Bowls'

A bowl shall not be accounted as outside the line unless it be entirely clear of it. This shall be ascertained by looking perpendicularly down upon the bowl or by placing a square on the green or by use of a string, mirror or other approved optical device.

Movement of Jack

39. A 'live' Jack in the Ditch

A jack moved by a bowl in play into the front ditch within the boundaries of the rink shall be deemed to be 'live'. It may be moved by the impact of a 'toucher' in play and also by the impact of a 'non-toucher' which remains in play after the impact, any movement of the jack by such incidents shall be valid. However, should the 'non-toucher' enter the ditch at any time after impact it shall be 'dead' and the jack shall be deemed to be 'displaced' by a 'dead' bowl and the provisions of Law 47 shall apply.

If the Jack in the ditch cannot be seen from the mat its position shall be marked by a 'white' indicator about 5 cm (2 in) broad and not more than 10 cm (4 in) in height, placed upright on the top of the bank and immediately in line with the place where the jack rests.

40. A Jack Accounted 'Dead' – Outdoor Version

Should the jack be driven by a bowl in play so that it passes beyond the face of the bank or comes to rest wholly beyond the side boundary of the rink, i.e. over the bank, or over the side boundary, or into any opening or inequality of any kind in the bank, or rebound to a distance of less than 18 m (19.7 yds) in direct line from the centre of the front edge of the mat to the jack in its rebounded position, it shall be accounted 'dead'.

41. 'Dead' End

When the jack is 'dead' the end shall be regarded as a 'dead' end and shall not be accounted as a played end even though all the bowls in that end have been played. All 'dead' ends shall be played anew in the same direction unless both skips or opponents in singles agree to play in the opposite direction. After a 'dead' end situation the right to deliver the jack shall always return to the player who delivered the original jack.

42. Playing to a Boundary Jack

The jack, if driven to the side boundary of the rink and not wholly beyond its limits, may be played to on either hand and, if necessary a bowl may pass outside the limits of the rink. A bowl so played, which comes to rest within the boundaries of the rink, shall not be accounted 'dead'.

If the jack be driven to the side boundary line and come to rest partly within the limits of the rink, a bowl played outside the limits of the rink and coming to rest entirely outside the boundary line, even though it has made contact with the jack, shall be accounted 'dead' and shall be removed to the bank by a member of the player's team.

43. A Damaged Jack

In the event of a jack being damaged, the umpire shall decide if another jack is necessary and, if so, the end shall be regarded as a 'dead' end and another jack shall be substituted and the end shall be played anew.

44. A Rebounding Jack

If the jack is driven against the face of the bank and rebounds on to the rink, or after being played into the ditch, it be operated on by a 'toucher', so as to find its way on to the rink, it shall be played to in the same manner as if it had never left the rink.

45. Jack Displacement

(a) **By a player**
If the jack be diverted from its course while in motion on the green, or displaced while at rest on the green, or in the ditch, by any one of the players, the opposing skip shall have the option of:
(i) restoring the jack to its former position;
(ii) allowing it to remain where it rests and playing the end to a finish;
(iii) or declaring the end 'dead'.
(b) **Inadvertently produced**
If the jack be moved at the time of measuring by a player it shall

be restored to its former position by an opponent.

46. Jack Displaced by a Non-player

(a) If the jack, whether in motion or at rest on the rink, or in the ditch, be displaced by a bowl from another rink, or by any object or individual not a member of the team, the two skips or the opponents in a singles game shall decide as to its original position, and if they are unable to agree, the end shall be declared 'dead'.
(b) If the jack is displaced by a marker or umpire, in the process of measuring or in any other circumstances, the displaced jack shall be restored as near as possible by the marker or umpire to its original position of which he shall be the sole judge.

47. Jack Displaced by 'Non-toucher'

A jack displaced in the rink of play by a 'non-toucher' rebounding from the bank shall be restored, as near as possible, to its original position by a player of the opposing team or by the marker in the singles game. Should a jack, however, after having been played into the ditch, be displaced by a 'dead' bowl it shall be restored to its marked position by a player of the opposing team or by the marker.

Laws 48–51 Fours Play

The basis of the game of bowls is fours play.
(See Players, page 170.)

Result of End

52. 'The Shot'

A shot or shots shall be adjudged by the bowl or bowls nearer to the jack than any other bowl played by the opposing player or players.

When the last bowl has come to rest, 30 seconds shall elapse, if either team desires, before the shots are counted.

Neither jack nor bowls shall be moved until each skip has agreed to the number of shots, except in circumstances where a bowl has to be moved to allow the measuring of another bowl.

53. Measuring Conditions to be Observed

No measuring shall be allowed until the end has been completed. All measurements shall be made to the nearest point of each object. If a bowl

requiring to be measured is resting on another bowl which prevents its measurement, the best available means shall be taken to secure its position, whereupon the other bowl shall be removed. The same course shall be followed where more than two bowls are involved, or where, in the course of measuring, a single bowl is in danger of falling or otherwise changing its position. When it is necessary to measure to a bowl or jack in the ditch, and another bowl or jack on the green, whenever possible, the measurement shall be made with a flexible measure.

54. 'Tie' – No Shot

When at the conclusion of play in any end the nearest bowl of each team is touching the jack, or is deemed to be equidistant from the jack, there shall be no score recorded. The end shall be declared 'drawn' and shall be counted a played end.

55.

Nothing in these laws shall be

deemed to make it mandatory for the last player to play his last bowl in any end, but he shall declare to his opponent or opposing skip his intention to refrain from playing it before the commencement of determining the result of the end and this declaration shall be irrevocable.

These laws are reprinted by permission of the World Bowls Board, World Indoor Bowls Council, International Women's Bowling Board and the World Indoor Bowls Council Ladies Section. A complete copy of the Laws of the Game, including laws 56–73, can be obtained from the World Bowls Board.

Bowled over
The aim of bowls is simply to deliver the bowl as close to the jack as possible, but this simple brief allows a huge range of alternative plays and tactical skills that make it a highly satisfying game.

Pétanque
Essentials

Ernest Pitiot, the inventor of pétanque, adapted the game of boule so that players with disabilities and abled-bodied players could compete on an equal basis. The new game meant that he could continue to enjoy matches with his friend Jules Le Noir, who had recently become disabled.

The balls in pétanque are called boules.

Area of play (the piste)

The game may be played on any terrain, although if a marked-out area is required, its dimensions must be: 15 x 4 m (49 x 13 ft) for national and international competitions. Variations down to 12 x 3 m (39 x 10 ft) may be allowed for other competitions.

Players

Three players against three (triples), two against two (doubles) or one against one (singles). In triples, each player uses two boules and in doubles and singles, each player uses three.

Accessories

A tape-measure is required to verify which of two boules is closer to the cochonnet. For greater precision in measuring distance, callipers are used. A notepad or hand-held score-keeper. People who have difficulty in bending down can retrieve their boules with the aid of a strong magnet attached to a string.

The boule

Metal, with a diameter of 7.05 – 8cm (approx 3 in) and a weight of 650–800 g (23–28 oz). The boule must not be weighted or sanded down or tampered with in any way.

The jack (or cochonnet)

Made entirely of wood and painted any colour. A diameter of 25–35mm (approx 1 in). Boules or cochonnet must not be changed during a game except when lost or broken.

HOW TO PLAY

The cochonnet is thrown to a spot within the playing area and then both teams try to place their boules as close to it as possible. After the first boule has been thrown by a member of the starting team, the second team plays until at least one of its boules is closer to the cochonnet than their opponents' boule. If they manage to do this before they run out of boules, the first team then resumes play until it is successful or has run out of boules. The sequence continues until all boules on either side have been played (an 'end'). The winner of the end starts the next end.

Officials

An umpire (for competitions).

Starting

A toss decides which team will choose the terrain and throw the cochonnet first. A member of the team winning the toss chooses the starting point and then traces a circle large enough for both feet to stay inside at this point. It must measure between 35 and 50 cm (14–20 in) in diameter. The circle must be at least 1 m (3 ft) from all obstacles and also the boundary of the playing area. The player then throws the cochonnet while standing inside the circle. A player throwing from a wheelchair must place it so that the circle is in the middle of the wheels.

How to win

Points are determined at the end of each end. The team that has won the end receives one point for each boule closer than any boule of the opposing team. The maximum score possible in any one end is six. The game ends when one team has gained 13 points.

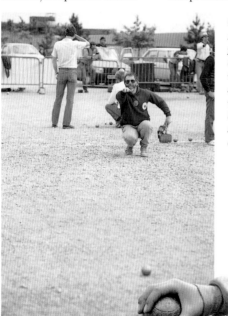

On a roll
Pétanque can be played on virtually any surface but it is usually played on a soft, dusty pitch on which the lines can be marked with a set of callipers called a 'baguette'.

The thrower can either throw the boule up in the air or roll it along the ground.

KEY RULES

• Boules must not be modified or tampered with in any way. The sanctions for breaking this rule are severe, including the possibility of a lengthy ban from competition sport.

• If the cochonnet is moved the game continues, provided that it does not roll beyond an agreed boundary, and that it remains visible from the circle. Beyond the boundary, or out of sight, the cochonnet is deemed 'dead' and the end is cancelled and replayed. However, if the cochonnet is knocked out of play when one team has thrown all its boules and the other team still has boules to play, the team with the boules gets one point for each one that it has not played. *See How to play, (page 174).*

• Once the cochonnet has been thrown, players have a maximum of one minute to play their boule. Both feet must be inside the circle when it is thrown and must remain so until the boule has hit the ground. No other part of the body may touch the ground outside the circle and all throws must be made from the same circle for the whole of an end. Whilst a player is preparing and executing his throw, the spectators and fellow players must observe total silence.
See Boules (page 176).

SKILLS AND TACTICS

Team members are likely to specialize as shooters *(tireurs)* or in placing the boule *(pointeurs)*, but individual players must be proficient in both areas. The tireur's goal is to knock an opponent's boule out of the game. The most successful shot is a *carreau*, in which the thrown boule replaces a boule on the ground. The pointeur's role is to get his boule as close to the cochonnet as possible.

A player's choice of boule may also affect his play. A pointeur may select a boule with striations, or grooves, which can help to give the boule more grip on the ground. A tireur may play with a softer boule as there will be less recoil following impact – a softer boule soaks up the impact with another boule, and does not rebound so easily.

Shooting boule
There are three main kinds of shot in pétanque. A 'point' is a boule thrown to roll along the ground and stop close to the jack. A 'boule portée' is a boule thrown through the air in an arc to stop close to the jack. A 'tir' is a boule thrown on the run intended to knock a specified target. With a tir the opposing team trace out an acceptable arc around the target with a baguette. This player is going for a boule portée.

PÉTANQUE THE RULES

General

Rules 1–4
Covered on pages 174–175.

Play

Rules 5 and 6
Covered on pages 174–175.

Rule 7
For the thrown cochonnet to be legal, the following conditions apply:
1) The distance from it to the nearest edge of the circle must be between:
– 4 m (13 ft) min and 8 m (26 ft) max for Minimes
– 5 m (16 ft) min and 9 m (30 ft) max for Cadets
– 6 m (20 ft) min and 10 m (32 ft) max for Juniors and Seniors.
2) The nearest edge of the circle must be 1 m from all obstacles and at least 1 m inside the boundary of the playing area.
3) The cochonnet must be at least 1 m minimum from all obstacles and from the boundary of the playing area.
4) The cochonnet must be visible to the player whose feet are entirely inside the circle and who is standing upright. In cases of dispute, the umpire will decide if the cochonnet is visible and there can be no appeal.
At the following end, the cochonnet is thrown from a circle drawn around the point where it finished at the previous end, except in the following cases:
(a) The circle would be less than 1 m from an obstacle or from the boundary of the playing area. In this case, the player will trace a circle in the nearest valid position from the obstacle and the boundary.
(b) The cochonnet could not be thrown out to all valid distances. In this case, the player may step back, in line with the previous end's line of play, until he or she is able to throw the cochonnet any valid distance up to the maximum distance allowed, and not beyond. This may only be done if the cochonnet cannot be thrown in any other direction to the maximum distance. If after three consecutive throws by the same team, the cochonnet has not been thrown correctly, it is then passed to the opposing team who also has three tries and who may move the circle back as described above. After this, the circle cannot be moved again even if this team has not succeeded with its three throws. In any case, the team who lost

the cochonnet after the first three tries plays the first boule.

Rule 8
If the cochonnet thrown is stopped by the umpire, a player, a spectator, an animal or any moving object, it is not valid and must be rethrown without being included in the three throws to which the player or the team is entitled. After the throwing of the cochonnet and the first boule, an opponent still has the right to contest the validity of the cochonnet's position. If the objection is valid, both the cochonnet and the boule are re-thrown. If the opponent has also played a boule, the cochonnet is deemed valid and no objection can be accepted. For the cochonnet to be thrown anew, both teams must have accepted the throw as being illegal or the umpire must have declared it so. In either case the cochonnet must be rethrown. Any team continuing otherwise would lose the throw of the cochonnet.

Rule 9
The cochonnet is deemed dead in the following six cases:
(1) When, after having been thrown, it is not within the limits as defined in Rule 7.
(2) When during an end, it is moved outside the boundary of the playing area (normally the dead boule line) even if it comes back on to the playing area. A cochonnet on the line of the boundary is still in play. It only becomes dead after having completely crossed the boundary. Where a cochonnet floats freely in water the area of the puddle is out of play.
(3) When still on the terrain, the moved cochonnet is not visible from the circle, as defined in Rule 7. The umpire may temporarily move a boule to ascertain whether the cochonnet is visible or not.
(4) When the cochonnet is displaced to more than 20 m (22 yds) or less than 3 m (10 ft) from the throwing circle.
(5) When the moved cochonnet cannot be found after a five minute maximum search time.
(6) When there is dead ground between the cochonnet and the throwing circle.

Rule 10
It is strictly forbidden for any player to remove, move or flatten any obstacle on the terrain within the boundaries of the playing area. However, the player

about to throw the cochonnet is allowed to test the ground by tapping it no more than three times with one of his or her boules. Furthermore, the player who is about to play or one of his partners may fill in the hole which was made by the last boule thrown.
For not observing the above rules, the players will incur the following penalties:
(1) Warning.
(2) Disqualification of the ball thrown or about to be thrown.
(3) Disqualification of the guilty team.
(4) Disqualification of both teams in case of complicity.

Rule 11
If, during an end, the cochonnet is completely obscured by a leaf, piece of paper etc. these objects are removed. If the stationary cochonnet is moved by the wind or slope of the terrain, it is put back in its place providing its position had been marked. The same applies if the cochonnet is moved accidentally by the umpire, a player, a spectator, a boule or cochonnet from another game, an animal or any moving object. To avoid any argument, the players should mark the cochonnet's position. No claim can be accepted regarding a boule or cochonnet whose position has not been marked.

Rule 12
If, during an end, the cochonnet is moved onto an area where another game is in progress, either on marked or unmarked terrain, the cochonnet is valid subject to Rule 9. The players using this cochonnet will wait for the players in the other game to finish their end before completing their own. The players concerned are asked to show patience and courtesy.

Rule 13
If, during an end, the cochonnet becomes dead, one of three cases can apply:
a) If both teams have boules to play, the end is void.
(b) If only one team has boules left to play, then this team scores as many points as it has boules to play.
(c) If neither team has boules to play, the end is void.

Rule 14
1) If the cochonnet, having been hit, is stopped by a spectator or by the umpire, it remains where it stops.

2) If the cochonnet, having been hit, is stopped by a player, his opponent has the choice of:
(a) leaving the cochonnet in its new position.
(b) putting it back in its original position.
(c) placing it anywhere on the extension of a line from its original position to the point where it is found, but only on the playing area, and so that the end can be continued.
Paragraphs (b) and (c) can only be applied if the position of the cochonnet was previously marked. If it was not marked, the cochonnet will remain where it lies. If the cochonnet, having been knocked on, crosses a boundary of the playing area (the dead boule line) but comes to rest on a permitted area, it is deemed dead and the rules defined in Rule 13 apply.

Rule 15
If, during an end, the cochonnet is moved outside the boundary of the playing area, the next end is started at the point from which it was displaced providing (see Rule 7):
(a) the circle can be traced at 1m (3 ft) from any obstacle and from the boundary of the playing area.
b) The cochonnet can be thrown at all valid distances.

Boules

Rule 16
The first boule of an end is thrown by a player belonging to the team that has won the toss or the last scoring end. The player must not use any object to give aid in playing a boule or draw a line on the ground to indicate or mark the point of landing. Whilst playing his or her last boule, he or she must not carry another boule in the other hand. It is forbidden to wet the boules or the cochonnet. If the first boule played goes out of play, the opponent plays and so on alternately while there are no boules in play. If after shooting or pointing no boules are left in play, the rules defined in Rule 29 apply.

Rule 17
During the time allowed for a player to throw a boule the spectators and the other players must observe total silence. The opponents must not walk, gesticulate or do anything that could disturb the player about to play. Only his or her team-mate/s may stand between the circle and the cochonnet. The opponents must remain beyond the cochonnet or behind the player

and, in both cases, to the side of the end's line of play and at a distance of at least 2 m (6.5 ft) from the one or the other. The players who do not observe these rules will be banned from the competition if, after a warning from the umpire, they persist in their conduct.

Rule 18
Once thrown, a boule may not be replayed; except that it must be replayed if it has been stopped or deviated accidentally from its course between the circle and the cochonnet by a boule or cochonnet coming from another game, or by an animal or by any other moving object (football. etc.), and also in the case defined in Rule 8, second paragraph. No one is allowed a practice throw during a game. If the terrains have been marked out by organizers (into separate pistes), the cochonnet must be thrown within the terrain (piste) allotted to each team. During an end, boules and cochonnets going outside the marked terrain are valid (except as in Rule 9 and 19). The following end is nevertheless played on the original marked terrain. If the terrains are surrounded by solid barriers, these must be a minimum of 30 cm (12 in) outside the dead ball line, which will surround the terrain at a maximum distance of 4 m (13 ft). These rules apply also to the 'Carré d'Honneur' (terrains used for finals, etc).

Rule 19
Any boule that goes entirely outside the boundary of the playing area (normally the dead boule line) is out of play. A boule straddling the boundary is valid. It only becomes dead after having completely crossed the boundary. If the boule subsequently comes back into the playing area, either because of the slope of the ground or by having rebounded from any object, moving or stationary, it is immediately taken out of the game. Anything that it has moved after re-entering the playing area is put back in place (if it has been previously marked). Any boule out of play must immediately be removed from the playing area, if it is not it will be deemed live as soon as the next boule has been played.

Rule 20
Any boule played that is stopped by a spectator or the umpire will remain where it comes to rest. Any boule played that is stopped by a player to whose team it belongs is deemed out of play. Any boule pointed that is stopped by an opponent can, on the decision of the player, be replayed or left where it comes to rest. If a boule shot or hit is stopped by a player, the opponent has a choice to: (a) leave it where it stopped, or (b) place it on the extension line from the original position where it (boule or cochonnet) was hit from where it is found, but only within the boundary of the playing area and if its position was previously marked. Any player purposely stopping a moving boule is immediately disqualified, along with his or her team, for the game in progress.

Rule 21
Once the cochonnet is thrown, each player has one minute at most to play his or her boule. This time starts from the moment when the preceding boule or cochonnet has stopped or, if a point has to be measured, from the moment the outcome has been decided. This rule also applies to the throwing of the cochonnet after each end. Players not respecting this rule will incur penalties as stated in Rule 10.

Rule22
If a stationary boule is moved by the wind or slope of the ground etc., it is put back in its place. The same applies to any boule accidentally moved by a player, the umpire, a spectator, an animal or any other moving object. To avoid any disagreement, the players should mark the positions of the boules and the cochonnet. No claim will be accepted for a boule or cochonnet which has not had its position marked, and the umpire will only give a decision according to the position of the boules and the cochonnet on the terrain.

Rule 23
A player who plays a boule other than his own receives a warning. The boule played is nevertheless valid but it must be immediately replaced, after measuring, if necessary. In the event of it occurring again during the game, the player's boule is disqualified, and everything that it has moved is put back in place. Before throwing a boule, the player should remove from it all traces of mud or any other substance.

Penalties for this rule are as stated in Rule 10. Players must not pick up the played boules before the completion of the end.

Rule 24
All boules thrown contrary to the rules are dead and everything they have moved is put back in place. The same applies to a boule played from a circle other than that from which the cochonnet was thrown. However, the opponent may play the advantage rule and count the erroneously played boule as valid. In this case, the boule pointed or shot and everything it may have displaced, is left in its new position. The team about to throw the cochonnet must erase any previous throwing circles located near the new one.

Points and measurements
Rule 25
To measure a point, it is permitted to move temporarily, after having marked their positions, the boules and any object situated between the cochonnet and the boule to be measured. After measuring, the boules and the objects moved are put back in place. If the objects cannot be moved, the measuring is done with the aid of callipers.

Rule 26
The measuring of a point is done by the player who played the last boule or by one of his or her team-mates. The opponents still have the right to re-measure the point. Whatever positions the boules may hold, and at whatever stage the end may be, the umpire may be called to adjudicate and his or her decision is final. Measuring must be done with appropriate equipment, which each team must possess. It is for instance forbidden to measure with one's feet. Players who do not observe these rules will be banned from the competition if, after a warning from the umpire, they persist in their conduct.

Rule 27
At the finish of an end, all boules picked up before the agreement of points are void if their positions were not marked. No claims can be made on this subject.

Rule 28
If, whilst measuring, one of the players moves the cochonnet or a boule being measured, his or her team loses the point. If, during a measure, the umpire disturbs or

moves the cochonnet or one of the boules and if, after re-measuring, the point is held by the boule which (the umpire) had originally judged to be on, then, in all fairness, he or she may declare it so. Even if the point is no longer held by that boule, the umpire may, in all fairness, still declare that it wins the point.

Rule 29
If two boules belonging to opposing teams are equidistant from, or touching the cochonnet, the end is declared void if there are no more boules to be played, and the cochonnet is thrown by the team winning the previous end or toss. If only one team has boules left to play, it plays them and scores as many points as it has boules closer to the cochonnet than the nearest opponent's boule. If both teams have boules to play, the team which played the last boule plays again, then the other team, and so on alternately until a boule is holding the point. When only one team has boules left, they play them as in the above paragraph. If, after completion of the end, no boules remain within the boundary of the playing area (normally the dead ball line), the end is declared void.

Rule 30
Any foreign bodies adhering to the boule or the cochonnet must be removed before measuring a point.

Rule 31
To be accepted, all claims must be made to the umpire. Claims made after the result of the game has been agreed cannot be considered. Each team is responsible for checking their opposing team (licenses, classification, terrain, boules, etc.).

DISCIPLINE
Rules 32–39
Deal with players' absence; late arrivals; replacement of players; the umpire's role and jurisdiction; penalties incurred for violation of the rules, violent behaviour or a lack of sporting spirit or respect; the role of the jury.

These abbreviated rules are reprinted by permission of the British Pétanque Association. A complete copy of the rules of pétanque is available from the B.P.A.

Athletics

A thletics are the oldest forms of organized sport, enjoying global popularity. They are contested between individuals or teams. Competitive track (as opposed to field) events consist of a range of running contests covering sprints, distance races, hurdles, steeplechases and relay events.

All races are run anti-clockwise

1,500 m start

Starting positions for 400 m
400 m hurdles
880m

The athletic field
The diagram shows the correct track markings and staggered starts for an eight-lane track.

3,000 m start

10,000 m start

Finsh line

200 m start

110 m hurdles start

Olympic stadium, Atlanta, Georgia, 1996.

Track and lane measurements

The length of a standard outdoor track is 400 m (440 yds). The track should be at least 7.32 m (24 ft) wide, representing six running lane widths (where each lane is 1.22 m (4 ft) wide, although lanes may be a maximum of 1.25 m in width. Eight lanes or more are normal for big events. There should be adequate

marking of the inner edge of the track. For cinder and other permanent (non-grass) tracks, this should be by a raised kerb at least 5 cm (2 in) wide and up to 5 cm (2 in) in height. Alternatively, the inner border can be marked with a 5-cm- (2-in)- wide white line, flagged or coned at intervals of 5 m (16.4 ft) to prevent competitors treading on

A running track should be level, not exceeding a maximum lateral inclination of 1:100, or an overall inclination in the running direction of 1:1000 downwards. The direction of running for competitors should be left-hand inwards.

In races up to and including 400 m (440 yds), competitors must stay in their own lanes, necessitating a staggered start to equalize the distance for each runner, except in the case of races up to 110 m (120 yds) which must be run on a straight course. Contests over 400 m (440 yds) and up to and including 800 m (880 yds) may be run in

Middle/long distance start
Line-up just before the gun for a 1000-metre event.

(220 yds) or less in length, the first two complete bends should be run in lanes, with a 'break' line distinctly marked on the track.

Stations

Stations for competitors should be drawn in all races. In straight course sprints, the competitor drawing No.1 should take the station on the left facing the finishing line. The next station is taken by the second-drawn runner and so on through the field. In events on the circular track, the first-drawn competitor should take the station nearest the centre, the second-drawn the next station and so on.

For reasons of safety and fairness, limits should be applied to the number of runners in races, with competitors being divided into heats at the discretion of the referee, and the event being run off accordingly.

The following rules are applicable for international competition at adult level. In some instances they may be at variance with rules applied for domestic and junior competition. If in doubt, the rulebook issued by the relevant national association (for example, the British Athletic Federation in the United Kingdom) should also be consulted.

the line itself. Lanes should be marked similarly by white lines, measured for width from the outside edge of one marking line, itself 5 cm (1/2 in) wide, to the outside edge of the next line (working outwards from the inner border of the track). For distance purposes, lanes should be measured 20 cm (8 in) outwards from their respective inner borders (or 30 cm(12 in) in the case of the inner edge of the track if there is a raised kerb).

lanes as far as the end of the first bend, again with compensatory adjustments to the starting point in each lane. A single finish line should serve all races at the end of one straight.

Indoor tracks are shorter than outside ones because of limited space. Banking of bends is permitted. Races up to and including 60 m (65 yds) must be run on a straight course in lanes. In a race of 400 m (440 yds) on a track 200 m

These rules should be followed wherever possible. Obviously, however, not all clubs, schools or individual athletics enthusiasts may be able to provide, or have access to, facilities and apparatus meeting the recommended standards. That should not deter adaptation or improvization – for example, laying out a 300-m (330-yd) outdoor running track if that is all that available space will allow.

Starting blocks

Starting blocks, against which runners place their feet to gain traction, may be used for all races up to and including 400 m (440 yds). This includes the first leg of a relay race, where that leg does not exceed 400 m (440 yds).

Starting blocks consist of two adjustable foot plates, mounted on a rigid frame. Their construction and use have to comply with several rules:

• they must be made entirely of rigid materials, and must not give any unfair advantage to the runner;

• they should be fixed to the track by a number of pins or spikes (arranged to minimize damage to the running surface), and should be easily and quickly removable;

• they may be adjustable but should allow no movement during the actual start;

• where runners use their own starting blocks, these must be approved by the starter; and

• when in position on the track, the starting block must not overlap the starting line or extend into another lane.

The surface of the foot plates may have slots or recesses, or may be covered with suitable material to accommodate the use of spiked shoes.

For major international competitions starting blocks must be linked to a false start apparatus. This provides an audible indication to the starter if an athlete's reaction time to the starting signal is less than 100/1000ths of a second. The starter has to recall the athletes in such circumstances.

The start

A white line, 5 cm (2 in) wide at right angles to the inner edge of the running track, should mark the starting point of a race, the distance of which should be measured from the edge of the starting line farther from the finish, to the edge of the finish line nearer to the start. In races which are not run in lanes, the starting line should be curved so that all the runners start the same distance from the finish.

All track events begin with the report of the starter's gun, or other approved starting apparatus, fired upwards into the air. Prior to this, the starter must be satisfied that the competitors have been placed correctly in their respective stations by other race officials (that is, 3 m (10 ft) behind the starting line or, in races run wholly or partly in lanes, behind each starting line) and that the timekeepers are ready.

In races up to and including 400 m (44 yds) (including relay events), the starter calls *"On your marks"*, then *"Set"* (when runners steady themselves motionless on their mark), and then fires the starting gun. In races longer than 400 m (440 yds), competitors approach the starting line (without touching it or touching the ground with their hands) on the 'On your marks' command. When all the competitors are steady, the starting gun is fired, there being no 'Set' command. The starter can order all runners to withdraw from their marks and reassemble if he or she is not satisfied that all is ready for the start of the race to proceed.

Unfair starts

Circumstances which could constitute a false start by a competitor in a race may include:

• failure to comply with the commands 'On your marks' or 'Set' within a reasonable space of time;

• disturbing fellow runners in a race, through sound or otherwise, after the 'On your marks' call; or

• moving after assuming a full and final set position and before the starting signal.

A competitor who is responsible for a false start must be given a warning. Two false starts, or three in the case of a combined event (the pentathlon, heptathlon, or decathlon), warrant disqualification. If the starter (or start recaller) thinks that the start was not fair, the competitors must be recalled with a second shot. When one or more competitors beat the gun, others are, in practice, inclined to follow – all of whom have made a false start according to the letter of the law. The starter should warn only such competitor or competitors who, in his or her opinion, were responsible for the false start. This may result in more than one competitor being warned. If an unfair start is not due to any competitor, obviously no warnings should be issued.

Right, crouch start and the use of starting blocks are com-pulsory under International Amateur Athletic Federation (IAAF) rules in all races up to and including 400 m.(440 yds). Competitors approach the starting line upon the "On your marks" command, assuming a crouching position within their allocated lanes and behind the starting line (which they must not touch). Each runner should have both hands and at least one knee in contact with the ground, and both feet on the foot plates of the block. On the "Set" command, competitors raise their knees from the track and arch to their final starting positions, with hands on the ground and feet on the blocks. Right, crouch start and the use of starting blocks are com-pulsory

Clothing and footwear

Athletes should wear clothing which is decent and presentable – vest and shorts (or equivalent), which are clean and non-transparent (even if wet). Competitors should not wear any attire that might impede the view of the judges. Distinctive number cards should be provided to competitors, corresponding with their numbers in the meeting programme list.

Shoes should give traction and protection with minimum weight, although athletes may compete in bare feet, or with footwear on one foot, if they wish. Shoes may not be constructed so as to give a competitor any additional assistance (for example, extra spring). Any number of spikes up to 11 may be used on the sole and heel of each shoe. In a competition taking place on a synthetic surface, the part of the spike projecting from the sole or heel must not exceed 9 mm (approx 1/2 in) or 12 mm in the high jump and javelin events. The spikes should have a maximum diameter of 4 mm. For non-synthetic surfaces the maximum spike length should be 25 mm (1 in), again with a maximum diameter of 4 mm. For track and field events other than the high jump, a shoe's sole and/or heel may be of any thickness. It may have grooves, ridges, or other design features, provided these are constructed of the same or similar material as the basic sole itself.

The race

In races run in lanes, competitors should keep in their assigned lane from start to finish. IAAF rules make it a mandatory disqualification if a runner, unless forced to do so by another competitor, steps on or over the inner line of the lane when running around any part of a bend. Running over the outside lane line does not constitute an infringement unless the action impedes another runner. Competitors who jostle, run across or impede others in a race risk disqualification. If a runner is so disqualified, the referee can order a race to be re-run (excluding that runner). The referee can also allow any competitor affected by an incident in a heat resulting in the disqualification of a fellow competitor to compete in a subsequent round of the event. Competitors on their marks may not be accompanied by an attendant, nor may they receive help in the course of a race. Runners are notified of the last lap usually by ringing a bell. In races of 200 m (220 yds) or less, the wind speed should be recorded wherever possible, with a gauge set up 50 m (55 yds) from the finish line, not more 2 m (2 yds) from the inner edge of the track, at a height of 1.22 m (4 ft) . The wind component should be measured for a 13-second period in hurdle events and for 10 seconds in others (starting in the 200 m (220 yds) when the first runner enters the straight). An aiding wind of more than 2 m (6.1/2 ft)

per second nullifies a record time.

The finish

The finishing line for a race should be 5 cm (2 in) wide and drawn across the track at right angles to the inner edge.

Except where their use may interfere with photo-finish equipment, two white posts may be placed along the prolongation of the line at least 30 cm (12 in) from the edge of the track. The posts should be about 1.4m (4 3/4 in) high, 8 cm (3 in) wide and 2 cm (2 in) thick. Competitors are placed in the order in which any part of the body (meaning the torso rather than the head and neck or limbs) reaches the vertical plane of the edge of the finish line nearer to the start.

Should a tie occur in any heat which affects the qualification of runners to compete in the following round or in the final of the event, the tying competitors should all qualify. (IAAF rules stipulate that, in determining whether there has been a tie for a qualifying place, it is acceptable to review the times recorded by the competitors to a finer margin than the official 1/100th of a second). Should there be a tie for first place in any final, the referee has the power to decide whether it is practicable to arrange for the tying competitors to run again. If the referee thinks otherwise, the results stands. Ties for placings other than first remain.

Timekeeping

A sufficient number of timekeepers for the number of competitors should be appointed, one of whom should be the chief timekeeper. Timekeepers must be in line with the finish, wherever possible on the outside of the track and at least 5 m (16 1/2 ft) from the outside lane. To ensure that they have an unimpeded view of the finish line and of the starter, an elevated position should be provided. A competitor's performance in a race should be timed from the flash of the starter's gun or other device to the instant when his or her body reaches the leading edge of the finish line (see *The finish*). In races of 800 m (880 yds) and over, lap times and the leader's number should be recorded, as should times at each 1000 m (1093 yds) in races of 3000 m (3279 yds) or more. In the case of a record claim, this information is essential. Only an official timekeeper or

Different track events require different running styles. Sprinters race to the finish line at top speed, involving high knee lift, free-swinging arm movements and a forward lean of some 25 degrees. Distance runners have to regulate their speed to avoid exhaustion. Knee action is less pronounced, the stride shorter and the forward lean less extreme.

other designated person may indicate intermediate times to competitors or give times to be announced over the public address system.

Fully automated timing

Fully automatic electrical timing is used at most important meetings and is a specific requirement in international competition, such as the Olympic Games or the World Championships.

For races up to and including 10,000 m (10,930 yds), the time read from the photo-finish picture should be recorded in 1/100ths of a second. Times for events longer than 10,000 m (10,930 yds), which are held entirely on the track, should be read in 1/100ths of a second and converted to the next longer tenth of a second. For races held partly or wholly outside the stadium the time should be read in 1/100ths of a second and recorded to the next longer whole second.

Fully automatic times should be regarded as official, unless the chief photo-finish judge deems otherwise, in which case the chief timekeeper should provide manual times taken by back-up timekeepers. A timing device which operates automatically at either the start or the finish, but not at both, cannot be used to register official times. If possible, two photo-finish cameras should be deployed, one on each side of the finish. They should be technically independent of each other.

Times for all finishing competitors should be recorded,

as should, where possible, lap times in races of 800 m (880 yds) and over and times at every 1,000 m (1093 yds) in contests of 3,000 m (3279 yds) or more.

Manual timing

Conventional watches (which have generally been superseded by manually operated electronic timers) may be used for timing races up to and including 3,000 m (3279 yds). Electronic timers may be used for hand timing in all races. For all hand-timed races on the track, timings recorded in 1/100ths of a second should be rounded up (unless ending in zero) to the next longer tenth of a second (for example, a timing of 10.13 seconds should be read as 10.2). The times for races partly or wholly outside the stadium should be converted to the next longer full second. Each timekeeper should act independently and declare the recorded time to the chief timekeeper who may inspect the readings for verification (which must be done if a record claim is involved). The chief timekeeper should then decide the official time for each competitor, applying as necessary the following provisions:
• when two out of three timekeepers timing one placing agree and one does not, the time shown by the two should be the official time;
• if all three timekeepers disagree, the middle time should be the official one;
• should only two times be available for any reason and

they disagree, the longer should be the official time.

Relay races

Relay races are for teams of four runners, each carrying a baton for a given distance or stage before passing it to the next team member. The handover needs to be accomplished with speed and dexterity within a defined take-over zone.

Lines should be drawn across the track to mark the distances of the relay stages and to denote what is called the scratch line. Lines drawn 10 m (11 yds) before and after the scratch line denote the take-over zone. These lines should be included in the zonal measurements.

In 4 x 100 m (110 yds) events (which should be run entirely in lanes) members of a team, other than the first runner, may not begin running more than 10 m (11 yds) outside the take-over zone. This extended limit should be marked distinctively in each lane.

In 4 x 400 m (440 yds) races (run in lanes for the first lap and for part of the second, although IAAF rules recommend only the first bend to be run in lanes if there are three or fewer competing teams), the outgoing runners must start their run within the take-over zone. The second runners in each team may break from their lanes immediately after passing the exit from the first bend (marked by a 5 cm (2 in) white line across the track). The runners in the third and fourth stages should, under official direction, place

themselves in their waiting position in the same order (from inside to out) as the order of their respective team members as they complete 200 m (220 yds) of their stages.

In other relay races, if lanes are not used, waiting runners can move to an inner position on the track as incoming team-mates arrive, provided another competitor's progress is not impeded.

If a runner drops the baton, he or she can retrieve it, leaving the lane to do so if necessary. However, other athletes must not be impeded and the distance to be covered must not be lessened, otherwise disqualification may result.

Once a team has started in a competition, only two additional athletes may be used as team substitutes for subsequent rounds. A substitution may only be made from among those athletes already entered for the meeting (whether for that or

Outdoor track events generally include:
sprints: 100-, 200-, 400-(110-, 220-,440-);
middle distance: 800-, 1,500- (880-, 1640-);
long distance: 5000-, and 10,000-m (5465-, 10,930-) runs;
steeplechase: 3000-m (3279-yds);
hurdles: 110- and 400-m (120- and 440- yds) (100 m (110 yds) for women); and the **relays:** 4 x 100- and 4 x 400-m (4 x 110- and 4 x 440 yds).

Passing the baton
Baton pass starts when it is first touched by the receiving runner and is completed the instant it is solely in the recipient's hand. It is only the position of the baton within the take-over zone, rather than the position of the body or limbs of the runners, that is decisive. Having passed on the baton, competitors should remain in their lanes or zones until the course is clear of other athletes, deliberate obstruction or jostling of members of another team warranting disqualification.

The baton
A rigid hollow tube, 12-13 cm (approx 5 in) in circumference. It should not be more than 30 cm (or less than 28 cm) (approx 12 in) in length, and not less than 50 gm (1 ¾ oz). It should be distinctly coloured to be visible during a race. In all relay races the baton should be passed between runners within the take over zone.

Hurdles

The standard outdoor hurdling distances for men are 110 m (120 yds) and 400 m (440 yds), and 100m (110 yds) and 400 m (440 yds) for women (50 m (55 yds) and 60 m (66 yds) indoors). All hurdle races are run in lanes, the hurdles in each lane being set out in accordance with the specifications in the chart opposite.

A hurdle is made of metal and wood, and consists of two bases and two uprights supporting a rectangular frame reinforced by one or more crossbars. The uprights are fixed at the extreme end of each

base, and the hurdle should be so placed on the track that the ends carrying the uprights are on the side of the competitor's approach.

The hurdle should be so designed that a force at least equal to the weight of 3.6 kg (7 lb) applied to

the centre of the top of the crossbar is needed to overturn it. It may be adjustable in height for each event. The counterweights should be adjustable so that at each height a force at least equal to the weight of 3.6 kg (7 lb) and not more than 4 kg (approx 9 lb) is required to overturn the hurdle. Where hurdles comply with these specifications, knocking down any

number in a race will not warrant a competitor's disqualification, nor any entitlement to claim a record.

A competitor should be disqualified if he or she:
• trails a foot or leg below the horizontal plane of the top of any hurdle at the instant of clearance;
• jumps any hurdle not in his or her own lane; or
• deliberately (in the referee's opinion) knocks down any hurdle by hand or foot.

Obstacle course
Hurdling events combine sprinting with clearing a series of obstacles called hurdles. A good hurdling style involves leaning far forward and clearing each hurdle in a smooth action without breaking the rhythm of the running stride.

Hurdle dimensions
The maximum width of an approved hurdle should be 1.2 m (4 ft) and the maximum length of the base should be 70 cm (27 ½ in). The top bar should be 7 cm (2 ¾ in) in width and between 1 cm (½ in) and 2.5 cm (1 in) thick, and should be striped in distinctive contrasting colours. The lighter stripes should appear at the end of the hurdle and should be at least 22.5 cm (9 in) wide.

Hurdle race specifications

Men

Distance of race	height of hurdle	distance from start line to first hurdle	distance between hurdles	distance from last hurdle to finish line
		outdoor		
110 m	1.067 m	13.72 m	9.14 m	14.02 m
400 m	0.914 m	45 m	35 m	40 m
		indoor		
50 m	1.067 m	13.72 m	9.14 m	8.86 m
60 m	1.067 m	13.72 m	9.14 m	9.72 m

Women

Distance of race	height of hurdle	distance from start line to first hurdle	distance between hurdles	distance from last hurdle to finish line
		outdoor		
100 m	0.840 m	13 m	8.5 m	10.5 m
400 m	0.762 m	45 m	35 m	40 m
		indoor		
50 m	0.840 m	13 m	8.5 m	11.5 m
60 m	0.840 m	13 m	8.5 m	13 m

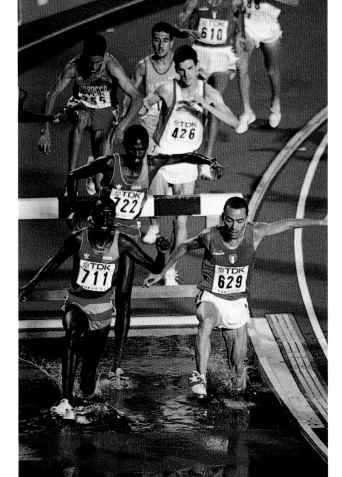

The steeplechase

The steeplechase combines long-distance running with hurdling. The two standard distances for the steeplechase are 2000m (2786 yds) and 3000m (3279 yds) (although it is also run over 1500 m (1640 yds). In a 3000 m (3279 yds) event there should 28 hurdle jumps and seven water jumps, while for 2000 m (2786 yds) there should be 18 and five respectively. For a 3000 m (3279 yds) course, there should be five evenly spaced jumps per lap, the fourth being the water jump.

Water jumps have to be constructed on an arena either inside or outside the track. This has the effect of shortening or lengthening the normal distance of the lap. It is not possible therefore to lay down any rule specifying the exact length of a steeplechase lap or to state exactly the position of the water jump.

To prevent overcrowding among competitors, there needs to be sufficient distance from the starting line to the first hurdle. In the 3000m (3279 yds) event, the distance from the start to the beginning of the first lap should not include any jumps (the hurdles being removed until the runners have entered the first lap). There should also be about 62.2 m 77 yds) from the last hurdle to the finish line. Competitors may go over each hurdle in any manner (for example, by jumping, vaulting or placing one or both feet on them). However, disqualification should result if a runner steps to one side or the other of the water jump, or if he or she trails a foot or leg below the horizontal plane of the top of any hurdle at the instant of clearance.

Steeple chase hurdle
Should be made of heavy timber, or of metal with a timber bar, so constructed that they cannot be easily overturned. They should be 91.4 cm (3 ft) in height 76.2 cm (2¹/₂ ft) for women's events) and at least 3.96 m (13 ft) in total width. The section of the top bar of hurdles, and the hurdle at the water jump, should be 12.7 cm (5 in) square. Weighing 80 – 100 kg,(176–220 lb) a hurdle should be placed on the track so that about 30 cm (12 in) of the top bar overlaps the track's inner edge into the field. The top bar should be striped in distinctive contrasting colours. The lighter stripes should appear at the end of the bar and should be at least 30 cm (12 in) wide.

Water jump
The water jump, including the hurdle, should be 3.66 m (12 ft) in length and width. The hurdle should be firmly fixed in front of the water and be the same height as the others in the event. The water should be 70 cm (2 ft) in depth at the hurdle end, remaining at that depth for a distance of 30 cm (12 in), and then rising to the level of the track at the farther end of the water jump. The bottom of the water jump should be covered at the farther end with a suitable material which ensures the safe landing of the runners. This should be at least the same width as the water jump and 2.5 m (18¹/₃ ft) in length, its thickness not exceeding 2.5 cm (1 in).

3.96 m minimum

0.914 m – men
0.762 m – women

12.7 cm

30 cm

1.2-1.4 m

Steeple chase hurdle

Fields events at an outdoor meeting comprise jumping and throwing disciplines – high jump, pole vault, long jump, triple jump, shot put, hammer throw, discus and javelin. The hammer, discus and javelin are unsuitable for indoor competition.

General conditions

For field events, where the aim is to out-jump or throw further than other contestants, a draw should first be made to decide the order in which the participants compete. Each throw or jump by a competitor is called a trial, a number of trials being allowed in each round of the competition. Except for the high jump and pole vault, competitors cannot hold over any of their trials to a subsequent round. In circumstances where competitors are entered in more than one event taking place simultaneously, the judges can allow them to take their trials in a different order to that decided upon at the initial draw. No competitor may have more than one trial recorded in any one round, except for the high jump and pole vault.

Once a competition has begun, athletes may not use runways, take-off areas or throwing sites for warm-up purposes or practice trials. In any field event, the referee has the power to change the place of the competition if conditions justify it. This should not be done in the course of a round.

All measurements should be made with a calibrated steel tape or with a scientific apparatus. The accuracy of any measuring equipment should be certified by an appropriate authority.

Qualifying rounds

A qualifying round should be held in field events when the number of competitors is too large for a single round. The participants should be divided into two or more groups, each group competing in turn unless facilities allow them to compete at the same time and under the same conditions. Those competitors who reach the pre-set standard of performance in the qualifying round go on to the competition. If less than the prescribed number of athletes achieve that standard, the group of finalists should be increased to that number by adding competitors according to their performances in the qualifying round.

Competitors should be

High jump – details on next page

allowed up to three trials each in a qualifying round (apart from the high jump and pole vault). Performance at this stage should not be considered part of the competition. Once a competitor achieves the qualifying standard, he or she shall not take any more trials.

Competitors who have qualified in preliminary rounds

or heats for further participation in any event, but do not then continue without giving the referee a valid reason, should be excluded from participating in any further events at the meeting. In meetings extending over more than one day, such an exclusion should apply to all subsequent events.

Vertical jumps

In the high jump and pole vault, competitors try to propel themselves over a crossbar, without knocking it off its supporting uprights, at successively greater heights. The

height at which the competition starts, and to what height the bar is raised at the end of each round, is decided by the judge.

Competitors may start at any of the heights above the minimum, and may do so at their own discretion at any subsequent designated height. Exit from the event follows three consecutive failures at any height (except in the case of a tie). Competitors may forgo their second or third trial at a particular height (after failing once or twice) but still attempt a subsequent height. However, if they forgo a trial, no subsequent attempt at that height may be made, except in the case of a tie.

A single remaining competitor can continue until three consecutive failures are recorded. In such a case, the height or heights to which the bar is raised rests with the official in charge after consultation with that competitor (not applicable for combined events competitions).

All height measurements should be made in whole centimetres perpendicularly from the ground to the lowest part of the upper side of the crossbar. Any measurement of a new height should be made before competitors attempt that height (and must be checked, in the case of a record claim, after it has been cleared). Unless only one competitor remains, the bar should not be raised by less than 2 cm (approx 1 in) in the high jump and 5 cm (2 in) in the pole vault after each round.

Ties

If there is a tie, the competitor with the lowest number of attempts at the height at which the tie occurs should be awarded the higher place. If it is

High jump construction

The diagram gives the specifications for the crossbar, uprights and supporting pegs in the high jump event. The uprights, of any style, must be rigid. The bar, made of fibre-glass, metal or other suitable material, should be circular in cross-section except for end pieces which rest on the pegs of the uprights. The front of the bar should be painted, and its weight should not exceed 2 kg.(4½ lb).

The pegs supporting the bar should be firmly fixed to the uprights, each facing the opposite upright so that the ends of the bar can rest on them. The pegs may not have any kind of springs, nor may they (or those parts of the bar which rest on them) be covered in any kind of friction-increasing material.

4 m · 100 mm minimum at maximum height · 30-35 mm · 15 cm-20cm · 6 cm · 1 cm · 4.02 m

Delay

A participant in a field event who unreasonably delays making a trial may have it disallowed and recorded as a fault. A second delay at any time during the competition may incur disqualification from taking any further trials (although performances up to that point still stand in the final result of the event). Although it is for the referee to decide what constitutes an unreasonable delay, the following times for each trial should not normally be exceeded:
* one and a half minutes for the high jump, long jump, triple jump, shot put, discus, hammer and javelin.
* two minutes for the pole vault (beginning when the uprights have been adjusted to the

satisfaction of the competitor).
* where only two or three participants remain in the competition in the high jump and pole vault, the above times should be increased to three minutes for the former and four minutes for the latter (and to five and six minutes respectively under IAAF rules when there is only one competitor left). This is not applicable in a combined events competition.
* the period between consecutive trials by the same athlete should be at least four minutes for the pole vault and three minutes for other field events.

If the time allowed elapses once the competitor has started his or her trial, that trial should not be disallowed.

Pole vault construction

The uprights for pole vaulting may be of any style provided they are rigid. They should be not less than 4.3 m (approx 14 ft), or more than 4.37 m, apart. The crossbar should be made of fibre-glass, metal or other suitable material, and should be circular in cross-section with a diameter of 29–31 mm (approx 1 in) except for end pieces (each 30-35 mm wide and 15–20 cm long) which rest on the supports of the uprights. The overall length of the bar should be between 4.48 m and 4.52 m (approx 15 ft), and its weight shall be 2.25 kg (5 lb).

The pegs supporting the bar should extend horizontally not more than 7.5 cm (3 in) from the face of the uprights on the side further from the runway. They should not be more than 13 mm in diameter. Alternatively the pegs may be positioned upon extension arms permanently attached to the uprights, so allowing the uprights to be placed wider apart without increasing the length of the crossbar, and lessening the chance of injury to competitors. The uprights should extend 35-40 mm above the supports. Neither the pegs nor the ends of the crossbar may be covered in any kind of friction-increasing material, and the pegs may not have any kind of springs.

still a tie, the lowest number of failures up to and including the height last cleared should prevail. If it is still a tie and concerns first place, the competitors should have one more jump, starting at the lowest height at which any of them failed. If no decision is reached, the bar should be raised or lowered 2 cm for the high jump and 5 cm (approx 1 in) for the pole vault, each competitor attempting one jump at each height until the tie is resolved. For other than first position, the competitors should be awarded the same place in the competition.

High jump

In this event the uprights should not be moved during a competition unless the referee thinks that the take-off and landing area has become unsuitable. This should not be done during a round. Competitors may place markers (which must not leave any indelible residue) to help them in their run-up and take-off.

Competitors are judged to have failed if they:
• take off from both feet;
• dislodge the crossbar so that it falls from the supports (pegs) on the uprights; or
• touch the ground, including the landing area, beyond the plane of the uprights (either between or outside them) with any part of the body without first clearing the bar (unless the judge considers no advantage has been gained).

Competitors may not wear shoes with a sole thickness of more than 13 mm ($\frac{1}{2}$ in) or a heel thickness over 19 mm ($\frac{3}{4}$ in).

The minimum length of the runway should be 15 m (16 yds) (or 20 m for more important competitions), and the landing area should measure not less than 5 m (5 $\frac{1}{2}$) in length and 3 m (3$\frac{1}{4}$ yds) in width. The take-off area should be level although there may be a maximum overall inclination of 1:250 in the direction of the centre of the crossbar.

Pole vault

Positioning the uprights

The following rules for the event apply in addition to the general conditions outlined opposite. Athletes may have the uprights moved in either direction, but not more than 40 cm (16 in) in the direction of the runway, and not more than 80 cm (31$\frac{1}{2}$ in) to the landing area from the prolongation of the inside edge of the top of the take-off box. (A white line 1 cm ($\frac{1}{2}$ in) wide may be drawn at right angles to the axis of the runway, at the level of the inside edge of the top of the box. It should be drawn as far as the outside edge of the uprights).

Pole vault

In pole vaulting a competitor aims to clear a high crossbar with the aid of a long flexible pole. Holding the pole a little way from its top, the athlete sprints along a runway towards the uprights and digs the end of the pole into a box sunk below ground level. He or she then swings upwards towards the bar, arching over it feet first and face down before dropping onto a thick, soft pad.

Before the competition starts, competitors should inform the appropriate official where they want the uprights to be for their first attempt, and that position should be recorded. If they subsequently want to make any changes, they should immediately inform the official before the uprights have been set in accordance with their initial wishes.

The jump

Athletes may place markers alongside the runway to help them in their run-ups and take-offs, but not on it. They may not use tape on their hands or fingers unless to cover an open wound, but can use an adhesive substance on their hands or on the pole to improve their grip. Competitors are judged to have failed in a vault if they:
• dislodge the crossbar so that it falls from the supports (pegs) on the uprights;
• touch the ground, including the landing area beyond the vertical plane of the upper part of the box, with any part of the body or with the pole, without first clearing the bar; or
• change grip after leaving the ground (moving the lower hand above the upper one or the upper hand

higher on the pole).

No one should be allowed to touch the pole unless it is falling away from the bar or the uprights. If it is touched, however, and the referee thinks that the bar would otherwise have been knocked off, the vault should be recorded as a failure. If a competitor's pole breaks during a vault, the attempt should not be recorded as a failure.

The runway should be level and not less than 40 m (44 yds) in length. As with a lane on a running track, the width should be not less than 1.22 m (4 ft) and not more than 1.25 m. For record purposes, the maximum allowance for lateral inclination of the runway should not exceed 1:100 and the overall inclination in the running direction 1:1000. The landing area should measure at least 5 m by 5 m (5$\frac{1}{2}$ yds by 5$\frac{1}{2}$ yds).

The pole

The pole may be of any material or combination of materials and of any length or diameter, provided that the basic surface is smooth. It may have a binding of not more than two layers of adhesive tape of uniform thickness and with a smooth surface. The lower 30cm of the pole may additionally have protective layers of tape to protect it when it strikes the back of the take-off box.

Pole vault box

The box in which the vaulter plants the pole for the take-off may be made of wood or metal. It should be sunk level with the runway and measure 1m in length along the inside of the bottom of the box. The width of the box should be 60cm at the front end, tapering to 15cm at the bottom of the stopboard. The base of the box should slope downwards from ground level at the front end to meet the stopboard at a depth of 20cm and at an angle of 105 degrees. If the box is made of wood, the bottom should be lined with 2.5mm sheet metal for 80cm from the front of the box.

Long jump/triple jump

General conditions

Where there are more than eight athletes in the competition, each should be allowed three trials and the eight competitors with the best valid jumps should be allowed three additional trials. If there is a tie for the eighth place, any competitor so tying should have three extra trials. If there are eight competitors or fewer, each should be allowed six trials.

As they complete their run-up, competitors take-off from a board, the 'take-off line' being the edge of the board which is nearer to the landing area. They may place markers alongside the runway to help them in their run-up and take-off, but may not mark the runway itself. Nor may they place any mark beyond the take-off line. Competitors are judged to have failed a trial if they:
* touch the ground beyond the take-off line with any part of the body, whether in the act of jumping or running up without jumping;
* take off from outside either end of the take-off board, whether beyond or before the extension of the take-off line;
* in the course of landing, touch the

ground outside the landing area at a point nearer to the take-off than the nearest break in the sand made by the jump;
* walk back through the landing area after a completed jump; or
* somersault in any fashion while in their run-up or in the act of jumping.

If an athlete takes-off before reaching the board, but within its width span, the jump should not be counted as a failure.

Measurement

The measurement of both a long jump and triple jump is made at right angles from the nearest break in the landing area made by any part of the competitor's body to the take-off line or its extension. Distances should be recorded to the nearest 1cm below the distance measured if the distance measured is not a whole centimetre.

In the case of a tie in the competition, the second best jump of the competitors tying should determine the result. Then, if necessary, the third best and so on. If the tie is still not resolved and it concerns first place, those competitors involved should compete again in the same order until the tie is decided. Each athlete should be credited with the best of all his or her jumps in the competition, including those achieved in deciding a tie for first place.

Wind speed

As for track events, the wind speed should be measured and recorded for both the long jump and triple jump wherever possible. A gauge should be set up 2 m (22 yds) from the take-off line, not more 2 m (6½ ft) from the edge of the runway, at a height of 1.22 m (4 ft). The wind component should be measured for a 5-second period from the time the competitor passes a mark positioned 40 m (44 yds) from the take-off board in the case of the long jump and 35 m (38 yds) for the triple jump. If the competitor's run-up is less than these distances, the reading should be taken from the time the competitor starts to run.

General specifications

The take-off board should be sunk level with the runway and rigidly fixed. Painted white, it should be made of wood, measuring 1.21 m to 1.22 m long (approx 4 ft), between 19.8 cm and 20.2 cm (approx 8 in) wide, and 10 cm deep. The minimum length of the runway should be 40 m (44 yds), with a minimum width of 1.22 m. For record purposes, the maximum allowance for lateral inclination of the runway should not exceed 1:100 and the overall inclination in the running direction 1:1000. Before a competition the sand in the landing area should be dampened, as this helps jumps to be accurately measured. The sand should be level with the top of the take-off board.

Tell-tale

Above, plasticine indicator board should, if possible, be positioned immediately beyond the take-off line for recording a competitor's footprint in the event of a foot fault. It should consist of a rigid board, between 9.8 cm and 10.2 cm (approx 4 in) wide and 1.21-1.22 m ((approx 38 in) long. Covered with plasticine, the surface should rise from the level of the take-off board at an angle of 30 degrees in the running direction to a maximum height of 7 mm (2¾ in) above the take-off board. If such an installation is not possible, soft earth or moist sand should be sprinkled to a height of 7 mm and for 10 cm (4 in) beyond the take-off board. The landing area should be between 2.75 m and 3 m wide and 9 m long (approx 3 by 10 yds)..

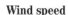

Triple jumpe in action – the hop stage.

Right: A gauge for measuring wind speed

Long jump

In addition to those rules already described, the take-off board in the long jump should be placed between 1–3 m (3–10 ft) from the nearer end of the landing area. There should also be a distance of at least 10 m (11 yds) between the take-off board and the far end of the landing area.

Runway

40-45 m

Take-off board

1-3 m

Landing area

10 m minimum

2.75-3 m

1.22-1.25 m

* These are the measurements for international competition. For any other competition they should be adjusted to the level of the competitors.

Runway

Take-off board

* 13 m minimum (men)
11 m minimum (women)

Landing area

All other measurements are as long jump

Triple jump

Similarly in addition to the general conditions outlined previously, the following rules apply in the triple jump. In the hop manoeuvre of the sequence competitors should land upon the same foot with which they took off; in the step phase they should land on the other foot from which, subsequently, the jump is performed. If, in performing the step, a competitor's 'sleeping' leg touches the ground, the jump is not considered a failure.

There should be a distance of at least 21 m (23 yds) between the take-off board and the far end of the landing area. It is recommended that the take-off board should not be less than 13 m (14 yds) for men and 11 m (12 yds) for women from the nearer end of the landing area.

The three stages of the triple jump

Arms used to keep balance

Arms and legs forward on landing

Body upright

Thigh level with runway

Hop

Step

Jump

Take-off and landing

In these events athletes try to clear the longest distance following a sprint along a runway up to a take-off board. While still in the air the long jumper throws both feet forward of the body before landing in a pit of sand. The triple jump involves a more complicated hop, step and jump sequence of actions before similarly landing in the sand. A jump is measured along a line from the front edge of the take-off board to the mark in the sand made closest to the take-off board by any part of the jumper's body on landing.

Long jumper

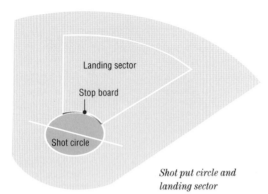

Shot put circle and landing sector

Throwing events

General conditions

The four standard throwing events in field competition – the shot put, hammer, discus and javelin – all involve the use of implements of various weights and shapes that are hurled for distance.

Where there are more than eight athletes in an event, each should be allowed three trials, and the eight competitors with the best valid throws should be allowed three additional trials. If there is a tie for the eighth place, those competitors should have three extra trials. If there are eight competitors or fewer, each should be allowed six throws.

In the case of a tie (other than that outlined above) in the competition, the second-best throw of the competitors tying should determine the result. Then, if necessary, the third best and so on. If the tie is still not resolved and it concerns first place, those involved should compete again in the same order until the tie is decided. Each athlete should be credited with the best of all his or her throws in the competition, including those achieved in deciding a tie for first place.

Athletes may not place any marker within the throwing sector. The taping of fingers (except in the hammer event) or use of any other means which may aid a competitor when making a throw should not be allowed. However, for a better grip, competitors may use an adhesive substance on their hands. They may also wear a belt of suitable material to help protect the spine.

Putting the shot

Putting the shot entails pushing, rather than throwing, a solid metal ball through the air for a maximum distance. Holding the shot in the throwing hand, the athlete rests that hand against the shoulder, with the shot positioned under the chin. The competitor then moves across the throwing circle in a twisting movement, and with gathering momentum, before rapidly straightening the arm and pushing the shot into the air within the throwing sector.

Each competitor may have two practice trials (from the throwing circle only) before the competition begins. Athletes may not wear gloves, nor apply any substance on their shoes or on the surface of the throwing circle.

The put
Competitors should commence their throws from a stationary position within the circle. Having started to make the throw, competitors may not touch the ground outside the circle, or the top of the circle rim, or the top of the stopboard (see opposite page) with any part of the body. To do so constitutes a foul throw, as does improperly releasing the shot in making any attempt. A foul throw should constitute a trial. A competitor should not leave the circle until the shot has touched the ground. When leaving the circle, the first contact with the top of the circle rim or the ground outside the circle has to be completely behind the white line which is drawn outside the circle and runs theoretically through its centre. Provided the above rules have not been infringed, a competitor may interrupt a trial once started, may lay the shot down inside or outside the circle, and may leave the circle (in the manner described above), before returning to a stationary position and beginning a fresh trial. Any such moves should be included in the maximum time normally allowed for a trial.

As a competitor takes his or her stance in the circle to begin a put, the shot should be near or touching the chin, and the hand must not be dropped below this position during the putting action. The shot must not be taken behind the line of the shoulders.

Measurement

For a put to be valid, the shot has to land completely within the inner edges of lines marking a sector of 40 degrees set out on the ground. It is measured from the nearest indentation in the ground made by the shot to the inside of the circumference of the throwing circle, along a line drawn to the centre of the circle. Measurements should be made immediately after each put, recorded to the nearest 1cm ($\frac{1}{2}$ in) below the distance measured if that distance is not a whole centimetre.

The shot

The shot should be made of any metal not softer than brass, or a shell of such metal filled with lead or other material, with a smooth finish. No unorthodox shot surface is permissible. The minimum weight of a shot should be 7.26 kg (16 lb) in men's competition and 4 kg (9 lb) in women's. In men's events, the shot should have a minimum diameter of 110 mm (4 $\frac{1}{4}$ in) and a maximum of 130 mm (5 in). For women's, the equivalents should be 95 mm (3$\frac{3}{4}$ in) and 110 mm (4$\frac{1}{2}$ in)

Indoor competition

In indoor competition the 40 degree landing sector should extend as far as the limitations of space allow, and should be of some suitable material on which the shot will make an imprint. There needs to be a stopping device at the end of the putting area. Specifications are the same as for outdoors, although special plastic or rubber cased shots may be used.

Below, shot put release; left and above left, different build-up styles

Safety is paramount in the throwing events in particular. They should be conducted only in a strictly controlled situation, with competition areas being adequately roped off. Whether in practice or competition, implements should be carried back to the starting area by hand and never thrown.

Shot circle construction

The interior of the shot circle should be constructed of concrete, asphalt or similar firm and non-slippery material. The surface of the inside of the circle should be level, and 14 mm–26 mm (½ in) lower than the upper edge of the circle rim (which should be level with the ground outside). The circle rim should be made of band iron, steel or other suitable material. Measured from inside the rim, the diameter of the circle should be 2.135 m (7 ft) (with a 5 mm (¼ in) tolerance either way). The rim (painted white) should be 6 mm (¼ in) thick. A white line, 5 cm wide (2 in), should be drawn from the top of the metal rim, extending for at least 75 cm (30 in) on either side of the circle. The plane of the line should form a theoretical bisection of the circle dividing it into front and rear halves, the rear edge of the line passing through the centre of the circle.

A stopboard, with a curved inner edge coinciding with the inner edge of the circle, should be positioned in the middle of the circumference of the front half of the circle (midway between the sector lines). The board, painted white, should be fixed firmly to the ground. Its dimensions should be as follows: 1.21–1.23 m (approx 4 ft) long on the inside, 11.2–11.4 cm wide, and 9.8–10.2 cm high in relation to the level of the inside of the circle.

Forty degree sector emanating from the centre of the throwing circle. It can be laid out accurately by making the distance between two points on the inside edge of the sector lines 20m from the centre of the circle exactly 13.68m apart (and 27.36m apart at 40m from the centre).

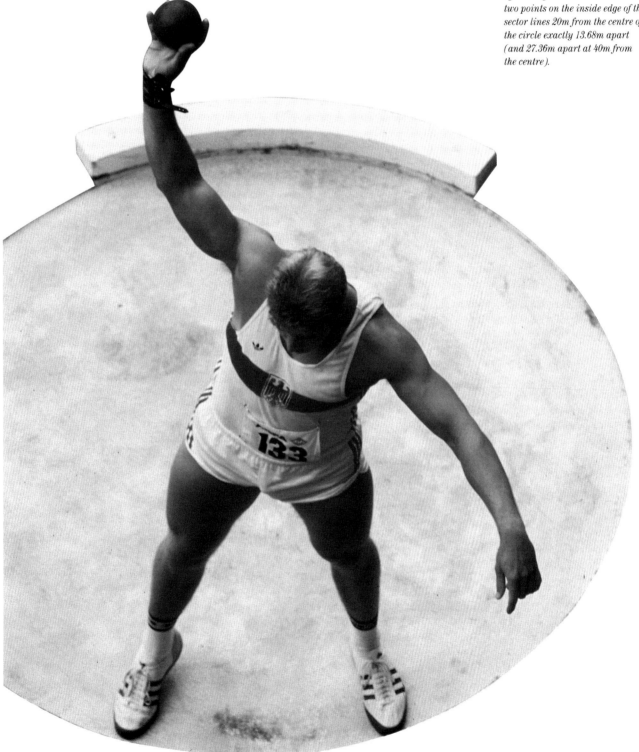

Throwing the hammer

In the hammer throw, the implement used is not a conventional hammer but a metal ball attached to a wire which has a handle at its other end. The competitor grips the handle with both hands and begins by whirling the ball around in a circle, passing above and behind the head and just below the knees. The thrower then spins around three or four times within the throwing circle, building up centrifugal force, before releasing the hammer upwards and outwards.

Landing sector

Hammer circle

40°

2.5 m

Hammer cage

The competition area should be roped off and, as in the discus event, throws should be made from an enclosure or cage to ensure the safety of spectators, officials and competitors. The cage should be capable of stopping a hammer moving at a speed of up to 32 m (105 ft) per second, and should be so arranged as to eliminate any danger of ricocheting or rebounding back towards the athlete or over the top of the cage. Provided it satisfies those requirements, any form of cage design and construction can be used.

Competition

Each competitor may have two practice trials only before competition begins. Athletes may wear gloves, and may tape individual fingers, but may not apply any substance to their shoes or to the surface of the throwing circle. They should

start their throws from a stationary position within the circle, at which point the head of the hammer may be on the ground either inside or outside the circle. Having started to make the throw, a competitor may not touch the ground outside the circle or the top of

the circle rim with any part of the body. To do so constitutes a foul throw (which is considered a trial). The head of the hammer may touch the ground during a competitor's preliminary swings and turns but, should the competitor then interrupt the throw so as to begin a trial again, it should be considered a foul throw. A competitor should not leave the circle until the hammer has touched the ground. When leaving the circle, the first contact with the top of the circle rim or the ground outside the circle has to be completely behind the white line which is drawn outside the circle and runs theoretically through its centre.

Provided the above rules have not been infringed, a competitor

may interrupt a trial once started, may lay the hammer down, and may leave the circle (in the manner described), before returning to a stationary position and beginning a fresh

trial. Any such moves should be included in the maximum time normally allowed for a trial.

For a throw to be valid, the hammer head must land completely within the inner edges of lines marking a sector of 40 degrees set out on the ground. If the hammer first strikes the cage before landing within the sector, the throw should not be considered invalid. If the hammer breaks during a throw or while in the air, the competitor may throw again. If such an incident results in the competitor losing balance and committing a foul, it should similarly not be counted.

Measurement

A throw is measured from the nearest indentation in the ground made by the head of the hammer to the inside of the circumference of the throwing circle, along a line drawn to the centre of the circle.

Measurements should be made immediately after each throw, recorded in even centimetre units to the nearest unit below the distance measured if that distance is not a whole even centimetre.

Left, hammer world championship competitor

Below, stages in the hammer throw build-up

1   2   3   4

5   6   7   8

Hammer circle and equipment
The specifications for the hammer circle are the same as for the shot put circle (but without a stopboard). The hammer should be made of any metal not softer than brass, or a shell of such metal filled with lead or other material. The steel wire, connected to the head by means of a swivel, should not be less than 3mm in diameter. The handle or grip on the other end of the wire may be of single or double

loop construction, but rigid and without hinging joints. The minimum weight of a hammer should be 7.26 kg (16 lb) in men's competition and 4kg (9 lb) in women's. In men's events, the hammer should have a minimum diameter of 110 mm (4¼ in) and a maximum of 130 mm . In women's, the equivalents should be 95 mm and 110 mm.

Throwing a discus

In this event the athlete holds the discus – a platter-shaped implement – against the palm of the hand and forearm of the throwing arm, with the finger ends around the edge. Facing away from the direction of the throw, he or she then rapidly makes one and half spins before propelling the discus into the air with a sidearm throw. For safety reasons, as in the hammer-throwing event, discus trials should be made from an enclosure or cage. Most of the specifications for the discus circle are the same as those for the hammer circle, except that the inside diameter of the circle should be 2.5 m (8 ft).

Competitors may have two practice trials only. They may not wear gloves, nor apply any substance on their shoes or in the throwing circle. Adopting any position they choose, athletes should commence their throws from a stationary position within the circle. It is a foul if, having started to make the throw, a competitor touches the ground outside the circle or

the top of the circle rim with any part of the body. A competitor should

not leave the circle until the discus has touched the ground. The rules relating to leaving the circle, or beginning a fresh trial, are the same as for the hammer and shot events outlined previously.

For a throw to be valid the discus should land completely within the inner edges of lines marking a sector of 40 degrees. If the discus first strikes the cage before landing within the

sector, the throw should not be considered invalid. If it breaks during a fair throw, it should not count as a trial.

Measurement

Immediately after a fair throw, the distance should be measured from the nearest mark in the ground made by the discus to the inside of the circumference of the circle, along a line drawn to the centre of the circle.

Measurements should be recorded in even centimetre units to the nearest unit below the distance measured if that distance is not a whole even centimetre.

Discus
Below, the body of the discus should be made of wood or other suitable material, with a metal rim, the edge of which should be circular. Each side should be identical, without any indentations or projections. The minimum weights should be 2 kg (2½ lb) for men and 1 kg (4½ lb) for women. The approved discus dimensions for men's and women's competition are shown in the diagram below.

Men 219-221 mm
Women 180-182 mm

Above, stages in the discus throw.

192 Athletics / field events *Essentials and rules / 5*

Throwing the javelin

A javelin is like a spear, thrown over the shoulder or upper part of the throwing arm by an athlete at the end of an approach run. It may not be slung or hurled, and no unorthodox styles are allowed.

No practice throws are permissible after the competition has begun, and gloves may not be worn. The javelin should be held in one hand only, and at the grip, so that the smallest finger is nearest to the point. Two parallel lines mark the javelin runway and competitors, during their run-up to throw, may not cross either of these lines. In the course of a throw, until the javelin has been launched, a competitor may not turn completely around so that his or her back is towards the throwing arc of the scratch line (the arc represents part of a circle drawn with a radius of 8 m (8¾ yds) with its centre in the middle of the runway).

If a competitor steps on or beyond the arc or extended scratch line in the course of a throw, it should be recorded as a foul. A foul throw, or letting the javelin go in an attempt, should count as a trial, but not if a javelin breaks during a fair throw. For a throw to be valid, the tip of the metal head must strike the ground before any other part of the javelin. It must also be within the inner edges of the landing sector. When the javelin has touched the

Landing sector

29 °

Throwing arc

Runway

30-36.5 m

4 m

ground, the competitor may leave the runway from behind the white line of the arc at right angles to the parallel lines.

Immediately after a fair throw, the distance should be measured from where the tip of the metal head first struck the ground, to the inside edge of the arc, along a line from the point of landing to the centre of the circle of which the arc is a part. Measurements should be recorded in even centimetre

units to the nearest unit below the distance measured if that distance is not a whole even centimetre.

The runway should be 30 –36.5 m (33 ft) in length. The parallel lines should be 5 cm (2 in) wide and 4 m (13 ft) apart. The throw should be made from behind the arc, a white strip 7 cm (2¾ in) wide and flush with the ground. From the extremities of the arc, 7 cm (2¾ in) wide white lines should be drawn for 75 cm (29½ in) at right angles to the parallel lines marking the runway. The landing sector should be marked with two white lines 5 cm (2 in) wide. It should be laid out by extending the inner edges of the lines from the centre of the circle of which the arc is a part, through the points at which the inner edges of the arc join the parallel lines marking the runway.

Javelin action.

Combined events

In combined events, athletes compete in several different disciplines over a period of up to two days. Athletes gain points for each event, and the one with the highest score at the end of the competition is the winner.

Combined events include the pentathlon, decathlon and heptathlon. The first may be contested at outdoor level by men and indoors by both men and women. Only male athletes contest the decathlon. The heptathlon is contested by men at indoor level, but only by women outdoors. The breakdown (and competing order) of events in each case is as follows:

* *Outdoor pentathlon (men):* one-day event – long jump, javelin, 200-m (220 yds) run, discus, and 1500-m (1640 yds) run.
* *Indoor pentathlon (men):* one-day event – 60-m (66 yds) hurdles, long jump, shot put, high jump, 1000-m (1093 yds) run.
* *Indoor pentathlon (women):* one-day event – 60-m (66 yds) hurdles, high jump, shot put, long jump, 800-m (880 yds) run.
* *Outdoor heptathlon (women):* two-day event – 100-m (10 yds) hurdles, high jump, shot put, 200-m (220 yds) run, long jump, javelin, 800-m (880 yds) run.
* *Indoor heptathlon (men):* two-day event – 60-m run (66 yds), long jump, shot put, high jump, 60-m (66 yds) hurdles,

pole vault, 1000-m (1093 yds) run.
* *Outdoor decathlon (men):* two-day event – 100-m run, long jump, shot put, high jump, 400-m (44 yds) run, 110-m (110 yds) hurdles, discus, pole vault, javelin, 1500-m ((1640 yds) run.

In combined competition, athletes should be allowed three trials only in the long jump and in each throwing event. There should, at the discretion of the referee, be an interval of at least 30 minutes between the time one event ends and another starts for an individual athlete. In running and hurdle races, competitors should be disqualified in any event in which they are responsible for three false starts. For the high

jump and pole vault, heights should be increased uniformly throughout the competition by 3 cm (approx 1 in) and 10 cm (4 in) respectively.

Any athlete who fails to participate in any of the required events may not participate further. In the event of a tie, the winner should be the competitor who, in the greater number of events, has received more points than the other competitor(s) tying. If that does not resolve it, the winner should be the athlete scoring the highest number of points in any one of the events (applicable also for any other place in the competition).

The javelin

A javelin comprises a metal shaft, with a pointed metal head fixed to it, and a cord grip. The finish of the shaft should be smooth and uniform. The cord grip, covering the javelin's centre of gravity, should not exceed the diameter of the shaft by more than 8 mm (⅓ in). The cross-section of the javelin should be regularly circular throughout, the maximum diameter of the shaft being immediately in front of the grip. From the grip, the javelin should taper regularly to the tip at the front and the tail at the rear.

2.2–2.3 m

2.6–2.7 m

Women's

Men's

Javelin's specifications in men's (and women's) competition:

minimum weight -
800 (600) gm

overall length -
2.6(2.2) m (min)
2.7(2.3) m (max)

length of metal head -
250(250) mm (min)
330(330) mm (max)

distance from tip of metal head to centre of gravity -
0.9(0.8) m (min)
1.06(0.95) m (max)

diameter of shaft at thickest point -
25(20)mm (min)
30(25)mm (max)

Golf
Essentials

The game of golf originated in Scotland during the late Middle Ages, probably on the grassy dunes of Scotland's eastern coast. In 1457, King James II of Scotland tried to ban his subjects from playing the game, because he felt that they were neglecting archery, a martial skill required to defend the realm. Nowadays, players of varying ability can legally enjoy a fair competition thanks to the handicap system.

The teams
Great flexibility – players can compete as individuals, with a partner against another pair, or in a field of competitors.

Officials
A marker records a competitor's score in stroke play. A fellow-competitor may act as a marker. In competitions, a referee decides on questions of fact and applies the rules.

Green

Fairway

Bunker

Rough

Teeing ground

Elements of a hole
Every hole consists of a teeing ground, a fairway, rough, hazards and a green.

Ryder cup –
major award for team golf, Europe versus USA.

The hole
The hole must be 4.25 in (108 mm) in diameter and at least 4 in (100 mm) deep.

The tee
A peg made of plastic or wood on which the ball is placed for the first stroke of each hole.

The ball
The maximum ball weight permitted is 1.62 oz (45.93 g) and the minimum size is 1.68 in (42.67 mm). Balls come in a variety of materials, ranging from the inexpensive one-piece Surlyn ball to the more costly balata-covered ball with a liquid centre bound with yarn. For regulations concerning usage and condition of the ball see Rule 5, The Ball (page 196). See also Rule 21, Cleaning Ball (page 203).

The course
A golf course normally consists of 18 holes, although short, 9-hole courses also exist. Each hole starts with a teeing ground. The fairway is an area of short grass that connects the tee to the green, an area of fine, well-maintained grass where the player putts the ball into the hole. The surrounding landscape of trees, rough grass, water features, and sand bunkers provide challenging obstacles to play.

Courses can vary in length, from around 5,500 to 7,000 yds (5,030 to 6,400 m). The length of each hole, and the sequence of long and shorter holes also varies from one course to another. Each hole is indicated by a flag.

Golfing Mecca
Augusta National, home of the U.S. Masters tournament.

On the green
Renowned for his driving, Greg 'the Great White Shark' Norman, would often get the ball on the green in a single stroke. But like every player he took immense care both choosing his iron and preparing his putting stroke on the green.

Golf bag
The bag stores clubs, balls and accessories such as a ball cleaner, pitch mark repairer, ball marker, towel, water bottle and snacks. Golf bags can be carried over the shoulder, or attached to a trolley for ease of transport across the course.

Clubs

Players take a set of clubs with them around the course, each designed for a certain type of stroke. There are two types of clubs – irons and woods – although most of today's woods are made of metal. The basic design of the club has changed little, but manufacturers have been experimenting with construction techniques and materials for over a century – woods such as persimmon and hickory gave way to steel, and other materials such as graphite, boron, and titanium are also now used.

Generally, woods are designed for power, and irons for precision. Each club has a different 'loft' or head angle, according to the required trajectory of the ball. Woods are normally numbered from 1 (the driver) to 9, and irons usually range from 1 to 10. In the range of clubs, the loft increases as the length of the trajectory decreases. The sand wedge has an extreme loft designed for getting the ball out of the bunker. Putters are designed for precision shots on the green. The maximum number of clubs that a player is permitted to take on a round of golf is 14.

Wood

Iron

Club class
Woods are designed for long drives; irons for accuracy over a short distance.

Dress

Smart dress is expected; jeans and T-shirts are banned by many clubs. A glove may be worn on the player's dominant hand to ensure a good grip on the club.

Buying equipment

Golf can be an expensive pastime, so it is best to buy a minimum amount of equipment before you commit yourself to the sport. You don't have to acquire a full set of clubs to start with – you may be able to buy suitable second-hand clubs. Basic Surlyn balls are fine for beginners. Even at an early stage, though, a pair of good quality shoes with leather uppers is well worth buying. Golf clubs insist that golf shoes (rather than, for instance, trainers) are worn.

HOW TO PLAY

Each hole starts at the teeing ground. The player strikes the ball with an appropriate club, selected for power or precision, aiming to land it on the green. The player then putts the ball into the hole. An 'ace', or hole-in-one, is quite a rare feat.

Good driving
Big hitter John Daly demonstrates excellent stance and posture before the downswing for a power drive. See also The swing, (pages 198–199).

How to win

There are two forms of golf: stroke play and match play. In stroke play, the final score is calculated according to the total number of strokes made over the 18 holes of the round. In match play, the players' score indicates the number of holes they have won; a player wins a hole by completing it using fewer strokes than his competitors.

The score card indicates the distance for each hole in yards or metres, as well as the par for that hole (the score that a scratch handicap player would be expected to achieve on that hole). In a handicap competition, the score is adjusted according to each player's handicap and the player with the lowest score wins.

A player's handicap is calculated by the club where the player is a member, on the basis of a series of completed score cards. A good player will have a lower handicap than a less proficient one. The handicap is deducted from the player's final score.

KEY RULES

• Golf has its own etiquette or code of behaviour, based on safety, honesty, and consideration for fellow players. The player should look around and behind before teeing off, to ensure that fellow-competitors or spectators will not be struck.

• If the player is responsible for marking a score card, as is frequently the case in non-competition golf, he is honour-bound to mark the card honestly and accurately.

• Fellow competitors must not disturb a player who is about to strike the ball, either by talking or by making any other noise or movement.

RULES OF GOLF

Rule 1. The Game

1-1. General
The game of golf consists in playing a ball from the teeing ground into the hole by stroke or successive strokes in accordance with the rules.

1-2. Exerting Influence on Ball
No player or caddie shall take any action to influence the position or the movement of a ball except in accordance with the rules.

1-3. Agreement to Waive Rules
Players shall not agree to exclude the operation of any rule or waive any penalty incurred.

1-4. Points Not Covered by Rules
If any point in dispute is not covered by the rules, the decision shall be made in accordance with equity.

Rule 2. Match Play

2-1. Winner of Hole; Reckoning of Holes
See How to win, (page 195).

2-2. Halved Hole
A hole is halved if each side holes out in the same number of strokes.

2-3. Winner of Match
A match (which normally consists of a stipulated round) is won by the side which is leading by a number of holes greater than the number of holes remaining to be played. For the purpose of settling a tie, the stipulated round may be extended to as many holes as are required for a match to be won.

2-4. Concession of Next Stroke, Hole or Match
When the opponent's ball is at rest or is deemed to be at rest under Rule 16-2, the player may concede the opponent to have holed out with his next stroke and the ball may be removed by either side with a club or otherwise.

A player may concede a hole or a match at any time prior to the conclusion of the hole or the match. Concession of a stroke, hole or match may not be declined or withdrawn.

2-5. Claims
In match play, if a doubt or dispute arises between the players and no duly authorized representative of the committee is available within a reasonable time, the players shall continue the match without delay. Any claim, if it is to be considered by the committee, must be made before any player in the match plays from the next teeing ground or, in the case of the last hole of the match, before all players in the match leave the putting green.

2-6. General Penalty
The penalty for a breach of a rule in match play is loss of the hole except when otherwise provided.

Rule 3. Stroke Play

3-1. Winner
The competitor who plays the stipulated round or rounds in the fewest strokes is the winner.

3-2. Failure to Hole Out
If a competitor fails to hole out at any hole and does not correct his mistake before he plays a stroke from the next teeing ground or, in the case of the last hole of the round, before he leaves the putting green, he shall be disqualified.

3-3. Doubt as to Procedure
a. Procedure
In stroke play only, when during play of a hole a competitor is doubtful of his rights or procedure, he may, without penalty, play a second ball. After the situation which caused the doubt has arisen, announce to his marker or his fellow competitor his decision to invoke this rule and the ball with which he will score if the rules permit.
b. Determination of Score for Hole
If the rules allow the procedure selected in advance by the competitor, the score with the ball selected shall be his score for the hole.

3-4. Refusal to Comply with a Rule
If a competitor refuses to comply with a rule affecting the rights of another competitor, he shall be disqualified.

3-5. General Penalty
The penalty for a breach of a rule in stroke play is two strokes except when otherwise provided.

Rule 4. Clubs
See also Clubs, (page 195).
4-1.
The player's clubs shall conform with the provisions of this rule and with the specifications and interpretations set forth in Appendix II (Design of Clubs).

If a player's club ceases to conform with Rule 4-1 because of damage sustained in the normal course of play, the player may:

(i) use the club in its damaged state, but only for the remainder of the stipulated round during which such damage was sustained; or
(ii) without unduly delaying play, repair it.

4-2. Playing Characteristics Changed
During a stipulated round, the playing characteristics of a club shall not be purposely changed by adjustment or by any other means.

4-3. Foreign Material
Foreign material must not be applied to the club face for the purpose of influencing the movement of the ball.

4-4. Maximum of Fourteen Clubs
See Clubs, (page 195).

Rule 5. The Ball
See also The ball, (page 194).
5-1. General
The ball the player uses shall conform to requirements specified in Appendix III (The Ball).

5-2. Foreign Material
Foreign material must not be applied to the ball for the purpose of changing its playing characteristics.

5-3. Ball Unfit for Play.
A ball is unfit for play if it is visibly cut, cracked or out of shape.

Rule 6. Player's Responsibilities

6-1.
The player is responsible for knowing the conditions under which the competition is to be played

6-2 Handicap
a. Match Play
Before starting a match in a handicap competition, the players should determine from one another their respective handicaps. If a player begins the match having declared a higher handicap which would affect the number of strokes given or received, he shall be disqualified.
b. Stroke Play
In any round of a handicap competition, the competitor shall ensure that his handicap is recorded on his score card before it is returned to the committee.

6-3. Time of Starting and Groups
a. Time of Starting
The player shall start at the time laid down by the committee.
b. Groups
In stroke play, the competitor shall remain throughout the round in the group arranged by the committee.

6-4. Caddie
The player may have only one caddie at any one time.

6-5. Ball
The responsibility for playing the proper ball rests with the player. Each player should put an identification mark on his ball.

6-6. Scoring in Stroke Play
a. Recording Scores
After each hole the marker should check the score with the competitor and record it. On completion of the round the marker shall sign the card and hand it to the competitor.
b. Signing and Returning Card
After completion of the round, the competitor should check his score for each hole and settle any

doubtful points with the committee. He shall ensure that the marker has signed the card, countersigning the card himself and return it to the committee.
c. Alteration of Card
No alteration may be made on a card after the competitor has returned it to the committee.
d. Wrong Score for Hole
The competitor is responsible for the correctness of the score recorded for each hole on his card. If he returns a score for any hole lower than actually taken, he shall be disqualified.

6-7. Undue Delay; Slow Play
The player shall play without undue delay and in accordance with any pace of play guidelines which may be laid down by the committee.

6-8. Discontinuance of Play
a. When Permitted
The player shall not discontinue play unless:
(i) the committee has suspended play;
(ii) he believes there is danger from lightning;
(iii) he is seeking a decision from the committee on a doubtful or disputed point; or
(iv) there is some other good reason such as illness.

Rule 7
Covers practice before or during rounds.

Rule 8. Advice; Indicating Line of Play

8-1. Advice
During a stipulated round, a player shall not give advice to anyone in the competition except his partner. A player may ask for advice during a stipulated round from only his partner or either of their caddies.

8-2. Indicating Line of Play
The 'line of play' is the direction which the player wishes his ball to take after a stroke, plus a reasonable distance on either side of the intended direction.
a. Other Than on Putting Green
A player may have the line of play indicated to him by anyone, but no one shall be positioned by the player on or close to the line or an extension of the line beyond the hole while the stroke is being played.
b. On the Putting Green
When the player's ball is on the putting green, the player, his partner or either of their caddies may, before but not during the stroke, point out a line for putting, but in doing so the putting green shall not be touched.

Rule 9. Information as to Strokes Taken.

9-1. General
The number of strokes a player

has taken shall include any penalty strokes incurred.
9-2. Match Play
A player who has incurred a penalty shall inform his opponent as soon as practicable.

An opponent is entitled to ascertain from the player, during the play of a hole, the number of strokes he has taken, and, after play of a hole, the number of strokes taken on the hole just completed.

If during the play of a hole the player gives or is deemed to give the wrong information as to the number of strokes taken, he shall incur no penalty if he corrects the mistake before his opponent has played his next stroke. If the player fails so to correct the wrong information, he shall lose the hole.
9-3.
A competitor who has incurred a penalty should inform his marker as soon as practicable.

Rule 10. Order of Play
10-1 Match Play
a. Teeing Ground
The side entitled to play first form the teeing ground is said to have the 'honour'.

The side which shall have the honour at the first teeing ground shall be determined by the order of the draw. In the absence of a draw, the honour should be decided by lot.
b. Other Than on Teeing Ground
When the balls are in play, the ball farther from the hole shall be played first. If the balls are equidistant from the hole, the ball to be played first should be decided by lot.
c. Playing Out of Turn
If a player plays when his opponent should have played, the opponent may immediately require the player to cancel the stroke so played and, in correct order, play a ball without penalty as nearly as possible at the spot from which the original ball was played.
10-2. Stroke Play
a. Teeing Ground
The competitor entitled to play first from the teeing ground is said to have the 'honour'.
See 10-1 (a) for the procedure for determining the honour.
b. Other Than on Teeing Ground
See 10-1 (b)
c. Playing Out of Turn
If a competitor plays out of turn, no penalty is incurred and the ball shall be played as it lies. If, however, the committee determines that competitors have agreed to play in an order other than that set forth in Clauses 2a and 2b of this rule to give one of them an advantage, they shall be disqualified.

10-3. Provisional Ball or Second Ball from Teeing Ground
If a player plays a provisional ball or a second ball from a teeing ground, he should do so after his opponent or fellow-competitor has played his first stroke. If a player plays a provisional ball or a second ball out of turn, Clauses 1c and 2c of this rule shall apply.
10-4. Ball Moved in Measuring
If a ball is moved in measuring to determine which ball is farther from the hole, no penalty is incurred and the ball shall be replaced.

Rule 11. Teeing Ground
11-1. Teeing
In teeing, the ball may be placed on the ground, on an irregularity of surface created by the player on the ground or on a tee, sand or other substance in order to raise it off the ground. A player may stand outside the teeing ground to play a ball within it.
11-2. Tee-Markers
Before a player plays his first stroke with any ball from the teeing ground of the hole being played, the tee-markers are deemed to be fixed.
11-3 Ball Falling Off Tee
If a ball, when not in play, falls off a tee or is knocked off a tee by the player in addressing it, it may be re-teed without penalty, but if a stroke is made at the ball in these circumstances, whether the ball is moving or not, the stroke counts but no penalty is incurred.
11-4. Playing from Outside Teeing Ground
a. Match Play
If a player, when starting a hole, plays a ball from outside the teeing ground, the opponent may immediately require the player to cancel the stroke so played and play a ball from within the teeing ground, without penalty.
b. Stroke Play
If a competitor, when starting a hole, plays a ball from outside the teeing ground, he shall incur a penalty of two strokes and shall then play a ball from within the teeing ground.

If the competitor plays a stroke from the next teeing ground without first correcting his mistake or, in the case of the last hole of the round, leaves the putting green without first declaring his intention to correct his mistake, he shall be disqualified.

Strokes played by a competitor from outside the teeing ground do not count in his score.
11-5. Playing from Wrong Teeing Ground
The provisions of Rule 11-4 apply.

Rule 12. Searching for and Identifying Ball
12-1. Searching for Ball; Seeing Ball.
In searching for his ball anywhere on the course, the player may touch or bend long grass or other vegetation, but only to the extent necessary to find and identify it, provided that this does not improve the lie of the ball, the area of his intended swing or his line of play.

In a hazard, if a ball is covered by loose impediments or sand, the player may remove as much thereof as will enable him to see a part of the ball. If the ball is moved in such removal, no penalty is incurred; the ball shall be replaced and, if necessary, re-covered.

If a ball lying in casual water, ground under repair or a hole, cast or runway made by an animal or bird is accidentally moved during search, no penalty is incurred; the ball shall be replaced, unless the player elects to proceed under Rule 25-1b.

If a ball is believed to be lying in water in a water hazard, the player may probe for it with a club or otherwise. If the ball is moved in so doing, no penalty is incurred; the ball shall be replaced, unless the player elects to proceed under Rule 26-1.
12-2. Identifying Ball
Except in a hazard, the player may, without penalty, lift a ball he believes to be his own for the purpose of identification. If the ball is the player's ball, he shall replace it. Before lifting the ball, the player must announce his intention to his opponent in match play or his marker or a fellow-competitor in stroke play and mark the position of the ball. He must then give his opponent, marker or fellow-competitor an opportunity to observe the lifting and replacement.

13-1. Ball Played as It Lies
The ball shall be played as it lies, except as otherwise provided in the rules.
13-2. Improving Lie, Area of Intended Swing or Line of Play
Except as provided in the rules, a player shall not improve or allow to be improved the position or lie of his ball, the area of his intended swing, his line of play or a reasonable extension of that line beyond the hole or the area in which he is to drop or place a ball by any of the following actions:
moving, bending or breaking anything growing or fixed, or removing or pressing down sand, loose soil, replaced divots, or

other irregularities of surface, except as follows:
as may occur in fairly taking his stance, in making a stroke or the backward movement of his club for a stroke, on the teeing ground in creating or eliminating irregularities of surface as provided in Rule 16-1a or on the putting green in removing sand and loose soil or in repairing damage as provided in Rule 16-1c.

The club may be grounded only lightly and shall not be pressed on the ground.
13-3. Building Stance
A player is entitled to place his feet firmly in taking his stance, but he shall not build a stance.
13-4. Ball in Hazard
Except as provided in the rules, before making a stroke at a ball which is in a hazard or which, having been lifted from a hazard, may be dropped or placed in the hazard, the player shall not:
a. Test the condition of the hazard or any similar hazard;
b. Touch the ground in the hazard or water in the water hazard with a club or otherwise; or
c. Touch or move a loose impediment lying in or touching the hazard.
Exceptions:
1. Provided nothing is done which constitutes testing the condition of the hazard or improves the lie of the ball, there is no penalty if the player (a) touches the ground or water in any hazard as a result of or to prevent falling, in removing an obstruction, in measuring or retrieving or lifting a ball under any rule or (b) places his clubs in a hazard.
2. The player after playing the stroke, or his caddie at any time without the authority of the player, may smooth sand or soil in the hazard, provided that nothing is done which improves the lie of the ball or assists the player in his subsequent play of the hole.

Rule 14. Striking the Ball
Definition
A 'stroke' is the forward movement of the club made with the intention of fairly striking at and moving the ball, but if a player checks his downswing voluntarily before the clubhead reaches the ball he is deemed not to have made a stroke.
14-1. Ball to be Fairly Struck at
The ball shall be fairly struck at with the head of the club and must not be pushed, scraped or spooned.
14-2. Assistance
In making a stroke, a player shall not accept physical assistance or protection from the elements.
➡ *page 200*

TACTICS

Arrive at the golf course in good time before the game, so that you can limber up and practice your drive and swing on the practice range. The tactics involved in golf are known as course management – this entails being able to judge which club to select for a shot, based on the need for power, precision, or loft. Pack a bottle of water and an energy-boosting snack in the golf bag to keep you going - a round of golf can last a long time.

Practice makes perfect
Players of all abilities seek regular practice and instruction. Below and right, golf coach, David Leadbetter, offers guidance.

Putters
Putters come in a variety of different shapes and weights to suit different greens. Heavier putters, for instance, are needed for slower greens.

A putting grip
The thumbs overlap facing directly down the putter handle.

Putting position
For a smooth putting action the golfer needs a completely stable stance with the knees slightly flexed and relaxed and the upper body weight firmly placed on the feet.

SKILLS

Developing a good *swing* (the arc made by the golf club before striking the ball) is the key factor in becoming a proficient golfer. The execution of the swing depends on the player's address (the posture adopted before the ball is struck), powers of concentration, and grip. As he swings, the player should keep his head still, looking down on the ball. Essentially, the swing comes from the arms, not the wrist.

Putting is the other essential skill; the player must be able to control his hands and deliver a delicate, accurate stroke to get the ball in the hole.

Although brute strength is not essential, and can even be counter-productive, exercises that develop the strength of the wrists, legs, and stomach are beneficial. Exercises designed to strengthen and protect the back are essential.

The swing (1)
Getting the swing right is something that obsesses every golfer and golfers may spend hours practising. One of the keys to success is the correct stance. The aim is to swing the arms, upper body and club so that the club head addresses the ball at the maximum possible speed. The stroke begins with the golfer addressing the ball with the face of the club to align it properly (1). The golfer then takes a half swing back to prepare the stroke. The swing then begins with the golfer swinging the club right back round his head, then forward to strike the ball in one smooth action (2) – see opposite.

1

2

GREY AREA

Rule 26-1 Ball in Water Hazard

This rule states that 'In order to treat the ball as lost in the [water] hazard, there must be reasonable evidence that the ball lodged in it'.

During play, there may be some difficulty in agreeing upon what constitutes 'reasonable evidence'. Further insight was given in the 1997 Decisions on the Rules of Golf:

The term 'reasonable evidence' in Rule 26-1 is purposely and necessarily broad so as to permit sensible judgements to be reached on the basis of all the relevant circumstances of particular cases. As applied in this context, a player may not deem his ball lost in a water hazard simply because he thinks the ball may be in the hazard. The evidence must be preponderantly in favour of its being in the hazard. Otherwise, the ball must be considered lost outside the hazard and the player must proceed under Rule 27-1. Physical conditions in the area have a great deal to do with it. For example, if a water hazard is surrounded by a fairway on which a ball could hardly be lost, the existence of reasonable evidence that the ball is in the hazard would be more likely than if there was deep rough in the area. Observing a ball splash in a water hazard would not necessarily provide reasonable evidence as splashing balls sometimes skip out of hazards. It would depend on all the circumstances.

Pitching and chipping
There are a number of other ways of striking the ball apart from a full swing drive and a putt. When the golfer is within 50 m (55 yds) of the green he needs a shot that will drop the ball on the green with the minimum of rolling after it lands. This is where the 'pitch stroke' comes into play, which uses a pitching wedge to gently loft the ball into the air in an action a bit like an underarm throw. Once within about 3 m (10 ft) of the green the golfer may use a 'chip shot' with a wedge to lift the ball over rougher grass so that it lands on the green.

The Swing (2)
After striking the ball the golfer swings, transferring his weight on to his front foot and unwinding his hips to push the ball away with smooth power (3). He then allows the club and his entire upper body to follow through freely to keep the action absolutely balanced (4). The club swings all the way around so that it ends up down the golfer's back. The aim is to make the entire swing into one smooth, continuous action, beginning with addressing the ball, and continuing with the take away, the backswing, the forward swing, the swing through and the follow through.

3

4

continued from page 197

14-3. Artificial Devices and Unusual Equipment
Except as provided in the rules, during a stipulated round the player shall not use any artificial device or unusual equipment:
a. Which might assist him in making a stroke or in his play; or
b. For the purpose of gauging or measuring distance or conditions which might affect his play; or
c. Which might assist him in gripping the club, except that:
   (i) plain gloves may be worn;
   (ii) resin, powder and drying or moisturising agents may be used;
   (iii) tape or gauze may be applied to the grip; and
   (iv) a towel or handkerchief may be wrapped round the grip.

14-4. Striking the Ball More than Once
If a player's club strikes the ball more than once in the course of a stroke, the player shall count the stroke and add a penalty stroke.

14.5 Playing Moving Ball
A player shall not play while his ball is moving.
Exceptions:
Ball falling off tee (11-3).
Striking the ball more than once (14-4).
Ball moving in water (14-6).
When the ball begins to move only after the player has begun the stroke or the backward movement of his club for the stroke, he shall incur no penalty under this rule for playing a moving ball, but he is not exempt from any penalty incurred under the following rules:
   Ball at rest moved by player (18-2a).
   Ball at rest moving after address (18-2b).
   Ball at rest moving after loose impediment touched (18-2c).
   (Ball purposely deflected or stopped by player, partner or caddie – see Rule 1-2).

14-6. Ball Moving in Water
When a ball is moving in water in a water hazard, the player may, without penalty, make a stroke, but he must not delay making his stroke in order to allow the wind or current to improve the position of the ball. A ball moving in water in a water hazard may be lifted if the player elects to invoke Rule 26.

Rule 15. Wrong Ball; Substituted Ball

Definition
A 'wrong ball' is any ball other than the player's:
a. Ball in play,
b. Provisional ball, or
c. Second ball played under Rule 3-3 or Rule 20-7b in stroke play.

15-1. General
A player must hole out with the ball played from the teeing ground unless a rule permits him to substitute another ball. If a player substitutes another ball when not so permitted, that ball is not a wrong ball; it becomes the ball in play and, if the error is not corrected as provided in Rule 20-6, the player shall incur a penalty of loss of hole in match play or two strokes in stroke play.

15-2. Match Play
If a player plays a stroke with a wrong ball except in a hazard, he shall lose the hole.

15-3. Stroke Play
If a competitor plays a stroke or strokes with a wrong ball, he shall incur a penalty of two strokes, unless the stroke or strokes played with such a ball were played when it was in a hazard, in which case no penalty is incurred.

The competitor must correct his mistake by playing the correct ball. If he fails to correct his mistake before he plays a stroke from the next teeing ground or, in the case of the last hole of the round, fails to declare his intention to correct his mistake before leaving the putting green, he shall be disqualified.

Strokes played by a competitor with a wrong ball do not count in his score.

If the wrong ball belongs to another competitor, its owner shall place a ball on the spot from which the wrong ball was first played.

Rule 16. The Putting Green

The 'line of putt' is the line which the player wishes his ball to take after a stroke on the putting green. Except with respect to Rule 16-1e, the line of putt includes a reasonable distance on either side of the intended line. The line of putt does not extend beyond the hole.

16-1. General
a. Touching Line of Putt
The line of putt must not be touched except:
   (i) the player may move sand and loose soil on the putting green and other loose impediments by picking them up or by brushing them aside with his hand or a club without pressing anything down;
   (ii) in addressing the ball, the player may place the club in front of the ball without pressing anything down;
   (iii) in measuring (10-4);
   (iv) in lifting the ball (16-1b);
   (v) in pressing down a ball marker;
   (vi) in repairing old hole plugs or ball marks on the putting green (16-1c); and
   (vii) in removing movable obstructions (24-1).

b. Lifting Ball
A ball on the putting green may be lifted and, if desired, cleaned. A ball so lifted shall be replaced on the spot from which it was lifted.

c. Repair of Hole Plugs Ball Marks and Other Damage
The player may repair an old hole plug or damage to the putting green caused by the impact of a ball, whether or not the player's ball lies on the putting green. If the ball is moved in the process of such repair, it shall be replaced, without penalty. Any other damage to the putting green shall not be repaired if it might assist the player in his subsequent play of the hole.

d. Testing Surface
During the play of a hole, a player shall not test the surface of the putting green by rolling a ball or roughening or scraping the surface.

e. Standing Astride or on Line of Putt
The player shall not make a stroke on the putting green from a stance astride, or with either foot touching, the line of putt or an extension of that line behind the ball.

f. Position of Caddie or Partner
While making a stroke on the putting green, the player shall not allow his caddie, his partner or his partner's caddie to position himself on or close to an extension of the line of putt behind the ball.

g. Playing Stroke While Another Ball in Motion
The player shall not play a stroke while another ball is in motion after a stroke from the putting green, except that, if a player does so, he incurs no penalty if it was his turn to play.

16-2. Ball Overhanging Hole
When any part of the ball overhangs the lip of the hole, the player is allowed enough time to reach the hole without unreasonable delay and an additional ten seconds to determine whether the ball is at rest. If by then the ball has not fallen into the hole, it is deemed to be at rest. If the ball subsequently falls into the hole, the player is deemed to have holed out with his last stroke, and he shall add a penalty stroke to his score for the hole; otherwise there is no penalty under this rule.

Rule 17. The Flagstick

17-1. Flagstick Attended, Removed or Held Up
Before and during the stroke, the player may have the flagstick attended, removed or held up to indicate the position of the hole. This may be done only on the authority of the player before he plays his stroke.

17-2. Unauthorized Attendance
a. Match Play
In match play, an opponent or his caddie shall not, without the authority or prior knowledge of the player, attend, remove or hold up the flagstick while the player is making a stroke or his ball is in motion.

b. Stroke Play
In stroke play, if a fellow-competitor or his caddie attends, removes or holds up the flagstick without the competitor's authority or prior knowledge while the competitor is making a stroke or his ball is in motion, the fellow-competitor shall incur the penalty for breach of this rule. In such circumstances, if the competitor's ball strikes the flagstick, the person attending it or anything carried by him, the competitor incurs no penalty and the ball shall be played as it lies, except that, if the stroke was played from the putting green, the stroke shall be cancelled, the ball replaced and the stroke replayed.

17-3. Ball Striking Flagstick or Attendant
The player's ball shall not strike:
a. The flagstick when attended, removed or held up by the player, his partner or either of their caddies, or by another person with the player's authority or prior knowledge; or
b. The player's caddie, his partner or his partner's caddie when attending the flagstick, or another person attending the flagstick with the player's authority or prior knowledge or anything carried by any such person; or
c. The flagstick in the hole, unattended, when the ball has been played from the putting green.

17-4. Ball Resting Against Flagstick
If the ball rests against the flagstick when it is in the hole, the player or another person authorized by him may move or remove the flagstick and if the ball falls into the hole, the player shall be deemed to have holed out with his last stroke; otherwise the ball, if moved, shall be placed on the lip of the hole, without penalty.

Rule 18. Ball at Rest Moved

A ball is deemed to have 'moved' if it leaves its position and comes to rest in any other place.

An 'outside agency' is any agency not part of the match or, in stroke play, not part of the competitor's side, and includes a referee, a marker, an observer and a forecaddie. Neither wind nor water is an outside agency.

18-1. By Outside Agency
If a ball at rest is moved by an outside agency, the player shall incur no penalty and the ball shall be replaced before the player plays another stroke.

18-2. By Player, Partner, Caddie or Equipment
a. General
When a player's ball is *in play*, if:

(i) the player, his partner or either of their caddies lifts or moves it, touches it purposely (except with a club in the act of addressing it) or causes it to move except as permitted by a rule, or

(ii) equipment of the player or his partner causes the ball to move, the player shall incur a penalty stroke. The ball shall be replaced unless the movement of the ball occurs after the player has begun his swing and he does not discontinue his swing.

b. Ball Moving after Address
If a player's ball in play moves after he has addressed it (other than as a result of a stroke), the player shall be deemed to have moved the ball and shall incur a penalty stroke.

c. Ball Moving After Loose Impediment Touched
Through the green, if the ball moves after any loose impediment, lying within a club-length of it has been touched by the player, his partner or either of their caddies and before the player has addressed it, the player shall be deemed to have moved the ball and shall incur a penalty stroke.

On the putting green, if the ball or the ball marker moves in the process of removing any loose impediment, the ball or the ball marker shall be replaced. There is no penalty provided the movement of the ball or the ball marker is directly attributable to the removal of the loose impediment.

18-3. By Opponent, Caddie or Equipment in Match Play
a. During Search
If, during search for a player's ball, the ball is moved by an opponent, his caddie or his equipment, no penalty is incurred and the player shall replace the ball.

b. Other Than During Search
If the ball is touched or moved by an opponent, his caddie or his equipment, except otherwise provided in the rules, the opponent shall incur a penalty stroke. The player shall replace the ball.

18-4. By Fellow-Competitor, Caddie or Equipment in Stroke Play
If a competitor's ball is moved by a fellow-competitor, his caddie or his equipment, no penalty is incurred. The competitor shall

replace his ball.
18-5. By Another Ball
If a ball in play and at rest is moved by another ball in motion after a stroke, the moved ball shall be replaced.

Rule 19. Ball in Motion Deflected or Stopped
19-1. By Outside Agency
If a ball in motion is accidentally deflected or stopped by any outside agency, it is a rub of the green, no penalty is incurred and the ball shall be played as it lies except:

a. If a ball in motion after a stroke other than on the putting green comes to rest in or on any moving or animate outside agency, the player shall, through the green or in a hazard, drop the ball, or on the putting green place the ball, as near as possible to the spot where the outside agency was when the ball came to rest in or on it, and

b. If a ball in motion after a stroke on the putting green is deflected or stopped by, or comes to rest in or on, any moving or animate outside agency except a worm or an insect, the stroke shall be cancelled, the ball replaced and the stroke replayed.

19-2. By Player, Partner, Caddie or Equipment
a. Match Play
If a player's ball is accidentally deflected or stopped by himself, his partner or either of their caddies or equipment he shall lose the hole.

b. Stroke Play
If a competitor's ball is accidentally deflected or stopped by himself, his partner or either of their caddies or equipment, the competitor shall incur a penalty of two strokes.

19-3. By Opponent, Caddie or Equipment in Match Play
If a player's ball is accidentally deflected or stopped by an opponent, his caddie or his equipment, no penalty is incurred. The player may play the ball as it lies or, before another stroke is played by either side, cancel the stroke and play a ball without penalty as nearly as possible at the spot from which the original ball was last played.

19-4. By Fellow-Competitor, Caddie or Equipment in Stroke Play
See Rule 19-1 regarding ball deflected by outside agency.

19-5. By Another Ball
a. At Rest
If a player's ball in motion after a stroke is deflected or stopped by a ball in play and at rest, the player shall play his ball as it lies.

In match play, no penalty is incurred. In stroke play, there is no penalty unless both balls lay on

the putting green prior to the stroke, in which case the player incurs a penalty of two strokes.
b. In Motion
If a player's ball in motion after a stroke is deflected or stopped by another ball in motion after a stroke, the player shall play his ball as it lies. There is no penalty unless the player was in breach of Rule 16-1g, in which he shall incur the penalty for breach of that rule.

Rule 20. Lifting, Dropping and Placing; Playing from Wrong Place
20-1. Lifting
A ball to be lifted under the rules may be lifted by the player, his partner or another person authorized by the player. In any such case, the player shall be responsible for any breach of the rules.

The position of the ball shall be marked before it is lifted under a rule which requires it to be replaced.

If a ball or ball marker is accidentally moved in the process of lifting the ball under a rule or marking its position, the ball or the ball marker shall be replaced. There is no penalty provided the movement of the ball or the ball marker is directly attributable to the specific act of marking the position of or lifting the ball.

20-2. Dropping and Re-Dropping
a. By Whom and How
A ball to be dropped under the rules shall be dropped by the player himself. He shall stand erect, hold the ball at shoulder height and arm's length and drop it.

If the ball touches the player, his partner, either of their caddies or their equipment before or after it strikes a part of the course, the ball shall be re-dropped, without penalty.

b. Where to Drop
When a ball is to be dropped as near as possible to a specific spot, it shall be dropped not nearer the hole than the specific spot which, if it is not precisely known to the player, shall be estimated.

A ball when dropped must first strike a part of the course where the applicable rule requires it to be dropped. If it is not so dropped, rules 20-6 and 20-7 apply.

c. When to Re-Drop
A dropped ball shall be re-dropped without penalty if it:

(i) rolls into a hazard;

(ii) rolls out of a hazard;

(iii) rolls onto a putting green;

(iv) rolls out of bounds;

(v) rolls to a position where there is interference by the condition from which relief was taken under 24-2 (immovable obstructions) or 25-1 (abnormal

ground conditions), or rolls back into the pitch mark from which it was lifted under 25-2 (embedded ball);

(vi) rolls and comes to rest more than two club-lengths from where it first struck a part of the course; or

(vii) rolls and comes to rest nearer the hole than its original position or estimated position (see 20-2b) unless otherwise permitted by the rules.

(viii) rolls and comes to rest nearer the hole than the point where the original ball last crossed the margin of the area or hazard (25-11c(i) and (ii)) or the margin of the water hazard (Rule 26-1b) or lateral water hazard (26-1c).

If the ball when re-dropped or placed under this rule is not immediately recoverable, another ball may be substituted.

20-3. Placing and Replacing
a. By Whom and Where
A ball to be placed under the rules shall be placed by the player or his partner. If a ball is to be replaced the player, his partner or the person who lifted or moved it shall place it on the spot from which it was lifted or moved. In any such case, the player shall be responsible for any breach of the rules.

If a ball or ball marker is accidentally moved in the process of placing or replacing the ball, the ball or the ball marker shall be replaced. There is no penalty provided the movement of the ball or the ball marker is directly attributable to the specific act of placing or replacing the ball or removing the ball marker.

b. Lie of Ball to Be Placed or Replaced Altered
If the original lie of a ball to be placed or replaced has been altered:

(i) except in a hazard, the ball shall be placed in the nearest lie most similar to the original lie which is not more than one club-length from the original lie, not nearer the hole and not in the hazard;

(ii) in a water hazard, the ball shall be placed in accordance with clause (i) above, except that the ball must be placed in the water hazard;

(iii) in a bunker, the original lie shall be recreated as nearly as possible and the ball shall be placed in that lie.

c. Spot Not Determinable
If it is impossible to determine the spot where the ball is to be placed or replaced:

(i) through the green, the ball shall be dropped in the hazard as near as possible to the place

➡ *page 202*

continued from page 201
where it lay but not in a hazard or on a putting green;

(ii) in a hazard, the ball shall be dropped in the hazard as near as possible to the place where it lay;

(iii) on the putting green, the ball shall be placed as near as possible to the place where it lay but not in a hazard.

d. Ball Fails to Come to Rest on Spot

If a ball when placed fails to come to rest on the spot on which it was placed, it shall be replaced without penalty. If it still fails to come to rest on that spot:

(i) except in a hazard, it shall be placed at the nearest spot not nearer the hole or in a hazard where it can be placed at rest;

(ii) in a hazard, it shall be placed in the hazard at the nearest spot not nearer the hole where it can be placed at rest.

If a ball when placed comes to rest on the spot on which it is placed, and it subsequently moves, there is no penalty and the ball shall be played as it lies, unless the provisions of any other rule apply.

20-4. When Ball Dropped or Placed Is in Play

If the player's ball in play has been lifted, it is again in play when dropped or placed.

A substituted ball becomes the ball in play when it has been dropped or placed.

20-5. Playing Next Stroke from Where Previous Stroke Played

The player shall proceed as follows: if the stroke is to be played from the teeing ground, the ball to be played shall be played from anywhere within the teeing ground and may be teed; if the stroke is to be played from through the green or a hazard, it shall be dropped; if the stroke is to be played on the putting green, it shall be placed.

20-6. Lifting Ball Incorrectly Substituted, Dropped or Placed

A ball incorrectly substituted, dropped or placed in a wrong place may be lifted, without penalty, and the player shall then proceed correctly.

20-7. Playing from Wrong Place

For a ball played from outside the teeing ground or from a wrong teeing ground, see 11-4 and -5.

a. Match Play

If a player plays a stroke with a ball which has been dropped or placed in a wrong place, he shall lose the hole.

b. Stroke Play

If a competitor plays a stroke with his ball in play (i) which has been dropped or placed in a wrong place or (ii) which has been moved and not replaced in a case

where the rules require replacement, he shall, provided a serious breach has not occurred, incur the penalty prescribed by the applicable rule and play out the hole with the ball.

If, after playing from a wrong place, a competitor becomes aware of that fact and believes that a serious breach may be involved, he may, provided he has not played a stroke from the next teeing ground or, in the case of the last hole of the round, left the putting green, declare that he will play out the hole with a second ball dropped or placed in accordance with the rules. The competitor shall report the facts to the committee before returning his score card; if he fails to do so, he shall be disqualified. The committee shall determine whether a serious breach of the rule occurred. If so, the score with the second ball shall count and the competitor shall add two penalty strokes to his score with that ball.

If a serious breach has occurred and the competitor has failed to correct it as prescribed above, he shall be disqualified.

Rule 21. Cleaning Ball

A ball on the putting green may be cleaned when lifted under Rule 16-1b. Elsewhere, a ball may be cleaned when lifted except when it has been lifted:
a. To determine if it is unfit for play (5-3);
b. For identification (12-2), in which case it may be cleaned only to the extent necessary for identification; or
c. Because it is interfering with or assisting play (22).

If a player cleans his ball during play of a hole except as provided in this rule, he shall incur a penalty for breach of Rule 20-3a, but no additional penalty under Rule 21 shall be applied.

22. Ball Interfering with or Assisting Play

Any player may;
a. Lift his ball if he considers that the ball might assist any other player; or
b. Have any other ball lifted if he considers that the ball might interfere with his play or assist the play of any other player, but this may not be done while another ball is in motion. In stroke play, a player required to lift his ball may play first rather than lift. A ball lifted under this rule shall be replaced.

Rule 23 Loose Impediments

Definition

'Loose impediments' are natural objects such as stones, leaves, twigs, branches and the like,

dung, worms and insects and casts or heaps made by them, provided they are not fixed or growing, are not solidly embedded and do not adhere to the ball.

Sand and loose soil are loose impediments on the putting green but not elsewhere.

Snow and natural ice, other than frost, are either casual water or loose impediments, at the option of the player. Dew and frost are not loose impediments.

23-1. Relief

Except when both the loose impediment and the ball lie in or touch the same hazard, any loose impediment may be removed without penalty. If the ball moves, see 18-2c.

When a ball is in motion, a loose impediment which might influence the movement of the ball shall not be removed.

Rule 24. Obstructions

Definition

An 'obstruction' is anything artificial, including the artificial surfaces and sides of roads and paths and manufactured ice, except:
a. Objects defining out of bounds, such as walls, fences, stakes and railings;
b. Any part of an immovable artificial object which is out of bounds; and
c. Any construction declared by the committee to be an integral part of the course.

24-1. Movable Obstruction

A player may obtain relief from a movable obstruction as follows:
a. If the ball does not lie in or on the obstruction, the obstruction may be removed. If the ball moves, it shall be replaced without penalty.
b. If the ball lies in or on the obstruction, the ball may be lifted, without penalty, and the obstruction removed. The ball shall through the green or in a hazard be dropped, or on the putting green be placed, as near as possible to the spot directly under the place where the ball lay in or on the obstruction, but not nearer the hole.

When a ball is in motion, an obstruction which might influence the movement of the ball, other than an attended flagstick or equipment of the players, shall not be removed.

24-2. Immovable Obstruction

a. Interference by an immovable obstruction occurs when a ball lies in or on the obstruction, or so close to the obstruction that the obstruction interferes with the player's stance or the area of his intended swing. If the player's ball lies on the putting green, interference also occurs if an immovable obstruction on the

putting green intervenes on his line of putt. Otherwise, intervention on the line of play is not, of itself, interference under this rule.

b. Relief

Except when the ball is in a water hazard or a lateral water hazard, a player may obtain relief from the interference by an immovable obstruction, without penalty, as follows:

(i) **Through the Green**: If the ball lies through the green, the point on the course nearest to where the ball lies shall be determined (without crossing over, through or under the obstruction) which (a) is not nearer the hole, (b) avoids interference (as defined) and (c) is not in a hazard or on a putting green. The player shall lift the ball and drop it within one club-length of the point thus determined on a part of the course which fulfils (a), (b), and (c) above.

(ii) **In a Bunker**: If the ball is in a bunker, the player shall lift and drop the ball in accordance with Clause (i) above, except that the ball must be dropped in the bunker.

(iii) **On the Putting Green**: If the ball lies on the putting green, the player shall lift the ball and place it in the nearest position to where it lay which affords relief from interference, but not nearer the hole nor in a hazard.

c) Ball Lost

Except in a water hazard or a lateral water hazard, if there is reasonable evidence that a ball is lost in an immovable obstruction, the player may, without penalty, substitute another ball and follow the procedure prescribed in 24-2b.

Rule 25. Abnormal Ground Conditions and Wrong Putting Green

'Casual water' is any temporary accumulation of water on the course which is visible before or after the player takes his stance and is not in a water hazard. Dew and frost are not casual water.

25.1 Interference

a. Interference by casual water, ground under repair or a hole, cast or runway made by an animal or bird occurs when a ball lies in or touches any of these conditions or when such a condition on the course interferes with the player's stance or the area of his intended swing.

If the player's ball lies on the putting green, interference also occurs if such condition on the putting green intervenes with his line of putt.

If interference exists, the player may either play the ball as it lies or take relief as provided in Clause b.

b. Relief

If the player elects to take relief, he shall proceed as follows:

(i) **Through the Green:** If the ball lies through the green, the point on the course nearest to where the ball lies shall be determined which (a) is not nearer the hole, (b) avoids interference by the condition, and (c) is not in a hazard or on a putting green. The player shall lift the ball and drop it without penalty within one club-length of the point thus determined on a part of the course which fulfils (a), (b) and (c) above.

(ii) **In a Hazard:** If the ball is in a hazard, the player shall lift and drop the ball either:

(a) Without penalty, in the hazard, as near as possible to the spot where the ball lay, but not nearer the hole, on a part of the course which affords maximum available relief from the condition; or

(b) Under penalty of one stroke, outside the hazard, keeping the point where the ball lay directly between the hole and the spot on which the ball is dropped, with no limit to how far behind the hazard the ball may be dropped. Exception: If a ball is in a water hazard, the player shall play the ball as it lies or proceed under 26-1.

(iii) **On the Putting Green:** If the ball lies on the putting green, the player shall lift the ball and place it without penalty in the nearest position to where it lay which affords maximum available relief from the condition, but not nearer the hole nor in a hazard.

c. Ball Lost Under Condition Covered by Rule 25-1

It is a question of fact whether a ball lost after having been struck toward a condition covered by Rule 25-1 is lost under such condition. In order to treat the ball as lost under such condition, there must be reasonable evidence to that effect. In the absence of such evidence, the ball must be treated as a lost ball and Rule 27 applies.

(i) **Outside a Hazard:** If a ball is lost outside a hazard under a condition covered by Rule 25-1, the player may take relief as follows: the point on the course nearest to where the ball last crossed the margin of the area shall be determined which (a) is not nearer the hole than where the ball last crossed the margin, (b) avoids interference by the condition and (c) is not in a hazard or on a putting green. He shall drop a ball without penalty within one club-length of the point thus determined on a part of

the course which fulfils (a), (b) and (c) above.

(ii) **In a Hazard:** If a ball is lost in a hazard under a condition covered by Rule 25-1, the player may drop a ball either:

(a) Without penalty, in the hazard as near as possible to the point at which the original ball last crossed the margin of the area, but not nearer the hole, on a part of the course which affords maximum available relief from the condition; or

(b) Under penalty of one stroke, outside the hazard, keeping the point at which the original ball last crossed the margin of the hazard directly between the hole and the spot on which the ball is dropped, with no limit to how far behind the hazard the ball may be dropped. Exception: If a ball is in a water hazard, the player shall play the ball as it lies or proceed under 26-1.

25-2. Embedded Ball

A ball embedded in its own pitch mark in the ground in any closely-mown area through the green may be lifted, cleaned and dropped, without penalty, as near as possible to the spot where it lay but not nearer the hole. The ball when dropped must first strike a part of the course through the green.

25-3. Wrong Putting Green

A player must not play a ball which lies on a putting green other than that of the hole being played. The ball must be lifted and the player must proceed as follows: The point on the course nearest to where the ball lies shall be determined which (a) is not nearer the hole and (b) is not in a hazard or on a putting green. The player shall lift the ball and drop it without penalty within one club-length of the point thus determined on a part of the course which fulfils (a) and (b) above.

Rule 26. Water Hazards

Water hazards (other than lateral water hazards) should be defined by yellow stakes or lines.

A 'lateral water hazard' is a water hazard or that part of a water hazard so situated that it is not possible or practicable to drop a ball behind the water hazard in accordance with Rule 26-1b. Lateral water hazards should be defined by red stakes or lines.

26-1. Ball in Water Hazard

It is a question of fact whether a ball lost after having been struck toward a water hazard is lost inside or outside the hazard. In order to treat the ball as lost in the hazard, there must be reasonable evidence that the ball lodged in it. In the absence of

such evidence, the ball must be treated as a lost ball and Rule 27 applies.

If a ball is in or is lost in a water hazard (whether the ball lies in water or not), the player may under penalty of one stroke:

a. Play a ball as nearly as possible at the spot from which the original ball was last played (see 20-5); or

b. Drop a ball behind the water hazard, keeping the point at which the original ball last crossed the margin of the water hazard directly between the hole and the spot on which the ball is dropped, with no limit to how far behind the water hazard the ball may be dropped; or

c. As additional options available only if the ball last crossed the margin of a lateral water hazard, drop a ball outside the water hazard within two club-lengths of and not nearer the hole than (i) the point where the original ball last crossed the margin of the water hazard or (ii) a point on the opposite margin of the water hazard equidistant from the hole.

26-2. Ball Played Within Water Hazard

a. Ball Comes to Rest in the Hazard

If a ball played from within a water hazard comes to rest in the same hazard after the stroke, the player may:

(i) proceed under Rule 26-1; or

(ii) under penalty of one stroke, play a ball as nearly as possible at the spot from which the last stroke from outside the hazard was played (see 20-5).

If the player proceeds under Rule 26-1a, he may elect not to play the dropped ball. If he so elects, he may:

(a) proceed under Rule 26-1b, adding the additional penalty of one stroke prescribed by that rule; or

(b) proceed under Rule 26-1c, if applicable, adding the additional penalty of one stroke prescribed by that rule; or

(c) add an additional penalty of one stroke and play a ball as nearly as possible at the spot from which the last stroke from outside the hazard was played (see 20-5).

b. Ball Lost or Unplayable Outside Hazard or Out of Bounds

If a ball played from within a water hazard is lost or declared unplayable outside the hazard or is out of bounds, the player, after taking a penalty of one stroke under Rule 27-1 or 28a, may:

(i) play a ball as nearly as possible at the spot in the hazard from which the original ball was last played (see 20-5); or

(ii) proceed under Rule 26-1b, or if applicable Rule 26-1c, by the

rule and using as the reference point the point where the original ball last crossed the margin of the hazard before it came to rest in the hazard; or

(iii) add an additional penalty of one stroke and play a ball as nearly as possible at the spot from which the last stroke from outside the hazard was played (see 20-5).

Rule 27. Ball Lost or Out of Bounds; Provisional Ball

If the original ball is lost in an immovable obstruction (24-2) or under a condition covered by Rule 25-1 (casual water, ground under repair and certain damage to the course), the player may proceed under the applicable rule. If the original ball is lost in a water hazard, the player shall proceed under Rule 26.

Definitions

A ball is 'lost' if:

a. It is not found or identified as his by the player within five minutes after the player's side or his or their caddies have begun to search for it; or

b. The player has put another ball into play under the rules, even though he may not have searched for the original ball; or

c. The player has played any stroke with a provisional ball from the place where the original ball is likely to be or from a point nearer the hole than that place, whereupon the provisional ball becomes ball in play.

27-1. Ball Lost or Out of Bounds

If a ball is lost outside a water hazard or is out of bounds, the player shall play a ball, under penalty of one stroke, as nearly as possible at the spot from which the original ball as last played (see 20-5).

27-2. Provisional Ball

a. Procedure

If a ball may be lost outside a water hazard or may be out of bounds, to save time the player may play another ball provisionally as nearly as possible at the spot from which the original ball was played (see 20-5). The player shall inform his opponent in match play or his marker or a fellow-competitor in stroke play that he intends to play a provisional ball, and he shall play it before he or his partner goes forward to search for the original ball. If he fails to do so and plays another ball, such ball is not a provisional ball and becomes the ball in play under penalty of stroke and distance (Rule 27-1); the original ball is deemed to be lost.

b. When Provisional Ball Becomes Ball in Play

The player may play a provisional ball until he reaches the place

➡ *page 204*

continued from page 203

where the original ball is likely to be. If he plays a stroke with the provisional ball from the place where the original ball is likely to be or from a point nearer the hole than that place, the original ball is deemed to be lost and the provisional ball becomes the ball in play under penalty of stroke and distance (Rule 27-1).

c. When Provisional Ball to Be Abandoned
If the original ball is neither lost outside a water hazard nor out of bounds, the player shall abandon the provisional ball and continue play with the original ball. If he fails to do so, any further strokes played with the provisional ball shall constitute playing a wrong ball and the provisions of Rule 15 shall apply.

Rule 28. Ball Unplayable
The player may declare his ball unplayable at any place on the course except when the ball is in a water hazard. The player is the sole judge as to whether his ball is unplayable.

If the player deems his ball to be unplayable, he shall, under penalty of one stroke:
a. Play a ball as nearly as possible at the spot from which the original ball was last played (see 20-5); or
b. Drop a ball within two club-lengths of the spot where the ball lay, but not nearer the hole; or
c. Drop a ball behind the point where the ball lay, keeping that point directly between the hole and the spot on which the ball is dropped, with no limit to how far behind that point the ball be dropped.

If the unplayable ball is in a bunker, the player may proceed under clause a, b or c. If he elects to proceed under clause b or c, a ball must be dropped in the bunker.

Rule 29. Threesomes and Foursomes
Definitions
Threesome: A match in which one plays against two, and each side plays one ball.

Foursome: A match in which two play against two, and each side plays one ball.

29-1 General
In a threesome or a foursome, during any stipulated round , the partners shall play alternately from the teeing grounds and alternately during the play of each hole. Penalty strokes do not affect the order of play.

29-2 Match Play
If a player plays when his partner should have played, his side shall lose the hole.

29-3 Stroke Play
If the partners play a stroke or strokes in incorrect order, such stroke or strokes shall be cancelled and the side shall incur a penalty of two strokes. The side shall correct the error by playing a ball in correct order as nearly as possible at the spot from which it first played in incorrect order (see Rule 20-5). If the side plays a stroke from the next teeing ground without first correcting the error or, in the case of the last hole of the round, leaves the putting green without declaring its intention to correct the error, the side shall be disqualified.

Rule 30, Three-Ball, Best-Ball and Four-Ball Match Play
Definitions
Three-Ball: A match play competition in which three play against one another, each playing his own ball. Each player is playing two distinct matches.

Best-Ball: A match in which one plays against the better ball of two or the best ball of three players.

Four-Ball: A match in which two play their better ball against the better ball of two other players.

30-1 Rules of Golf Apply
The Rules of Golf, so far as they are not at variance with the following special Rules, shall apply to three-ball, best-ball and four-ball matches.

30-2 Three-Ball Match Play
a. Ball at Rest Moved by an Opponent
Except as otherwise provided in the Rules, if the player's ball is touched or moved by an opponent, his caddie, or equipment other than during search, Rule 18-3b applies. That opponent shall incur a penalty stroke in his match with the player, but not in his match with the other opponent.

b. Ball Deflected or Stopped by an Opponent Accidentally
If a player's ball is accidentally deflected or stopped by an opponent, his caddie or equipment, no penalty shall be incurred. In his match with that opponent the player may play the ball as it lies or, before another stroke is played by either side, he may cancel the stroke and play a ball without penalty as nearly as possible at the spot from which the original ball was last played (see Rule 20-5). In his match with the other opponent, the ball shall be played as it lies.
Exception: Ball stroking person attending flagstick – see Rule 17-3b.

(Ball purposely deflected or stopped by opponent – see Rule 1 2).

30-3 Best-Ball and Four-Ball Match Play
a. Representation of Side
A side may be represented by one partner for all or any part of a match; all partners need not be present. An absent partner may join a match between holes, but not during play of a hole.
b. Maximum of Fourteen Clubs
The side shall be penalised for a breach of Rule 4-4 by any partner.
c. Order of Play
Balls belonging to the same side may be played in the order the side considers best.
d. Wrong Ball
If a player plays a stroke with a wrong ball except in a hazard, he shall be disqualified for that hole, but his partner incurs no penalty even if the wrong ball belongs to him. If the wrong ball belongs to another player, its owner shall place a ball on the spot from which the wrong ball was first played.
e. Disqualification of Side
(i) A side shall be disqualified for a breach of any of the following by any partner:
Rule 1-3; Rule 4-1, -2, -3; Rule 5-1 or -2; Rule 6-2a; Rule 6-4; Rule 6-7; Rule 14-3; Rule 6-3; Rule 6-8.
f. Effect of Other Penalties
If a player's breach of a Rule assists his partner's play or adversely affects his opponent, the partner incurs the applicable penalty in addition to any penalty incurred by the player.

In all other cases where a player incurs a penalty for breach of a Rule, the penalty shall not apply to his partner. Where the penalty is stated to be loss of hole, the effect shall be to disqualify the player for that hole.
g. Another Form of Match Played Concurrently
In a best-ball or four-ball match when another form of match is played concurrently, the above special Rules shall apply.

Rule 31. Four-Ball Stroke Play
In four-ball stroke play, two competitors play as partners, each playing his own ball. The lower score of the partners is the score for the hole. If one partner fails to complete the play of a hole, there is no penalty.
31-1. Rules of Golf Apply
The Rules of Golf, so far as they are not at variance with the following special Rules, shall apply to four-ball stroke play.
31-2. Representation of Side
A side may be represented by either partner for all or any part of a stipulated round; both partners need not be present. An absent competitor may join his partner between holes, but not during play of a hole.

31-3. Maximum of Fourteen Clubs
The side shall be penalized for a breach of Rule 4-4 by either partner.
31-4. Scoring
The marker is required to record for each hole only the gross score of whichever partner's score is to count. The gross scores to count must be individually identifiable; otherwise the side shall be disqualified. Only one of the partners need be responsible for complying with Rule 6-6b. (Wrong score – see Rule 31-7a.)
31-5. Order of Play
Balls belonging to the same side may be played in the order the side considers best.
31-6 Wrong Ball
If a competitor plays a stroke or strokes with a wrong ball except in a hazard, he shall add two penalty strokes to his score for the hole and shall then play the correct ball. His partner incurs no penalty even if the wrong ball belongs to him.

If the wrong ball belongs to another competitor, its owner shall place a ball on the spot from which the wrong ball was first played.
31-7. Disqualification Penalties
a. Breach by One Partner
A side shall be disqualified from the competition for a breach of any of the following by either partner:
Rule 1-3; Rule 3-4; Rule 4-1, -2 or -3; Rule 5-1 or -2; Rule 6-2b; Rule 6-4; Rule 6-6b;Rule 6-6d; Rule 6-7; Rule 7-1; Rule 14-3; Rule 31-4.
(b) Breach by Both Partners
A side shall be disqualified:
(i) for a breach by both partners of Rule 6-3 (Time of Starting and Groups) or Rule 6-8 (Discontinuance of Play) or
(ii) if, at the same hole, each partner is in breach of a Rule the penalty for which is disqualification from the competition or for a hole.
c. For the Hole Only
In all other cases where a breach of a Rule would entail disqualification, the competitor shall be disqualified only for the hole at which the breach occurred.
31-8. Effect of Other Penalties
If a competitor's breach of a Rule assists his partner's play, the partner incurs the applicable penalty in addition to any penalty incurred by the competitor.

In all other cases where a competitor incurs a penalty for breach of a Rule, the penalty shall not apply to his partner.

Rule 32. Bogey, Par and Stableford Competitions
32-1. Conditions
Bogey, par and Stableford

competitions are forms of stroke competition in which play is against a fixed score at each hole. Generally the Rules for stroke play apply, but there are some special conditions. For details, see *The Rules of Golf.*

Rule 33. The Committee
33-1. Conditions; Waiving Rule
The Committee shall lay down the conditions under which a competition is to be played.

The Committee has no power to waive a Rule of Golf.

Certain special rules governing stroke play are so substantially different from those governing match play that combining the two forms of play is not practicable and is not permitted. The results of matches played and the scores returned in these circumstances shall not be accepted.

In stroke play the Committee may limit a referee's duties.
33-2. The Course
a. Defining Bounds and Margins
The Committee shall define accurately:

(i) the course and out of bounds.

(ii) the margins of water hazards and lateral water hazards.

(iii) ground under repair, and

(iv) obstructions and integral parts of the course.
b. New Holes
New holes should be made on the day on which a stroke competition begins and at such other times as the Committee considers necessary, provided all competitors in a single round play with each hole cut in the same position.

Exception: When it is impossible for a damaged hole to be repaired so that it conforms with the Definition, the Committee may make a new hole in a nearby similar position.

Note: Where a single round is to be played on more than one day, the Committee may provide in the conditions of a competition that the holes and teeing grounds may be differently situated on each day of the competition, provided that, on any one day, all competitors play with each hole and each teeing ground in the same position.
c. Practice Ground
Where there is no practice ground available outside the area of a competition course, the Committee should lay down the area on which players may practise on any day of a competition, if it is practicable to do so. On any day a stroke competition, the Committee should not normally permit practice on or to a putting green

or from a hazard of the competition course.
(d) Course Unplayable
If the Committee or its authorized representative considers that for any reason the course is not in a playable condition or that there are circumstances which render the proper playing of the game impossible, it may, in match play or stroke play, order a temporary suspension of play or, in stroke play, declare play null and void and cancel all scores for the round in question. When play has been temporarily suspended, it shall be resumed from where it was discontinued, even though resumption occurs on a subsequent day. When a round is cancelled, all penalties incurred in that round are cancelled. (Procedure in discontinuing play – see Rule 6-8.)
33-3. Times of Starting and Groups
The Committee shall lay down the times of starting and, in stroke play, arrange the groups in which competitors shall play.

When a match play competition is played over an extended period, the Committee shall lay down the limit of time within which each round shall be completed. When players are allowed to arrange the date of their match within these limits, the Committee should announce that the match must be played at a stated time on the last day of the period unless the players agree to a prior date.
33-4. Handicap Stroke Table
The Committee shall publish a table indicating the order of holes at which handicap strokes are to be given or received.
33-5 Score Card
In stroke play, the Committee shall issue for each competitor a score card containing the date and the competitor's name or, in foursome or four-ball stroke play, the competitors' names.

In stroke play, the Committee is responsible for the addition of scores and application of the handicap recorded on the card.

In four-ball stroke play, the Committee is responsible for recording the better-ball score for each hole and in the process applying the handicaps recorded on the card, and adding the better-ball scores.

In bogey, par and Stableford competitions, the Committee is responsible for applying the handicap recorded on the card and determining the result of each hole and the overall result or points total.
33-6. Decision of Ties
The Committee shall announce the manner, day and time for the decision of a halved match or of a tie, whether played on level terms

or under handicap.

A halved match shall not be decided by stroke play. A tie in stroke play shall not be decided by a match.
33-7. Disqualification Penalty: Committee Discretion
A penalty of disqualification may in exceptional individual cases be waived, modified or imposed if the Committee considers such action warranted.

Any penalty less than disqualification shall not be waived or modified.
33-8. Local Rules
a. Policy
The Committee may make and publish Local Rules for abnormal conditions if they are consistent with the policy of the Governing Authority for the country concerned as set forth in Appendix I to these Rules.
b. Waiving Penalty
A penalty imposed by a Rule of Golf shall not be waived by a Local Rule.

Rule 34. Disputes and Decisions
34-1. Claims and Penalties
a. Match Play
In match play, if a claim is lodged with the Committee under Rule 2-5, a decision should be given as soon as possible so that the state of the match may, if necessary, be adjusted.

If a claim is not made within the time limit provided by Rule 2-5, it shall not be considered unless it is based on facts previously unknown to the player making the claim and the player making the claim had been given wrong information (Rules 6-2a and 9) by an opponent. In any case, no later claim shall be considered after the result of the match has been officially announced, unless the Committee is satisfied that the opponent knew he was giving wrong information.

There is no time limit on applying the disqualification penalty for a breach of Rule 1-3.
b. Stroke Play
Except as provided below, in stroke play, no penalty shall be rescinded, modified or imposed after the competition has closed. A competition is deemed to have closed when the result has been officially announced, or in stroke play qualifying followed by match play, when the player has teed off in his first match.
Exceptions: A penalty of disqualification shall be imposed after the competition has closed if a competitor:

(i) was in breach of Rule 1-3 (Agreement to Waive Rules); or

(ii) returned a score card on

which he had recorded a handicap which, before the competition closed, he knew was higher than that to which he was entitled, and this affected the number of strokes received (Rule 6-2b); or

(iii) returned a score for any hole lower than actually taken (Rule 6-6d) for any reason other than failure to include a penalty which, before the competition closed, he did not know he had incurred; or

(iv) knew, before the competition closed, that he had been in breach of any other Rule for which the prescribed penalty is disqualification.
32-2. Referee's Decision
If a referee has been appointed by the Committee, his decision shall be final.
34-3. Committee's Decision
In the absence of a referee, any dispute or doubtful point on the Rules shall be referred to the Committee, whose decision shall be final.

If the Committee cannot come to a decision, it shall refer the dispute or doubtful point to the Rules of Golf Committee of the Royal and Ancient Golf Club of St. Andrews, whose decision shall be final.

If the dispute or doubtful point has not been referred to the Rules of Golf Committee, the player or players have the right to refer an agreed statement through the Secretary of the Club to the Rules of Golf Committee for an opinion as to the correctness of the decision given. The reply will be sent to the Secretary of the Club or Clubs concerned.

If play is conducted other than in accordance with the Rules of Golf, the Rules of Golf Committee will not give a decision on any question.

The rest of the rule book consists of: **Appendix I** Local Rules; **Appendix II** Design of Clubs; **Appendix III** The Ball; **Rules of Amateur Status** (defines amateur status); and **Royal & Ancient Policy On Gambling.**

These rules are reprinted by permission of the copyright holders, the Royal and Ancient Gold Club of St Andrews. Free copies of the rules are available from the sponsors of *The Rules of Golf,* Royal Sun Alliance, Level One, 70 Price Street, Birkenhead, Wirral, Cheshire L41 3Q2.

Boxing
Essentials

The rules published by the Marquess of Queensberry in 1867 form the basis of the modern sport – both professional and amateur. The latter, which we present here, are a much stricter, more safety-conscious code. Players must wear headguards and bouts are limited to five rounds, as opposed to the maximum of twelve in professional contests.

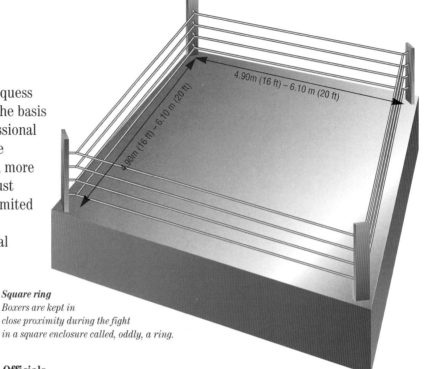

4.90m (16 ft) – 6.10 m (20 ft)

4.90m (16 ft) – 6.10 m (20 ft)

The ring

Minimum 4.90 m (16 ft) square, maximum 6.10 m (20 ft) square. Fitted with four corner posts and a floor covered with felt, rubber or other approved material. Three or four ropes of thickness 3–5 cm (approx 1.5 in) are tightly drawn from the corner posts at 40 cm (1.3 ft), 80 cm (2.6 ft)and 1.30 m (4.3 ft) high.

Square ring
Boxers are kept in close proximity during the fight in a square enclosure called, oddly, a ring.

Officials

A referee (in the ring), five judges and a timekeeper.

Dress

Light boots or shoes, gloves (weighing 284 g (10 oz), socks, shorts and vests. (For top level competitions, boxers must wear either a red or a blue singlet, depending on the colour of their corner. Soft surgical bandaging only may be worn underneath gloves for protection.

Harmful or objectionable products may not be worn. Beards are forbidden and long hair must be always covered by the headguard.

Boxing gloves

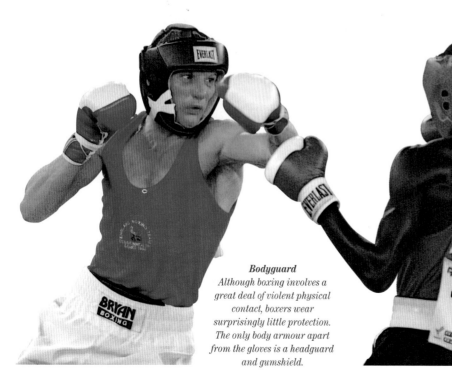

Bodyguard
Although boxing involves a great deal of violent physical contact, boxers wear surprisingly little protection. The only body armour apart from the gloves is a headguard and gumshield.

Players

Two players. Each boxer is also allowed two 'seconds'. (Only one may enter the ring.) The seconds service the boxer, clear the ring of towels, buckets and so on prior to a round and may retire their boxer or throw the towel into the ring if they consider he is having difficulties.

The international weight classifications are as follows:

Light Fly:
Up to 48 kg (106 lb).
Fly:
Over 48 kg and up to 51 kg (112 lb).
Bantam:
Over 51 kg and up to 54 kg (119 lb).
Feather:
Over 54 kg and up to 57 kg (126 lb).
Light:
Over 57 kg and up to 60 kg (132 lb).
Light Welter:
Over 60 kg and up to 63.5 kg (140 lb).

Welter:
Over 63.5 kg and up to 67 kg (148 lb).
Light Middle:
Over 67 kg and up to 71 kg (157 lb).
Middle:
Over 71 kg and up to 75 kg (165 lb).
Light Heavy:
Over 75 kg and up to 81 kg.
Heavy:
Over 81 kg and up to 91 kg (179 lb).
Super Heavy:
Over 91 kg (201 lb).

Contestants must weigh in, stripped, on the day of a competition.

HOW TO PLAY

Two opponents score points with blows to one another, using the knuckle part of their gloves. Hits must land on the front or sides of the head, or anywhere on the body above the belt.

Starting

At the start of the bout, everyone, apart from the referee and the two boxers, must leave the ring. The opponents shake hands and then wait in their separate corners until the timekeeper announces the round and strikes the bell or gong to start it.

How to win

A boxer can win in a number of different ways. The most easily recognized is the knockout, although this occurs less frequently in amateur boxing than in professional contests. Otherwise, a bout is won on points. An electric scoring system is now used at all AIBA (Association Internationale de Boxe Amateur) competitions. Judges feed correct hits into a computer by pressing the relevant buttons and a final result is calculated automatically. The winner is the boxer who has scored the most correct hits, the final result being based only on blows that have been fed in simultaneously by at least three of the five judges. In the case of a boxer being disqualified or outclassed (unable to continue in the opinion of the referee), his opponent wins the bout.
See Rule XVI, Decisions (page 208).

The referee raises the hand of the winning boxer at the end of the bout.

KEY RULES

Bouts consist of five rounds of two minutes each, with a one minute interval between rounds. (Some international contests may consist of three or four rounds of three minutes each, or six rounds of two minutes each.)

• When a boxer knocks his opponent to the floor he is sent to a corner by the referee, where he must remain while the referee counts out ten seconds aloud, indicating each second with his hand to the boxer on the floor. If this boxer fails to resume boxing after ten seconds have passed and the referee has given the command "Box", a knockout is declared.
See Rule XIX, Down (page 209).

• Boxers must not hit below the belt, on the back of the neck or in the kidneys. They must not hit with an open glove nor hit an opponent who is down or in the act of rising. When a referee breaks up a clinch with the command "Break", both boxers must cease boxing and step back one pace before continuing. Failure to obey any of these rules is a foul and will result in a warning. A third warning brings automatic disqualification.
See Rule XVIII, Fouls (page 209).

SKILLS

Sharp reflexes, speed and the ability to concentrate and commit to two minutes of intense, one-on-one combat. Boxers train to be able to score maximum points with well-placed hits to target areas, while also dodging and blocking the blows of an opponent.

The *jab* is a short, sharp punch, the *uppercut* is delivered from below and aimed at the body or the lower part of the face and the *hook* is a heavy blow, usually to the head. Combination punching makes use of all these in varying order, usually in rapid

Jab on the jaw
The most common blow in boxing is the jab – a short, sharp punch, often aimed at the jaw, one of a boxer's weak points. Here the boxer is a 'south-paw' who leads with his right foot and also his right arm. This unortho-dox combination can be tricky for opponents to deal with.

The 'champ'
There is no world body for professional boxing, and there may be four 'world champions' at a particular weight. Above are professional boxers – hence no headgear.

THE RULES

RULE I: The Ring
See The Ring (page 206)
RULE II: Gloves
Rule III: Bandages
Rule IV: Dress
See Dress (page 206)
Rule V: Ring Equipment
Rule VI: Medical Examination and Weigh-in For International Competitions

RULE VII: Draws and Byes
A. The Draw. The draw shall take place after the medical examination and weigh-in. The draw must take place in the presence of official representatives of the teams concerned, and must ensure, where practicable, that no competitor shall box twice in the competition before all other competitors have boxed at least once. In special situations, the Executive Committee of A.I.B.A. has the right to depart from this rule. The draw shall proceed first for the boxers to box in the first series and then for the byes. However, no boxer may be awarded a World or Continental Championship or Olympic Games Medal without having boxed.

B. Byes. In competitions where there are more than four competitors, a sufficient number of byes shall be drawn in the first series to reduce the number of competitors in the second series to four, eight, 16 or 32. Competitors drawing a bye in the first series shall be the first to box in the second series. If there is an odd number of byes, the boxer who draws the last bye will compete in the second series against the winner of the first bout in the first series. Where the number of byes is even, the boxers drawing byes shall box the first bouts in the second series in the order in which they are drawn. No medal shall be awarded to a boxer who has not boxed at least once.

C. Order of the Programme. In World Championships, the Olympic Games, and Continental Championships, the order of the program should be arranged as far as practicable in the order of weights so that in each series the lightest weights will be run off first and thence in order of weights up to the heaviest weights in that series followed by the lightest weights in the next series, and so on.

RULE VIII: ROUNDS
See Key Rules (page 207).

RULES IX – XV
Deal with the appointment and duties of the seconds, referee, judges, jury and timekeeper.

Winning
Most contests are decided on points – that is, on points awarded to each boxer by the judges up to the end of the contest. Only rarely is a bout decided by a knockout.

RULE XVI: Decisions
A. Types. Decisions shall be as follows:

1. Win on Points. At the end of a contest, the boxer who has been awarded the decision by a majority of the judges shall be declared the winner. If both boxers are injured, or are knocked-out simultaneously, and cannot continue the contest, the judges shall record the points gained by each boxer up to its termination, and the boxer who was leading on points up to termination, or the actual end of the contest, shall be declared the winner.

2. Win by Retirement. If a boxer retires voluntarily owing to injury or other cause, or if he fails to resume boxing immediately after the rest between rounds, his opponent shall be declared the winner.

3. Win by Referee Stopping Contest:

a. Outclassed. **RSC** is a term used to stop a bout when a boxer is outclassed or is unfit to continue. If a boxer, in the opinion of the referee is being outclassed or is receiving excessive punishment, the bout shall be stopped and his opponent declared the winner.

b. Injury. If a boxer, in the opinion of the referee, is unfit to continue because of injury sustained from correct blows or other action or is incapacitated for any other physical reasons, the bout shall be stopped and his opponent declared the winner. The right to make this decision rests with the referee, who may consult the doctor. Having consulted the doctor, the referee must follow his advice. It is recommended that the referee checks the other boxer for injury also before he makes this decision. The Ringside Medical Officer has the right to request that the bout be suspended if he thinks, for medical reasons, the bout should not be allowed to continue. He must first inform the Jury President and the latter shall inform the referee that the bout shall be suspended. The suspension shall last a maximum of one minute by the referee for examining the fitness of a boxer by the Medical Officer.

4. Win by Disqualification. If a boxer is disqualified, his opponent shall be declared the winner. If both boxers are disqualified, the decision shall be announced accordingly.

5. Win by Knockout. If a boxer is 'down' and fails to resume boxing within ten seconds, his opponent shall be declared the winner by a knockout.

6. No Contest. A bout may be terminated by the referee inside the scheduled distance owing to a material happening outside the responsibility of the boxers, or the control of the referee, such as the ring becoming damaged, the failure of the lighting supply, exceptional weather conditions etc. In such circumstances, the bout shall be declared "no contest" and in the case of Championships, the jury shall decide the necessary further action.

7. Win by Walkover. Where a boxer presents himself in the

ring fully attired for boxing and his opponent fails to appear after his name has been called out by the public address system, the bell sounded and a maximum period of three minutes has elapsed, the referee shall declare the first boxer to be the winner by a 'Walkover'. He shall first inform the judges to mark their papers accordingly, collect them and then summons the boxer to the centre of the ring and after the decision is announced, raise his hand as winner.

8. A Draw (Dual Matches Only). Two clubs or two Nations in a friendly dual match may agree to a draw decision, when the majority of judges scored the competition equally. Likewise, an injury in the first round may result in a draw in dual matches.

9. Incidents in the Ring Outside the Control of the Referee.

a) If something happens that does not allow the bout to continue within one minute after the bell has rung for the beginning of the first or second round (e.g. power failure), the bout shall be stopped and the boxers will box again in the last bout of the same session.

b) If the incident occurs in the third round of a bout, the contest shall be terminated and the judges are asked to give a decision as to the winner of the bout.

c) If the incident occurs in the last three bouts of a session on the programme, the boxers shall be asked to box the first bout on the programme of the next session. The boxers shall be weighed and medically examined again for that bout.

RULE XVII: Awarding of Points
See How to Win (page 207).

RULE XVIII: Fouls
A. Cautions, Warnings, Disqualifications. The competitor who does not obey the instructions of the referee, acts against the boxing rules, boxes in any unsportsmanlike manner, or commits fouls, can, at the discretion of the referee, be cautioned, warned or disqualified without warning. A referee may, without stopping a contest, caution a boxer at some safe opportunity. If he intends to warn a boxer, he shall stop the contest, and will demonstrate the infringement. He will then point to the boxer and to each of the five judges. A referee having once administered a warning for a particular foul, e.g. holding, cannot issue a caution for the same type of offence. A third

Out for the count
When the boxer is on the canvas or outside the ropes the referee will count the seconds. If the boxer is not back on his feet by the count of ten, the bout ends as a knockout.

caution for the same type of foul will mandatorily require a warning to be issued. Only three warnings may be given to the same boxer in one contest. The third warning brings automatic disqualification.

B. Types of Fouls. The following are fouls:

1. Hitting below the belt, holding, tripping, kicking, and butting with foot or knee.

2. Hits or blows with head, shoulder, forearm, elbow, throttling of the opponent, pressing with arm or elbow in opponent's face, pressing the head of the opponent back over the ropes.

3. Hitting with open glove, the inside of the glove, wrist or side of the hand.

4. Hits landing on the back of the opponent and especially any blow on the back of the neck or head and kidney punch.

5. Pivot blows.

6. Attack whilst holding the ropes or making any unfair use of the ropes.

7. Lying on, wrestling and throwing in the clinch.

8. An attack on an opponent who is down or who is in the act of rising.

9. Holding.

10. Holding and hitting or pulling and hitting.

11. Holding, or locking, of the opponent's arm or head, or pushing an arm underneath the arm of the opponent.

12. Ducking below the belt of the opponent in a manner dangerous to his opponent.

13. Completely passive defence by means of double cover and intentionally falling to avoid a blow.

14. Useless, aggressive or offensive utterances during the round.

15. Not stepping back when ordered to break.

16. Attempting to strike the opponent immediately after the referee has ordered "Break" and before taking a step back.

17. Assaulting or behaving in an aggressive manner towards a referee at any time.

18. Spitting out gumshield (teeth protector).

19. Keeping the advanced hand straight in order to obstruct the opponent's vision.

C. Seconds. Each boxer is responsible in the same way for his second.

D. Referee Consults judges. If a referee has any reason to believe that a foul has been committed which he himself has not seen, he may consult the judges.

RULE XIX: Down
A. Definition. A boxer is considered 'down':

1. if he touches the floor with any part of his body other than his feet as the result of a blow or series of blows, or

2. if he hangs helplessly on the ropes as a result of a blow or series of blows, or

3. if he is outside or partly outside the ropes as the result of a blow or series of blows, or

4. if following a hard punch he has not fallen and is not lying on the ropes, but is in a semi-conscious state and cannot, in the opinion of the referee, continue the bout.

B. The Count. In the case of a knock-down, the referee shall immediately begin to count the seconds. When a boxer is 'down' the referee shall count aloud from one to ten with intervals of a second between the numbers, and shall indicate each second with his hand in such a manner that the boxer who has been knocked down may be aware of the count. Before the number "one" is counted, an interval of one second must have elapsed from the time when the boxer has fallen to the floor, and the time of announcing "one". If the opponent should not go to the neutral corner on the command of the referee, the referee shall stop counting until the opponent has done so. The counting shall be then continued where it has been interrupted.

C. Opponent's Responsibilities. If a boxer is down, his opponent must at once go to the neutral corner as designated by the referee. He may only continue against the opponent who is knocked down after the latter has got up and on the command "Box" of the referee.

D. Mandatory Eight Count. When a boxer is 'down' as the result of a blow, the bout shall not be continued until the referee has reached the count of eight, even if the boxer is ready to continue before then.

E. The Knockout. After the referee has said "ten" and the word "out", the bout ends and shall be decided as a 'knock-out'. (Points F – J of RULE XIX give further details of the Down Rule.)

These rules are abridged and reprinted here by permission of the International Amateur Boxing Association (AIBA). A complete copy of the Rules of Boxing, including Rules XX to XXVIII and Appendices I – VII, can be obtained from the Association.

GREY AREA

Q. Can a medical officer stop a fight for medical reasons?

A. No. A new rule, XVI, A 3b, adopted in 1994, stated that the medical officer has the right to request that the bout be suspended for medical reasons. Some people interpret this rule as saying that the medical officer has the right to stop the bout. In fact the rule goes on to state that he must inform the Jury President who in turn instructs the referee to stop the bout; he cannot stop it himself.

Karate
Essentials

Karate translates from Japanese as 'empty hand' and is a form of unarmed self-defence which first evolved during the 16th Century on the island of Okinawa. Denied the right to carry weapons by their overlords, the Okinawans secretly developed a system of combat which relied on the power of their hands and feet. The sparring form of karate involving two opponents in combat, delivering kicks, punches or blocking one another's blows, is called Kumite. Another form, using a set of movements and techniques as if in combat with an imaginary opponent, is called Kata. A Karate tournament may comprise Kumite and/or Kata competitions.

The competition area

A flat, matted area, 8 m (26 ft) square, which may be elevated to a height of up to 1 m (3 ft) above the floor. A referee's line, 0.5m (1½ ft) long, is drawn 2 m (3¼ ft) from the centre of the area and two lines, each 1 m long, are drawn at right angles to this and 1.5 m (5 ft) from the centre. These are for positioning the competitors. A line is drawn 1 m (3 ft) on the inside of the competition area and the area enclosed by it may be in a different colour.

1 m

Contestant

3 m

2 m

Contestant

Referee

Competition area 8m x 8 m

Safety area must extend 10 m outside competition area

Players

Two contestants. The Kumite competition can be divided into team and individual matches. Each team must have an odd number of contestants. Individual matches are divided further into weight divisions and open category and each weight division is divided into bouts between opposing pairs of team members.

Karate kids

Karate has become very popular with young children inspired by movies such as The Karate Kid.

Dress

A white, unmarked gi, comprising jacket (at least hip length) and trousers (must cover at least two-thirds of the shin). One contestant wears a red belt, the other a white belt. Mitts and gumshields are compulsory and boxes and soft shin pads may also be worn. Shin/instep protectors are forbidden.

To avoid injury, fingernails must be kept short and contestants must not wear glasses or any other potentially dangerous objects.

Degrees of achievement are recognized by the colour of a contestant's belt – the highest being the black belt (or Dan) which, in itself, is divided into ten grades of proficiency.

Side kick
One of the most powerful strokes in karate is the 'yoko-geri', here used as an attacking move. The yoko-geri can either be a thrust kick in which the foot travels in essentially a straight line, or a snap kick where the foot travels up in an arc.

Officials

One referee (shushin), two judges (fukushin) and one arbitrator (kansa). Timekeepers, caller-announcers and record-keepers facilitate the operation of matches.

HOW TO PLAY

Two contestants meet on the square mat. Each tries to score points (or half points) by attacking particular areas of their opponent's body. Physical contact is never excessive and certain parts of the body are out of bounds.

Starting

The two opponents take their place on the mat and, facing each other, with their feet touching their starting lines, bow formally. When they are ready, the referee announces "Shobu sanbon hajime!" to start the bout.

How to win

Contestants score either full points (ippon) or half points (waza-ari). A half point is awarded for a technique which is not quite worthy of an ippon; for example, it may have lacked precision or conviction in its delivery. The first contestant to gain sanbon (three points – whether they are comprised of three ippons or six waza-ari or a combination of both) wins the bout. Contestants may also win the bout if their opponent is given a hansoku (for a foul), a shikkaku (disqualification) or a kiken (if he is absent, withdraws or is withdrawn).

GREY AREA

Scoring in karate depends on the judges' subjective view of what happens in a bout. They must make a skilled assessment of a technique, considering the following criteria:
• Would the technique have worked in real combat?
• If so, was it delivered on time?
• If two opponents seem to have delivered a technique almost simultaneously, which was the first to do so and should therefore score?
• In this way, scoring depends very much on the personal interpretation of events by a judge.

KEY RULES

• A karate bout is three minutes long for senior male contestants and two minutes long for women and junior bouts. A warning buzzer sounds 30 seconds before the end of a bout.

• Each time a contestant scores, the referee calls "yame!" and the clock is stopped. The referee uses hand signals to indicate the points awarded and the fighting then resumes with the call "tsukete hajime!".
See Article 13, Starting, Suspending and Ending of Matches (page 213).

• For the sake of safety, contestants may only attack certain target areas on the body. These include the head, face, neck, abdomen, chest, back (excluding shoulders) and side. They must not attack the throat, groin, joints or instep. Nor must excessive force be used, especially in attacks to the head and neck. All techniques must be extremely controlled.
See Article 8, Prohibited Behaviour (page 212).

• Scoring is based on the quality of a technique. A blow must have good form. It must be made with a good attitude, a good sense of timing and from the correct distance. Judges take all these things, and more, into account when awarding points.
See Article 6, Scoring (page 212).

• Penalty points may be awarded to an opponent for misconduct. The scale of penalties is given in *Article 9, Penalties (page 212).*

SKILLS AND TACTICS

Years of hard work and self-discipline are required to acquire a black belt. Speed, technique and strength are the key components of karate expertise. The beginner must first acquire the basic chops, punches, kicks and blocking techniques. The next step is to learn a series of combinations of these basic techniques.

Overall fitness is crucial, but warming up and stretching exercises prior to any karate practice are essential in order to avoid injury. Deep-breathing techniques are also an important part of the karate attack.

The key to success in competition is a finely-tuned control over the delivery of kicks and punches as well as a keen sense of timing, alertness and the ability to surprise.

In focus
Karate is a very elaborate discipline and it is practised in three distinct ways – Kata, Kumite and Kihon – and involves performing set drills over and over again with the emphasis on absolute perfection. In all kinds of practise a number of different elements are essential: 'kime' which is about achieving a mental focus of power; 'kokyu' which is breath control; and 'zanshin', which is an almost meditative state of total awareness.

KUMITE KARATE THE RULES

This is an abridged version of the official Rules of Karate Competition.

Article 1: Competition Area
See The Competition area (page 210).

Article 2: Official Dress
See Dress (page 210).

Article 3: Organization of Kumite Competitions

Article 4: The Referee Panel

Article 5: Duration of Bout
See Key rules (page 211).

Article 6: Scoring

6.1 The result of a bout is determined by either contestant scoring three ippons, 6 waza-ari, or a combination of the two totalling sanbon, or obtaining a decision, or by a hansoku, shikkaku, or kiken imposed against a contestant.

6.2 It must be noted that an Ippon is worth two waza-ari.

6.3 An ippon is awarded on the basis of the following:

6.3.1 A scoring technique counts as an ippon when it is performed according to the following criteria to a scoring area.

6.3.1.1 Good form.

6.3.1.2 Correct attitude.

6.3.1.3 Vigorous application.

6.3.1.4 Zanshin (perfect finish).

6.3.1.5 Proper timing.

6.3.1.6 Correct distance.

6.4 An ippon may also be awarded for techniques deficient in one of the above criteria but which conform to the following schedule:

6.4.1 jodan kicks or other technically difficult techniques.

6.4.2 Deflecting an attack and scoring to the unguarded back of the opponent.

6.4.3 Sweeping or throwing followed by a scoring technique.

6.4.4 Delivering a combination technique, the individual components of which each score in their own right.

6.4.5 Successfully scoring at the precise moment the opponent attacks.

6.5 A waza-ari is awarded for a technique almost comparable to that needed to score ippon. The refereeing panel must look for ippons in the first instance and only award a waza-ari in the

second instance.

6.6 A victory over an opponent who has been given a hansoku or shikkaku will be worth sanbon (3 full points or ippons). If a contestant is absent, withdraws, or is withdrawn, the opponent will be credited with a win by kiken (sanbon, or three ippons).

6.7 Attacks are limited to the following areas:

6.7.1 Head.

6.7.2 Face.

6.7.3 Neck.

6.7.4 Abdomen.

6.7.5 Chest.

6.7.6 Back (but excluding shoulders).

6.7.7 Side.

6.8 An effective technique delivered at the same time that the end of the bout is signalled, is considered valid. An attack, even if effective, delivered after an order to suspend or stop the bout shall not be scored and may result in a penalty being imposed on the offender.

6.9 No technique, even if technically correct, will be scored if it is delivered when the two contestants are outside the competition area. However, if one of the opponents delivers an effective technique while still inside the competition area and before the referee calls "yame", the technique will be scored.

6.10 Simultaneous effective scoring techniques delivered by both contestants the one on the other, shall not score.

Article 7: Criteria for Decision

7.1 In the absence of a sanbon score, or of a defeat caused by kiken, hansoku, or a shikkaku during the bout, a decision is taken on the basis of the following considerations:

7.1.1 Whether there have been any ippons or waza-ari awarded.

7.1.2 The attitude, fighting spirit or strength demonstrated by the contestants.

7.1.3 The superiority of tactics and techniques.

7.2 In individual category where there is no score superiority, then the following procedure will be followed:

7.2.1 If, at the end of a bout, the two contestants have no score, the winning decision shall be given by hantei (judgement).

7.2.2 If, at the end of a bout, the two contestants have scored equally, the decision for victory shall be given by hantei.

7.2.3 If, at the end of a bout, neither contestant has established a superiority, then

the decision for the bout shall be a draw ('hikiwake') and encho-sen (an extension) should be announced.

7.2.4 A penalty or warning incurred in the bout will be carried forward to the encho-sen.

7.3 In team competition the winning team is the one with the most bout victories.

7.4 If two teams have the same number of victories, the winner is the one whose contestants have scored the most points, taking both winning and losing fights into account.

7.5 If two teams have the same number of victories and scores, a deciding bout must be held between representatives of the two teams. In the event of a continuing tie, there is an extension ('encho-sen'). The first contestant to score ippon or waza-ari is declared the winner.

7.6 If there is no decision after a bout of an individual match, an extension ('encho-sen') will be fought. In the event of a tied encho-sen, the majority decision of the panel will be announced by the referee.

Article 8: Prohibited Behaviour

8.1 The following are forbidden:

8.1.1 Techniques which make contact with the throat.

8.1.2 Techniques which make excessive contact, having regard to the scoring area attacked. All techniques must be controlled. Any techniques which impacts the head, face or neck and results in visible injury must be penalized, unless caused by the recipient.

8.1.3 Attacks to the groin, joints, or instep.

8.1.4 Attacks to the face with open hand techniques ('teisho' or 'nukite').

8.1.5 Dangerous throws which by their nature preclude or prejudice the opponent's ability to land with safety.

8.1.6 Techniques which by their nature, cannot be controlled for the safety of the opponent.

8.1.7 Direct attacks to arms or legs.

8.1.8 Repeated exits from the competition area (jogai), or movements which waste too much time. Jogai relates to a situation where a contestant's body, or part thereof touches the floor outside of the area. An exception is when the contestant is actually pushed or thrown from the area by his opponent.

8.1.9 Wrestling, pushing or

seizing without an immediate technique.

8.1.10 mubobi is the term used to describe a situation where one or both contestants display a lack of regard for his, or their own safety.

8.1.11 Feigning of injury to gain advantage.

8.1.12 Any discourteous behaviour from a member of an official delegation can earn the disqualification of the offender or the entire team delegation from the tournament.

Article 9: Penalties

9.1 The following scale of penalties shall operate.

9.1 Atenai Yoni: may be imposed for intended minor infractions or for the first (Warning) instance of a minor infraction.

9.2 Keikoku: this is a penalty in which waza-ari is added to the opponent's score. Keikoku is imposed for minor infractions for which a warning has previously been given in that bout, or for infractions not sufficiently serious to merit hansoku-chui.

9.3 Hansoku-chui: this is a penalty in which ippon is added to the opponent's score. Hansoku-chui is usually imposed for infractions for which a Keikoku has previously been given in that bout.

9.4 Hansoku: this is imposed following a very serious infraction. It results in the opponent's score being raised to sanbon. Hansoku is also invoked when the number of hansoku-chuis and keikokus imposed raise the opponent's score to sanbon.

9.5 Shikkaku: this is a disqualification from the actual tournament, competition, or match. The opponent's score is raised to sanbon. In order to define the limit of shikkaku, the referee council must be consulted. Shikkaku may be invoked when a contestant commits an act which harms the prestige and honour of karate-do and when other actions are considered to violate the rules of the tournament.

Article 10: Injuries and Accidents in Competition

10.1 Kiken or forfeiture is the decision given when a contestant or contestants are unable to continue, abandon the bout, or are withdrawn on the order of the referee. The grounds for abandonment may include injury not ascribable to the opponent's actions.

10.2 If two contestants injure

each other at the same time or are suffering from the effects of previously incurred injury and are declared by the tournament doctor to be unable to continue, the bout is awarded to the contestant who has amassed the most points score at that time. If the points score is equal, than a decision (hantei) will decide the outcome of the bout.

10.3 An injured contestant who has been declared unfit to fight by the tournament doctor cannot fight again in that competition.

10.4 An injured contestant who wins a bout through disqualification due to injury is not allowed to fight again in the competition without permission from the doctor. If he is injured, he may win a second bout by disqualification but is immediately withdrawn from further kumite competition in that tournament.

10.5 When a contestant is injured, the referee shall at once halt the bout and call the doctor. The doctor is authorized to diagnose and treat injury only.

10.6 Any competitor who falls, is thrown, or knocked down, and does not fully regain his feet within ten seconds, is considered unfit to continue fighting and will be automatically withdrawn from the tournament.

Article 11: Protest

11.1 No one may protest about a judgement to the members of the refereeing panel.

11.2 If a refereeing procedure appears to contravene these rules, the official representative is the only one allowed to make a protest.

11.3 The protest will take the form of a written report submitted immediately after the bout in which the protest was generated. The sole exception to this is when the protest concerns an administrative malfunction. The area controller should be notified immediately the administrative malfunction is detected.

11.4 The protest must be submitted to a representative of the referee council. In due course the council will review the circumstances leading to the protested decision. Having considered all the facts available, it will produce a report and shall be empowered to take such action as may be called for.

11.5 Any protests concerning application of the rules must be made in accordance with the complaints procedure defined by

the World Karate Federation Directing Committee (WKF-DC) and submitted in writing on an approved form and signed by the official representative of the team or contestant(s).

11.6 The complainant must deposit a sum of money as may be agreed by the WKF-DC, with the treasury and a duplicate receipt will be issued. The protest, plus a copy of the receipt, must be lodged with the chairman of the referee council.

Article 12: Power and Duties of the Referee Council, Match Area Controllers, Referees, Judges, and Arbitrators.

Refers to officials.

Article 13: Starting, Suspending, and Ending of Matches.

13.1 The terms and gestures to be used by the referee and judges in the operation of a match shall be specified in Appendices 1 and 2.

13.2 The referee and judges shall take up their prescribed positions and, following an exchange of bows between the contestants, the referee will announce "Shobu sanbon hajime!" and the bout will commence.

13.3 The referee will stop the bout by announcing "Yame!" when a scoring technique is seen.

13.4 The referee will order the contestants to take up their original positions.

13.4.1 The referee returns to his position and the judges indicate their opinion by means of a signal.

13.4.2 The referee identifies the relevant score, awards waza-ari or ippon and supplements the announcement with the prescribed gesture.

13.4.3 The referee then restarts the bout by calling "Tsuzukete hajime!".

13.5 When a contestant has scored sanbon during a bout, the referee shall call "Yame!" and order the contestants back to their standing lines as he returns to his. The winner is then declared and indicated by the referee raising a hand on the side of the winner and declaring "Shiro (aka) no kachi". The bout is ended at this point.

13.6 When time is up and the scoring situation tied:

13.6.1 The referee shall call "Yame!" and return to his position.

13.6.2 The referee will call "Hantei" and following his signal

(by whistle) the judges will indicate their opinions.

13.6.3 The majority decision will be taken. The judges and referee have one vote each at hantei.

13.7 The referee will award the decision and announce the winner, or give a draw ("Hikiwake").

13.8 In the event of a tied individual bout, the referee will announce "Encho-sen"and start the extension with the command "Shobu hajime!"

13.9 When faced with the following situations, the referee shall announce "Yame!"and halt the bout temporarily. The bout will subsequently be restarted.

13.9.1 When both or either of the contestants are out of the area (or when a judge signals a jogai). The referee will order the two contestants to their initial positions.

13.9.2 When the referee orders the contestant to adjust his gi.

13.9.3 When the referee notices that a contestant appears about to contravene the rules, or when a signal concerning same from a judge is perceived.

13.9.4 When the referee notices that a contest has contravened the rules, or when the referee perceives a signal from a judge regarding same.

13.9.5 When the referee considers that one or both of the contestants cannot continue with the bout owing to injuries, illness or other causes. Heeding the tournament doctor's opinion, the referee will decide whether the bout should be continued.

13.9.6 When a contestant seizes his opponent and does not perform an immediate effective

technique, the referee will separate them.

13.9.7 When one or both contestants fall or are thrown and no effective techniques are immediately forthcoming.

These rules are reprinted here by permission of the English Karate Governing Body. A complete copy of the rules, including notes, explanations and guidelines, as well as the rules governing Kata competition are available from the Karate Governing Body.

Untouchable
The aim in karate is to break through your opponent's defence with a punch or a kick which stops just short of touching him.

Judo
Essentials

Judo developed from an ancient Japanese method of unarmed combat known as jujutsu, also spelled jujitsu. It is a sport in which a contestant uses balance, leverage and timing to pin or throw an opponent.

Combat team
In judo, contest bouts are fought by each of the six team members

Competition area

Must be a minimum of 14 m (15 yds) square and a maximum of 16 m (17 ½ yds) square. Must be covered by tatami or a similarly acceptable material, generally green in colour. The competition area is divided into two zones. The area between these two zones is called the 'danger zone' and is indicated by a red area, approximately 1 m (3 ft) wide, parallel to the four sides of the competition area. The area within and including the danger zone is called the 'contest area' and must be a minimum of 8 m (26 ft) square or a maximum of 10 m (33 ft) square. The area outside the danger zone is called the 'safety area' and must be 3 m (10 ft) wide. A red tape and a white tape must be fixed on the centre of the contest area 4 m (13 ft) apart, to indicate the positions at which the contestants must start and end the contest. The red tape must be to the referee's right and the white to the referee's left. A free zone, a minimum of 50 cm (19 ½ in), must be maintained around the competition area.

On the mat
The aim in judo is to achieve a decisive throw which keeps an opponent on the mat for a particular time.

The contestants

Two contestants participate in a contest.

Competition area 14-16 m

Starting positions

Danger zone 1 m

4 m

Contest area 8-10 m

Officials

Generally, the contest is conducted by one referee (who must generally stay within the contest area) and two judges (sitting opposite each other at two corners outside the contest area), assisted by contest recorders and timekeepers.

Close contest
Combatants engage when the referee announces 'hajime'.

Equipment

The following technical equipment is needed for a contest: two chairs for the judges, each chair with a red and a white flag; two scoreboards; one timing clock for contest duration, and two for osaekomi; timekeepers' flags – one yellow for contest stop, one blue for osaekomi.

Dress

The contestants must wear judogi (judo uniform) made of cotton or similar material. The judogi must be in good condition and white, off-white or blue in colour. The jacket must be long enough to cover the thighs and reach at least down to the fists when the arms are fully extended downwards. The trousers must be long enough to cover the legs and at their maximum reach to the ankle joint and at their minimum to 5 cm (2 in) above the ankle joint. A strong belt of 4 to 5 cm wide must be worn over the jacket at waist level and tied with a square knot, tight enough to prevent the jacket from being too loose and long enough to go twice around the waist.

HOW TO PLAY

Starting

The contestants must stand facing each other on the contest area at the red or white tape according to the sash they are wearing. They must make a standing bow and take one step forward. The referee announces "Hajime" to start the contest.

Duration of contest

The duration of the contest for World Championships and Olympic games is five minutes for men, and four minutes for women. A bell or similar audible device indicates to the referee the end of the time allotted for the contest. Contestants are entitled to rest for a period of ten minutes between contests.

How to win

A contestant wins the contest if they score an ippon. If no one scores an ippon, the contestant with the highest score wins the contest.

Scoring

Points are not cumulative (except for a waza-ari). An ippon scores ten points, and wins the contest. A waza-ari scores seven points, and two waza-ari achieve an ippon. A yuko scores five points, and a koka scores three points.

Thrown
Combatants are judged on their throwing technique (nagewaza) and holding technique (katamewaza).

KEY RULES

• *Ippon* is achieved:

a) When a contestant, with control, throws the other contestant largely on his back with considerable force and speed.

b) When a contestant holds with osaekomi the other contestant, who is unable to get away for 30 seconds after the announcement of osaekomi.

c) When a contestant gives up by tapping twice or more with his hand or foot or says "maitta" (I give up), generally as a result of grappling technique, shime-waza (strangle) or kansetsu-waza (armlock).

d) When the effect of a strangle technique or armlock is sufficiently apparent.

e) If one contestant gains two waza-ari in one contest, the contestant is awarded an ippon (called a 'waza-ari awasete ippon').

• *Waza-ari* is awarded:

a) When a contestant, with control, throws the other contestant, but the technique is partially lacking in one of the elements necessary for an ippon.

b) When a contestant holds with osaekomi the other contestant who is unable to get away for 25 seconds or more, but less than 30 seconds.

• *Yuko* is awarded:

a) When a contestant, with control, throws the other contestant, but the technique is partially lacking in two of the other three elements necessary for an ippon.

b) When a contestant holds with osaekomi the other contestant who is unable to get away for 20 seconds or more but less than 25 seconds.

• *Koka* is awarded:

a) When a contestant, with control, throws the other contestant onto his thigh(s) or buttocks with speed and force.

b) When a contestant holds with osaekomi the other contestant who is unable to get away for ten seconds or more but less than 20 seconds.

Penalties

Like points, penalties are not cumulative; however, the awarding of a second or subsequent penalty automatically cancels an earlier penalty. When a contestant has already been penalized, any succeeding penalties must be awarded in higher value than the existing penalty. When a contestant is given a penalty, the opponent gains points.

Shido is given to any contestant who has committed a slight infringement. Slight infringements include:

– To make an action designed to give the impression of an attack but which clearly shows that there was no intent to throw the opponent (false attack).

– To put a hand, arm, foot or leg directly in the opponent's face. If one contestant is penalized shido, the other contestant is awarded koka.

Chui is awarded to any contestant who has committed a serious infringement (or having been awarded a shido commits a second slight infringement). Serious infringements include:

- To kick with the knee or foot, the hand or arm of the opponent, in order to make the opponent release their grip.

- To bend back the opponent's finger(s) in order to break the opponent's grip.

When one contestant is penalized chui, the other contestant is awarded yuko.

Keikoku is awarded to any contestant who has committed a grave infringement (or who having been penalized chui, commits a further slight or serious infringement). Grave infringements include:

– Making any action which might injure or endanger the opponent, or may be against the spirit of judo.

– Disregarding the referee's instructions.

When one contestant is penalized keikoku, the opponent is awarded waza-ari.

Hansoku Make is awarded to any contestant who has committed a very grave infringement (or having been penalized keikoku, commits a further infringement of any degree). Very grave infringements include:

– Intentionally falling backwards when the opponent is clinging to the contestant's back and when either contestant has control of the other's movement.

– Wearing a hard or metallic object (covered or not).

If a contestant is penalized hansoku-make, their opponent is awarded ippon.

The ultimate aim in a judo bout is to score an ippon, hurling one's opponent flat on his back.

SKILLS

There are four key combat techniques used in judo contests:

Nage-komi-waza – throwing an opponent.

Osaekomi-waza – pinning an opponent to the ground.

Kansetsu-waza – armlocking an opponent.

Shime-waza – choking an opponent.

These are not the full rules of judo, but a resumé. Full rules are available from judo associations.

Fencing *Essentials*

Fencing originated in the techniques of swordsmanship used in duelling. During the Renaissance, the vigorous Italian style of fencing, based on the use of the rapier, predominated in Europe, . The épée, or small sword, was invented in France during the Eighteenth Century, giving rise to a more formal, restrained style of fencing. The rules of modern fencing are for the most part derived from the French style, and many of the sport's technical terms are French words.

There are three forms of fencing, defined by the type of weapon used: foil, épée, and sabre.

Officials

Bouts are judged by a referee who applies the right-of-way rules and awards touches.

The referee is assisted by two ground-judges; when non-electric weapons are used, there are four ground-judges.

The referee has the authority to halt a bout if the play of the competitors is dangerous or contrary to the rules, or if one of the competitors is disarmed or leaves the piste.

Left, foil.

20 cm max
18 cm max
110 cm max

15 cm blade insulation for electric foil

Making a point
The épée is an old duelling weapon which is bound by none of the conventions which govern the foil and the sabre. Double hits are valid.

Players
Forms of Competition

Two opponents. A fencing contest between two adversaries is called a 'bout'. In individual competitions, the result of a competition is the aggregate of the bouts.

In team competitions, the aggregate of the bouts fought between the fencers of two different teams is called a 'match'. The winner of a team competition is decided on an aggregate of the matches.

Competitions are distinguished by weapons, by the competitors' sex, age or occupation (e.g. military, students) and by whether they are for individuals or for teams.

Competitions are said to be by 'direct elimination' when the competitors are eliminated as soon as they have received their first defeat, or after their second if the rules specify a system 'with repêchage'. A pool is the meeting of several competitors (or of all the competitors) each of whom fences all the others in order to establish their classification.

Centre line

On gaurd line

Start of 2 m signal area

Last 2m of piste

Rear limit

Extensions of piste

14 m

2 m

3 m

2 m

Point to point
Fencers must combat each other within a narrow strip called the 'piste'.

The piste
The field of play is known as the piste. It measures 14 m (46 ft) in length and is from 1.5 to 2 m (5 to 6½ ft) wide. It may be made of various materials, such as cork, rubber, or plastic. In competitions where electrical apparatus is used to detect hits, a metallic mesh covers the piste.

Equipment

The three types of weapon are called the foil, épée, and sabre. The blades of all three are made of tempered steel, the blunted end forming the so-called 'button'. A variety of handles exist, including the Italian grip which has a crossbar and is used with a wrist strap, and the French grip, which is slightly curved and has a pommel (or knob) at the end.

As it is light and flexible, the *foil* is used by most beginners. The épée is similar to the foil, but it has a larger hand guard, and is heavier and more rigid. The design of the *sabre* is based on that of the cavalryman's weapon, and it requires a cut-and-thrust technique based on military sword play.

A fencer wears a protective face mask made of fine wire mesh, and a jacket, over which the plastron, a metallic chest protector, is worn. Women wear breast protectors made of metal or other rigid material. The sword hand is protected by a glove. The jacket, which must be white or a pale colour, overlaps breeches or trousers. These must be buttoned or fastened below the knee or at the ankle, respectively.

Electrical weapons are used in formal competitions to increase the accuracy of scoring in bouts. The weapons are wired. When the weapon blade's button makes contact with the opponent's metallic plastron, electricity is conducted to a body wire. The hit registers on

an electrical scoring apparatus: when a touch is scored, a light flashes on a screen on the sidelines. The referee awards touches accordingly.

Because fencing is a potentially hazardous sport, participants have to take on responsibility for safety, both for themselves and for others. Weapons and protective clothing must meet prescribed safety standards. Before competitions, clothing and weapons are submitted to a control office for checking. As well as checking for safety, the officers will ensure that electrical components such as the body wire will register touches accurately.

Caption, below.

HOW TO PLAY

Fencing tactics depend on fundamental stances and movements; defensive and attacking motions lead on from the basic 'on-guard' position, in which the knees are flexed, the rear arm crooked upwards, and the sword arm partly extended towards the opponent. The 'lunge', the basic attacking action, is executed by stabbing at the target with the sword arm and thrusting forward on the front leg.

A defensive movement of the blade intended to block an attack is called the 'parry'. There are eight main parries in foil and épée fencing, each one designed to protect a different part of the target against attack. In sabre fencing, there are just five parries. The parries bear the names of the Old French words meaning 'first' to 'eighth'– prime, seconde, tierce, quarte, quinte, sixte, septime, and octave. The return thrust made immediately after a parry is known as a 'riposte'. The 'counter-riposte' is an offensive action made by the fencer who has parried the riposte.

How to win

Points are scored in fencing by touching valid parts of the opponent's body with the blade. In foil fencing, only the touches to the torso count, whereas in épée fencing the entire body is valid. In sabre fencing, only touches above the 'saddle line' can be counted – a line running across the top of the hips.

When non-electric weapons are used, thrusts with the point must reach their target clearly and distinctly to be counted as a hit.

The effective duration of a bout is: at épée for one hit (in pentathlon): 3 minutes; at all weapons, for five hits: 4 minutes; for 15 hits: 9 minutes – consisting of up to three sets, each lasting 3 minutes.

KEY RULES

• The competitors fence in their own ways and at their own risk with the one condition that they must observe the fundamental rules of fencing.
• All bouts or matches must preserve the character of a courteous and frank encounter. All irregular actions (flèche attack which finishes with a collision jostling the opponent, disorderly fencing, a fall, irregular movements on the piste, hits achieved with undue violence, hits made while falling) are strictly forbidden.
• Before the beginning of the bout the two fencers must perform a fencing salute to their opponent, to the spectators and to the referee. The fencing salute is performed by lifting the weapon guard up to the chin. If one of the two fencers does not comply with this rule, he will receive a red card from the referee. When the final hit has been scored, the bout is not ended until the two fencers have saluted each other, the audience, and the referee.
• At foil it is forbidden, during the course of fencing, to advance the shoulder of the non-sword arm in front of the shoulder of the sword-arm.
• The fencer, whether on or off the piste, must keep his mask on until the referee calls halt.
• Bodily contact between the competitors (known as corps à corps) is forbidden, even without brutality or violence.
• It is forbidden to turn oneís back on one's opponent during the bout.

SKILLS

Concentration, alertness, precision, and anticipation are, of course, essential.

The technique of finger-play, or *doigté*, is important: manipulating the weapon using the thumb and first finger in such a way that the blade will move as and when required by the shortest possible route in the quickest possible time.

An associated skill is blade-sense, or *sentiment du fer*. For an experienced fencer, the weapon feels like an extension of his own body. With this heightened sense of feeling, he can perceive his opponent's dexterity, strength, speed, and temperament.

TACTICS

A competitor who takes the offensive may choose from a number of attacking techniques to overcome his opponent's parries. A rapid, single cut or thrust of the blade may hit the target before the defender can parry. A more complex tactic involves making a compound attack requiring several blade movements – the initial movements, deceptively suggesting an area of attack, may mislead the opponent into parrying in a different direction from the one in which the attack is finally made. An opponent may also be caught unawares by a running attack, or flèche. However, a competitor on the defensive may catch an opponent by surprise by making a 'stop-thrust', a counter-attack made by thrusting without lunging. Another offensive technique is to beat or press the opponent's blade aside before attacking.

Winning hit
In top-level matches the winner is the fencer who scores the most hits in three rounds of five hits in six minutes. In foil and épée, hits are scored with the point; in sabre, with the edge too.

Association Croquet

Essentials

Traditionally seen as a genteel pastime for the country house, croquet is actually a rapidly developing international sport, with the average age of competition players now frequently around 25. Often likened to snooker on grass, it is a subtle game in which tactics and cunning are more important than strength.

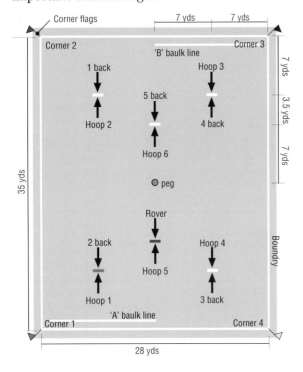

Equipment and accessories

Six hoops, metal, painted white, fixed firmly in, and measuring 12 in (30 cm) in height above the ground. The first hoop has a blue crown and the final hoop (the rover) has a red crown. A centre-peg – wooden, 18 in (46 cm) high, with a diameter of $1\frac{1}{2}$ in (4 cm). Four balls, coloured blue, black, red and yellow, each with a diameter of $3\frac{5}{8}$ in (9 cm) and a weight of 1 lb (0.45 kg). (Alternative colours green, brown, pink and white are permitted.) Clips, the same colour as the balls, are placed on the hoop or peg next in order for each ball. A mallet with a head usually made of wood and two identical end faces.

Players

Two for singles – the striker and the outplayer – or four for doubles. The striker is the player whose turn it is to strike the ball. Each player has two balls for singles, or one ball each for doubles.

Officials

A referee.

Dress

Generally white. Men wear a shirt and trousers or shorts and women may substitute a skirt. Suitable flat sports shoes.

The court

A rectangular lawn, 35 yds (32 m) by 28 yds (25.5 m) or smaller for non-competition games. The boundary marked with a continuous white line. Imaginary yard-lines (not marked) lie one yard in from the boundary. The area contained within these is the yard-line area. Corners may be marked with flags. There is a baulk-line at each end, consisting of 13 yds (12 m) of the yard-line, measured out from the corners.

Follow-through
In most strokes, follow-through is important for achieving accuracy and distance.

Point of law
One of the many issues which sometimes needs the decision of a referee is whether the ball has passed completely through a hoop. No part of the ball may show on the playing side of the hoop, so that a straight edge run down the playing side of the hoop will not disturb the ball. The playing side is the one on which the ball lay when it was struck towards the hoop.

HOW TO PLAY

Both players or teams try to hit their balls with the head of their mallets through each of the six hoops on the court twice, and then against the centre peg, thus completing the course, before their opponent(s) does. The six hoops form a circuit that must be completed in a set order in one direction and then in a reverse sequence.

Starting

The winner of the toss decides whether to opt for a choice of colours (to play the blue and black or the red and yellow) or to start the game. The player starting then places a ball anywhere on a baulk line and strikes it to begin the game. The opposing player does the same. Then two more alternating turns are taken so that all four balls are in play.

How to win

Each time a ball passes through a hoop in order a point is scored, as is also the case when the ball hits the centre peg at the completion of the circuit. The points scored therefore total 13 for each ball. The winner is the player or team who makes his balls score these 12 *hoop points* and one *peg point* (26 in total) before his or her opponent.

KEY RULES

• Players have alternate turns. Either of a player's two balls may be played; at the beginning of each turn he chooses a *striker's ball* and this ball is played exclusively throughout that turn.

• Each turn consists of one initial stroke. However, if in this first stroke the ball scores a hoop point., the player is allowed another stroke (a *continuation stroke*).

• A player earns two extra strokes if he makes a roquet (hits another ball with his ball). For the first of these (the *croquet stroke*) he places his ball in any position, providing it is in contact with the roqueted ball, and then strikes his own ball ensuring that both balls move. After this he takes a continuation stroke and, if this does not result in a roquet or a hoop point, his turn ends.

• Within one turn, each of the other balls may be roqueted and croqueted only once. But, if the player is able to score by hitting his ball through the next hoop in order he is entitled to roquet and croquet each ball anew.

• If during play a ball goes off the court (i.e. beyond the boundary line) or comes to rest in the yard-line area, it is retrieved and placed on the yard-line at a point nearest to where it left the court.

• A turn ends when a player has no strokes left to him. It also ends if, *in a croquet stroke,* a ball goes over the boundary or, if the player commits a fault. This occurs, for example, if he pushes his ball, hits his ball more than once (a *double tap*), squeezes his ball against a hoop or the peg (a *crush*), touches a ball other than his own with his mallet or fails to move or shake the croqueted ball in a croquet stroke. In addition to the turn being ended, a fault also means that a point cannot be scored off that particular stroke and the balls are replaced in their previous positions on the court.

• A ball must pass completely through a hoop (and stay there) to score a point. If a ball other than the striker's ball passes through the next hoop in order (*peeled* through the hoop) it also scores a hoop point. When a ball has completed both circuits of six hoops and has scored 12 points, it becomes a

A croquet shot
Having roqueted the red ball, this striker now plays his croquet stroke. You may roquet and croquet not only your own partner ball, but also those of your opponent.

rover ball. It must then be *pegged-out* by being hit against the centre peg directly (or by another rover ball) for a peg point, after which it is removed from the court.

SKILLS AND TACTICS

As with snooker, a high degree of accuracy is needed when taking a shot. Because croquet is played over a relatively large area and the balls are only $\frac{1}{8}$ in

(3 mm) narrower than the hoops, a player needs to be accurate to within 6 in (15 cm) over 35 yds (32 m).

The same kind of strategy used in snooker also applies. As well as trying to get his own ball through the hoops, a player must do everything he can to prevent his opponent from completing the circuit before him. Play therefore needs to be determinedly positive and tactically defensive. Skilled players use spin, angle shots and apply just the right amount of strength to place not only their own ball, but also their opponent's ball, using roquet and croquet strokes. They try to retain the initiative in play whilst disadvantaging the opponent and think as much about what a particular shot might give away as what gain it will achieve. Advanced players use such finely-tuned and elaborate tactics that they need to be constantly planning up to 20 strokes ahead, ideally to build and maintain a four ball break.

These are not the full Laws of Croquet, but a simplified resumé. The full laws and other books are available from the Croquet Association.

Easy roquet
This player strikes his yellow ball towards the red in order to make a roquet. Once that's achieved, he plays the croquet shot (see above) in order to position his yellow in a good hoop-running position.

Index

Addresses of sports governing bodies

American football
British American Football
Association
22A Market Place
Still Lane
Boston
Lincs PE21 6EH
U.S. governing body:
National Football League
tel: 001 212 450 2000 /fax:
001 212 681 7599

Athletics
British Athletic Federation
225A Bristol Road,
Edgbaston, Birmingham B5
7UB

Australian rules football
Australian Football
Foundation Box 1449N, GPO
Melbourne 3001

Badminton
International Badminton
Association Manor Park
Place, Rutherford Way,
Cheltenham GL51 9TU

Baseball
British Baseball Association
66 Belvedere Road
Hessle
North Humberside
HU13 9JJ

Basketball
International Basketball
Federation (FIBA) PO Box
70 06 07, Boschetsrieder
Str. 67, D-81379 Munchen,
Germany

Bowls
World Bowls Board
17 Sun Court, Rye Close,
Worthing, West Sussex
BN11 5EG

Boxing
International Amateur
Boxing Association (AIBA)
PO Box 0141, 10321 Berlin

Cricket
Marylebone Cricket Club
(MCC) Lords Cricket
Ground, London NW8 8QN

Fencing
Amateur Fencing
Association 1 Barons Court,
33-35 Rothschild Road,
London W4 5HT

Football
The Football Association
16 Lancaster Gate, London
W2 3LW

Golf
English Golf Union The
National Golf Centre, The
Broadway, Woodhall SPA,
Lincs, LN1 6PU

Handball
The British Handball
Association 40 Newchurch
Road, Rawtenstall,
Rossendale, Lancs BB4 7QX

Hockey
International Hockey
Association Avenue des
Arts 1 (BOX5), 1210
Brussels

Ice hockey
British Ice Hockey
Association
Second Floor
Suite, 517
Christchurch
Road, Boscombe,
Bournemouth,
BH1 4AG

Judo
British Judo Association 7A
Rutland Street, Leicester
LE1 1RB

Karate
English Karate Governing
Body 58 Bloomfield Drive,
Bath, Avon, BA2 2BG

Korfball
British Korfball Association
PO Box 179
Maidstone
Kent ME14 1LU

Lacrosse (men's)
English Lacrosse
Association 4 Western
Court, Bromley Street,
Birmingham, B9 4AN

Lacrosse (women's)
English Lacrosse
Association 4, Western
Court, Rowley Street,
Birmingham B9 4AN

Netball
All England Netball
Association Netball House,
Paynes Park, Hitchin, Herts,
SG5 1EH

Pétanque
The British Pétanque
Association
18 Ensign Business Centre
Westwood Park
Coventry CV4 8JA
tel: 01203-421408

Rounders
National Rounders
Association 3 Denehurst
Avenue, Nottingham, NG8
5DA

Rugby League
Rugby Football League Red
Hall, Red Hall Lane, Leeds
LS17 8NB

Rugby Union
International Rugby
Football Board Hugenot
House, 35-8, St. Stephen's
Green, Dublin

Softball
International Softball
Federation Oklahoma, USA;
tel: 001 405 424 6714
(Oklahoma)

Squash
World Squash Federation 6
Havelock Road, Hastings,
East Sussex TN34 1BP

Table tennis
English Table Tennis
Association Third Floor,
Queensbury House,
Havelock Road, Hastings,
East Sussex, TN34 1HF

Tennis
International Tennis
Federation Palliser Road,
London, W14 9EN

Volleyball
English Volleyball
Association 27 South Road,
West Bridgford,
Nottingham, NG2 7AG

Editorial Director Andrew Duncan
Art Director Mel Petersen
Chief compiler Angela Koo
Assistant compilers Sarah Barlow, Richard German and Huw Jones
Captions by John Farndon
Assistant Editors Nicola Davies and Sarah Barlow
Designers Chris Foley and Beverley Stewart
Illustrations Julian Baker
Photography Allsport Picture Library